CAFÉ du MiDi

Francis Leroux • Chef de Cuisine

Mary Kozicz • Sous-chef

Cafe du Midi serves Mediterranean style French cuisine, one that relies heavily on fresh herbs in order to attain the assertive flavors of southern French cooking. At the core of Mediterranean cuisine lies a Provencal heart, with its free use of garlic and olive oil, often in conjunction with basil, thyme, marjoram and rosemary, but the essential aspect is the freshness of all its separate ingredients and its reliance on fish, seafood, and capers — all endemic to the Mediterranean Sea. North African influences can also be seen (cumin seed and sesame seed) as well as Italian and Spanish, reflecting the central influence of the Mediterranean. The area in France known as the "Midi" extends from the western Pyrenees to the eastern coastal area abutting both the Alps and Italy.

———————— ✦ ————————

Chef Leroux came to America from France in 1965 and opened his first restaurant in 1973 at 858 W. Armitage in Chicago. "Gare St. Lazare" was a friendly little place with its rustic dining room tucked away behind a long bar. The food was "bistro style" and was acclaimed over the years by Jeff Smith (the "Frugal Gourmet"), Karla Kelson, Sherman Kaplan, and many others. In 1980, a second restaurant, "Chez Chose", was opened in a 105-year old frame house at 3048 W. Diversey, previous home of the Creole House.

Cafe du Midi Restaurant • 2118 N. Damen Ave. • Chicago, Il 60647

W9-CPF-934

Cover Photo by John Rizzo

THE MENU CHICAGO & VICINITY

A Menu Guide to the Top 200
Restaurants in Chicago
& Vicinity

PAT BRUNO

David Thomas Publishing

To my wife Gale
who shares my passion for good food

T H E
MƐΠU

is the perfect business gift—useful, tasteful, and appreciated. Special editions, including customized covers and full-color pages showcasing your product or service, are available for your clients, prospects, or employees.

Find out how simple and affordable this unique marketing program can be for your company.

Please call today and ask for Frank Alvey at:

1-800-755-MENU (6368)

during regular business hours
(Pacific standard time), or write:

Mr. Frank Alvey
Vice President, Sales and Marketing
David Thomas Publishing/Menubooks, Inc.
733 N.W. Everett St., Box 12
Portland, Oregon 97209

Printed on Recycled Paper with Soy Based Inks

Cover Design & Illustrations
by Heather Kier

733 NW Everett St., Box 12, Studio 5E
Portland, Oregon 97209
(503) 226-6233

Table of Contents

Restaurants by Cuisine

I have been writing about restaurants in this city for nearly ten years, yet my appetite is still being stirred and my taste buds tantalized. To put it more succinctly, my stomach is still on its toes when it comes to eating out around town. I constantly look forward to visiting the new and bold and revisiting the old and the beautiful. Chicago is that kind of restaurant town--no matter what kind of food mood you're in, it grabs you, pulls you in and makes you feel right at home at the table.

The depth and breadth of culinary diversity in our town is as good as it gets. From Greektown to Chinatown, from River North to Near North, from Uptown to downtown, from the suburbs to somewhere over the rainbow, there is a melting pot of magnificent eating that knows no bounds.

Seas and oceans are nowhere in sight around here, but we enjoy the freshest of seafood, as there are plenty of well-managed and well-stocked distributors for our restaurants to choose from. Our straightforward approach to cooking seafood is as it should be; no emperor in fool's clothes here.

We are in the deep freeze four or five months a year, but that doesn't stop our great restaurants from serving the finest fresh vegetables, fresh fruits and choice fresh herbs. Chicago's chefs probably seek out freshness with greater vigor than those who have it at their feet every day.

We may not have the experience of Europeans when it comes to mastering the art of al fresco dining, but from May through late September, Chicago restaurants put on an outdoor eating show that is the epitome of al fresco finery.

And how Chicago restaurants love to entertain. Hundreds of thousands of tourists and conventioneers descend on this city in the course of a year, and Chicago's restaurants treat them royally. Visitors show their loyalty by returning year after year to their favorite dining spots.

Chicago is still a bargain restaurant town. You can still get a great meal around here at a sensible price. Top-rated restaurants like Ambria, Everest, Carlos' and Le Français leave nothing to be desired, yet let you leave with an arm and leg intact. ("That was a great meal, but it cost me an arm and a leg" is a cliche not heard very often around here.)

Pound for pound, Chicago steakhouses weigh in with the best that this country has to offer. From old and estimable places like Gene & Georgetti and Eli's, to the sizzling and sensational places like Morton's, The Palm, and the Chicago Chop House, the turf (and surf) run deep and delicious, tender and terrific.

And how we love our Italian restaurants. When I arrived in Chicago in 1966 I nearly went crazy trying to find good Italian food. Now my pasta bowl runneth over and then some with the best that Italian cooking offers. We are knee deep in sauce, up to our ears in artichokes, rolling in risotto, and pan for pizza like prospectors at Fort Knox.

Hotel fine dining is not an oxymoron in this city; Chicago boasts some of the finest hotel dining in this country, a fact that millions of visitors to this city will attest to and swear by.

And on it goes: Greek and Thai, Polish and soul food, Chinese and Continental, Mexican and Mediterranean...the great eats go on and on and on.

It wasn't an easy thing, paring the hundreds and hundreds of fine restaurants in Chicago and its suburbs down to but 200, but when all has been said and eaten I know that my choices are sound and well thought out. More important, though, is the enjoyment that I know you will get from dining at any of the fine restaurants listed in this book.

Pat Bruno
Chicago, Illinois
July, 1993

Publisher's Note

Everyone's a critic. No experience more perfectly echoes that sentiment than dining out. It never fails — whenever someone finds out that I publish restaurant guides, they immediately proceed to tell me about their favorite places to eat. My mouth waters as they describe, in vivid detail, the dish they ordered, as well as what everyone else in their party ordered. In other words, they describe the restaurant's menu.

It follows that a great way to choose a restaurant would be to read its menu, provided the place is well recommended. In the last few years, it has been my pleasure to discover that literally thousands of readers like yourself share this same conclusion. As you enjoy using this book, please keep three items in mind:

1. NO ONE PAID TO BE IN THIS BOOK.
   Neither Pat Bruno nor the publisher, nor any of their associates, allow fees to be charged to any of the restaurants featured in the book, nor is inclusion in the book subject to any favors, trade-outs, book purchases, or any such promotional fees whatsoever.

2. MENUS AND PRICES CHANGE.
   Most all of the restaurants in this book change their menu and/or prices frequently, many even daily. We have tried to feature menus that accurately reflect the style and approach of the chef.

3. YOU CAN'T PLEASE EVERYONE.
   Even with no strings attached, we do (on rare occasion) encounter a restaurant who is either unwilling or unable to provide us with menus and other information, and thus, reluctantly, must be excluded.

Putting this book together was no small task. My heartfelt thanks go out to Deanna Demaree, Cordy Jensen, Heather Kier, Susan Fishback, Frank Alvey, Lynn Burgess, Alicia Geiger, Rex Nurnberg, Scott Deusebio, Jeannette Schilling, Barbara Disciacio, John Rizzo, and especially Pat Bruno.

We are continually striving to improve our product. To do so, we need your feedback. To that end, you will find a tear-out Reader Survey inside the back cover. Please take a moment to fill it out and mail it (pre-paid) to my attention. I would love to hear from you.

Here's hoping that, as a fellow food lover, you not only find THE MENU to be a useful handbook of your favorite places, but also a tempting map to new gastronomical discoveries.

Tom Demaree
Publisher

Features Guide

The following table will answer the most often asked questions about the services offered by a particular restaurant. Please keep in mind that just as menus and prices change, so do amenities. It is always best to confirm those features important to you when making your reservation.

A few explanatory notes:

Types of Cuisine — The restaurants are grouped alphabetically by type of cuisine, starting with *Afghanistan*, all the way through *Vietnamese*. The cuisine category is referenced at the top right of each two-page spread. Index by Cuisine can be found on page 432.

Geographic Location — The address of the restaurant is located at the bottom of the left page on each menu. When there are additional locations, the best known or original location address is given, followed by the statement: (call for additional locations). Restaurants located in Chicago are listed by their district or neighborhood, all others by their city name. Geographical index begins on page 437.

Hours — Dinner hours are listed at the bottom of the right page on each menu. A quick reference icon appears at the bottom right showing which meals a restaurant serves. See icons on next page.

100% Non-Smoking — Restaurants that do accommodate smoking guests generally offer non-smoking areas as well.

Wheelchair access — Most all of the restaurants without full wheelchair access are still able and happy to accommodate the special needs of any of their guests.

Dress — The three categories of dress referred to are only an indication of how *most* people dress for dinner. If you have a question, call ahead.

Personal Checks — Restaurants which accept personal checks require proper I.D.

Features Guide

On each lower right-hand page you will notice a row of symbols that represent certain features or services that a particular restaurant may offer. These "icons" are designed to give you a quick reference to the features that you may be looking for in a restaurant—at a glance.

Below is a list of the icons and what they represent:

♿ — Wheelchair Access

⊗ — 100% Non-Smoking

💳 — Major Credit Cards (Restaurants differ—see Features Guide)

🍸 — Full Bar

🍳 — Breakfast

🍴 — Lunch

🍽 — Dinner

🥂 — Sunday Brunch

👔 — Jacket/Tie (May be required - call to be safe)

🎵 — Live Entertainment

Features Guide

17

Features Guide

Restaurant	Pg.	Wheelchair Access	100% Non-Smoking	Visa/Master Card	American Express	Discover	Diners Club	Checks Accepted	Beer & Wine	Full Bar	Live Entertainment	Sunday Brunch	Breakfast	Lunch	Dinner	High Chairs	Take Out	Valet Parking	Private Parties	Informal Dress	Casual Dress	Jacket/Tie	Reserv. Recom.	Reserv. Required	Reserv. Not Taken
Casbah, The	126	♦		♦	♦			♦	♦	♦					♦		♦		♦	♦	♦		♦		
Catch 35	372	♦		♦	♦	♦	♦		♦	♦	♦			♦	♦	♦	♦	♦	♦	♦	♦		♦		
Charlie's Ale House	52	♦		♦	♦	♦	♦		♦	♦			♦	♦	♦	♦	♦		♦	♦	♦				♦
Chez Paul	182			♦	♦	♦	♦		♦	♦				♦	♦		♦	♦		♦		♦			
Chicago Chop House	400			♦	♦	♦	♦			♦	♦			♦	♦		♦	♦		♦		♦			
City Tavern	54	♦		♦	♦	♦	♦					♦	♦	♦	♦	♦									
Club Gene & Georgetti	402	♦		♦	♦		♦			♦				♦	♦			♦	♦		♦		♦		
Club Lago	274									♦				♦	♦	♦	♦		♦		♦		♦		
Club Lucky	276			♦	♦				♦	♦				♦	♦	♦	♦	♦	♦		♦				♦
Como Inn	278	♦		♦	♦	♦	♦	♦	♦	♦	♦			♦	♦	♦	♦	♦	♦	♦	♦		♦		
Cottage, The	56	♦		♦				♦		♦				♦	♦	♦	♦		♦		♦	♦	♦	♦	
Courtyards of Plaka	232	♦	♦	♦	♦	♦	♦	♦	♦	♦	♦			♦	♦	♦	♦	♦			♦				
Cricket's Restaurant and Bar	58	♦		♦	♦	♦	♦	♦		♦	♦	♦	♦	♦	♦	♦		♦	♦		♦		♦		
Cuisines	60	♦		♦	♦	♦	♦			♦				♦	♦	♦		♦	♦		♦		♦		
D.B. Kaplan's Delicatessen	158	♦		♦	♦	♦				♦			♦	♦	♦	♦	♦		♦		♦				♦
Davis Street Fishmarket	374	♦		♦	♦			♦	♦	♦			♦	♦	♦	♦	♦				♦				
Dining Room, The	184	♦		♦	♦	♦	♦		♦	♦	♦	♦		♦	♦		♦					♦		♦	
Don Roth's in Wheeling	'62	♦		♦	♦	♦	♦		♦	♦				♦	♦			♦	♦		♦				
Dos Hermanos Mexican	344	♦		♦	♦	♦	♦			♦				♦	♦	♦	♦		♦		♦		♦		
Eccentric, The	64	♦		♦	♦	♦	♦		♦	♦	♦			♦	♦	♦	♦	♦	♦	♦	♦		♦		
El Jardin	346	♦		♦	♦	♦	♦		♦	♦	♦		♦	♦	♦	♦	♦	♦	♦		♦				♦
El Nuevo Mexicano	348			♦	♦	♦	♦			♦				♦	♦	♦	♦		♦		♦				
Eli's the Place for Steaks	404	♦		♦	♦	♦	♦		♦	♦				♦	♦		♦	♦	♦		♦	♦			
Emilio's Tapas Bar and Rest.	394	♦		♦	♦	♦			♦	♦				♦	♦	♦				♦		♦			
Emperor's Choice Rest.	134	♦		♦	♦	♦				♦				♦	♦	♦	♦				♦				
Everest	186	♦		♦	♦	♦	♦			♦					♦			♦	♦			♦		♦	
Franco's Ristorante	280			♦					♦					♦	♦	♦				♦	♦				♦
Froggy's	188		♦		♦	♦	♦	♦	♦	♦				♦	♦	♦	♦		♦		♦				♦
Frontera Grill	350	♦		♦	♦	♦	♦		♦					♦	♦	♦		♦	♦		♦				
Galan's	424			♦	♦	♦		♦	♦	♦	♦			♦	♦	♦	♦		♦		♦	♦	♦		
Gandhi India Restaurant	248	♦		♦	♦	♦	♦			♦				♦	♦	♦			♦		♦				
Geja's Cafe	66			♦	♦	♦	♦			♦	♦				♦				♦		♦				
Gibsons Steakhouse	406	♦		♦	♦	♦			♦	♦	♦				♦	♦	♦	♦	♦	♦	♦				
Golden Ox	224	♦		♦	♦	♦	♦			♦	♦			♦	♦	♦	♦	♦	♦		♦		♦		
Goose Island Brewing Co.	68	♦		♦	♦	♦			♦	♦			♦	♦	♦	♦			♦		♦		♦		
Gordon	70	♦		♦	♦	♦	♦			♦		♦	♦	♦	♦			♦	♦		♦		♦	♦	
Greek Islands	234	♦		♦	♦	♦	♦		♦	♦				♦	♦	♦	♦	♦	♦		♦		♦		
Green Door Tavern, The	72			♦	♦			♦	♦	♦	♦		♦	♦	♦		♦		♦		♦				
Greenery, The	164			♦	♦	♦	♦		♦	♦					♦	♦	♦	♦			♦	♦			
Hard Rock Cafe	74	♦		♦	♦				♦	♦	♦			♦	♦	♦	♦		♦		♦				♦
Harry Caray's Restaurant	76	♦		♦	♦	♦	♦		♦					♦	♦	♦		♦	♦		♦	♦	♦		♦
Hat Dance	352	♦		♦	♦	♦	♦	♦	♦	♦				♦	♦			♦	♦		♦		♦		
Heartland Cafe	426	♦		♦	♦		♦	♦	♦	♦	♦		♦	♦	♦	♦	♦		♦	♦	♦		♦		
Heaven on Seven	78	♦											♦	♦		♦	♦			♦		♦			♦
Heidelberger Fass	226	♦		♦	♦			♦		♦				♦	♦	♦	♦		♦		♦	♦			

RESTAURANT	PG.	Wheelchair Access	100% Non-Smoking	Visa/Master Card	American Express	Discover	Diners Club	Checks Accepted	Beer & Wine	Full Bar	Live Entertainment	Sunday Brunch	Breakfast	Lunch	Dinner	High Chairs	Take Out	Valet Parking	Private Parties	Informal Dress	Casual Dress	Jacket/Tie	Reserv. Recom.	Reserv. Required	Reserv. Not Taken
Helmand, The	24	◆		◆	◆		◆		◆	◆					◆	◆			◆		◆		◆		
Home Bakery and Rest.	166		◆					◆	◆			◆	◆	◆	◆	◆	◆			◆	◆			◆	
Home Run Inn	282	◆		◆	◆				◆	◆				◆	◆	◆	◆			◆	◆				◆
Honda Japanese Rest.	334	◆		◆	◆		◆		◆	◆				◆	◆	◆	◆	◆			◆		◆		
Hong Min Restaurant	136		◆											◆	◆		◆				◆				◆
House of Hunan Mich. Ave.	138	◆		◆	◆	◆	◆		◆	◆				◆	◆	◆	◆		◆		◆		◆		
Ina's Kitchen	80	◆	◆									◆	◆	◆		◆	◆		◆		◆				◆
It's Greek to Me	236	◆		◆	◆	◆	◆		◆	◆				◆	◆	◆	◆	◆	◆		◆		◆		
Jackie's Restaurant	190	◆		◆	◆	◆			◆	◆				◆	◆			◆	◆	◆			◆		
Jaxx Restaurant	82	◆		◆	◆	◆	◆		◆	◆	◆	◆	◆	◆	◆	◆			◆		◆		◆		
Jerry's Kitchen	386	◆		◆			◆						◆	◆	◆	◆	◆				◆		◆		
Jim N' Johnnys'	284	◆		◆					◆	◆				◆	◆	◆	◆	◆	◆		◆				
Jimmy's Place	192	◆	◆	◆		◆	◆		◆	◆				◆	◆			◆	◆				◆	◆	
Kanval Palace	250	◆		◆	◆	◆	◆		◆	◆				◆	◆	◆	◆		◆		◆		◆		
Kiki's Bistro	194	◆		◆	◆	◆	◆		◆					◆	◆			◆			◆				
Kinzie Street Chophouse	84	◆		◆	◆				◆	◆				◆	◆		◆		◆		◆		◆		
Klay Oven	252	◆	◆	◆	◆		◆							◆	◆		◆		◆				◆	◆	
Konak	422	◆		◆	◆				◆	◆				◆	◆	◆			◆		◆		◆		
L'Escargot	196	◆		◆	◆	◆	◆			◆				◆	◆			◆	◆	◆	◆	◆	◆		
La Bella Pasteria	286	◆		◆	◆		◆		◆	◆				◆	◆	◆	◆	◆	◆		◆		◆		
La Cantina	288			◆	◆	◆	◆	◆	◆	◆				◆	◆	◆	◆	◆	◆		◆	◆	◆		
La Locanda	290	◆		◆	◆	◆	◆		◆	◆				◆	◆		◆	◆	◆		◆	◆			◆
La Paella	396	◆		◆	◆				◆	◆					◆						◆		◆		
La Strada Ristorante	292	◆		◆	◆	◆	◆		◆	◆	◆			◆	◆			◆	◆				◆	◆	
La Tour	198	◆		◆	◆	◆	◆		◆	◆	◆	◆	◆	◆	◆			◆	◆				◆	◆	
Lawry's the Prime Rib	86	◆		◆	◆	◆	◆			◆				◆	◆		◆	◆	◆		◆		◆		
Le Bistro	428	◆		◆	◆				◆	◆				◆	◆	◆	◆		◆		◆		◆		
Le Français	200	◆		◆	◆	◆	◆		◆	◆				◆	◆			◆				◆	◆		
Le Mikado	202	◆		◆	◆	◆	◆		◆	◆				◆	◆			◆		◆		◆	◆		
Le Perroquet	204	◆		◆	◆		◆		◆	◆				◆	◆			◆				◆		◆	
Le Titi de Paris	206	◆		◆	◆	◆	◆	◆	◆					◆	◆			◆	◆			◆		◆	
Le Vichyssois	208	◆		◆			◆	◆	◆	◆				◆	◆		◆			◆	◆			◆	
Little Bucharest	168		◆	◆			◆		◆	◆	◆			◆	◆	◆			◆		◆		◆		
Lou Mitchell's Rest. & Bakery	88											◆	◆	◆		◆	◆		◆	◆	◆	◆			
Machu Picchu	366	◆		◆										◆	◆			◆			◆		◆		
Maggiano's	294			◆	◆	◆	◆			◆		◆		◆	◆		◆			◆	◆		◆		
Mandar-Inn Restaurant	140			◆	◆	◆	◆	◆	◆	◆				◆	◆		◆		◆	◆	◆	◆	◆		
Michael Jordan's	90	◆		◆	◆	◆			◆	◆				◆	◆	◆	◆	◆	◆		◆				◆
Mirabell	228	◆		◆	◆				◆	◆				◆	◆	◆	◆		◆		◆		◆		
Mirador	92	◆		◆	◆	◆	◆		◆	◆	◆				◆		◆		◆		◆				
Mity Nice Grill, The	94	◆	◆	◆	◆	◆	◆	◆	◆	◆				◆	◆	◆				◆	◆				
Montparnasse	210	◆		◆	◆	◆	◆			◆				◆	◆			◆			◆	◆	◆		
Morton's, The Steakhouse	96	◆		◆	◆		◆			◆					◆				◆		◆	◆	◆		
Mrs. Levy's Delicatessen	160	◆							◆			◆	◆		◆	◆			◆		◆				◆
Nick's Fishmarket	376	◆		◆	◆	◆	◆	◆	◆	◆				◆	◆			◆	◆			◆	◆		

Features Guide

Restaurant	Pg.	Wheelchair Access	100% Non-Smoking	Visa/Master Card	American Express	Discover	Diners Club	Checks Accepted	Beer & Wine	Full Bar	Live Entertainment	Sunday Brunch	Breakfast	Lunch	Dinner	High Chairs	Take Out	Valet Parking	Private Parties	Informal Dress	Casual Dress	Jacket/Tie	Reserv. Recom.	Reserv. Required	Reserv. Not Taken
Nuevo Leon Restaurant	354									◆		◆		◆	◆	◆	◆		◆			◆		◆	
O'Briens	152	◆		◆	◆				◆	◆	◆			◆	◆		◆	◆		◆			◆		
Oak Tree Restaurant	98	◆		◆					◆		◆	◆	◆	◆	◆	◆	◆			◆			◆		◆
Old Carolina Crab House	376	◆		◆	◆	◆	◆			◆		◆	◆	◆	◆	◆	◆			◆			◆		
Oo-La-La	212	◆		◆					◆	◆		◆			◆		◆	◆	◆	◆					
Original A-1 Border, The	356	◆		◆	◆	◆	◆		◆					◆	◆		◆			◆					
Original Pancake House	100											◆	◆	◆		◆				◆					◆
Palm, The	408	◆		◆	◆		◆		◆	◆				◆	◆	◆	◆	◆	◆				◆		
Papagus Greek Taverna	238	◆		◆	◆	◆	◆		◆	◆				◆	◆	◆	◆	◆	◆				◆		
Parthenon	240	◆		◆	◆	◆	◆		◆	◆				◆	◆	◆	◆	◆		◆			◆		
Pattaya Thai Restuarant	418	◆		◆	◆	◆	◆		◆	◆				◆	◆	◆	◆			◆			◆	◆	◆
Pegasus Restaurant	242	◆		◆	◆	◆			◆					◆	◆	◆	◆			◆			◆		
Phil Smidt & Son, Inc.	380	◆		◆	◆		◆		◆					◆	◆	◆			◆				◆		
Philander's	382			◆	◆	◆	◆		◆	◆	◆				◆	◆			◆	◆			◆		
Pine Yard Chinese Rest.	142	◆							◆					◆	◆		◆			◆					
Pizzeria Uno	296			◆	◆	◆				◆				◆	◆	◆	◆			◆					◆
Prairie	102	◆		◆	◆	◆	◆		◆	◆		◆	◆	◆	◆			◆	◆				◆	◆	
Primavera Ristorante	298	◆		◆	◆	◆	◆		◆	◆	◆	◆	◆	◆	◆			◆	◆	◆			◆		
Printer's Row	104			◆	◆	◆	◆		◆	◆				◆	◆			◆		◆		◆	◆	◆	
Pump Room, The	106			◆	◆	◆	◆		◆	◆	◆	◆	◆	◆	◆			◆				◆		◆	
R. J. Grunt's	108			◆	◆	◆			◆	◆		◆		◆	◆	◆	◆			◆			◆		
Relish	110	◆		◆	◆		◆		◆	◆				◆	◆		◆	◆		◆			◆		
Robinson's No. 1 Ribs	130	◆	◆	◆	◆			◆						◆	◆	◆	◆		◆						◆
Rosebud on Taylor	300	◆		◆	◆	◆	◆		◆	◆				◆	◆	◆	◆	◆	◆	◆	◆		◆	◆	
Ruth's Chris Steakhouse	410	◆		◆	◆	◆	◆			◆				◆	◆			◆					◆	◆	
Sage's Sages	112	◆		◆	◆	◆	◆	◆		◆	◆		◆	◆	◆	◆	◆	◆	◆	◆			◆		
Saloon, The	412			◆	◆				◆	◆	◆		◆	◆	◆		◆			◆			◆		
Santorini Restaurant	244	◆		◆	◆	◆	◆			◆				◆	◆		◆	◆		◆			◆		
Sayat Nova	128			◆	◆	◆	◆		◆	◆				◆	◆	◆	◆			◆			◆		◆
Scoozi	302			◆	◆	◆	◆			◆				◆	◆		◆					◆			◆
Shaw's Crab House	384			◆	◆	◆	◆			◆				◆	◆		◆						◆		
Shilla Restaurant	336	◆		◆	◆			◆						◆	◆	◆	◆	◆	◆		◆		◆		◆
Spiaggia	304	◆		◆	◆	◆	◆			◆	◆			◆	◆	◆			◆				◆	◆	
Standard India	254	◆		◆	◆		◆		◆			◆		◆	◆	◆	◆		◆	◆					
Star Top Cafe	114			◆	◆					◆					◆						◆		◆		
Streeterville Grille & Bar	116	◆		◆	◆	◆	◆	◆		◆				◆	◆	◆		◆	◆				◆	◆	
Su Casa	358	◆		◆	◆	◆			◆	◆	◆	◆		◆	◆		◆	◆	◆	◆			◆		
Szechwan House	144	◆		◆	◆	◆	◆		◆					◆	◆	◆	◆	◆	◆	◆			◆		
T'ang Dynasty	146	◆		◆	◆	◆			◆		◆			◆	◆	◆	◆	◆	◆	◆			◆		
Tania's	156	◆		◆	◆	◆	◆	◆		◆	◆			◆	◆	◆	◆	◆	◆	◆				◆	
Tecalitlan	360	◆								◆		◆	◆	◆	◆	◆				◆					◆
Tehran Restaurant	364	◆		◆	◆	◆	◆							◆	◆	◆	◆	◆	◆		◆		◆		
Thai Borrahn	420			◆	◆				◆	◆				◆	◆	◆	◆		◆		◆		◆		
Topo Gigio	306	◆		◆	◆				◆	◆				◆	◆	◆				◆	◆		◆		
Topolobampo	362	◆		◆	◆	◆	◆		◆					◆	◆	◆			◆	◆			◆		

Features Guide

Restaurant	Pg.	Wheelchair Access	100% Non-Smoking	Visa/Master Card	American Express	Discover	Diners Club	Checks Accepted	Beer & Wine	Full Bar	Live Entertainment	Sunday Brunch	Breakfast	Lunch	Dinner	High Chairs	Take Out	Valet Parking	Private Parties	Informal Dress	Casual Dress	Jacket/Tie	Reserv. Recom.	Reserv. Required	Reserv. Not Taken
Toulouse	214	◆		◆	◆		◆			◆	◆				◆			◆	◆				◆	◆	
Trattoria Bellavia	308	◆		◆	◆					◆				◆	◆	◆			◆		◆		◆		
Trattoria Gianni	310	◆		◆				◆	◆	◆		◆		◆	◆	◆	◆	◆	◆		◆		◆		
Trattoria No. 10	312	◆		◆	◆	◆	◆			◆				◆	◆	◆			◆	◆	◆		◆		
Tucci Benuuch	314		◆	◆	◆	◆	◆			◆				◆	◆			◆			◆		◆		
Tucci Milan	316		◆	◆	◆	◆	◆			◆				◆	◆			◆					◆	◆	
Tufano's Vernon Park Tap	318							◆	◆	◆				◆	◆	◆	◆		◆	◆			◆		◆
Tuttaposto	338	◆		◆	◆	◆	◆		◆	◆				◆	◆	◆	◆	◆	◆		◆		◆		
Twin Anchors	118			◆	◆		◆			◆				◆	◆	◆	◆		◆		◆				◆
Un Grand Cafe	216	◆		◆	◆	◆	◆		◆	◆					◆		◆			◆		◆			
Va Pensiero	320	◆		◆	◆	◆			◆	◆				◆	◆	◆		◆	◆			◆	◆		
Via Veneto	322	◆		◆	◆	◆	◆			◆				◆	◆	◆	◆		◆		◆		◆		
Village, The	324			◆	◆	◆	◆	◆	◆	◆				◆	◆	◆	◆	◆	◆		◆		◆		
Vinci	326	◆		◆	◆					◆					◆	◆		◆	◆		◆		◆		
Vinny's	328	◆		◆	◆		◆		◆	◆				◆	◆	◆	◆	◆	◆	◆	◆		◆		
Vivere	330	◆		◆	◆	◆	◆	◆	◆	◆				◆	◆	◆		◆	◆		◆		◆		
Wayside Manor, The	218	◆		◆						◆					◆				◆	◆			◆		
Wishbone	120	◆		◆		◆		◆	◆	◆		◆	◆	◆	◆	◆	◆	◆							
Yoshi's Cafe	220	◆		◆	◆		◆								◆			◆	◆		◆	◆	◆		
Yvette	122	◆		◆	◆		◆		◆	◆	◆				◆			◆	◆				◆		
Yvette Wintergarden	124	◆		◆	◆		◆		◆	◆				◆	◆				◆			◆	◆		
Zaven's	154	◆		◆	◆	◆	◆	◆	◆	◆				◆	◆	◆	◆		◆		◆		◆	◆	
Zum Deutschen Eck	230	◆		◆	◆	◆	◆		◆	◆	◆			◆	◆	◆	◆		◆		◆		◆		

The Restaurants

A pleasant atmosphere amid a forest of green plants, impeccable service and carefully prepared food make Chicago's only Afghan restaurant a dining oasis not to be missed.

The Helmand

Menu Changes Seasonally

══════ APPETIZERS ══════

AUSHAK. *Afghan ravioli filled with leeks, served on yogurt-mint and topped with ground beef sauce.* — 2.95

MANTWO, *Homemade pastry shells filled with onions and beef, served on yogurt and topped with carrots, yellow split peas and beef sauce.* — 2.95

BOWLAWNI. *Pan-fried twin pastry shells filled with leeks and spiced potatoes, garnished with yogurt and mint.* — 2.95

BANJAN BORAWNI, *Pan-fried eggplant seasoned with fresh tomatoes and spices, baked and served on yogurt garlic sauce.* — 2.95

KADDO BORAWNI, *Pan-fried and baked baby pumpkin seasoned with sugar and served on yogurt garlic sauce.* — 2.95

══════ SOUPS ══════

AUSH, *Home-made noodle soup served with beef sauce and mint yogurt.* — 2.25

MASHAWA, *Beef, mung beans, chick peas, black-eyed peas and yogurt soup.* — 2.25

SHORWA, *Lamb, fresh vegetables and bean soup.* — 2.25

ENTREES

KABULI, *Pallow (Afghan style rice) baked with chunks of Lamb Tenderloin, raisins and glazed Julienne of carrots.* *9.50*

DWOPIAZA, *Season Tenderloin of Lamb cooked with onions, sauteed with yellow split-peas and tossed with onions lightly marinated in vinegar. Served with pallow.* *9.50*

AUSHAK, *Afghan ravioli filled with leeks, served on yogurt and topped with ground beef and mint.* *8.50*

MANTWO, *Home-made pastry-shell filled with onions and beef, served on yogurt and topped with carrots, yellow split-peas and beef sauce.* *8.50*

SABZY CHALLOW, *Spinach sauteed with chunks of beef and Afghan seasonings, served with challow.* *8.50*

KOURMA CHALLOW, *Beef sauteed with Afghan seasonings and variety of vegetables, served with challow.* *8.50*

MOURGH CHALLOW, *Chicken sauteed with spices and yellow split-peas, served with challow.* *7.95*

SEEKH KABAB, *Char-broiled marinated lamb tenderloin served with pallow.* *9.95*

KOUFTA CHALLOW, *Combination of lamb and beef meatballs seasoned with sun dried baby grapes, paprika, turmerik in hot green pepper, green peas and fresh tomato sauce and served with challow.* *8.50*

Dinner: Mon - Thurs 5 - 10:30, Fri - Sat 5 - 11:30, Sun 4 - 9

One of Chicago's few restaurants with viewing pleasure inside and out. The multi-level dining room has a casual plush about it, and there's not a bad seat in the house from which to enjoy Chicago's spectacular lakefront. The American concept menu changes seasonally, and you can always count on some interesting food ideas.

Menu Changes Seasonally

APPETIZERS

COLD

Cured salmon cake with asparagus salad; sherry and black pepper vinaigrette   10.00

Pheasant confit with oven-roasted tomatoes and green beans; rosemary and mustard dressing   9.75

Spring vegetable terrine with smoked chicken and mixed greens; herb shallot vinaigrette   9.50

HOT

Broiled smelts on a bed of crispy potatoes; crème fraîche and chive   9.75

Salmon, ricotta and mushrooms rolled in pasta with creamed spinach   13.00

Sautéed quail with wheatberries, sun-dried tomatoes and fontinella cheese; caramelized onion demi-glace   16.50

Dungeness crabmeat wrapped in fillo pastry; jalapeño and garlic mayonnaise   11.75

SALADS

Bibb lettuce with goat cheese and pine nuts; sun-dried tomato vinaigrette 6.75

Grilled radicchio with field greens; lemon grass vinaigrette 6.50

Asparagus salad; Parmesan vinaigrette 6.50

MAIN COURSE SELECTIONS

Honey and ginger glazed salmon with chilled rice noodles; sesame soy sauce 29.00

Sautéed grouper with marinated spring vegetables; saffron sauce 28.00

Seared Ahi tuna on a bed of greens; basil and orange infused oil 32.50

Poached halibut with julienned vegetables; spicy vegetable broth 27.00

Steamed green lip mussels with angel hair pasta; tomato and saffron broth 24.00

Sautéed breast of chicken; pear and shallot compote 24.00

Grilled pork tenderloin with okra hash; pablano pepper sauce 24.00

Grilled marinated quail with wild rice stuffing; cranberry orange demi-glace 29.75

Roasted rack of lamb with rosemary potatoes and tapenade; natural juices 39.00

Dinner: Sun - Thurs 5:30 - 10, Fri 5:30 - 11, Sat 6 - 11

Ann Sather

A wonderful breakfast (the cinnamon rolls are great) is the signature meal of this group of restaurants, but the homey atmosphere and the upgraded menu make lunch and dinner viable contenders.

ANN SATHER

HOT SANDWICHES

Veggie Burger (Lacto-Ovo)	$4.95
Jumbo Burger	$5.25
Reuben Sandwich	$5.95
Marinated Grilled Chicken Breast Sandwich	$5.95
Tuna Melt or Patty Melt	$5.95
Grilled Cheese	$3.75
Swedish Meatball Sandwich	$4.50

***Choose One** from Our "Side Dishes" or Fresh Fruit, Mashed Potatoes with Gravy, French Fries, Hash Browns, Swedish Potato Salad, or Pasta Salad*

Extra Toppings!!! 50¢ each
Sautéed Mushrooms; Mozzarella, Cheddar, Swiss, Blue, or American Cheese; Bacon, Ham, Avocado, Guacamole, Sprouts

COLD SANDWICHES

Served on Homemade White or Swedish Limpa Rye or Whole Wheat Bread, Lettuce & Tomato, Pickle, ANN SATHER Coleslaw

Chef's Market Ham, Roast Beef, Corned Beef, or Turkey	$5.25
Smoked Liver Sausage	$4.25
Red Sockeye Salmon Salad	$5.50
White Albacore Tuna Salad	$5.25
Chicken Salad	$5.25
Bacon, Lettuce & Tomato	$4.50
Turkey Club Sandwich	$5.95
Open Faced Veggie Sandwich	$4.95

SALADS

Chicken Salad Bowl	$5.95
Fresh Spinach Salad Choose Bacon or Sun-dried Tomatoes	$5.95
Crabmeat & Seafood Salad	$6.95
Grilled Chicken Breast Salad	$6.95

Above Salads Include Cheddar & Swiss Cheese, Hard Boiled Egg, Tomato, Pickled Beets, Mushrooms, Carrot, and Red Cabbage

Fresh Fruit with Chicken Salad Tropical Fruit with our World Famous Chicken Salad	$5.95
Stuffed Tomato Whole Tomato, stuffed with Chicken, Salmon, or Tuna Salad (Salmon Salad add 50¢)	$5.95
Caesar Chicken Tortellini Salad With Romaine Lettuce & Cheese Tortellini	$6.95
Vegetarian Pasta Salad	$5.95
Deluxe Garden Salad	$3.95
Tossed House Salad With Sandwich Order	$1.75 $1.00

HOMEMADE SOUP OF THE DAY

Bowl	$1.75
With sandwich order or large salad	$1.00

DINNERS

Complete Meals: *Include Starter, Entree, Two Side Dishes, Dessert, & Beverage*

Lite Meals: *Include Starter, Lite Portion Entree, One Side Dish, & Beverage*

A Selection of Homemade Breads Accompanies Every Dinner!

Swedish Sampler (Side dishes predetermined)   **$11.95**
Roast Duck, Lingonberry Glaze, Meatball,
Potato Sausage Dumpling, Sauerkraut, & Brown Beans

Catch of the Day	Selection & Price Vary Daily
Fresh Fish	Please Ask Your Server

	Complete Meals	Lite Meals
Roast Duck With Sauerkraut, Dumpling, & Lingonberry Glaze (Side dishes predetermined)	$9.95	$7.95
Swedish Potato Sausage A Mild Blend of Veal, Pork, & Potatoes	$9.50	$7.50
Swedish Sirloin of Beef Steak Thinly Sliced with Onions	$8.50	$6.50
Swedish Meatballs With Butter Noodles and Brown Gravy	$8.50	$6.50
Roast Loin of Pork With Celery Dressing, Gravy	$9.95	$7.95
Pan Fried Pork Chops (2) Center Cut	$9.95	$7.95
Baked Spring Chicken (¼) With Celery Dressing, Gravy	$8.50	$6.50
Roast Tom Turkey With Celery Dressing, Gravy	$9.50	$7.50
Chopped Beef Steak Rare, Medium, or Well Done; with Fried Onions	$8.95	$6.95
Veal Steak Lightly Breaded, with Gravy & Almonds	$9.50	$7.50
Pan Fried Beef Liver With Fried Onions	$8.75	$6.75
Baked Meat loaf With Brown Gravy	$8.95	$6.95
Boneless Breast of Chicken Marinated	$9.50	$7.50

STARTERS

Homemade Soup of the Day

Chilled Swedish Fruit Soup

Pickled Herring

Tossed House Salad

Cottage Cheese

Fruit Gelatin

Cranberry Juice and Sherbet Float

SIDE DISHES

Swedish Brown Beans

Mashed or Boiled Potatoes

Candied Sweet Potatoes

Mixed Vegetables

Caraway Seed Sauerkraut

Creamed Peas

Pickled Beets

Cranberry Sauce

Homemade Applesauce

Wild Rice Medley

Pasta Salad

Dinner: 7 Days a Week until 10

Now into its 20th year, Arnie's, where the New American cuisine took root, has a special appeal for diners who enjoy quality fare at a reasonable price. And the Art Deco ambiance is special unto itself.

Appetizers

Fried Calamari, Cocktail Sauce   5.50

Grilled Shrimp Remoulade   7.95

Sizzling Chicken, Tai Peanut Sauce   4.50

Crab Cake, Lobster Dill Sauce   4.95

Escargot & Shitake Mushrooms en Croute, Garlic Cream   4.95

Wild Mushrooms in Phyllo Pouch   4.95

Appetizer Selection   7.50 (2 person minimum)
Grilled Shrimp, Thai Chicken, Escargot en Croute, B.B.Q. Ribs & Pizza

Soups

Soup du Jour
Served by the Bowl

Baked Onion Soup, Gruyere

Black Bean Soup
In our Onion Loaf, Sour Cream & Onions

3.50

Salads

Caesar
Creamy Garlic & Parmesan Dressing, Romaine & Toasted Croutons

Spinach Salad
Warm Virginia Bacon Dressing

Arnie's
Blue Cheese Dressing, Egg & Anchovy

3.95

Pasta

Pasta Primavera   12.95
*A Sunburst of Fresh Vegetables Blended with Imported Spaghetti
in a Creamy Parmesan Cheese & Butter Sauce*

Angel Hair Pasta with Shrimp & Scallops   14.95
Vegetables Julienne, Fresh Basil Sauce

Trios

Grilled Shrimp Remoulade, Roast Lobster Pasta & Chef's
Seafood Selection   17.95
Ginger Shallot Rice

Petite Filet Mignon, Sauce Bearnaise, Shrimp
Alex & Sizzling Chicken, Thai Peanut Sauce   18.95
Horseradish Mashed Potatoes

Crab Cake, Lobster Dill Sauce, Shrimp Tempura & Lobster en Croute   15.95
Chef's Vegetable Selection

Specialties

22 oz. Porterhouse Steak   25.95
Prime New York Strip Steak   24.95
Filet Mignon, Sauce Bearnaise   20.95
B.B.Q. Baby Back Ribs   12.95
Cottage Fried Potatoes

Sauteed Whole Dover Sole   22.95
Sauce Meuniere or Almondine, Served Tableside

Garden Veal Chop   19.95
Breaded in Croissant Crumbs, Topped with Assorted Greens Vinaigrette

Chicken with Eggplant Duxelle   12.95
Shitake Mushroom Brandy Sauce   12.95
Sauteed Lake Superior Whitefish   12.95
Fresh Lemon & Capers

Vegetables

Asparagus, Hollandaise   4.95
Baked, Mashed or Au Gratin Potatoes   2.50
Sauteed Spinach & Mushrooms   2.95

Sunday Brunch; Dinner: Sun - Thurs 5:30 - 10, Fri - Sat 5:30 - 11:30

This restaurant, like Rodney Dangerfield, doesn't get enough respect. The people in the neighborhood know its worth, though, and like the down-to-earth mix of good sandwiches and interesting entrees.

APPETIZERS

*Chips, Guac and Salsa   5.50
Crispy corn tortilla chips, thick, rich guacamole and zesty salsa-all made fresh daily from authentic recipes. Sour cream on the side.

*Combination Platter   Cost per person: 5.95
A tasty assortment of Potato Skins, Nachos, Cajun chicken tenders and our world famous hot wings. (minimum 2 people)

SALADS

Blackened Chicken Salad   6.95
Fresh boneless breast of chicken seared with Cajun spices, and served chilled with a mixture of fresh grilled vegetables and tomato on a bed of shredded lettuce. Served with Balsamic Vinaigrette dressing.

*Grilled Turkey Breast with Bow Tie Pasta   6.95
Hearty chunks of freshly grilled turkey breast and homemade bow tie pasta tossed in a lite sour cream dressing with cucumbers, fresh dill, carrots, celery and red radishes.

"WINGS, WINGS, WINGS"

All of our wings carry the Perdue mark of excellence!

Regular Basket	**Large Basket**	**Super Basket**
5.50/10 Wings	9.95/20 Wings	14.95/30 Wings

Barbequed Chicken Wings
Slowly smoked over real Applewood then finished off on the grill and basted with our homemade BBQ sauce. Served with a pile of oven browned potatoes with BBQ sauce on the side.

San Antonio Chicken Wings
A recipe from the deep in the heart of Texas. These wings are breaded, deep fried and then covered with San Antonio sauce, made of honey and picante. Served with a pile of oven browned potatoes.

RIBS AND CHICKEN

*Baby Back Ribs
Full Slab (1 1/2 pounds)   13.95
Half slab   10.95

Bigsby's Beef Ribs   14.95
Cut right from the prime rib. These ribs are big, meaty and full of flavor.

Baby Back Rib & Chicken Combo   13.95
Choice of Barbequed Chicken or Sweet Garlic Chili Sauce Chicken

& SHRIMP

Fried Shrimp   10.95
Succulent Shrimp lightly breaded and deep fried to a golden brown. Served
with oven browned potatoes, homemade coleslaw, BBQ, cocktail and tartar sauces.

*Cajun Peel 'N Eat Shrimp   10.95
A whole pile of succulent shrimp cooked to order in our secret recipe Cajun Sauce.
Served with oven browned potatoes and homemade coleslaw.

CHICKEN BREAST SPECIALTIES

*Blackened Chicken Breast   10.95
An 8 oz. boneless breast of chicken seared in our Cajun spices and brushed
with a mild Cilantro butter.

Barbequed Chicken Breast   10.95
An 8 oz. boneless breast of chicken grilled to perfection and basted
with our homemade BBQ sauce.

BURGERS BURGERS & MORE BURGERS

All of our burgers are hand-patted daily from one half pound of USDA
choice ground chuck, lightly seasoned and grilled to order. Served with your
choice of sesame bun, whole wheat bun or black bread, along with oven
browned potatoes, lettuce, tomato, sliced red onion and homemade coleslaw.

Bigsby's Cheddar Bacon Burger   5.95
Topped with Cheddar cheese and hickory smoked bacon.

Jack McDowell's California Burger   6.25
Topped with guacamole, Monterey Jack and Cheddar cheeses.

*André Dawson's North of the Border Burger   6.50
Topped with grilled Canadian bacon, Cheddar cheese, sauteed mushrooms and onion.

*Indicates Popular Items

Dinner: Sun - Thurs until 10, Fri - Sat until 11

This is the huddling and deal-making place that Loop business types and politicos are drawn to. The Old World atmosphere and the savvy waitstaff definitely add to the appeal. The turtle soup is practically a legend in Chicago.

B I N Y O N ' S

Menu Changes Seasonally

Soups

TURTLE .... 2.25   CHICKEN NOODLE 2.25

Salad Entrees

HOLLYWOOD COBB SALAD	9.95
SPINACH SALAD	7.50
GARDEN SALAD	7.95
PASTA SALAD PRIMAVERA	8.95
JULIENNE SALAD	8.95
CAESAR SALAD	7.25
SEAFOOD CAESAR	9.95
CHICKEN ARTICHOKE CAESAR SALAD	8.95
SEAFOOD PASTA SALAD	10.95

Pasta Entrees

FETTUCINI OR LINGUINI
SERVED: BOLOGNESE
          MARINARA
          ALFREDO
      OR OLIVE OIL and GARLIC 8.95
    WITH: SHRIMP............................. 12.95
          PRIMAVERA 10.95
          MARINATED CHICKEN 11.95
          Pasta Entrees include House Salad

Fish and Seafood

FRESH FISH OF THE DAY	MARKET
LAKE SUPERIOR WHITEFISH	11.95
SHRIMP DE JONGHE	13.95
FRENCH FRIED SHRIMP	12.95
STUFFED TROUT	11.50
BAY SCALLOPS	11.50
BROILED ORANGE ROUGHY	11.50
FARM RAISED CATFISH	10.95
IMPORTED ENGLISH DOVER SOLE	21.00

Poultry and Veal

MARINATED LEMON CHICKEN 10.95
CHICKEN MARSALA 11.95
SAUTEED CALF'S LIVER 12.95
VEAL MARSALA 12.95
VEAL PARMAGIANA 12.95
VEAL PICCATA 12.95
ROAST LONG ISLAND DUCKLING 13.95

Beef, Lamb and Chops

ROAST PRIME RIB OF BEEF 17.50
LADIES CUT PRIME RIB 13.50
FILET MIGNON 19.95
PETITE FILET 13.95
STEAK & SHRIMP 18.95
N.Y. CUT SIRLOIN 19.95
DELMONICO STEAK 14.95
PEPPER STEAK 12.95
PORK CHOPS 12.95
CHOPPED SIRLOIN 9.95
ROAST BABY RACK OF LAMB 22.00

All Entrees include Soup or Salad, Fresh Vegetable and Choice of Potato or Rice

½ Caesar or ½ Spinach Salad with Entree 2.95

*Dressing Choices: Thousand Island, Creamy Bleu Cheese or
Lo-Cal Ranch, Lo-Cal French or Lo-Cal Italian
Dry Bleu Cheese 1.00 Additional*

Dinner: Mon - Sat 4:30 - 9

35

Blackhawk Lodge

The atmosphere is a mix of country lodge and city plush with the best screened-in porch outdoor eating outside of New Orleans. A new approach to the daily specials has lifted the eating interest immensely.

BLACKHAWK
LODGE

Menu Changes Seasonally

APPETIZERS

GOAT CHEESE SOUFFLÉ *bedded on mixed greens* 4.95

WARM GRILLED WILD MUSHROOMS *watercress and parsley* 5.95

SHRIMP COCKTAIL *roasted tomato-horseradish sauce* 9.95

GRILLED EGGPLANT AND MOZZARELLA *served chilled with tomato-basil sauce* 4.95

APPLEWOOD-SMOKED STURGEON AND CURED SALMON *grilled brioche* 8.95

SAUTÉED CRAB CAKE *baby lettuces, scallion-tartar sauce* 7.95

SMOKED-BABY BACK RIBS, FRIED CHICKEN WINGS, AND BRAISED DUCK
 plenty for sharing 10.50

CARPACCIO OF BEEF *arrugula, romano cheese, and extra-virgin olive oil* 5.95

BAKED CHEESE GRITS *tasso ham and mushroom sauce* 4.95

GRILLED CALAMARI *capers, roasted peppers, lemon-garlic olive oil* 5.95

SOUPS AND SALADS

SEAFOOD-CORN CHOWDER *bacon, potatoes, and Southern Comfort* 3.95

BARLEY AND BEAN SOUP *with vegetables* 3.50

ASPARAGUS AND CUCUMBERS *Maytag blue cheese and lemon-olive oil* 4.50

TOMATO AND AVOCADO SALAD *onions and red-wine vinaigrette* 6.95

BLACKHAWK LODGE SALAD *olives, sage croutons, and mustard dressing* 3.95

CAESAR SALAD *garlic croutons and shaved parmesan cheese* 7.95
 With grilled chicken breast 8.95

---

41 East Superior • Near North/Gold Coast • (312) 280-4080

36

MAIN COURSES

ROASTED GARLIC AND HERB CHICKEN *grilled vegetables* 12.95

LEMON PEPPER FRIED CHICKEN *vegetable cole slaw* 12.95

ROASTED TURKEY FILET *mashed potatoes, rhubarb chutney, and sage cream* 13.50

GRILLED PORK CHOPS *apple rings, thin fried onions and mustard sauce* 15.95

SEASONAL VEGETARIAN PLATTER *grilled, braised, and roasted vegetables with lemon* 12.95

SAUTÉED WHITEFISH *cabbage and bacon, red-wine butter sauce* 13.95

GRILLED FILLET OF SALMON *asparagus, boiled potatoes, and tomato-dill hollandaise* 16.95

SAUTÉED RAINBOW TROUT *lemon, shallots, and capers* 13.95

BARBEQUED WHOLE RED SNAPPER *marinated in lemon, garlic and herbs; served with vegetables* 18.95

LINGUINE WITH SEAFOOD *shrimp, clams, mussels, squid, cherry tomatoes, garlic, white wine* 10.95   *Appetizer portion* 5.95

RIGATONI AND SMOKED CHICKEN *chard and herbed cheese sauce* 12.95   *Appetizer portion* 6.95

ASPARAGUS AND RICOTTA RAVIOLI *grilled pancetta and roasted plum tomatoes* 11.95   *Appetizer portion* 6.95

GRILLED LAMB LOIN *celery root-mashed potatoes and sautéed spinach* 16.95

BLACKHAWK HAMBURGER *lettuce, tomato, and buttermilk onion rings* 7.95

DRY AGED NEW YORK STEAK *wild mushrooms and pearl onions* 21.95

HICKORY-SMOKED BABY BACK RIBS *cole slaw* 15.95   *Half slab* 11.95

DRY AGED PRIME RIB OF BEEF *horseradish cream* 19.95   *California cut* 16.95

VEGETABLES AND SIDES

GRILLED ASPARAGUS 3.75

CELERY ROOT MASHED POTATOES 3.25

BUTTERMILK FRIED ONION RINGS 2.95

SAUTÉED SPINACH WITH LEMON AND GARLIC 3.50

WHITE BEANS WITH ROMANO CHEESE, SAGE, OLIVE OIL 3.95

HOUSE CUT FRIES 2.95

GRILLED AND ROASTED SEASONAL VEGETABLES 3.75

Bones

Casual no-frills atmosphere, a friendly waitstaff, and some of the best ribs around have made this Lincolnwood "cottage" restaurant a winner, one that probably gets more repeat customers than any in the area.

HOME SMOKED BBQ

Appetizers

SPINACH FINGERS	$3.75	GARLIC CHICKEN FINGERS	$3.95
FRIED CALAMARI	$4.25	BUFFALO CHICKEN FINGERS	$3.95
ONION STRINGS	$2.50	POTATO SKINS	$4.25
BUFFALO CHICKEN WINGS	$4.95	STUFFED MUSHROOMS	$4.95
BBQ WINGS	$4.95	FRIED SHRIMP	$5.95
ORIENTAL CHICKEN WINGS	$4.95	GARLIC SHRIMP	$5.95

POTATO PANCAKES (As many as you can handle) . . . .$1.00 each

Combos

WINGS
BBQ , Buffalo & Oriental
Small Combo $5.95
Large Combo $8.95

SHRIMP
BBQ , Garlic & Fried
Small Combo $5.95
Large Combo $10.95

FINGERS
Garlic Chicken, Buffalo & Spinach
Small Combo $3.95
Large Combo $6.95

BBQ
Shrimp & Wings
Small Combo $5.95
Large Combo $10.95

Sandwiches

HAMBURGER	$6.35
CHEESEBURGER	$6.35
BONESBURGER, blue cheese sauce, marlboro onions	$6.50
GOURMET BURGER, mushrooms, onions, swiss cheese, bordelaise sauce	$6.50
BBQ BEEF SANDWICH, "Brisket Slowly Smoked"	$6.50
BBQ PORK SANDWICH, slowly smoked pork loin	$6,50
BBQ CHICKEN SANDWICH, shredded chicken simmered in BBQ sauce with grilled onions	$6.35
GRILLED TURKEY BREAST, teriyaki glaze, onion roll	$6.50

Sandwiches served with coleslaw, choice of double baked potato, or Bones fries.
Choice of raw, grilled or marlboro onions.

7110 West Lincoln Ave • Lincolnwood • (708) 677-3350

38

Whitefish, Salmon, & Shrimp

FRESH LAKE SUPERIOR WHITEFISH
Broiled $11.95
Mustard Glazed $11.95
Blackened $11.95
Herbed $11.95

SHRIMP
Fried $14.95
BBQ $14.95
Garlic $14.95

SALMON FILET
Broiled $14.95
BBQ $14.95
Mustard Glazed $14.95

Served with soup of the day or salad or coleslaw.
Choice of boiled new potatoes, double baked or Bones fries.

Bones Specialities

SIMA'S WHOLE GARLIC CHICKEN (white meat only $2.00 extra), choice of potato $12.95
WHOLE BROILED CHICKEN (white meat only $2.00 extra), choice of potato $12.95
ROASTED BRISKET, home-made potato pancake $12.95
BRAISED SHORT RIBS AND POT ROAST, braised vegetable and horseradish
whipped potatoes $12.95
SWEET AND SOUR STUFFED CABBAGE, horseradish whipped potatoes $9.95
CENTER CUT SKIRT STEAK, grilled onions, choice of potato $14.95
T-BONE STEAK, 16 oz., grilled or marlboro onions, choice of potato $16.95
Specialities served with soup of the day or salad or coleslaw.
Order of potato pancakes 3 with any of the above...... $3.00 extra.

Pasta

BOW TIE PASTA, grilled chicken breast, light wild mushroom broth $9.95
MEDITERRANEAN CHICKEN, served with pasta $11.95
SHRIMP LINGUINE, tomato and basil sauce $12.95
CHICKEN SAUSAGE PASTA, spicy chicken sausage, light tomato sauce $11.95
Pasta served with soup of the day or salad.

BBQ Specialties

BBQ BABY BACK RIBS, slow smoked over hickory $14.95
WHOLE BBQ CHICKEN (white meat only $2.00 extra) $12.95
BBQ BEEF RIBS $11.50
BBQ BRISKET PLATE $12.95
BBQ TURKEY BREAST $11.95
BBQ items served with soup of the day or salad or coleslaw.
Choice of double baked potato, or Bones fries.

16% Gratuity added to parties of five or larger.
There will be times when quality will not meet our specifications and
an item on the menu will not be served.

Please refrain from pipe and cigar smoking in dining areas.

These items are prepared from recipes that meet the fat and cholesterol guidelines of the
American Heart Association of Metropolitan Chicago for healthy adults.

Sunday Brunch; Dinner: Mon - Thurs until 11, Fri - Sat until 12, Sun 3 - 10

Serving only breakfast and lunch, this cozy cottage, which is surrounded by light industry, offers some heavy-duty eating. The homemade scones and muffins are wonderful, and so are the daily specials.

Specials

Steak Au Vin 7.95
7 oz STRIP STEAK sauteed with fresh mushrooms, a fabulous teriaki and red wine sauce - served w/ Couscous and Peapods

Pasta Primavera 6.50
mushrooms, broccoli, Red Pepper, peas tossed with Linguini in our delicious Parmesan Sauce

Grecian Chicken 7.25
3 tender pieces of chicken (1/2 chicken) in a lemon/oregano seasoning - served with Rice Pilaf and fresh vegetable

Meatloaf 5.95
Served w/ mashed potatoes, gravy and fresh vegetable

Fresh Lake Perch 7.25
"The best you'll ever eat!" served with Homemade potato pancakes, fresh green beans, lemon and tartar sauce

Oriental Vegetable Stir Fry 5.95
a wonderfully fresh combination of mushrooms, broccoli, zucchini, yellow squash, red peppers, onions, in a fabulous light sauce - served w/ a platter of Brown Rice & warmed tortilla

Beans and Rice 5.95
Black Beans slowly simmered with cilantro and other seasonings served w/ Brown Rice (this is the perfect food balance)

Veggie Burger - smart 5.95
a garden-vegetable and grains burger on-a-bun w/ lettuce, tomatoes, our special, special mustard sauce

Roast Loin of Pork   6.95
tender roast of pork, served with mashed potatoes, gravy and fresh green beans

Chicken Stir Fry   7.50
an array of fresh vegetables, including mushrooms, broccoli, zucchini, squash, onion, peppers, (and more) - sautéed in a lite-delicious sauce, topped w/ crunchy noodles & a broiled Chicken Breast

Avocado, Swiss Cheese and Mango Chutney   5.95
an exotic mixture of avocado, Swiss, chutney, lettuce and tomato on Multi-Grain Bread

Burgers & Sandwiches
Sandwiches served with French fries, lettuce and tomato

Breakfast Club Burger, grilled and served on a sesame seed bun $5.25

Breakfast Club Cheeseburger, grilled, with choice of cheeses $5.50

Bacon Cheeseburger, with your choice of cheese $5.75

Cheese & Mushroom Burger, with your choice of cheese $5.75

Cajun Burger, topped with melted cheese, sauteed onions, and bell peppers $5.95

Our Famous Club Sandwiches, choose from BLT, Turkey, or Ham & Cheese, served on Greek bread $5.75

Barbequed Chicken Breast Sandwich, topped with grilled onions and cheddar and served on a sesame seed bun $6.75

Cordon Bleu Chicken Sandwich, grilled chicken breast with Ham & Swiss $6.75

New Orleans Cajun Chicken Breast Sandwich $6.75

Turkey and Swiss, *lettuce and tomato,* on French or Multi Grain bread $5.75

Tuna Salad, on French or Multi Grain bread $5.95

The Big Cheese, three cheeses, bacon and tomato grilled on Multi Grain bread $4.95

Veggie Melt, fresh vegetables, grilled with mozzarella cheese, and served on Multi Grain bread $5.75

Salads

Warm Chicken Breast Salad, grilled chicken, julienned, served over lettuces and served with our own Honey Mustard dressing $6.95

Chicken Caesar Salad, grilled chicken breast, served over our delicious Caesar salad $6.95

Breakfast; Lunch: Mon - Fri 6 - 3, Sat - Sun 7 - 3

Owner Brett Knobel has put together an interesting restaurant. The food is California-style, light and easy. The decor is a combination of simple and elaborate. And most everybody applauds the totally smoke-free environment.

Menu Changes Weekly

SOUP

Carrot Ginger   3.95

HOUSE SALAD

Spinach, charred onion, cured black olives and citrus vinaigrette   3.95

APPETIZERS

Cornmeal dusted calamari with spinach
and corn risotto   5.95

Grilled shrimp with black bean and Jack
torte with cilantro and chili oils   6.25

Goat cheese and caraway filo with wild mushroom
and red onion salad and red pepper coulis   4.50

Cumin roast chicken quesadilla with
tomatillo salsa   4.25

MAIN COURSE

Braised skate, corn-baked Bibb and bacon
balsamic vinaigrette   13.95

Grilled adobo spiced pork chop, sweet potato
pecan cakes and jicama/orange pico de gallo   13.95

Grilled flank steak, roast garlic, whipped
potatoes, braised collards and barbecue jus   15.95

Roast salmon over salad of roast beets,
cucumber linguini, Great Northern beans,
parsley horseradish oil   14.95

Savoy cabbage strudel, braised leeks and
tomato cous cous parfait, celery broth   10.95

Linguini with arugula, mozzarella, roast
garlic and tomato broth   10.95

We now offer a special dessert "sampler" featuring an
assortment selected from our dessert table, for $5.00
per person

Bub City Crabshack

Down home and delightful, Bub City, despite its cavernous and retro-chic decor, is a great spot to roll up your sleeves and whack away at fresh crab or a tangy barbecue. The live country music and dancing are appealing too.

Cold Appetizers

Our Famous Guaranteed Crab Claws $6.95
Fresh Shucked Cockenoe Oysters, half shell .... ½ doz. $5.95 .... doz. $10.95
Gussied-up Blue Crab Fingers $5.25
Gulf Shrimp Cocktail (We peel) .... $5.95 .... (You peel) $4.95
Mumbo Jumbo Combo—enough shrimp, oysters, crab claws & crab fingers for 2 .... $11.95

Hot Appetizers

Blue Crab Fritters, rémoulade sauce $4.25
Pick 'n' Lick Garlic Shrimp (We Peel) .... $5.95 .... (You Peel) $4.95
Pick 'n' Lick Hot 'n' Spicy Shrimp (We Peel) $5.95 .... (You Peel) $4.95
Pick 'n' Lick BBQ Shrimp (We Peel) .... $5.95 .... (You Peel) $4.95
Baked Oysters Ralphie Boy; Ralphie's special 3-cheese sauce $6.95
Baked Clams with tomato and basil $5.95
Buffalo Chicken Tenders $5.95
Who Do's Swimmin' Chicken Wings $4.50
Texas Torpedos—fried jalapeños with cheese .... ½ $4.50 .... full $8.75
Fried Calamari with spicy marinara $4.95
Cajun Popcorn Shrimp $5.95
Beer Battered Onion Mum $3.95

Soups & Salads

Seafood Gumbo .... cup $2.50 .... bowl $3.75
Homemade Soup .... cup $2.50 .... bowl $3.75
Snapper Stew .... cup $2.50 .... bowl $3.75
Gertie's Garbage Salad $4.95
    With Grilled Chicken $6.95
    With Grilled Shrimp $7.95

Crabs & Shrimp

Guaranteed Crab Claws, cold with mustard sauce $12.95
Guaranteed Crab Claws, hot steamed in garlic butter $12.95
Blue Crabs, garlic or hot 'n' spicy .... 1/2 .... $8.95 .... full $14.95
Whole Dungeness Crab, drawn butter, garlic or hot & spicy $19.95
Snow Crab Legs $16.95
Pick 'n' Lick Garlic Shrimp (We Peel) .... $13.95 .... (You Peel) $11.95
Pick 'n' Lick Hot 'n' Spicy Shrimp (We Peel) $13.95 .... (You Peel) $11.95
Pick 'n' Lick BBQ Shrimp (We Peel) .... $13.95 .... (You Peel) $11.95
Baked Shrimp with crab-and-shrimp stuffing $12.95
Famous Alaskan Snow Crab Claws, garlic, hot n spicy or BBQ $19.95
New Orleans Jumbo BBQ Shrimp $15.95
French-Fried Shrimp with two dipping sauces $12.95

BUB CITY'S FRESH FISH GUARANTEED 7 WAYS

TEX MEX
Marinated in fresh lime, cilantro
& chiles. Grilled over the coals

BBQ STYLE
Broiled with our special
BBQ Seafood Sauce

BLACKENED
Seared on a flat grill
with a spicy coating

JAMAICAN JERK
A Blend of Lime, Ginger, Garlic,
Jalepeno & Thyme. Grilled over the coals

BUB STYLE
Original Bub City Marinade.
Grilled over the coals

GULF STYLE
Remoulade Marinade.
Grilled over the coals

Spaghetti

	Li'l Bit	Lot More
With Crab Sauce—Man, ya gotta taste!	$5.95	$8.95
With Red Seafood Sauce—(shrimps, scallops, crab)	$6.95	$9.95
With Seafood Cream Sauce	$6.95	$9.95

Sandwiches

BBQ Brisket, chopped	$4.95	Hickory Burger with trimmings...	$4.75
BBQ Pork, chopped	$4.95	Bayou Burger	$4.95
BBQ Chicken Cut up	$4.95	Blackened Chicken	$5.95
Tex-Mex Chix Sandwich	$5.95	Too Good's Fish Sandwich	$3.95

★★★
BUB CITY'S NEVER-FAIL
1-lb. TEXAS T-BONE
★★★

★★★
COWBOY'S CUT
RIBEYE STEAK
★★★

Dinner: Mon - Thurs 5 - 11, Fri - Sat 5 - 12, Sun 4 - 10

Buckingham's Steak House

They don't make dining rooms like this anymore (who could afford to?). Stately, comfortable and quiet, Buckingham's continues to look for the right menu fit, but no matter what, the food is meticulously prepared and expertly served.

Menu Changes Seasonally

APPETIZERS

"Buckingham's Crab Cake"
*Fresh Crabmeat Cake, Baked to Perfection
and served with Dry Mustard Mayonnaise
and Tartar Sauce*
$6.95

Steak Tartar
*Beef Tenderloin Ground to Order with Egg,
Capers, Onion, Olive Oil and Rye Toast*
$6.95

SOUPS AND SALADS

Seafood Gumbo
*Traditional House Recipe Includes
Fresh Vegetables, Spices and Seafood*
$3.95

Buckingham's Ceasar Salad
$3.95

Soup of the Day
$2.75

Shrimp Bisque
$3.95

POULTRY

Grilled Breast of Chicken
*Light Cream Sauce
Garnished with Wild Mushrooms*
$13.95

Roasted Half Chicken
*Sundried Tomato,
Roasted Garlic and Fresh Rosemary*
$13.50

PASTA FRESCA

Bowtie Pasta
*Fresh Pasta with Tender Chicken,
Mushrooms, Scallions, Roasted Pinenuts,
Smothered in a Pesto Cream Sauce*
$10.95

Grilled Shrimp & Sea Scallops
*Served on a Bed of Angel Hair Pasta
with a Tomato Basil Sauce*
$18.95

720 South Michigan Ave • Downtown/Loop • (312) 922-4400 ext 4376

FROM THE BROILER

All Of Our Steaks Are U.S.D.A. "Chef Selection". The Best Steak You Will Ever Eat!

All Entrees served with "Buckingham's Signature Potato and Vegetable".
Baked Potato or Rice are available and may be substituted upon request.

Filet Mignon
6 oz. Center Cut $16.50
10 oz. Center Cut $19.95

Grilled Veal Medallions
Covered in a Rich Sauce
with Chanterelles, Bacon and Pearl Onions
$21.50

Prime Rib
Served with Natural Juice and Horseradish Sauce
8 oz. $13.50
12 oz. $18.50

Surf & Turf
6 oz. Filet Mignon &
6 oz. Lobster Tail
$26.95

Porterhouse Steak
Our 20 oz. Select Cut
$19.95

Rack of Lamb
Roasted Domestic Lamb, Au Jus
$22.95

STEAKHOUSE SPECIALTIES

New York Strip
10 oz. $17.95
14 oz. $23.95

Buckingham's T-Bone
18 oz. $23.95

Steakhouse Specialties are U.S.D.A. "Prime" Aged Beef.

SEAFOOD

Swordfish Vesuvio
Marinated and Grilled Swordfish in a Light Cream Sauce
Flavored with Olive Oil, Garlic, White Wine & Roasted Peppers
$17.95

Crab Cakes
"Our Recommended Seafood Specialty"
Fresh Crabmeat Cakes Baked to Perfection and
served with Dry Mustard Mayonnaise and Tartar Sauce
$16.50

Your Server will be delighted to tempt you with our Pastry Chef's Special Desserts.
Watch for our Dessert Cart $4.75.

Dinner: 7 Days a Week 5:30 - 9:30

There's a lot of Polish food at this very popular "American" restaurant, but no matter how it's classified, the food is cheap and the portions are huge, which means value spelled with a capital "V".

Busy Bee
RESTAURANT

Deluxe Sandwiches
Served with French Fries and Pickle

HAMBURGER DELUXE	2.25
CHEESEBURGER DELUXE	2.50
SLICED TURKEY ROLL DELUXE	3.25
REUBEN W/COLE SLAW	4.25

Club Sandwiches
Served with French Fries and Pickle

BACON, LETTUCE & TOMATO CLUB	3.50
HAM & CHEESE CLUB SANDWICH	3.75
ROLL TURKEY "CLUBHOUSE"	3.50

Hot Sandwiches
Served with Mashed Potatoes, Gravy & Vegetable of the Day

HOT ROAST BEEF	3.50
HOT ROAST PORK	3.50
HOT HAMBURGER	2.75
HOT BREADED VEAL PATTIE	3.25
HOT BREADED PORK	3.50
HOT CHICKEN	3.50
HOT MEATLOAF	3.25

Plain Sandwiches
Served with Lettuce and Pickles on Bread or Bun

GRILLED RIBEYE Steak Sandwich	4.00
ROAST BEEF	2.50
SLICED "KRAKUS" HAM	2.50
POLISH SAUSAGE	2.00
HAM & EGG	2.75
TUNA FISH	2.75
CHEESEBURGER	1.75
AMERICAN CHEESE	1.25
BACON LETTUCE & TOMATO Plain Sandwich	2.25
ROAST PORK	2.50
CORNED BEEF	2.75

Side Orders

Small Lettuce Salad	1.25
Vegetables	.75
Beet or Cucumber Salad	.80
Cottage Cheese	.75
French Fries	1.00

Polish Specialties

CHEESE BLINTZES 4.00
POTATO PANCAKES 4.00
FLACZKI, Bowl w/BREAD & BUTTER 2.50
BIGOS (Hunters Stew)
  With Boiled or Mashed Potatoes 4.00
COMBINATION POLISH PLATE
STUFFED cabbage, 3 Dumplings, Old
  Fashioned Hamburger, Polish Sausage
  and Sauerkraut served with Mashed
  Potatoes & Gravy 7.00

Salad Plate

Served with Crackers, Bread or Toast & Butter

LOW CALORIE PLATE - Beef Patti,
  Cottage Cheese & Fruit Cocktail 3.50
JULIENNE SALAD BOWL - Ham,
  Cheese, Chicken, Boiled Egg and
  Tomato Wedges 4.50
STUFFED TOMATO with Tuna or
  Egg Salad 4.00
TUNA OR EGG SALAD Cottage Cheese or
  Potato Salad 3.75

Regular Dinners

	A La Carte	Dinner
GRILLED SHORT STEAK	7.25	8.50
GRILLED RIB EYE STEAK	4.50	5.75
HAMBURGER STEAK	4.50	5.75
GROUND VEAL STEAK	5.50	6.75
ROAST BEEF	4.75	6.00
ROAST PORK	4.75	6.00
GRILLED PORK CHOPS, 2 pieces with apple sauce	5.25	6.50
BREADED PORK 2 pieces Brown Gravy	4.75	6.00
BREADED VEAL, 2 Patties	4.50	5.75
BAKED HAM	4.25	5.50
FRIED BEEF LIVER with Onions	3.75	5.00
FRIED CHICKEN, one Quarter	3.75	5.00
STEWED CHICKEN, one Quarter	3.75	5.00
SMOKED POLISH SAUSAGE	4.00	5.25
KISZKA with Mashed Potatoes	3.50	4.75
STUFFED CABBAGE	4.25	5.50
SPAGHETTI with Meat Sauce	4.00	5.25
CHICKEN CROQUETTES	3.75	5.00

Seafood

	A La Carte	Dinner
FRENCH FRIED SHRIMP With Cocktail Sauce	5.00	6.25
BREADED FISH STICKS With Tartar Sauce	3.50	4.75
BREADED FISH PATTIE With Tarter Sauce	3.50	4.75

Dinner: 7 Days a Week until 8

One of the oldest and best rib places in a city where ribs tickle the fancy of not only Chicagoans but out-of-towners, too. The well-placed locations in the city and suburbs add to the popularity and accessibility.

CARSON'S®
The Place for Ribs

In The Beginning...

Your dining experience at Carson's, The Place for Ribs, begins with a basket of assorted breadstuffs. Then comes a generous helping of our award-winning Cole Slaw. To accompany your entree, choose either French Fries, Potato Skins, Baked Potato or our fabulous Potatoes au Gratin. A Garden Salad is available in place of Cole Slaw for $1.95. Our Home-made dressings include House (Anchovy Sour Cream), Bleu Cheese, Thousand Island, Creamy Garlic, French or Caesar.

—Our famous ala carte Garbage Salad 6.95—
—Greek Salad 6.95—
—Chef's Salad 6.95—
Smaller salads with entree 3.50
—Beefsteak Tomatoes & Onions 3.50—

—Deep Fried Onions 3.50—

Prime Steaks

Pepper Steak 14.95
(Sliced Filet Mignon sauteed in wine & fresh vegetables)

12 oz. Filet Mignon 16.95

One Pound N.Y. Steak 19.95

Giant (22 oz.) N.Y. Steak 24.95

Charcrust highly recommended

612 North Wells • River North • (312) 280-9200 • Call for Additional Locations

Barbeque

BBQ BABY BACK RIBS

Full Slab 14.95   Half Slab 10.95
BBQ Baby Backs & BBQ Chicken 13.95
BBQ Baby Backs & America's Cut Pork Chops 15.95
BBQ Baby Backs & Prime N.Y. Steak 18.95
America's Cut BBQ Pork Chops 13.95
BBQ Chicken
Whole 11.95   Half 8.95
(All White Meat 2.00 extra)

Etcetera

Prime Rib 16.95
A man-sized cut cooked fresh daily.
Served until we run out.

BBQ Pork Brochette 13.95
Half Greek Chicken 9.95
Broiled Orange Roughy 14.95

Sandwiches

BBQ Pork 5.95
Boneless Breast of Chicken 5.95
½ lb. Hamburger, Cheeseburger, Oliveburger
5.95
New York Steak Sandwich 10.95

Served With Cole Slaw &
French Fries.

Charlie's Ale House

Tavern fare (the pork chops are great) with all the bells but not the whistles, a neighborhood atmosphere and a serene outdoor dining patio attract not only the young and breathless but the middle-aged and restless as well.

Menu Changes Seasonally

Appetizers

The Blaze 103.5 Buffalo Chicken Wings...... single 4.95 ....double 8.95
Chunky blue-cheese dip, celery, carrot sticks. Your choice, hot or barbecued

Fried Calamari 5.95
Lightly breaded, topped with Parmesan, homemade cocktail sauce

Four Cheese Spinach Dip 5.95
Creamy cheese sauce blended with spinach; toasted black bread

WNUA's 95.5 Crab Cakes..5.95
Twin golden crab-packed cakes, homemade tartar sauce

Soups and Salads

Charlie's Chowder................................cup 2.25............................bowl 3.95
Spicy thick tomato-based chowder with fresh fish, potatoes and carrots

Bernie's Kick Ass Chili............................cup 2.50............................bowl 4.50
Chunky sirloin tips and our spicy seasonings with kidney beans and a side of chopped onion, sour cream and cheddar cheese

---

1224 West Webster St • Lincoln Park/DePaul • (312) 871-1440

• ┣━━━┫ *Sandwiches* ┣━━━┫ •

served with coleslaw and Suzy's Lumpy Spuds

Drew's ⑦ Burger 6.50
*Half a pound of seasoned round with your pick of cheese, bacon,
mushrooms, and/or grilled onions; onion roll or black bread*

Loop 98 Grilled Chicken Club 7.50
*Grilled chicken breast with bacon, tomato, spinach, and Swiss
on black bread with mustard sauce*

The Point's 100.3 Roasted Vegetable Hero 6.95
*Creamy goat cheese and a bevy of seasoned roasted vegetables
on lightly grilled French bread with caesar dressing*

Oven Baked Meatloaf Sandwich 6.95
Served warm with melted mozzarella and sautéed mushrooms on an onion roll

• ┣━━━┫ *Entrees* ┣━━━┫ •

Franchise's Homestyle Pot Roast (T.O.'s favorite)...............9.50
*Braised in a dark gravy with carrots, onion, and celery; served
with corn on the cob and lumpy spuds*

Us. 99 BBQ Baby Back Ribs.................................Full 13.50
*A tender slab glazed with our homemade barbecue sauce;
served with lumpy spuds and cole slaw*

Seashore Fish Grill 11.95
Fresh fish of the season grilled and served with rice

Today's Pasta...9.95
Ask your server - it might be hip or it might be homey

WGN's 720 AM Meatloaf..8.95
Topped with mushroom gravy and served with lumpy spuds and peas

Chicken Pot Pie 9.95
Chock full of chicken, potatoes, carrots and peas ; topped with pastry crust and baked

The XRT Porterhouse...14.95
*One pound of charcoal grilled prime T-bone smothered in
sautéed onions and mushrooms; served with lumpy spuds and peas*

This is a tavern where the lunch crowd in this part of the Loop loves to congregate. The clubby atmosphere and the excellent burgers add to the appeal.

Tavern Pastas

SEAFOOD PASTA Rock shrimp, sea scallops and salmon sauteed in olive oil and garlic served on linguine with fresh tomato and basil. 12.95

MUSHROOM STUFFED RAVIOLI Mushroom and ricotta cheese stuffed ravioli sauteed with spinach, garlic and plum tomatoes, finished in a light chicken broth. 9.95

PAPPARDELLE PASTA Wide ribbons of black pepper pasta with chicken, arugula, tomatoes, red peppers, cured olives, wild mushrooms and sun-dried tomatoes in a light chicken broth. 9.95

SALMON FETTUCINE ALFREDO Atlantic salmon sauteed in olive oil with garlic and sun-dried tomatoes then tossed with tri-colored fettucine in a light cream sauce. 10.95

SPAGHETTI AND MEATBALLS Spaghetti with homemade meatballs and marinara served with garlic toast. 7.95

Brick Oven Pizzas

GARLIC CHICKEN PIZZA Roasted garlic chicken, plum tomatoes, spinach and provolone cheese. 7.95

GRILLED VEGETABLE PIZZA Oak fired seasonal vegetables, sun-dried tomatoes and goat cheese. 7.95

ROCK SHRIMP PIZZA Rock shrimp, plum tomatoes, fresh basil and provolone cheese. 7.95

TAVERN TRADITIONAL PIZZA Mild Italian sausage and mozzarella cheese. 7.95

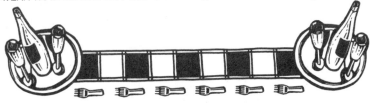

33 West Monroe • Downtown/Loop • (312) 280-2740

Chef Specialties

OVEN ROASTED SALMON The best market fresh salmon of the day is selected by our Chef then seasoned and roasted in our woodburning ovens. 15.95

AHI TUNA Steak cut ahi tuna pan seared and served with a warm tomato and ginger salsa and vegetable of the day. 13.95

MEATLOAF "TAVERN STYLE" Thick sliced meatloaf served with garlic roasted mashed potatoes and gravy. 7.95

PETITE FILET 6 oz. center cut filet grilled to order, served with mushroom caps and the fresh vegetable of the day. 14.95

City Sandwiches

ATLANTIC SALMON SANDWICH Charcoal-grilled salmon with toasted garlic and dill mayonnaise, served open face on vegetable bread. 10.95

CITY CHICKEN MELT Oak roasted chicken breast with asparagus, provolone cheese, and sun-dried tomato mayonnaise, served open face on a focaccia bread. 8.95

FRESH GROUND CHICKEN BURGER Fresh ground chicken with basil and egg white, then we charcoal-grill it to perfection and serve it on a sesame bun. 7.95

STEAK SANDWICH Chargrilled marinated skirt steak served on sourdough bread with sauteed onions and homemade steak sauce. 7.95

TUNA SALAD SANDWICH Fresh tuna mixed with herb dressing served on your choice of bread. 5.95

CHICKEN SALAD SANDWICH Whole chunk chicken tossed in herb dressing served on your choice of bread.6.50

CT'S FAMOUS STUFFED BURGER One-half pound of ground beef with cheddar cheese inside and topped with Tavern BBQ sauce. 6.95

TRADITIONAL BURGER One-half pound of ground beef with your choice of toppings.6.50

TURKEY SANDWICH Hand carved roasted turkey breast served on sourdough bread with roasted garlic mayonnaise, smoked bacon and monterey jack cheese. 7.95

Tavern Temptations

TOLLHOUSE SUNDAE Chocolate Chip tollhouse cookie topped with white chocolate chip ice-cream, hot fudge, chopped nuts and whipped cream. 3.95

PECAN PIE Served with a caramel whipped cream. 3.95

KEY LIME PIE Served with whipped cream. 3.95

BREAD PUDDING Served with a whiskey sauce. 2.95

Dinner: Mon - Sat 4 - 9

Creative dishes, a cozy atmosphere, a working fireplace, and country-spun decor are all just part of the charm and popularity of this preeminent south suburbs charmer. And the wine list, put together by owner Jerry Buster, is one of the most complete around.

Menu Changes Seasonally

— Appetizers —

SMOKED ATLANTIC SALMON $6.95
Red Onions, Capers, Lemon Creme Fraiche

BAKED HELIX SNAILS EN CROUTE $5.95
Herb Garlic Butter

CHAMPAGNE COUNTRY PATE $6.95
Traditional Garniture

LOUISIANA CRAB CAKE AND BAY SCALLOPS $7.95
Roasted Yellow Pepper Sauce

DOMESTIC LAMB SAUSAGE AND MIXED BEAN SALAD $5.95\8.95
Roasted Garlic Rosemary Sauce

GRILLED SCAMPI AND SPINACH FETTUCCINI $7.95
Spicy Tomato Coulis

FRESH SHUCKED SEASONAL OYSTERS $6.95
Mignonette Sauce

THYME   GARLIC   PARSLEY   SAGE   MINT   BASIL

— Soups & Salads —

DAILY SELECTION WILL BE EXPLAINED BY SERVER $3.95

(A Flower of Boston Lettuce Salad included with all full entrees)

A FLOWER OF BOSTON LETTUCE $2.95
*Garnished with fruits, nuts, and a lively Balsamic vinaigrette
with walnut oil*

MELANGE OF SEASONAL BABY GREENS $2.95
Sherry Vinaigrette, Cherry Tomatoes

— Entrees —

COTTAGE SCHNITZEL $8.95/16.95
*pork tenderloin medallions dipped in a light egg batter
with lemon butter sauce*

HERB CRUSTED RACK OF NEW ZEALAND LAMB $9.95/18.95
Ratatatouille, Sauce Pinot Noir

STEAMED 1½ LIVE MAINE LOSTER $19.95
Seasonal Vegetables, Sauce Americaine

GRILLED FILET OF FARM RAISED STURGEON $17.95
Napa Cabbage, Julienne Carrots, Citrus Caper Sauce

ROASTED FREE RANGE CHICKEN $14.95
Roasted Potatoes, Fresh Thyme and Parsley Sauce

STEAK MADAGASCAR A LA COTTAGE $9.95/18.95
*8 ounces of Prime Wisconsin Beef Tenderloin,
Green Peppercorn Sauce*

THREE WAY RIBS $8.95/15.95
*Baby Back Ribs braised in beer with fresh herbs,
marinated in honey, then grilled with a spicy tomato glaze*

OSSO BUCCO $13.95
Braised Lamb Shank, Cabernet Sauce, turnips and carrots

— Table D'Hote Menu on Back —
— See Blackboard for Daily Chef's Table —

Please do not smoke cigars or pipes while dining at "The Cottage"

Dinner: Tues - Thurs 6 - 10, Fri 6 - 11, Sat 5 - 11, Sun 4 - 8

Cricket's Restaurant and Bar

This is a power restaurant bar none, and the power tools—model planes, trains, trucks and such—hanging from the ceiling reinforce the whole idea. After a period of nonchalance, the kitchen is again back in full form.

STARTERS

TORTILLA SOUP
Grilled Chicken, Avocado
and Cheddar Cheese
3.75

ATLANTIC SALMON
House-Cured, Lemon Caper Relish, Creme
Fraiche and Sesame Bagel Chips
7.25

**ROAST LOBSTER AND
GOAT CHEESE ENCHILADA**
Yellow Tomato Pico de Gallo
and Chinese Parsley Cream
8.50

**PAN-FRIED MARYLAND
STYLE CRAB CAKES**
Curried and Cayenne Tartars, Peach and
Pumpkin Seed Chutney
9.75

HUDSON VALLEY FOIE GRAS
Smoked with Crisp Pancetta, Savoy
Cabbage, Blackberry Vinaigrette
12.50

GRILLED QUAIL
Spinach and Arugula,
Walnuts, Beet Vinaigrette
9.75

SALADS

SMOKED SCALLOP SALAD
Arugula, Hothouse Watercress, Pinenuts,
Sauvignon Blanc Sauce
8.50

ICEBERG LETTUCE SALAD
Hearts of Palm, Tomato and Cucumber,
Avocado Dressing
3.75

PORTOBELLA MUSHROOM SALAD
Grilled, with Baby Greens and Basil Shallot
Vinaigrette
7.25

TRADITIONAL CAESAR SALAD
Housemade Dressing
5.25

PLUM TOMATO AND SMOKED MOZZARELLA
Basil Vinaigrette
6.75

---

100 East Chestnut • Near North/Gold Coast • (312) 280-2100

MAIN COURSES

GRILLED RED SNAPPER
*Coriander Lime Vinaigrette, Smithfield
Ham and Black Bean Relish*
21.50

PRIME RIB OF BEEF
*Mustard and Pepper Crusted, Horseradish
au Jus, Roast Garlic Mashed Potatoes*
24.50

CHARBROILED ATLANTIC SALMON
*Orange Basil Vinaigrette,
Root Vegetable Chips*
18.50

VEAL CHOPS CALLOPINI
*Sauteed with Fresh Tomato, Basil and Three
Cheeses, Farfalle Pasta*
27.50

ILLINOIS RACK OF LAMB
*Broiled, Tarragon and Mustard Seed Crust,
Fennel and Pinot Noir Essence, Fried Potato
Spring Roll*
27.50

ROAST FARMHOUSE HALF CHICKEN
*Herbed Garlic Cream Cheese
Stuffing, Natural Pan Gravy,
Roast Garlic Mashed Potaoes*
16.50

GRILLED WISCONSIN CALVES LIVER
*Raspberry Vinaigrette, Applewood Smoked
Bacon and Bermuda Onions, Roast Garlic
Mashed Potatoes*
16.50

OVEN ROASTED PORK CHOP
*Calvados Peppercorn Sauce,
Granny Smith Apples*
22.50

SMOKED LONG ISLAND DUCK
*Boneless Breast and Braised Leg with Juniper
Berry Gravy, Red Bell Pepper Polenta*
22.50

PRIME NEW YORK SIRLOIN
*Grilled, California Merlot Sauce, Roast
Garlic Mashed Potatoes*
27.50

GULF PRAWNS
*Barbecued, Honey-Smoked Tomato Glaze,
Blackeyed Peas and White Rice Compote*
19.50

WHOLE MAINE LOBSTER TAIL AND PRIME RIB OF BEEF
*Broiled with Lemon Butter Sauce
and Baked Potato*
39.50

SWEET ENDINGS

PEACH AND BREAD PUDDING
*Toasted Almonds, Black
Jack Vanilla Anglaise*
4.75

DEEP DISH KAHLUA PECAN PIE
Caramel Candy, Fresh Vanilla Bean Sauce
4.75

CHOCOLATE BOURBON TORTE
Baileys and Milk Chocolate Fudge Sauce
3.75

WARM APPLE TART
*Cheddar Cheese Crust,
Vanilla Ice Cream*
4.50

Dinner: 7 Days a Week 6 - 10:30

Cuisines

Some of the best Mediterranean-influenced cuisine in Chicago. The impeccable service and a handsome, crisp, well-appointed dining room that exudes romanticism add to the allure.

MENU CHANGES SEASONALLY

LUNCH

STARTERS

VEGETABLE AND PASTA SOUP WITH PESTO $4.75

ROASTED EGGPLANT AND GARLIC SOUP WITH REGGIANO AND TOMATO $4.25

FIELD GREENS WITH QUAIL EGGS AND PROSCIUTTO CRACKLINGS $5.25

BEEF CARPACCIO WITH SHAVED PARMESAN, VIRGIN OLIVE OIL AND CAPERS $5.25

GRILLED SMALL PIZZA WITH OVEN DRIED TOMATOES, COPPA AND RICOTTA SALATA $5.25

GRILL AND GREENS

GRILLED PROSCIUTTO AND BOCCONCINI MOZZARELLA WITH $8.95
FIELD GREENS, CURED OLIVES AND GARLIC TOAST

HARDWOOD GRILLED PRIME RIB EYE WITH HEARS OF ROMAINE $12.95
GORGONZOLA-CABERNET VINAIGRETTE

ROSEMARY GRILLED BREAST OF CHICKEN AND GREENS, CITRUS VINAIGRETTE $10.95

SPICED SHRIMP, HARICOTS VERTS AND ARUGULA WITH BASIL VINAIGRETTE $11.95

ENTREES

CRABMEAT AND SEA SCALLOPS LASAGNA, BASIL TOMATO SAUCE $12.95

LEMON PEPPER LINGUINE, WILD MUSHROOM, SPICY SAUSAGE AND CILANTRO $8.95

GRILLED SWORDFISH, OYSTERS AND FRIED CALAMARI $12.95
WITH ROASTED EGGPLANT REMOULADE

MEDITERRANEAN SEAFOOD AND FISH SOUP WITH AIOLI AND GARLIC BREAD $13.50

GRILLED TUNA WITH MUSTARD VINAIGRETTE AND CRISPY ONIONS $11.95

GRILLED BEEF FILET WITH FOUR CHEESE RAVIOLO AND PORTOBELLO MUSHROOMS $13.95

PAPPARDELLE, GRILLED PRAWNS AND SCALLOPS WITH PLUM TOMATO, $13.95
FRESH BASIL AND SHAVED PARMESAN

TORTELLINI WITH GORGONZOLA CHEESE, WALNUTS AND FRESH SAGE $9.50

HARDWOOD GRILLED CHICKEN BREAST WITH ROSEMARY AND CAPER BUTTER $9.95

MOROCCAN CHICKEN "TAJINE" WITH CANDIED LEMON, GINGER AND SAFFRON, $10.25
MINTED COUSCOUS

DESSERTS $4.50

---

1 West Wacker Dr • Downtown/Loop • (312) 372-7200 ext 3410

DINNER

STARTERS

BEEF CARPACCIO WITH SHAVED PARMESAN, VIRGIN OLIVE OIL AND CAPERS $5.25

AHI TUNA CARPACCIO WITH ARTICHOKE CHIPS, CHIVE AND TRUFFLE OIL $6.95

LOBSTER AND GRILLED PORTOBELLO WITH ARUGULA IN ALMOND OIL AND LEMON $12.25

STEAMED CLAMS IN A WHITE WINE, ITALIAN PARSLEY AND GARLIC BROTH $5.95

THINLY SLICED ROASTED VEAL WITH TUNA CAPER SAUCE $5.95

SELECTION OF ICED SHRIMP, OYSTERS AND CRAB $9.95

PROSCIUTTO ANTIPASTO WITH PAPAYA RELISH AND GRILLED FOCACCIA BREAD $6.95

CRABMEAT AND MANCHEGO CHEESE IN FILLO WITH FRIED BASIL $6.95
SMOKED TOMATO COULIS

GRILLED PROSCIUTTO AND BOCCONCINI MOZZARELLA, CURED OLIVES, $6.95
GARLIC TOAST AND BASIL OIL

VEGETABLE AND PASTA SOUP WITH PESTO $4.75

MEDITERRANEAN CREAMY FISH SOUP, ROUILLE AND OLIVE OIL CROUTON $4.95

FIELD GREENS WITH QUAIL EGGS AND PROSCIUTTO CRACKLINGS $5.25

HEARTS OF BUTTER LETTUCE AND RADICCHIO $5.75
SUN DRIED TOMATO VINAIGRETTE

ROMAINE SALAD WITH GARLIC, ANCHOVY AND OLIVE OIL DRESSING $5.50

ENTREES

VEAL MEDALLIONS, WILD MUSHROOMS AND HOMEMADE EGG NOODLES, PORCINI CREAM $18.

ROASTED SALMON TOURNEDOS WITH ALMOND PEPPER CRUST, $17.95
BEURRE ROUGE AND STRAW POTATOES

GRILLED BABY CHICKEN, BRAISED LEEKS, TOMATO FONDUE AND STRING POTATOES $15.95

HARDWOOD GRILLED PRIME SIRLOIN STEAK $22.95
WITH ROSEMARY ROASTED POTATO AND MERLOT SAUCE

GRILLED LOBSTER TAIL IN HERBS DE PROVENCE WITH POLENTA FRIES $24.95
AND OLIVE OIL TOSSED SPINACH

SAUTEED RED SNAPPER ON A RAGOUT OF ARTICHOKES, LEEKS, $15.95
TOMATOES AND MUSCAT

OREGANO AND POTATO ENCRUSTED LAMB CHOPS WITH BAKED EGGPLANT $21.95

PAPPARDELLE, GRILLED PRAWNS AND SCALLOPS WITH PLUM TOMATO, $18.95
FRESH BASIL AND SHAVED PARMESAN

VEAL SCALOPPINE "SALTIMBOCCA" WITH SAGE, PROSCIUTTO AND MARSALA $16.95

DESSERTS $4.50

NICOLA TORRES, CHEF DE CUISINE   DENNIS KOLODZIEJSKI, EXECUTIVE CHEF

Dinner: 7 Days a Week 6 - 10

Legendary restaurateur Don Roth has put his name on the sign, so it has to be good, and it is. I call this a "safe" restaurant, as you can always count on top-quality food and first-rate service.

DON ROTH'S

IN WHEELING

Appetizers

Jumbo Shrimp Cocktail
6.95

Crispy Calamari
To share.
5.25

Fresh Artichoke
(when available)
COLD: served with light vinaigrette dressing.
HOT: with hollandaise sauce and melted butter
4.25

French Onion Soup
(A great recipe) topped with Swiss Gruyere cheese.
3.95

Entrees

The Blackhawk's Famous Spinning Salad Bowl comes to you complimentary with your entree.

Roast Prime Ribs of Beef
"WHILE IT LASTS"
The beef that made the Blackhawk famous, aged properly & roasted to perfection - served with freshly whipped horseradish sauce. Be sure to add the au jus (natural juices).

Regular or English	Diamond Jim	Slim Jim
19.95	24.50	16.95

61 North Milwaukee Ave • Wheeling • (708) 537-5800

Steak——Steak——Steak

Sirloin Strip
The king of them all - thick, juicy, tender, closely trimmed.
12 oz. - 19.95
8 oz. - 16.95

Filet Mignon
An old favorite - served with sauteed mushrooms and bearnaise sauce.
19.95
Petit version 16.95

Beef Oskar
A tender filet mignon, crabmeat, asparagus, & bearnaise sauce.
18.95

(Steaks blackened upon request.)

Chicken Marsala
Sauteed breast of chicken in a light marsala wine sauce topped with mushrooms - as prepared at Longhi's Restaurant on the island of Maui.
14.95

Roasted Baby Rack of Australian Lamb
Served with a sherry & garlic demi-glaze.
19.95

1/2 Chicken, Blackhawk
Roasted with herbs, assorted spicy peppers, olive oil & a hint of garlic.
14.95

B-B-Q Baby Back Ribs (Whole 1 1/2 lb. slab)
With our tangy sauce.
15.95

1/2 Slab Ribs and 1/4 B-B-Q Chicken
14.75

Fish and Seafood

Our Very Famous Fresh Boston Scrod
A Blackhawk tradition - as prepared at Anthony's Pier 4 & Jimmy's Harbor Side, Boston.
15.75

Swordfish Steak Oskar
Crabmeat, asparagus & bearnaise sauce.
18.95

Lobster Tail
The tender, succulent kind from the cold water areas of the world.
Market Price

Seafood Platter
French fried jumbo gulf shrimp, scallops, fillet of Boston Scrod, homemade tartar and cocktail sauces.
16.50

Please save room for one of our legendary *Hot Fudge Sundaes.*

Oprah Winfrey's restaurant, with its artsy atmosphere and eclectic fare, brings in customers by the busload. It may seem a bit off-center at times, but the fare is steady and conventional. A don't-miss dish is Oprah's potatoes.

the ECCENTRIC

★ **"An American Brasserie"** ★

Menu Changes Seasonally Along With Daily Specials

Salads

House Salad of Mixed Greens, choice of dressing 2.95

Chopped Salad, mixed greens, tomato, blue cheese, avocado, bacon, mustard vinaigrette. 4.25

Grilled Chicken Caesar, tender breast sliced thin over classic Caesar. 6.95

The Eccentric Cobb Salad, chopped salad with grilled and chunked chicken breast 7.95

Pasta

	APPETIZER	ENTRÉE
Vegetables and Bowties	3.95	7.95
fresh vegetables and an herbed chicken broth		
Linguini and Red Sauce, fresh parmesan, classic and simple.	3.95	7.95
Sausage and Pepperoni Penne	4.95	8.95
tossed with mozzarella cheese and a spiced tomato-fresh basil sauce		
Gulf Shrimp and Linguini	6.95	12.95
seasoned with garlic, olive oil, fresh basil and tomatoes		

Steaks, Chops and Grills

Grilled Fresh Salmon Fillet

We direct-ship only the freshest salmon available from either coast.
Choose one of three styles...15.95

Lemon-Herb Butter	♥ **Bar-B-Que**	**Snappy Mustard Glaze**
rice pilaf	with dill	rice pilaf
and fresh vegetables	potato salad	and fresh vegetables

Grilled Breast of Chicken 10.95
served with oven-roasted tomatoes, eggplant and cous-cous

Thick and Juicy Pork Chop, mustard marinade 13.95
cured ham and apple relish, Oprah's potatoes and fresh vegetables

Grilled House-smoked Filet Mignon 18.95
onion strings, fresh vegetables and roasted new potatoes

Char-broiled Double-cut Lamb Chops 19.95
oven-roasted vegetables, fresh spinach, roasted red potatoes, herbed au jus

Char-broiled Prime Aged New York Sirloin 21.95
onion strings, fresh vegetables and roasted new potatoes

Grilled Center-cut Veal Chop, herb marinated 21.95
oven-roasted vegetables and new potatoes, fresh spinach, herbed au jus

159 West Erie St • River North • (312) 787-8390

HOME-STYLE SPECIALTIES

House Specials

One-half Oven-roasted Chicken, rubbed with fresh herbs and slow-roasted 10.95
Oprah's potatoes, fresh vegetables, natural chicken juices
Roast Turkey, "The American Way", all white meat carved off the bone 12.95
traditional stuffing and light gravy, Oprah's potatoes, sweet potatoes, cranberry relish
Crispy Coconut Shrimp 13.95
rice pilaf, onion strings, cole slaw, sweet and sour sauce
Fritzel's Pepper Steak 15.95
cubes of filet mignon, bell peppers, onions and mushrooms, served over rice pilaf

Chef's Specials

Boston Sea Scallop Ceviche Appetizer
Fresh Sea Scallops, Flown in from Boston, Marinated in Absolut Citron Vodka, Lime Juice,
Garlic and Cilantro. Served with Fresh Tomato and Avocado
5.95
Bogle, Sauvignon Blanc $4.50

Planked Lake Superior Whitefish
Roasted in a Pure Old World Manner, Planked, Crusted and Served with Duchess Potatoes.
13.95
Pinot Grigio, Bollini $4.25

Smoked Salmon and Capellini Pasta
Hickory wood Smoked Salmon, Served on a bed of Angel Hair Pasta
Tossed with a Light Mustard Cream Sauce, Sun-Dried Tomatoes and Asparagus
14.95
Reisling, Piesporter $4.50

Grilled Pacific Mahi Mahi and Fresh Tomato Relish
Fresh Pacific Mahi Mahi, Served with a Tomato, Basil, Chive and Garlic Relish,
Roasted New Potatoes and Julienne Summer Squash
15.95
Chardonnay, Franciscan $5.95

Roasted Prime Rib of Beef

We select aged prime ribs, cook them in our exclusive slow roasting ovens
to seal in the natural flavors and juices, then carve to order.

Our House Special Cut, 14 ounces. 18.95
Chicago Style Thick Cut, 18 ounces 22.95

★ ★ Oprah's Potatoes ★ ★

"The Original"	♥ **Light**	**"Simply Mashed"**	**"Ultimate"**
whipped and mashed Idaho potatoes served LIVE! with horseradish	*no-fat sour cream, margarine and horseradish*	*whipped and mashed Idaho potatoes **without** the LIVE! horseradish*	*A crispy potato skin stuffed with bacon and cheddar cheese*
2.95	2.95	2.95	3.95

★ ★ ★ ★ ★

Often noted as one of the most romantic restaurants in Chicago, Geja's is still doing fondue and flamenco guitar, which says something about its popularity. The owner has a thriving wholesale wine business on the side, so the wine list is rather special.

CHEESE FONDUE

Imported Gruyere Cheese blended with white wine, Kirsch, and spices. Served with red and golden apple wedges, grapes and crusty chunks of pumpernickel and onion bread for dipping. Geja's salad included.
SERVED FOR 2 OR MORE
10.50 per person
Side Order: Fresh mushrooms, red, yellow and green peppers, broccoli and onion rings
3.95
Special Side Order: Zucchini, cauliflower and broccoli
3.95

CHEESES OF THE WORLD

Cheese Wedges served on a board with fresh French and black bread - plus whipped butter.

SHARP	ROBUST	MILD
Denmark	**France**	**France**
Danish Blue	Brie	Gourmandaise
England	Camembert	**Italy**
Cheshire	**Wisconsin**	Bel Paese
France	Maplewood	**Wisconsin**
Roquefort	Smoked Cheddar	Baby Longhorn
Wisconsin	Havarti Dill	Monterey Jack
Aged Cheddar	Jalapeno	Muenster
Aged Swiss	Pepper Jack	**Holland**
Canada	**Switzerland**	Edam
Black Diamond	Gruyere	Gouda

GOURMET PLATTER

A combination of imported Krakus Polish Ham, Usinger Landjaeger, Milwaukee Braunschweiger and your choise of 3 of Geja's cold cheeses. Served with apple wedges, grapes, French and black bread, Dijon mustard and Geja's salad.
for one 8.75 for two 14.50
Minimum food order per person 6.00

DESSERTS
CHEESE AND CHOCOLATE FONDUE SPECIAL
Salad, Cheese Fondue, Flaming Chocolate Dessert Fondue, and Coffee.
14.75 per person

FLAMING CHOCOLATE DESSERT FONDUE
Flamed with orange liqueur, and served with fresh strawberries, apples, melon, pineapple, banana slices, pound cake and marshmallows for dipping.
SERVED FOR 2 OR MORE
$7.95 per person

340 West Armitage • Lincoln Park/DePaul • (312) 281-9101

PREMIER FONDUE DINNERS

All Premier Fondue Dinners include our Famous Cheese Fondue Appetizer, Geja's Salad, assorted fresh vegetables*, 8 sauces for dipping, our Flaming Chocolate Dessert Fondue and Geja's Fresh Ground Coffee.

All Premier Dinners served for a minimum of 2 people - each person may select any entree. Each Premier Fondue entree is available a la carte for $4.00 less.
*Vegetables include sliced red, yellow and green peppers, onions, mushrooms, broccoli and Irish potatoes.

INTERNATIONAL FONDUE
25.95 per person
Combination of Aged Beef Tenderloin, Boneless Breast of Chicken and Jumbo Gulf Shrimp.

CHICKEN AND LOBSTER FONDUE
24.95 per person
Combination of Boneless Breast of Chicken and Lobster Tail

CHICKEN AND SHRIMP FONDUE
24.95 per person
Combination of Boneless Breast of Chicken and Jumbo Sea Scallops.

BEEF AND SCALLOP FONDUE
23.95 per person
Combination of Aged Beef Tenderloin and Jumbo Sea Scallops.

SCALLOP FONDUE
23.95 per person
Jumbo Sea Scallops.

LOBSTER AND SHRIMP FONDUE
Market Price
Combination of Lobster Tail and Jumbo Gulf Shrimp

CHICKEN AND SCALLOP FONDUE
21.95 per person
Combination of Boneless Breast of Chicken and Jumbo Sea Scallops.

CHICKEN FONDUE
19.50 per person
Boneless Breast of Chicken.

FRESH VEGETABLE FONDUE
18.50 per person
Mushrooms, Red, Yellow and Green Peppers, Onions, Zucchini, Cauliflower, Eggplant, Broccoli and Irish Potatoes.

CONNOISSEUR FONDUE
26.95 per person
Combination of Aged Beef Tenderloin, Lobster Tail and Jumbo Gulf Shrimp.

SEAFOOD FONDUE
26.95 per person
Combinationof Lobster Tail Jumbo Gulf Shrimp and Sea Scallops.

BEEF AND LOBSTER FONDUE
26.95 per person
Combination of Aged Beef Tenderloin and Lobster Tail

BEEF AND SHRIMP FONDUE
26.95 per person
Combination of Aged Beef Tenderloin and Jumbo Gulf Shrimp.

Each Premier Fondue entree is available a la carte for $4.00 less.

Dinner: Mon - Thurs 5 - 10:30, Fri 5 - 12, Sat 5 - 12:30, Sun 4:30 - 10

Goose Island Brewing Co.

While most brew pubs around town are tapped out, this combination brewery and restaurant, sprawling across several comfortable dining rooms, is still holding its own with its excellent home brew and decent food.

ppetizers

Thin Crust Pizza

Spinach, Tomato and Gorgonzola	4.95
Rock Shrimp, Sweet Peppers and Pesto	6.95

Beer Batter Onion Rings 3.25
Overflowing basket of onions deep fried in Golden Goose Pilsner batter

Traditional Nachos 4.95
Served on shredded lettuce with jalapenos, sour cream and Pico de Gallo (Goose Island's own salsa of chopped tomatoes, onions, jalapenos and cilantro)

Quesadillas
Stuffed flour tortillas served with pico de gallo

Brie, Mushroom and Garlic	3.95
Shrimp and Jalapeno	4.25

Grilled Calamari 5.95
Tender calamari charcoal grilled with olive oil and served with a lime

**Buffalo Style
Chicken Wings** 4.50
Extra hot, served with celery, blue cheese dressing and hot sauce.

alads

Choice of dressings made fresh daily:
Light Italian, Blue Cheese, Caesar, Mustard Vinaigrette or Thousand Island.

House Salad 2.50

Grilled Chicken Salad 6.95
Grilled breast on mixed greens

Caesar Salad	5.95
With grilled chicken breast	7.95

Grilled Seafood Salad Market
Fresh chosen grilled seafood over greens, topped with avocado vinaigrette, served with a side of black bean salsa.

E*ntrees*

Home Smoked
Babyback Ribs   13.95
Half Slab   7.95

Our ribs slowly smoked,
dunked in our sauce, then
finished on the grill. Served with
french-fried potatoes, cole slaw
and plenty of napkins.

Armando's Chicken Tacos 7.95

Armando mixes chicken,
tomatoes, onions, sweet and hot
peppers and little extras.
Served with refried
beans and pico de gallo.

S*andwiches*

All Goose Island sandwiches come
with cole slaw and a pickle.

Choice of hand cut french-fries,
mustard fries, cucumber salad, or
baked beans, $.50 extra

Grilled Fresh Fish
on Italian Bread   7.95

Chosen daily, with mustard
mayonnaise.

Grilled Klement's
Bratwurst   5.25

Wisconsin's finest sausage, served
on an onion roll. Sauerkraut
and grilled onions available
on request.

Texas Beef Brisket   7.50

Slowly smoked, covered in
barbecue and served on
an onion roll.

Chicken Lasagne   9.95

Tri-color pasta layered with
chicken and garden vegetables, and
covered with roasted garlic and
parmesan sauce. Served with
house salad and bread.

Pasta   Market

An ever-changing array of pastas
with traditional sauces, served with
house salad and bread.
Half order available a la carte

Fish of the Day   Market

With house salad, chef's vegetable
and new potatoes.

Carolina Pulled Pork
Barbecue   7.50

Authentic tangy Coastal barbecue
with cole slaw on an onion roll.

Classic Club on Whole
Wheat Toast   7.95

Grilled chicken breast and smoked
bacon with lettuce, tomato and
mayonnaise.

Grilled Half-Pound Burger 5.95

Pure Angus beef topped with your
choice of cheese (Wisconsin
cheddar, blue, Swiss, jalapeno jack
or American), bacon, mushrooms,
grilled onions and anything else you
can think of, all on an onion roll.

Chicken Breast   6.95

Grilled, blackened or barbecued,
on a twist roll.

Despite the fact that Gordon goes through something on the order of a chef a year, the consistency and creativity of the food never wavers thanks to the watchful supervision of owner Gordon Sinclair. The atmosphere is a mix of serene and surreal, and the service is nothing less than impeccable.

GORDON

APPETIZERS

The Original Artichoke Fritters *with bearnaise sauce* 5.95

Gazpacho Vegetable Ravioli *with black olive-caperberrie salad and tomato vinaigrette* 6.95

Sashimi of Ahi Tuna, *salad of tri-pepper ribbons and mango-persimmon relish* 8.50

Poached and Sliced Sea Scallops *on a bed of bulgar-couscous pilaf with arugula greens* 7.50

Crispy Confit Duck *with jicama-watercress salad, roasted beets and a light orange vinaigrette* 7.25

SALADS

Endive and Cucumber Salad *with orange segments, tarragon, and four citrus vinaigrette* 5.95

Summer Salad of Red and Golden Beets, *asparagus, mache, and chive vinaigrette* 6.75

Caesar Style Salad, *whole baby romaine, shaved parmesan, and pumpernickel toast* 5.75

MAIN COURSES

Steamed Wheel of Salmon *with red bliss potatoes, broccoli rabe, and shallot-herb vinaigrette* 21.95

Pan-Fried Sturgeon, *crispy potato cakes, onion puree and a hearty potato-chive broth* 21.95

Chilean Sea Bass *with red lentils, cucumber, and herbed yogurt* 22.95

Seared Amish Chicken Breast *with grilled asparagus and morel mushrooms* 18.95

Roasted Muscovy Duck Breast *with grilled portobellos, yucca-tortilla torte, ancho chili sauce* 23.95

Tournedos of Beef *with hazelnut crusted sweetbreads, herbed spaetzle, and madeira scented onions* 23.95

Grilled Veal Chop *with a salad of watercress, chickpeas, proscuitto, and shiitake mushrooms* 25.95

Chef's Spring Harvest Vegetable Preparation: *corn bread with oven roasted tomatoes, bean fricassee and sauteed spring vegetables* 17.95

"IF

YOU

OBEY ALL

THE RULES

YOU MISS

ALL THE

FUN."

Katharine Hepburn

D E S S E R T S

Warm Seasonal Fruits and Berries *5.95*

**An Assortment of Homemade Ice Creams
    and Sorbets** *4.95*

Lime Tartlet with blackberry coulis and fresh
    blackberries *6.25*

Warm Flourless Chocolate Cake *with chocolate sauce and
    vanilla ice cream (please order with main
    course)* *6.95*

Peaches and Custard *between layers of crispy phyllo* *6.50*

Baked Meringue *with passion fruit, raspberries,
    and citrus sauce* *6.25*

Rum and Coconut Creme Brulee *6.95*

D E S S E R T   W I N E S

By the Half Bottle

Muscato St. Supery, *Napa Valley, 1992* *12.00*

Sauternes, *Chateau Cru D'Arche 1986* *25.00*

Black Muscat, *"Elysium," Andrew Quady 1990* *12.00*

Moscato d'Oro, *Robert Mondavi 1991* *13.50*

Muscat Canelli, *"Vin de Glaciere," Bonny Doon 1990* *30.00*

C O F F E E S   A N D   T E A S

All are available decaffeinated, if you prefer

Fresh Ground House Blend *1.65*

Espresso *1.95*

Double Espresso *2.95*

Cappuccino *2.50*

Selection of Herbal and Fine Teas *1.65*

OUR PRIVATE DINING ROOMS accommodate groups of 2
to 180 for business meetings, dinners, luncheons, cocktail
parties and weddings. Please ask for our brochure.

Please, no pipe or cigar smoking in the dining room.

Dinner: Mon - Thurs 5:30 - 9:30, Fri - Sat 5 - 12

There is no mistaking the charm of this tavern-cum-restaurant (the building dates back to 1872). The kitsch and kaboodle of old signs, pictures and posters make for nostalgic reading, and the tavern fare—burgers, ribs, homemade soups, chili—makes for good eating.

Menu Changes Seasonally

M   E   N   U

★SANDWICHES

Turkey Burger	$ 6.25
Patty Melt	$ 5.75
Chicken Breast	$ 6.50
G.D.T. B.L.T.	$ 5.75
G.D.T. Turkey Club	$ 6.25
Tuna Melt	$ 5.75
Sunkist Turkey	$ 6.25
3-Decker Grilled Cheese	$ 5.75
Hot Veggie Sandwich	$ 5.75
Grilled Cashew Butter	$ 5.75
G.D.T. Ham/Kraut	$ 5.75

★SALADS

Special House Salad	Large	$ 6.95
	Small	$ 5.75
Red Flannel Salad		$ 7.50
Mexican Salad		$ 6.95
Chicken Breast Salad		$ 7.50
Spinach Salad		$ 6.95
G.D.T. Greek Salad		$ 6.95

★TEXAS CHILI w/ garlic toast

Cup - $ 2.95   Bowl - $ 4.25
- Beans, jalapenos & onions - no charge
- Grated Cheddar - $.50 Extra

★BAR-B-QUE RIBS (After 5PM)

Full Slab (1 1/2 lbs.) .... $ 12.95
Half Order .... $ 8.95
Ribs served with choice of pasta or potatoes, coleslaw, bread & butter.

★3 EGG OMELETTES

Designer Omelette
Select your own ingredients:
Cheddar, brick, brie*, muenster, swiss, ham, chili, bacon, spinach, broccoli, mushrooms, green peppers, onions, jalapeno, black olives, tomatoes, & zucchini.
*Brie-$ 1.00 Extra
Eggs only = $ 5.25
Any 4 items = $ 5.75 Any 5 = $ 6.25
Any 6 items = $ 6.50

★APPETIZERS

Quesadilla .... $ 6.50
- Chili/Cheese
- Chicken/Cheese/Jalapenos
- Veggie/Cheese
- Three Cheese

Nachos Supreme .... $ 6.25
Chili-French Fries .... $ 4.50

★DINNER SPECIALS

Dinner specials are available each evening.
Selections & prices are posted.
Dinners include choice of soup or dinner salad, bread & butter.

★DESSERTS

Ask your server for our daily selection of homemade desserts.

Dinner: Mon - Thurs until 11, Fri - Sat until 12, Sun until 9

Hard Rock Cafe

Long before sunset, especially on summer weekend evenings, the line starts to form. What is amazing is that the mix of people is as broad as the line is long. Inside, the din can be deafening, but after a period of adjustment it becomes obvious that the food is as good as the music is loud.

Menu Changes Seasonally

APPETIZERS

All our soups, guacamole and onion rings are homemade daily with the freshest of ingredients.

ONION RINGS	2.95
HARD ROCK AND ROLL CHILI - HOMEMADE	CUP 3.75 BOWL 4.95
HOMEMADE H.R.C. NACHOS - ENOUGH TO SHARE 5.95	

SALADS

All our salads on every plate are made with fresh hearts of romaine.

GRILLED CHICKEN BREAST SALAD   6.95
marinated sliced chicken served on a mound of tossed California greens, sliced fresh peppers and our Sherry Vinaigrette dressing.

HARD ROCK CAESAR SALAD   5.95
hearts of romaine lettuce with homemade croutons and our Caesar dressing.
[with grilled Sliced chicken breast.]   7.95

SPECIALTIES OF THE HOUSE

If you've been to the Hard Rock and haven't had our lime chicken or watermelon ribs, then you haven't been to the Hard Rock!

LIME BAR-B-Q CHICKEN   8.95
one half of a whole chicken marinated in our special lime marinade and then grilled and served with fries and a green salad.

H.R.C. FAMOUS BABY ROCK WATERMELON RIBS   11.95
Texas style ribs basted in our special Watermelon BBQ sauce, grilled and served with fries and a green salad.
[COMBO RIBS and CHICKEN - served with fries and a salad.]   9.95

63 West Ontario • River North • (312) 943-2252

THE T-BONE STEAK   12.95
> 16 oz., aged T-bone steak. Served with your choice of baked potato or fries and a green salad.

THE HARD ROCK FAJITA   9.95
> 1/2 pound of chicken, beef or a combination, served with pico de gallo, cheddar cheese, fresh guacamole, shredded lettuce and hot tortillas.

H.R.C. VEGGIE FAJITA   7.95
> 3/4 pound of fresh grilled vegetables, served with pico de gallo, cheddar cheese, fresh guacamole, sour cream and hot tortillas.

BURGERS and SANDWICHES

All our beef and turkey burgers are served with fries, a fresh green salad and your choice of our made from scratch dressings - 1,000 island, blue cheese, french, ranch or house vinaigrette.

H.R.C.'s GRILLED "BEEF or TURKEY" BURGERS   5.95
> 1/3 pound of the finest hand patted chopped steak or ground turkey breast.

1/3 pound with our Hard Rock and Roll Chili.   6.75

1/3 pound with crisp bacon, fresh guacamole and melted Jack cheese.   6.95

HARD ROCK NATURAL VEGGIE BURGER   5.95
> fresh vegetables, rice, nuts and spices, grilled on a whole wheat bun with lettuce, tomato and Bermuda onion. Served with salad, fries or watermelon.

GRILLED CHICKEN BREAST SANDWICH   6.95
> tender breast of chicken with melted natural Swiss cheese, fresh guacamole on whole wheat bun. Served with fries and salad.

THE COUNTRY CLUB SANDWICH   6.95
> marinated grilled chicken, crisp bacon, tomato, mayo, and two kinds of lettuce. Served with fries.

SODA FOUNTAIN AND DESSERTS

H.R.C. country ice creams, vanilla bean, coffee, chocolate and strawberry are specially made for the Hard Rock Cafe with the freshest and finest ingredients.

THICK COLD SHAKES
(WE MAKE "EM RIGHT!)   2.95
chocolate, strawberry, vanilla or coffee.

HARD ROCK COFFEE FLOAT   2.95
> iced sweetened coffee and coffee ice cream, topped with whipped cream.

H.R.C. FAMOUS CHEESECAKE   3.75
> New York style with fresh strawberries.

THE CAFE HOT FUDGE SUNDAE   3.75
> ice cream topped with our own famous homemade hot fudge, pure homemade whipped cream and toasted almonds.

HOMEMADE CHOCOLATE DEVIL'S FOOD CAKE   3.50
> rich and delicious, triple layer with ice cream.

Dinner: 7 Days a Week until 11:30

Harry Caray's Restaurant

Chicago's inimitable sports announcer actually does frequent his eponymous restaurant. And so do his fans and those looking for excellent food in big portions at reasonable prices. Note that the always busy bar is the same length as the distance from pitcher's mound to home plate.

·APPETIZERS·

FRESH OYSTERS (in season) .... DOZEN 11.95	....HALF DOZEN	6.95
FRESH CLAMS ....DOZEN 8.95	....HALF DOZEN	5.95
SAUTEED JUMBO SHRIMP WITH MARSALA WINE		8.95
CHEF ABRAHAM'S CALAMARI		7.95
GRILLED PULPO		7.95
MOZZARELLA MARINARA		5.95
HARRY'S BRUSCHETTA		4.95

·ITALIAN FAVORITES·

FETTUCCINE ALFREDO 9.95
    WITH PRIMAVERA VEGETABLES 11.95
MEAT RAVIOLI WITH MEAT SAUCE 8.95
CHEESE RAVIOLI WITH MARINARA SAUCE 8.95
    RAVIOLI WITH MEATBALLS OR ITALIAN SAUSAGE 10.95
LINGUINE CARBONARA 10.95
LINGUINE WITH SHRIMP MARINARA 17.95
CAPELLINI, FETTUCCINE, SPAGHETTI, MOSTACCIOLI, LINGUINE OR CAVATELLI
    WITH MEAT SAUCE OR MARINARA SAUCE 8.95
    WITH MEAT BALLS OR ITALIAN SAUSAGE 9.95
    WITH GARLIC AND OIL 7.95
EGGPLANT PARMIGIANA 9.95
ITALIAN SAUSAGE AND PEPPERS 10.95

·STEAKS AND CHOPS·

We Serve Prime, Dry-Aged Beef, Exclusively.

FILET MIGNON (13 OZ) 21.95
(9 OZ) 18.95
NEW YORK SIRLOIN STEAK (16 OZ) 25.95
WITH PEPPERCORNS 27.95
VESUVIO STYLE 27.95
PORTERHOUSE STEAK (23 OZ) 26.95
BEEF FILET PEPPERSTEAK 16.95
BROILED LAMBCHOPS, PLAIN OR OREGANATO (3-6 OZ) 25.95
PORK CHOPS, ITALIAN STYLE (3-6 OZ) 17.95
VEAL CHOP, SICILIAN STYLE (12 OZ) 22.95

·VEAL·

VEAL PARMIGIANA 17.95
LUNCHEON PORTION: AVAILABLE LUNCH ONLY 12.95
VEAL MARSALA 17.95
VEAL SCALLOPINI 17.95

·CHICKEN·

CHEF ABRAHAM'S CHICKEN VESUVIO 12.95
(ALL WHITE MEAT ADD $3.00)
BONELESS BREAST OF CHICKEN VESUVIO 15.95
LUNCHEON PORTION: AVAILABLE LUNCH ONLY 9.95
BONELESS BREAST OF CHICKEN MARSALA 12.95
LUNCHEON PORTION: AVAILABLE LUNCH ONLY 9.95
CHICKEN PARMIGIANA 12.95
LUNCHEON PORTION: AVAILABLE LUNCH ONLY 9.95

·FISH·

BROILED LOBSTER TAIL (10 OZ), PLAIN 27.95
VESUVIO STYLE 29.95
ITALIAN STYLE SALMON 17.95

Dinner: Mon - Fri 5 - 10:30, Sat - Sun 5 - 12

An unbelievably successful place (be prepared for a line at lunch unless you get there early) that started as a coffee shop and blossomed into a full-blown restaurant. The Cajun specialties featured at lunch are excellent and most authentic.

"HEAVEN ON SEVEN"

Menu Changes Daily

Cajun and Creole Specialties . . .

Louisiana Soft Shell Crab Po' Boy Sandwich
served with Cajun Coleslaw and cup of soup .... $ 8.95
Southern Fried Louisiana Soft Shell Crab Salad
with Honey Jalapeno Dressing served with cup of soup .... $ 8.95
Linguini with New Orleans Style BBQ Shrimp
served with cup of soup or salad .... $ 8.95
Mardi Gras Jambalaya
served with cup of soup or salad .... $ 8.50
Linguini with New Orleans Style BBQ Oysters
served with cup of soup or salad .... $ 8.95
Cajun Fried Oyster Salad with Honey Jalapeno Dressing
served with cup of soup .... $ 8.95
Southern Fried Oyster Po' Boy Sandwich
served with Cajun Coleslaw and cup of soup .... $ 8.95
Cajun Fried Shrimp Salad with Honey Jalapeno Dressing
served with cup of soup .... $ 8.95
Louisiana Soft Shell Crawfish Po' Boy Sandwich
served with Cajun Coleslaw and cup of soup .... $ 8.95
Red Beans and Rice
entree portion served with soup or salad .... $ 7.50
side order .... $ 4.50
Hoppin' John (Blackeye Peas)
entree portion served with cup of soup or salad .... $ 7.50
side order .... $ 4.50

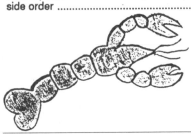

111 North Wabash • Downtown/Loop • (312) 263-6443

Cajun Fried Chicken Salad with Honey Jalapeno Dressing
served with cup of soup .... $ 8.95
Louisiana Crab Cakes
served with Cajun Coleslaw and cup of soup or salad .... $ 8.95
Louisiana Shrimp Po' Boy Sandwich
served with Cajun Coleslaw and cup of soup .... $ 8.95
Louisiana Catfish Po' Boy Sandwich
served with Cajun Coleslaw and cup of soup .... $ 8.95
Southern Fried Chicken Po' Boy Sandwich
served with Cajun Coleslaw and cup of soup .... $ 8.50
Andouille Sausage Po' Boy Sandwich
served with Cajun Coleslaw and cup of soup .... $ 8.50
Baton Rouge Omelet
served with cup of soup .... $ 6.95
Creole Omelet
served with cup of soup .... $ 6.95
Cajun Tasso Ham Omelet
served with cup of soup .... $ 6.95
Andouille Sausage Omelet
served with cup of soup .... $ 6.95

For that extra something . . .

Jalapeno Cheddar Corn Muffin ..... $1.50   Cajun Fried Onion Rings $2.50
Corn Muffin .... $1.25   Collard Greens $2.50
Cajun Coleslaw .... $1.50   Cheese Grits $2.50

Desserts worth waiting for . . .

Georgia Peach Pie .... $2.95   Sweet Potato Pecan Pie $3.25
Chocolate Peanut Butter Pie .... $3.25   Sweet Potato Pie $2.95
Key Lime Pie .... $3.25   Bread Pudding $2.95
Pecan Pie .... $2.95   New Orleans Chicory Coffee .... $ .75

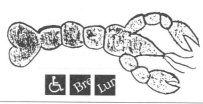

Lunch: Mon - Fri until 5, Sat until 3

It took the town by storm with its home cooking and homey atmosphere. Ina Pinkney and Elaine Farrell, the owners, always seem to be around to greet and seat the loyal locals who don't mind queuing up to sample the goodies, especially the delicious pastries and cakes.

Ina's Kitchen

Our Granola	3.50	Steel Cut Oatmeal	3.25
with yogurt	3.75	with brown sugar	
with fruit	4.00	with fruit	3.75

Basket of Breakfast Sweets 3.50

Ina's Pancakes	with maple syrup	6.25
	with fruit of the day	6.50
Heavenly Hots	sour cream pancakes with fruit compote	6.25
Whole Wheat Oatmeal Pancakes	with maple syrup	6.25
Vegetable Hash	with 2 poached eggs	6.75
Corn, Black Bean & Cheese Scrapple	with eggs and chorizo sausage	6.75
Noodle & Vegetable Frittata	with lightly sauteed tomato sauce	6.75

Omelette - *3 eggs with your choice of 2 fillings:*
herbed cheese, swiss, cheddar, spinach, tomatoes,
bacon or mushrooms, addt'l ingredients .60 each   7.25

Eggs -   *Your way with potatoes*   4.25
     with your choice of meat   7.00
     Egg substitute available

Side Dishes

Potatoes	1.25
Scrapple	3.00
Hash	3.00
Fruit	1.75/3.00
Yogurt	1.00
Peanut butter	1.00
Bacon	3.00
Chorizo sausage	3.00
Andouille sausage	3.00
Veal Chive sausage	3.00
Maple syrup	1.00
Bread basket with Jelly	2.50

Beverages
Freshly squeezed:

Orange juice	2.00	Coffee	1.25	Espresso	2.00
Grapefruit juice	2.00	Tea	1.25	Cappuccino	2.25
Soda	1.00	Milk	1.00	Hot Chocolate	1.75

Jaxx Restaurant

With floor-to-ceiling windows overlooking Michigan Avenue, the dining room is smashing in a casual sort of way. A perfect place to relax before or after the rigors of shopping or to hide away for a power breakfast or lunch.

Menu Changes Seasonally

SOUPS AND SALADS

CORN CHOWDER 4.25
with Apple Bacon
and Smoked Chicken

CREAM OF TOMATO 3.95

CAESAR SALAD 8.95
with Grilled Chicken

WARM SPINACH SALAD 10.75
with Grilled Scallops
and Poppyseed Vinaigrette

LEMON B.B.Q. CHICKEN SALAD 9.75
with Thin Green Beans, Tomatoes, Corn,
Roasted Turnips and Balsamic Vinaigrette

CHARRED LAMB SALAD 10.75
with Goat Cheese-Garlic Fritters
Fried Leeks and Warm Ginger Dressing

PEPPERED SALMON SALAD 11.50
with Roasted Sweet Peppers

PIZZA

LUMP CRAB AND PROSCIUTTO 8.95
with Stewed Leeks, Spinach and
Aged Jack Cheese

VEAL BACON AND PESTO 8.95
With Provolone Cheese and Plum Tomatoes

GRILLED CHICKEN AND MUSHROOM 8.95
with Fresh Roma Tomatoes

SPICY SAUSAGE AND ONION 8.50
with Buffalo Mozzarella

FROM THE OVEN AND GRILL

WOOD-ROASTED PRIME RIB OF BEEF
With Yorkshire Pudding and Fresh Horseradish
English Cut 18.50   American Cut 19.95

ROASTED YOUNG CHICKEN 15.75
With Escalloped Turnips
and Wood-Roasted Cider Onions

ROASTED RACK OF LAMB 23.50
Baked in A Sesame Crust
With Barley Risotto and
Homemade Garlic Jam

ROASTED LOIN OF PORK 15.50
Basted with Beer Bacon Jus
and Whiskey Apple Compote

THIS EVENING'S ROAST
Served with an Array of Fresh Garden Vegetables
21.00

ENTRECOTE STEAK 18.95   **FILET STEAK 20.50**

MIXED GRILL 21.00
Lamb Chops, Kidney, Filet, Sausage,
Bacon, Mushroom, Tomato and Egg

SPRING LAMB CHOPS 22.50
With Fresh Mint Sauce

PORK CHOPS 17.00
With Applesauce and Roasted Garlic

SEAFOOD

GRILLED JUMBO PRAWNS 21.00
With Tomato Relish and
Warm Spinach Salad

GRILLED SWORDFISH 19.95
With Papaya Relish

OVEN-ROASTED SALMON 18.75
Basted with Garlic and Italian Parsley

MEDALLIONS OF PEPPERED SALMON 22.00
With Spinach, Asparagus
and Shrimp Bordelaise

SEAFOOD MIXED GRILL 23.50
Sesame Fried Lake Trout, Peppered Salmon,
B.B.Q. Shrimp, Lobster and Scallops
with Two Relishes

Dinner: Sun - Thurs 6 - 10, Fri - Sat 5 - 11

Kinzie Street Chophouse

It used to be called the Kinzie Street Bistro, but Chicago is undergoing a steaks and chops renaissance, affecting a slight change in menu and attitude for this cozy spot close to the Merchandise Mart.

STARTERS

Crab Cakes with 2 Sauces	5.95
Fried Calamari	4.95
Ravioli of the Day	5.95
Wild Mushroom & Goat Cheese Tart	4.95
Greg's Garlic Shrimp with Scampi	7.95
Steamed Mussels	5.95
Tuna Tartare	5.95
Blackened Scallops	5.95
Goat Cheese & Pesto Pizza	6.95
Spicy Buffalo Chicken Wings	5.95
Asparagus Vinaigrette	5.95
Shrimp Cocktail	7.95
Smoked Salmon Platter	7.95
Carpaccio	5.95
Assorted Seafood Platter per person	7.95
Tasty Kinzie Chophouse T-shirt	13.50

SOUP/CHILI

Black Bean	1.95/2.95
The Other Soup	1.95/2.95
Black Angus Chili	2.95/5.95

SMALL SALADS

Wedge of Iceberg	1.95
House Salad	2.95
Spinach and Mushroom	3.95

LARGE SALADS

Caesar Salad with Chicken	6.95
Garbage Salad	6.95
Salad Nicoise with Fresh Grilled Tuna	8.95
Spinach and Mushroom	6.95
Shrimp Salad	8.95
Steak and Potato Salad	8.95
Caesar Salad with Calamari	7.95

DESSERTS

Mile High Apple Pie	3.95
.... Ala Mode	.95
Hot Fudge Brownie Sundae	3.95
Creme Brulee	3.95
Cheesecake	3.95
Fresh Fruit	4.95

SPAGHETTI/PASTA

Spaghetti with Roasted Peppers, Pine Nuts Fresh Tomatoes and Olive Oil	9.95
Penne with Asiago Cheese, Chicken Sundried Tomatoes, Broccoli	9.95
Spaghetti Marinara	9.50
Spaghetti and Meatballs	9.95
Rigatoni with Mushroom Ragu	9.95
Angel Hair with Grilled Chicken, Sundried Tomato Basil Pesto	9.95

400 North Wells St • River North • (312) 822-0191

Herb Crusted Skirt Steak on
Black Pepper Pasta 9.95

Smoked Mozzarella and
Roast Chicken Ravioli 9.95

Five Cheese Ravioli, Spicy
Vegetable Marinara 9.95

Seafood Fettuccini with
Spicy Marinara 10.95

Lasagna of the Day .... Market

All pastas are made on premise

BLACKBOARD SPECIALS

Chicken Hash 10.95
Chicken Pot Pie......................................9.95
Meatloaf with Smashed Potatoes 8.95
Today's Fresh Grilled Fish ......(Priced Daily)
BBQ St. Louis Baby Back Ribs 1/2 9.95
Full..13.95
Grilled Chicken Breast with
Peppers & Onions 9.95
Mixed Grill .... Market

FRESH FISH/SEAFOOD

Herb Crusted Salmon............................14.95
Sesame Crusted Yellowfin Tuna 14.95
Grilled Swordfish, Homemade
Red Pepper Tartar Sauce 14.50
Lobster Tail per lb. 35.00
Swordfish & Tuna Stirfry 15.95
Greg's Garlic Shrimp Scampi 15.95

STEAKS/CHOPS

Filet Mignon 8 oz. 14.95
Filet Mignon 14 oz. 19.95
New York Sirloin 10 oz. 15.95
Kansas City Sirloin 18 oz. 19.95
Pork Chop 1 lb......................................13.95
Blackened Double Cut
Lamb Chops 21.95

20 oz. Porterhouse.................................23.95
Stuffed Veal Chop..................................21.95
Blackened Rib Eye 16.95
48 oz. Porterhouse (for two)
per person..24.50
Surf & Turf .... Market
Giant Surf & Turf .... Market

Rare: Very red, cool center.
Medium Rare: Red warm center.
Medium: Pink center.
Medium Well: Broiled throughout,
no pink.

Sorry, we are not responsible for steaks
ordered past medium

BAR MENU

Available all day in the bar.

Saloon Burger 10 oz. 6.95
with Choice of Cheese

Grilled Chicken Sandwich with
Mozzarella and Roast Peppers 6.95

Roast Chicken Tostada 6.95
Salmon Club Sandwich 9.95
Chop House Turkey Ruben 6.95

SIDES

Bacon Scallion Smashed Potatoes 1.95
Crispy Onions 1.95
French Fries 1.95
Half Onion/Half Fries 1.95
Hashed Browns 1.95
Baked Potato 1.95
Spinach and Mushrooms 1.95
Potato Skins 1.95
with Cheddar Cheese ....+.95
Broccoli 2.95
Asparagus cold with vinaigrette
or hot with hollandaise 5.95
Macaroni & Cheese................................1.95
Grilled Vegetables 3.95

Dinner: Mon - Sat until 10

85

Lawry's the Prime Rib

Located in the former McCormick mansion, it is unusually elegant for a basic meat and potatoes restaurant. But the meat (the fork-tender prime rib) and the potatoes (real whipped) are some of the best around. And the perky service people are sure and swift.

LAWRY'S
THE PRIME RIB

A LA CARTE & BEVERAGE

LAWRY'S BAKED POTATO	2.75

Amply sized—with butter, bacon, chives and sour cream . . . easily shared

CREAMED SPINACH	2.25

Our world-famous spinach is subtly seasoned with spices, bacon and onion

CREAMED CORN	2.25
BUTTERED PEAS	2.25

DESSERTS

ENGLISH TRIFLE	3.95

Rum and brandy laced cake layered with vanilla cream, strawberries, whipped cream and topped with sherry.

SOUR CREAM APPLE PIE	3.95

Sliced Granny Smith apples mixed with sour cream and topped with cinnamon crumbs.

BITTERSWEET CHOCOLATE CAKE	3.95

A flourless chocolate cake served with a vanilla cream sauce.

100 East Ontario St • River North • (312) 787-5000

For over five decades, Lawry's The Prime Rib has been internationally recognized for serving the finest quality beef available. Every standing rib roast is carefully selected by meat experts, then dry-aged 14 to 21 days for natural tenderness. Following a traditional recipe, the beef is roasted to perfection on a bed of rock salt, thus assuring each portion is as flavorful and juicy as the next.

THE CALIFORNIA CUT   17.95
A smaller cut for lighter appetites

THE ENGLISH CUT   19.95
Deftly carved in thinner slices to heighten the rich beef flavor

THE LAWRY CUT   21.95
The traditional—our generous portion—since 1938

THE "CHICAGO" CUT   24.95
An extra-thick portion that includes the rib bone

Our expert carver brings the beef tableside in a stainless steel cart, then slices it to order—rare to well done, center or end cut. Dinner at Lawry's The Prime Rib also includes . . .

DINNER ACCOMPANIMENTS

THE FAMOUS ORIGINAL SPINNING BOWL SALAD
A blend of crisp Romaine lettuce, iceberg lettuce and watercress, lightly tossed with shredded beets, chopped eggs and croutons. Our exclusive Vintage dressing is added with flourish as the salad is spun on a bed of crushed ice

MASHED POTATOES
The American favorite—whole potatoes, cooked, then whipped with milk until smooth and creamy

YORKSHIRE PUDDING
The second traditional accompaniment, baked in small skillets until puffy and golden brown—uniquely Lawry's

WHIPPED CREAM HORSERADISH
This surprisingly mild blend of freshly ground horseradish root and whipped cream enhances your beef

Dinner: Mon - Thurs 5 - 11, Fri - Sat 5 - 12, Sun 3 - 10

Lou Mitchell's Restaurant & Bakery

The logging camp atmosphere is so enjoyable it's hard to push away after enjoying the great French toast, the big omelet, the fat pancakes, the homemade pastries and the rich coffee. Lou himself has abdicated, and so has the effervescent Nick Noble, but their footprints are still much in evidence.

Fruit, Juices and Cereals

Freshy Squeezed Orange or Grapefruit Juice .90-1.60

Pure California Tomato Juice .80-1.10   Ice Cold Melon 1.75

California Santa Clara Stewed Prunes 1.25   Jumbo Orchard Grapefruit (half) 1.75

Michigan Apple Juice .80-1.10   Fresh Fruit Cup in Season 2.75

CEREALS: Cold with Milk — 1.50

Cooked Cereal — 1.75

with Hot Apples and Cinnamon .75 Extra

with Sliced Bananas .40 extra   with Sunkist Raisins .25 extra

Fluffy Pancakes and Waffles

MELTAWAY PANCAKES with Country Fresh Butter, Maple Syrup........ 3.10

MALTED MILK BELGIAN WAFFLE with Country Fresh Butter,

    Maple Syrup... 3.10

FLUFFY ROLLED PANCAKES	GRILLED THICK
or	FRENCH TOAST
MALTED BELGIAN WAFFLE	OR GOLDEN NUGGETS
with Cooked Fruit of the Day,	3.10
Fresh Sour Cream, Maple Syrup	with Cooked Fruit of the Day
4.25	4.25

---

565 West Jackson Blvd • Downtown/Loop • (312) 939-3111

Fresh All Butter Handrolled Homemade Pastries

*All Our Pastries are Prepared in Our Oven **FRESH DAILY***
Only the Finest Ingredients are Used

Country Fresh Eggs

TWO EGGS, as you like them..3.00
TWO EGGS with CRISP BACON or PURE PORK SAUSAGE LINKS or
    HONEY CURED HAM..4.15
ONE EGG, as you like it...2.25
ONE EGG with CRISP BACON or PURE PORK SAUSAGE LINKS or
    HONEY CURED HAM..3.20
FLUFFY FRESH "EGG WHITES CHOLESTERAL FREE".............3.20

Served in Skillet, all Egg Orders Served with Toasted
Homemade Greek Bread, Homemade Orange Marmalade, Hash Brown Potatoes

Fluffy Jumbo Omelettes

Denver...5.75
Michigan Sugar Sweet Apples and Old English Cheddar Cheese............5.75
Fresh Sour Cream or Cottage Cheese, Bacon Bits and Tomato..............5.75
Garden Fresh Spinach, Greek Feta Cheese and Onion....................5.75
Fresh Mushroom, Swiss Cheese, Tomato and Onion......................5.75
Fresh Tomato, Green Pepper, Onion and Greek Feta Cheese..............5.75
Homemade Greek Sausage, Tomato, Green Pepper.......................5.75
California Broccoli and Old English Cheddar Cheese.....................5.75
Salami and Swiss Cheese...5.40
Diced Ham and Cheddar Cheese.....................................5.40
Imported Greek (Feta) Cheese.......................................5.00
Spanish Omelette..5.00
Garden Fresh Spinach..5.00
Fresh Mushroom...5.00
Garden Fresh Zucchini and Tomato..................................5.00
Fresh Mushroom, Green Pepper, Tomatoes
    and Bermuda Onion...5.75

All Omelettes can be Prepared with Egg Whites

.50 extra for Each Additional Ingredient in Omelettes

Homemade Raisin Toast .40 extra	**Side Order of Crisp Bacon 1.90**
Fresh Hash Brown Potatoes	**Fried Ham or Sausage Links 2.25**
(Pan Fried in Butter) 1.25	

Michael Jordan's

Hey, the Great One has his own private (glass-enclosed) dining room in this stadium-size restaurant, so if Michael eats here, so will (sooner or later) most Chicagoans. It's the place to be right now.

Menu Changes Seasonally

D I N N E R

A P P E T I Z E R S

Crab Cake 7.50	Wood Grilled Sea Scallops 5.95
Shrimp Cocktail 7.95	Grilled Portobello Mushrooms 5.25
Chilled Asparagus with Stone Ground Mustard Vinaigrette 4.50	Crispy Fried Calamari 5.95
	Onion Loaf 3.95
Panned Mussels Arrabiatta 6.50	Baked House Mozzarella, Wrapped in Prosciutto 4.95

S O U P S

Wild Mushroom 3.25	Today's Soup 2.75

500 North LaSalle • River North • (312) 644-DUNK

SALADS

Seasonal Field Greens 2.75

Caesar with Garlic
Herbed Croutons 3.95

Grilled Chicken Caesar 7.95

Beefsteak Tomato with Red
Onion and House Mozzarella 4.50

Joe's Giant Chopped Salad 6.95

Seafood with Feta on Greens 9.95

Grilled Vegetable Plate 6.50

Seared Tuna on Wilted Spinach
with Caramelized Onions and
Roasted Peppers 11.95

Balsamic Vinaigrette,
Stone Ground Mustard Vinaigrette,
and Caesar

STEAKS, CHOPS & SEAFOOD

Filet Mignon, 13 oz. 21.95

Small Filet, 10 oz. 15.95

MJ's Prime New York Strip, 18 oz. 26.95

Small New York Strip, 12 oz. 18.95

Gene's Porterhouse, 22 oz. 26.95

Veal T-Bone, 16 oz. 22.95

Lamb T-Bone 21.95

Grilled Salmon with
Avocado Relish 16.95

Michael's Sauteed Sole with
Lemon Thyme Butter 14.95

Grilled Swordfish 18.95

Grilled Ahi Tuna with
Ginger Vinaigrette 16.95

Grilled Shrimp 15.95

SPECIALTIES

Hickory Smoked
Baby Back Ribs 12.95

Juanita's Macaroni and Cheese   7.95

Chicken Scaloppine
with Artichoke Hearts 9.95

Crab Cakes 14.95

Spit Roasted Chicken 10.95

The Hamburger
with Choice of Cheese,
Bacon or Fried Onions 6.95

Turkey Burger 6.95

Bowtie Pasta with Grilled
Chicken and Prosciutto 10.50

Seafood Linguine Arrabiatta 12.95

Fusilli Primavera 8.95

Dinner: Mon - Thurs 5 - 11, Fri - Sat 5 - 12, Sun 5 - 10

Mirador

The crowd is cool, suave and hip. The decor is simple, serious and sane. The food is delicious and au courant but in a pleasing, uncomplicated way. Daily specials are really special and have pizzazz. And the upstairs Blue Room is just the place for after-dinner music and an after-dinner drink.

Menu Changes Weekly

STARTERS

Always, a Fabulous Soup! 3.95

Grilled Fresh Asparagus, Wild Mushrooms
and Teardrop Tomatoes 5.95

Amy's Absolute Favorite... Caviar Caviar Caviar...
Black Osetra 23   Golden Osetra 30

Warm Baked Brie from Illinois
Sundried Tomato Vinaigrette and Sweet
Peppered Pecans 5.95

Sauteed Calamari with Artichokes, Frisee
and Spicy Roasted Tomato Vinaigrette 5.95

Great Grilled Salmon, Cured with Fennel
Served with Shallots, Eggs, Creme Fraiche
and Toast Points 6.50

Yellow and Red Vine Ripened Tomato
and Fresh Mozzarella Terrine
with Basil Oil and Balsamic 5.95

California Artichoke Stuffed with
Dungeness Crab Salad 6.95

1400 North Wells • River North • (312) 951-6441

SALADS

Salad of Mixed Lettuces with Walnut Vinaigrette 4.25
with Goat Cheese add 1.00

Caesar Salad 4.95

Asparagus and Endive Salad with Radicchio
and Oven Roasted Tomatoes with Mustard Vinaigrette 5.50

ENTREES

Fresh Water Shrimp, Lemon Black Pepper Pasta,
Shallot Broth 16.95

Grilled Alaskan Salmon with Shiitake Mushrooms, Spinach
and Wild Leeks 15.95

Whole Young Chicken served Moroccan Style
Vegetable Couscous and Roasted
Red Pepper Sauce 13.95

Vegetarian Strudel, Essence of Madly
Wild Mushrooms 12.95

Fettuccine with Garlic, Vine-ripened Tomatoes,
Capers and Olive Oil 10.95

Lively, Grilled Swordfish Steak with Chermoula,
a Spicy Moroccon Relish 17.95

Pork Tenderloin, Italian Broccoli and Stewed
Tomatoes in Natural Gravy 14.95

Filet Mignon, Herbed Potatoes and
Baby Spring Vegetables 18.95

Dinner: Sun - Thurs 6 - 10:30, Fri - Sat 6 - 11:30

I can't say enough about this place. The atmosphere is comfortable, the service is first-rate, the prices are right, and the food is, well, just plain good— home cooking good from the meat loaf dinner to the homemade pies.

Appetizers

Shrimp Cocktail	5.95
Crispy Calamari	4.95
Penne Primavera	3.95
Home Smoked Salmon, Toast Points	5.95
Linguini, White Clam Sauce	4.95
Baked Onion Soup	3.95
Vegetarian Chili	Cup 1.50 Bowl 2.95
Today's Soup	Cup 1.95 Bowl 2.95

Small Salads

House Salad	2.95
Nicer Salad	3.95
Sliced Tomato, Onion	2.95

Large Salads

Caesar Salad, Minute Chicken	7.95
Cobb Salad	7.95
Oriental Chicken Salad	7.95
Boulevard Salad	8.25
Steak Salad	9.95

All Caesars Available Enlightened

Specialty Plates

EVERYDAY: Meatloaf, Mashed Potatoes, Vegetable	7.95
MONDAY: Roast Pork Loin, Mashed Potatoes, Vegetable	8.95
TUESDAY: Turkey Steak, Mashed Potatoes, Vegetable	7.95
WEDNESDAY: Lasagna, Marinara or Italian Sausage Sauce	8.95
THURSDAY: Pot Roast, Mashed Potatoes, Vegetables	8.95
FRIDAY: Lake Perch Fry, French Fries, Cole Slaw	9.95
SATURDAY: Grilled Skirt Steak, Mashed Potatoes	8.95
SUNDAY: Roast Turkey, Dressing, Give Thanks	7.95

Italian Specialties

Penne Primavera	7.95
Rigatoni, Sausage, Eggplant, Tomato	8.95
Linguini, White Clam Sauce	9.95
Angel Hair, Shrimp, Tomato, Broccoli	9.95

835 North Michigan Ave, Water Tower Place • Near North/Gold Coast • (312) 335-4745

Fish & Seafood

Lake Superior Whitefish,
  Broiled 8.95
Lake Superior Whitefish,
  Griddled 8.95
Lemon Sole, Lemon, Capers 8.95
Lemon Sole, Florentine..............9.95
Jumbo Fried Shrimp Platter,
  Fries, Slaw 9.95

Vegetables & Grains

String Beans, Steamed 1.95
Broccoli, Lemon 1.95
Cous Cous 1.95
Spinach, Creamed 2.95
Spinach, Steamed 2.95
Asparagus, Steamed 2.95

Salad Platters

Stuffed Tomato, Tuna Fish 6.95
Stuffed Tomato,
  Chicken Salad 6.95
Smoked Salmon, Creamed
  Cheese, Bagels.........................7.95
Drugstore Combo Chicken,
  Tuna, Eggless Egg...................7.95

Chicken

Minute Chicken 7.95
Griddled Chicken, Lemon,
  Capers 7.95
Half Roasted Chicken 7.95
Half Roasted Chicken, Garlic.....8.95
Half Roasted Chicken,
  Peppers, Onions 8.95

Potatoes

Real Mashed Potatoes 1.95
Potato Strings............................ 1.95
Baked Idaho 2.25
French Fried 1.95
Onion Strings 1.95

Hamburgers & Patty Melts

Hamburger 6.45
Cheddar Hamburger 6.85
Hamburger Club 6.95
Bacon Cheddar Hamburger 6.95
Blue Cheese Hamburger........... 6.80
Mushroom Hamburger 6.85
Hamburger Patty Melt 6.95
Turkey Burger 6.95

Popular Sandwiches

Turkey Club 6.95
Grilled Chicken Cheddar,
  Onions 6.95
Eggless Egg Salad 5.95
Tunafish 5.95

French Fries Accompany
Your Sandwich

Guiltless Desserts

Low Fat Vanilla Yogurt............... 2.25
Low Fat Vanilla Yogurt,
  Strawberries 3.50
Low Fat Vanilla Yogurt, No
  Fat Hot Fudge 2.95
Bowls of Seasonal Fresh Fuit ... 2.95
No Fat Yogurt Available

Morton's of Chicago, The Steakhouse

The steaks are prime eating, and so are the veal chops, the lobster and the great potatoes. This is one of Chicago's premier steakhouses. With an atmosphere as jubilant and as straightforward as the food, there is no question that this is the place for the power hitters—local and far-flung.

THE STEAKHOUSE

DINNER MENU

APPETIZERS

Gulf Shrimp Cocktail	8.95
Cockenoe Oysters on the Half Shell	7.95
Smoked Pacific Salmon	8.95
Fresh Lump Crabmeat Cocktail, *Remoulade Sauce*	8.50
Broiled Sea Scallops Wrapped in Bacon, *Apricot Chutney*	8.50
Black Bean Soup	4.25

SALADS

Morton's Salad or Spinach Salad	4.75
Caesar Salad	4.95
Sliced Beefsteak Tomato & Purple Onion or Blue Cheese	4.95

1050 North State St • Near North/Gold Coast • (312) 266-4820

ENTREES

Prime Rib of Beef, Double Cut, *Whipped Horseradish*	24.95
Double Filet Mignon, *Sauce Bearnaise*	25.95
Porterhouse Steak, 24 oz.	28.95
New York Strip Sirloin, 20 oz.	28.95
Ribeye Steak	19.95
Tenderloin Brochette, *Diablo Sauce*	18.95
Sicilian Veal Chop	21.95
Domestic Rib Lamb Chops	23.95
Grilled Fresh Swordfish Steak, *Sauce Bearnaise*	21.95
Shrimp Alexander, *Sauce Beurre Blanc*	17.50
Lemon Oregano Chicken	15.95
Fresh Fish of the Day	17.95
Whole Baked Maine Lobster	Market Price

VEGETABLES

Sauteed Fresh Spinach & Mushrooms	3.95
Sauteed Mushrooms	3.95
Steamed Fresh Broccoli, *Sauce Hollandaise*	4.25
Steamed Fresh Asparagus, *Sauce Hollandaise*	6.50
Baked Idaho® Potato, Hashbrown Potatoes, Potato Skins, Lyonnaise Potatoes	3.95

DESSERTS

Fresh Strawberries, *Sabayon Sauce*	3.95
Fresh Raspberries, *Sabayon Sauce*	5.95
New York Cheesecake	4.50
Country-Style Pecan Pie	4.50
Chocolate Velvet Cake	4.50
Souffle for Two, *Chocolate, Grand Marnier, Lemon*	9.25
Coffee, Decaffeinated, Tea	1.75

Oak Tree Restaurant

The unlikely move from its longtime location on Oak Street to a luxury vertical shopping mall on North Michigan Avenue has not affected the good food attitude of this well-respected Chicago "coffee shop".

CARNEGIE DELI FAVORITES

Papa's Pastrami
peppered & cured beef piled high
on your choice of bread, Mardi
Gras slaw & Katie's potato salad
7.75

The Reuben
corned beef, swiss cheese &
sauerkraut served hot on grilled rye,
Mardi Gras slaw and Katie's potato salad
8.25

New York Grille
pastrami & swiss cheese grilled on
dark pumpernickel bread, served with
thousand island dressing, Mardi Gras
slaw & Katie's potato salad
8.25

Corned Beef
thinly sliced, Mardi Gras
slaw & Katie's potato salad
7.75

BLUE PLATE SPECIALS

Turkey Burritos
two warm flour tortillas laced with fresh
roasted turkey, avocado & homemade salsa
7.50

Turkey Hash
freshly roasted turkey meat
sauteed with onions, green &
red pepper & potatoes
7.95

Chicken or Tuna Delight
chicken or tuna salad nested on an
English muffin, topped with cheddar
cheese and tomato slices, broiled
& served with hand-cut French Fries
7.25

Salmon Grill
char-grilled vegetables tossed with
Wasabi-Soy basted & flaked salmon
9.75

Turkey Grill
char-grilled vegetables tossed with fresh
roasted turkey
8.25

Hot Turkey
homemade mashed potatoes & gravy
7.95

Turkey Club
hand-cut French Fries
7.75

---

900 North Michigan Ave, Sixth Floor • Near North/Gold Coast • (312) 751-1988

COOL BREEZE GARDEN SALADS

Fresh Fruit Plate
yogurt or cottage cheese
date nut bread
7.95

Windy City Chopp
turkey, mixed greens, swiss cheese,
hard boiled egg, tomato & bacon tossed
with thousand island dressing
7.75

Tuna Salad Platter
cucumber, tomato, hard-boiled
egg & cottage cheese or fresh fruit
7.25

Grilled Ivy Salad
char-grilled vegetables & chicken
tossed with garden greens
8.25
with shrimp
9.25

Salmon Salad
on a bed of marinated
cucumber slices
7.25

Curry Chicken Salad Platter
with fresh fruit
7.75

GREEN SALADS

Mesclun Greens & Salmon
baby spring greens tossed with
Wasabi Soy dressing and topped
with grilled & flaked salmon
9.25

Papaya & Chicken
tossed with boston bibb, papaya seed
dressing & slivered toasted almonds
8.25

**Char-Grilled Asparagus
& Chicken**
on a bed of Boston Bibb served with
raspberry or ginger vinaigrette
8.25

Cashew Chicken
chicken, cashews, & grapes
tossed with romaine & a
light French Mustard dressing
7.75

Molokai Tuna
albacore Tuna, pineapple & toasted
almond slivers tossed with romaine
& pineapple vinaigrette
7.75

Chin Chin
grilled chicken, rice noodles,
wonton & lettuce tossed
with our Far East dressing
7.25

Chopped Spinach
mushrooms, bacon & egg tossed
with Sweet Mystery dressing
6.75

Char-Grilled Chicken Breast
bed of mixed greens
7.75

Dinner: Sun - Thurs until - 9, Fri - Sat until 10

It's not much more than a shack on a street of million-dollar condos, but this is one of my favorite breakfast spots. The hash browns are great, but the baked apple pancake is superb.

YEASTY OLD FASHIONED BUCKWHEAT PANCAKES
Whipped Butter, Hot Syrup
3.95

BUTTERMILK PANCAKES
Whipped Butter, Hot Syrup
3.25

CHOCOLATE CHIP PANCAKES
Powdered Sugar, Whipped Butter & Hot Syrup
3.95

DUTCH BABY
An Oven Baked German Pancake with Fresh Lemon & Powdered Sugar to Stir.
5.45
Filled with Fresh Strawberries and Banana Slices, Served with Homemade Strawberry Syrup.
6.95

49'ER FLAP JACKS
From the Famous Mother Lode Country Strike of the Century
THIN - CHEWEY GOOEY
4.35

APPLE BUTTERMILK PANCAKES
Fresh Apples with Cinnamon Sugar
3.95

SWEDISH PANCAKES
With Imported Lingonberries and Butter
4.45

WAFFLES

BLUEBERRY WAFFLE 4.30
Served with Fresh Blueberry Compote

COCONUT WAFFLE 4.25
Topped with Toasted Coconut

PECAN WAFFLE 4.55
Topped with Fresh Toasted Georgia Pecans

STRAWBERRY WAFFLE 5.55
Topped with Strawberries and Real Whipped Cream

CREPES

FRENCH CREPES 5.10
Rolled with Fresh Frozen Strawberries
                        Single Crepe 3.50

CONTINENTAL CREPES 5.10
Rolled with Sour Cream and Cointreau, a Gourmet's Delight
                        Single Crepe 3.50

CHERRY KIJAFA CREPES 5.10
Filled with Montmorency Cherries, Simmered in Cherry Kijafa
                        Single Crepe 3.50

MANDARIN CREPES 5.10
The Crepe Suzette of the Orient - Mandarin Orange Segments,
Tropical Syrup, Tempered with Cointreau
                        Single Crepe 3.50

---

22 East Bellevue • Near North/Gold Coast • (312) 642-7917

OUR HOUSE ORIGINALS

HAWAIIAN HAM STEAK.. 6.25
8 oz. Slice of Hickory Smoked Dry Cured Ham, Served with
Pineapple Slices, Prunes and Three Potato Pancakes

THE TWO BY FOUR 3.75
Two Fried Eggs, Four Buttermilk Pancakes, Syrup & Butter

THREE LITTLE PIGS IN BLANKETS.............................. 4.35

JUNIOR PLATE (for Juniors of all Ages) 2.85
Three Buttermilk Pancakes with a choice of Sausage Link or Patty,
or One Egg, Whipped Butter & Hot Syrup

SOUR DOUGH FRENCH TOAST.................................. 4.45
Thick Sliced Sourdough French Bread dipped in an Egg Batter
with a Touch of Almond Essence. Dusted with Powdered Sugar.

10 DOLLAR PANCAKES, with Whipped Butter & Hot Syrup 2.95

EGG SPECIALTIES

Extra Large Grade AA White Eggs

HAM & EGGS 4.95
A Thick Slice of Hickory Smoked Ham, Two Large
Fresh Ranch Eggs and Three Buttermilk Pancakes

DICED HAM & SCRAMBLED EGGS 4.70
Served with Three Buttermilk Pancakes

CANADIAN BACON & EGGS 4.95
Served with Three Buttermilk Pancakes

SAUSAGE (Patty) & EGGS..................................... 4.70
Served with Three Buttermilk Pancakes

LINKS AND EGGS.. 4.70
Served with Three Buttermilk Pancakes

OMELETTES

MUSHROOM OMELETTE 6.40
Our Famous Fluffy Omelette filled with Fresh
Mushrooms and topped with a Rich Sherry Sauce,
served with Potato Pancakes

SPANISH OMELETTE 6.40
Direct from Barcelona. Omelette Espanole. Our
Famous Fluffy Omelette filled with Fresh
Mushrooms and smothered with a Spicy, Peppery,
Tangy Sauce, served with Potato Pancakes

FRESH VEGETARIAN OMELETTE........................... 6.20
Filled with Fresh Broccoli, Tomatoes, Mushrooms,
Onions and Cheddar Cheese

CHICKEN CREPE

Chunks of Chicken Breast, Ripe Olives
and Green Pepper Blended into our
Mushroom Sherry Sauce and Topped
with Toasted Almonds. Served with
Potato Pancakes.
5.35

CORNED BEEF HASH

Freshly Ground Corned Beef, Idaho
Potatoes, Diced Spanish Onions
and a Blend of Spices. Served with
2 Grade AA Eggs and your choice of
Buttermilk Pancakes or Toast.
6.35

EGGS MICHAEL

Canadian Bacon or Sausage Patties
and Poached Eggs on an English Muffin,
covered with our Mushroom Sherry
Sauce. Served with Potato Pancakes
5.65

Lunch: Mon - Fri 7am - 3pm, Sat - Sun 7am - 5pm

Prairie

There's a Frank Lloyd Wright feel to this place which sets the tone for the comfort and style of the room as well as the menu, a marvelous pastiche of food that focuses on midwestern produced and grown products.

Menu Changes Seasonally

STARTERS

Ginger Chicken Broth with Alphabets, Fiddleheads and Sunchokes....$4.50

Starburst of Yellow, Green and Red Tomato Soups Served Chilled
with Sour Cream and Hackleback Caviar....$4.50

Saute of Wild Mushrooms in a Crispy Sweet Potato Basket
with Roasted Corn and Basil Sauces....$8.00

Cornish Pasty Filled with Crayfish, Artichokes and Tarragon
in a Paprika Butter Sauce....$6.50

Grilled Quail with Huckleberry Relish and Cardamon Croutons....$7.00

Parslied Pheasant Terrine with Spicy Zucchini Piccalilli
and Purple Plum Ketchup....$7.50

Layered Terrine of Smoked Fresh Water Fish with Deviled Egg,
Bagel Chips and Gherkin Mayonnaise....$7.50

SALADS

Wilted Spinach and Watercress Salad with Apple Caraway Kraut
and Smoked Pork Tenderloin....$10.00
Small Salad....$7.00

Medley of Baby Lettuces tossed in Raspberry Dressing with Bass Lake Farms
Goat Cheese and Pumpkin Bread Toast....$11.00
Small Salad....$8.00

FROM THE GRILL

Boneless Center Cut Iowa Pork Chop with Barbeque Butter....$15.00
Half Portion....$9.00

One Pound Chargrilled Kansas City Sirloin Strip Steak with
Natural Juices and an Assorted Vegetable Kabob....$23.00

Hasselbring Buffalo Steak with Roasted Shallot Sauce and Jerky....$24.00
A Smaller Steak....$17.00

Grilled Baby Coho Salmon with Country Bacon, Smothered Fennel
and Missouri Black Walnuts....$18.00

Wood Grilled Honey Mustard Chicken with Assorted Bean
Sprouts and Scallions....$14.00

Half Portion....$8.00

MAIN COURSES

Provimi Veal Chops with Mushrooms, Peas and
Sherried Sweet Onion Broth....$22.00

Wood Roasted Rack of Lamb with Natural Juices and
Garlic-Cilantro Custard....$25.00

Boneless Duck Breast Pan Roasted Medium Rare In
Dried Cherry Port Wine Sauce....$17.00
Half Portion....$11.00

Baked Walleye Pike Stuffed with Wild Rice and Vegetables
in an Asparagus Puree....$18.00

Filet of Sturgeon Topped with Tender Herbs and Horseradish
Presented in a Stewed Bell Pepper Broth....$20.00
Half Portion....$14.00

Pan Roasted Lake Superior Whitefish on a Bed of Steamed Basil
with Fried Leeks and Golden Tomato Sauce....$17.00
Half Portion....$11.00

DESSERTS

Walnut and Caramel Schaum Torte with Seasonal Berries....$4.50

Homemade Sweet Potato Praline Cheesecake in a Graham Cracker Crust....$4.50

Warm Rhubarb Crumble with Apple Cinnamon
Ice Cream in a Crispy Almond Tulip....$4.50

Bittersweet Hot Fudge Sundae....$4.00

Dinner: Sun - Thurs 5:30 - 10, Fri - Sat 5:30 - 11

Michael Foley, one of Chicago's most innovative chefs, has his restaurant firmly in hand these days. The pleasant room hums with the murmur of happy eaters, and the service is as expert as it gets.

PRINTER'S ROW

Menu Changes Seasonally

APPETIZERS

Lemongrass Soup
Spinach, sesame seeds and glass noodles
$5.00

Jamaican Black Bean Soup
Pureed, mildly spicy, accented with tamarind
$4.50

Shrimp Dumplings
In a saffron ginger broth
$7.00

Terrine of Portabella Mushrooms with Goat's Cheese
Fennel bulb and pear salad
$6.50

Potato Gnocchi Tossed with Calamari
Finished with oven-dried tomatoes, arugula, parmesan and Italian parsley
$7.00

SALADS

Grilled Asparagus Salad
With vermouth, grapefruit, sage and extra virgin olive oil
$6.50

Caesar Salad with Two Romaines
Tossed with traditional dressing, served in a roast garlic wafer cup,
$5.50

Endive Salad
A variety of endives tossed with sherry vinaigrette and served over marinated cucumbers
$6.00

Printer's Row Salad
A selection of lettuces sprinkled with toasted fennel seed, balsamic vinaigrette
$4.50

ENTREES

BBQ Salmon with "Creole" Styled Risotto
Inspired by the cuisine of New Orleans
$17.50

Crab Cakes, Shoestring Potatoes
Flavored with chives, accented with caramelized onions and a hint of smoked bacon
$15.50

Grilled Beef Tenderloin, Black Pepper Sauce
Roast shallot mashed potatoes finished with blue cheese
$18.50

Roast Pork Chop, Juniper Jus
Seared with rosemary, roasted new potatoes
$15.50

Grilled Vegetable Brochette, Cilantro Oil
Seasonal vegetables served over curried quinoa
$12.50

Rare Roasted Tuna with Mustard and Green Peppercorns
Served with tarragon couscous and orange butter sauce
$18.00

Sautéed Veal Medallions, Black Olive Sauce
Seasoned with marjoram, lemon fettucini
$18.50

Sea Scallop with a Poppy Seed Crust
Pan roasted, with braised young leeks, Dijon mustard sauce
$17.50

Paillard of Capon with Spring Onion
Over wilted mixed greens, balsamic vinegar, extra virgin olive oil, and herbs
$15.00

Combination of Duck, Natural Jus
Roast breast, sweet corn and duck hash
$17.50

Dinner: Mon - Thurs 5 - 10, Fri - Sat 5 - 11

This illustrious room, more than 50 years old now, is worth a visit if for no other reason than to study the photos of famous people that line the walls of the entrance. Then again, the food and nightclub decor deserve a visit, too.

Menu Changes Seasonally

Dinner

Appetizer

Pate or Terrine Selection 5.95

Escargot, Mixed Greens, Mushrooms, Celery Root, Crispy Potatoes 7.95

♥ **Selected Oysters on the Halfshell,** Soy, Wasabi, Pickled Ginger 8.50

Chilled Jumbo Shrimp, Roast Tomato Chili Sauce, Fresh Horseradish 9.50

Petrossian Smoked Salmon, Lobster Vinaigrette, Pumpernickle Toasts 13.50

Iced Russian Beluga Caviar "Malossol" 75.00

The Chef's Featured Pasta of the Day

Soups and Salads

Lobster Bisque, Dry Sherry 5.00

Black Angus Salad, Anchovy Dressing 4.50

Crisp Caesar Salad, Parmesan Pepper Croutons 5.00

Pump Room Salad, Spinach, Bacon, Egg, Radish, Mustard Vinaigrette 5.00

Mixed Lettuces, Tomato, Cucumber, Goat Cheese, Roasted Garlic Dressing 4.50

Entrees

Rosemary and Sage Roast Chicken, Natural Chicken Jus **17.95**
Roast Prime Rib of Beef, Horseradish Cream, Yorkshire Pudding **19.95**
(Limited Quantities Nightly)
Sauteed Calf's Liver, Roasted Onion, Bacon, French Lentil Broth **15.00**
♥ **Oven Roasted Salmon,** Lemon Pepper Crust, Bell Pepper Chutney **22.50**
Herb Crusted Lamb Chops, Red Pesto Orzo, Lamb Jus **25.95**
Grilled Veal T-Bone, Apple Mushroom Sauce, Waffled Sweet Potato **25.95**
Crispy Roast Duck, Four Grain Rice, Tart Cherry Pinot Noir Sauce **18.95**
Broiled Filet Mignon, Roasted Garlic and Shallot Ale Sauce **24.50**
New York Cut Prime Sirloin, Wild Mushrooms, Red Onion Confit **26.95**

Potatoes and Vegetables

Garlic and Horseradish Whipped Red Potatoes 3.50
Baked Idaho Potato 2.95
Double Baked Potato 3.95
♥ **Natural Spinach 3.95**
Creamed Spinach 3.95
Pump Room Vegetable Selection (Market Price)
Winter Squash, Maple Toasted Macadamia Nuts 4.00

Andrew Selvaggio, Executive Chef

In fairness to our other guests, please refrain from cigar and pipe smoking.
There will be times when quality does not meet our standards, and an item on the menu
will not be served.
An 18% gratuity will be added to checks of parties of eight or more.
♥ Prepared in accordance with the American Heart Association Guidelines

This is the place that started the Lettuce Entertain You crop of innovative and world-famous eating places. Still one of the best burgers in town to be enjoyed amid the counterculture markings of the '60s.

R.J. GRUNTS®

SANDWITCHES

1. HAMBURGER
All burgers are char-broiled!
Juicy chopped Sirloin served on a sesame bum escorted by a heaping portion of cottage fries, sloppy cole slaw and a very dull pickle. Yeah! **$5.75**

1a. CHEEZEBURGER
Absolutely the same as the above, forementioned #1 with one extremely gooey exception. You guessed it. CHEEZE! **$5.75**
* Your choice. No extra charge

2. GRUNTBURGER *UNGH!*
The Kosmic Kornerstone of Kulinary Karma. Karefully hand krafted with fried onions, blue cheese and all that other Grunts stuff.
And the word is OMmmm **$5.95**

3. THE *Gormet* BURGER
For effete snobs of the burger coterie. Features mushrooms, onions, Swiss cheese and an aristocratic, if not esoteric, brown sauce. The fee? **$5.95**

4. BACON CHEDDAR BURGER
Our juicy cheddarcheeze burger topped with a rasher of maple-cured bacon and just about anything else you can imagine. Sooooeee! **$5.95**

♥ **5. WHAT A TURKEYBURGER!**
You'll have no beef with lean ground white turkey topped with grilled tomatoes and onions. **$6.25**

6. MR. NATURAL BRISKET
Thin sliced brisket steeped in its own gravy & piled up on a sesame bun or Italian bread. Includes fried onions, fries and pickle. **$6.25**

7. BARBIE Q. MEETS MR. NATURAL !!!
Xactly like #6 but its ZAPPED up with B.B.Q. sauce. One taste and you'll know that Barbie will go down in history.....Yeah right. **$6.25**

8. STEAK TERIYAKIWICH
Charcoal broiled and served on garlic bread w/a side of Teri Yaki sauce and fries.
Teri creates this special sauce in the privacy of her own home. **$6.95**

? COULD BE QUICHE
Could be this. Could be that. Chef Martin is just as confused as the rest of us so your guess is as good as mine. Maybe not **$5.75**

With onion soup, soup of the day or chili the salad bar is **$3.95** extra.

SPECIAL NOTE ♫
You are now reading the LUNCH MENU but feel free to order anything from the flip side (DINNER).
If this is the case why (you might ask) is there a distinction?
Good Question.
peace & love,
R.J.

YAS. OH YASSSSS!!

13. CHICKEN·IN·A BASKET *Is this DEJA-VU or What?*
You get half a chicken. You get fries. You get a biscuit. You get a basket. You get confused !! So what else do you want? **$6.25**

NOW IS THE CENTER OF ALL THINGS
THIS, HOWEVER, IS THE CENTER OF THE MENU.

14. THE UN·BURGER
A burger with no meat? Wow! What a concept!
Yummy de-boned breast of chicken plus lots of other things. What things? Got me. Ask your waitress. I'm tired... **$6.25**

VEGETARIAN THINGS zzzzz

THE SALAD BAR
From 11:30 till DINNER MONDAY thru SATURDAY you may help yourself to the salad bar with your sandwich. **$2.95** BUT just salad is **$5.95**

15. ♥HEART HEALTHY PASTA
Our homemade marinara with fresh ground turkey herbs and spices over a bed of tasty pasta **$5.95**
AND REMEMBER !!!
Everything on this menu is available for carry out.

2056 Lincoln Park West • Lincoln Park/DePaul • (312) 929-5363

NOTICE TO DINNER EATERS

All dinners come with Cobblestone bread and our **WORLD** (?) **FAMOUS** salad table featuring an eco-climactic assortment of mouth watering dressings, toppings and lots of stuff you've never seen before. Take a look. The salad bar is right over there. Nice, huh? It's calling you... Wooooo...

Yes, you may order any of our sandwiches from the other side of the menu **BUT** the salad will be an extra... **$3.95** With onion soup, Soup of the day or chili, salad goes for **$4.95**

But if all you want to do is blow your beets on salad the damage will run to... **$6.50**

♥ These items meet the fat and cholesttrol guidelines of the American Heart Assoc. of Metropolitan Chicago for healthy Adults.

CHARCOAL HEARTH

20. CHOPPED STAKE
Juicy chopped steak quickly seared over glowing charcoal to seal off all the natural goodness one expects. Broiled to your taste (as opposed to the person sitting next to you), and served with bordelaise..... **$8.95**

21. RJ's SPECIAL CHOP STEAK
Even juicer! AND it's covered with fresh green peppers, mushrooms and onions! Select either rare, medium rare, semi-medium rare, medium rare, medium-medium well, well, or well well........ **$9.95**

23. LONDON BROIL
We marinate it, we sear it, we roll it in cracked pepper, we cook it in its own natural juices (as opposed to its own un-natural juices) and serve it with Aw juice and a veggie & potato. **$10.50** But then... wouldn't you? 5-92

24. FILET MIGNON ★
Leanest, tenderest, juiciest, prettiest and everything and real fine. Yes. **$14.95** **OR** have it Herb's way with garlic/herb butter and topped with sauteed mushrooms and **KRISPY** onions. 50¢ **EXTRA**

25. RIBS:
A full slab of tender, meaty succulent ribs, extra fancy with lots of "de Gooey"..... **$13.95**

FIBS: ① The way to a man's heart is through his stomach. ② Anything anybody said in 1968

CHICKEN STUFF

26. ♥ CHICKEN MILANESE "Heart Healthy"
START with boneless breast of chicken rolled in Italian bread crumbs & spices THEN saute in olive oil and fresh lemon. NoW chew & swallow **$9.95**

27. CHEEZIE CHICKEN?
Lovely breast of chicken topped with a creamy parmesan sauce and nestled on a bed of our special Italian noodles. Orgasmic. **$9.95**

28. ITALIAN CHICKEN KABOB
Boneless breast of..... (you guessed it) with spicy Italian sausage, mushrooms, peppers, onions, zucchini tomato slapped on a pile of WILD rice. **$10.95**

29. BBQ CHICKEN
RJ's favorite dish is half a baked chicken broiled with B.B.Q. sauce. Me too! **$9.50**

18. FRENCH..... ONION SOUP!
Our own homemade onion soup covered with krunchy krootons and melted cheezes. Served in a crock. **$3.25**

19. CHICAGO'S BEST CHILI
The winner of "The Great Chicago Chili Cook off." Served with grated cheeze and SOUR cream. Also # 1 on the New York Times bestsmeller list. **$3.95**

WHEN THE SPOON IS IN THE SEVENTH MOUTH

33. TURKEY PARMESAN
Fresh, juicy breast of turkey that's breaded and sauteed in olive oil with fresh herbs and spices and served over a bed of linguini with marinara and mozzarella cheeze. **$8.25**

PASTA

34. RIGATONI ARTICHOKI
♥ Features artichokes, capers, black olives, tomatos, fresh basil and...... Olive Oyl. One taste and you'll shout..."Sono queste la sue seno?!" **$9.95**

Relish

The name is apt. You savor and eat with gusto at chef/owner Ron Blazek's place. This space has seen many restaurants, but none have put the focus on food quite as well. And the refurbished interior is a welcome change.

Menu Changes Weekly and Seasonally

APPETIZERS

Morel and Potato Won Ton lemon aioli and asparagus	4.50
Seared Sea Scallop tomatillo relish and annetto oil	4.75
Wild Mushroom Strudel with arugula pesto and roast garlic	5.00
Shrimp and Pinenut Ravioli crispy leeks and a lobster basil essence	5.25
Quesadilla of Duck mango, brie and roast poblanos	4.50
Antipasto five mini salads with varying flavors	5.50
Crab and Basil Cake sun dried tomatoes and candied onions	6.50
Spicy Chicken Pizza with rosemary crust, leeks and shiitaki's	6.25
Ratatouille Pizza red onions and Roma tomatoes	5.75
Walnut and Blue Cheese Pizza with brie and celery	6.00

PASTAS

B.B.Q. Chicken Lasagna mozzarella, charred vegetables and basil	9.50
Duck Fettucine brie, walnuts and port glaze	8.50/14.50
Black Trumpet and Hedgehog Mushroom Linguini olive oil	7.25/1250
Penne Pasta spicy lamb sausage, toasted cumin seed, eggplant	5.75/11.50

2044 North Halsted • Lincoln Park/DePaul • (312) 868-9034

110

SOUPS AND SALADS

Black Bean a touch spicey , served with cilantro and citrus cream   3.75

Today's Soup your wait person will give you all the details   3.75

Watercress and Endive Salad hazlenuts and blue cheese   4.25

Relish our Greens with a balsamic vinaigrette   3.75

Tomato and Roast Bell Peppers arugula, house mozzarella   5.00

Asparagus Salad with oven roast cherry tomatoes and lemon thyme   4.50

Caesar Salad parmesan and sour dough croutons   4.75

Grilled Vegetable Salad drizzled with a honey basil vinaigrette   5.50

ENTREES

Goat Cheese Chicken Breast with black bean cake and cilantro oil   9.75

Pan Seared Chicken Breast asiago mashed potatoes and basil   11.95

Toasted Cumin Seed Crusted Swordfish, corn relish and polenta   14.75

Rack And Leg of Lamb rosemary, roasted shallots and fennel   16.75

Indian Style Glazed Duck citrus infused lentels and crispy pasta   16.50

Marinated Grilled Venison wild mushroom risotto and red wine sauce   15.75

Roast Salmon and Shrimp Cake with Asian flavors   14.50

Grilled Rib Eye Steak bliss potatoes and charred vegetables   14.75

Grilled Vegetable Platter always different and always interesting   10.50

Pepper Marinated Tuna olive and tomato salsa with shrimp skewer   15.50

Roast Loin of Pork with blue cheese and roast butternut squash   13.50

Sage's Sages

Owner Gene Sage has been in the restaurant business for a long time, and it shows: Attention to detail—on and off the plate—is meticulous, and the atmosphere is comfortable and relaxing.

Menu Changes Daily and Seasonally

APPETIZERS

♥ Venison and Wild Mushrooms in a delicate Merlot Sauce	4.95	Jumbo Shrimp Cocktail	7.95
Goat Cheese Tempura, Garlic Tomato Sauce	3.95	Smoked Salmon and Buckwheat Crepes with Creme Fraiche and American Caviars	7.95
Crab Cakes, Chili Mayonnaise	5.95	Fresh Oysters of the Season	4.95
Stuffed Jumbo Shrimp with Cajun Crabmeat	5.95	Domestic Caviar	9.95
Oysters of the Season, Rockefeller	4.95	Imported Caviar	At Market
Escargot in Puff Pastry	5.95		

SOUPS

Three Cheese Onion Soup	2.95	Soup Du Jour	1.95

A LA CARTE SALADS

Caesar Salad	4.95	Caesar Salad with Shrimp	9.95

Sage's Salad with Hearts of Palm, Artichoke Hearts, Asparagus, Mushrooms, and Tomatoes on Bibb Lettuce with Sage's Mustard Roquefort Dressing   5.95
Sage's Salald with Shrimp 10.95

Beefsteak Tomato, Cucumber, and Red Onion   3.95

♥ Indicates Heart Healthy Preparations

75 West Algonquin Road • Arlington Heights • (708) 593-6200

STEAKS & CHOPS

The Sirloin Steak (20 ounces), Sweet Onion Rings and Mushroom Caps	23.95 / 17.95
Filet Mignon (three-quarters pound), Sweet Onion Rings, Mushroom Caps	19.95 / 12.95
The **Southwestern Sirloin Steak**, pan-seared and served with a spicy sauce of Tomato, Cilantro, and Jalepeno	17.95
♥ **Double-Rib Lamb Chops** and Rosemary Sauce served with roasted Peppers	19.95 /12.95
Prime Veal Chop, seared, and served Forestiere with Chantrelle Mushrooms, Green Onions and a hint of Garlic. (Also available grilled au natural)	19.95
♥ **Pork Chop Porterhouse**, grilled, and served with a Country Apple Fritter	14.95

SEAFOOD

♥ **Grouper**, grilled, and served with Roasted Garlic Sauce and Imported Mushrooms with fresh Leaf Spinach	15.95
Salmon, seared, accompanied by Sweet Corn, Shiitake Mushrooms, Chives, and Balsamic Vinaigrette Sauce	16.95
♥ **Ahi Tuna** coated with Peppercorns and Fennel, grilled over charcoal, Orange Ginger Sauce	14.95

PASTA AND . . .

Giant Fresh-water Shrimp served with Linguine with Shallots, Plum Tomatoes, and Garlic	17.95 / 10.95
Stone Steak, a Filet Mignon (three-quarters pound) coated with Romano Cheese and Garlic, broiled, and served atop Fettucine with Sweet Peppers, Onions and Mushrooms	19.95 / 12.95
Boneless Breast of Chicken dusted with Parmesan Bread Crumbs, served on Linguine with Tomato Basil Sauce	14.95 / 8.95

AND . . .

Roasted Half-Chicken Diable accompanied by Roasted Peppers and a tangy Diable Sauce with Shallots, Tarragon, and Peppercorns (also available broiled)	8.95
Shellfish Medley with Giant Shrimp, Sea Scallops and Maine Lobster broiled, Citrus Butter	19.95
Lobster Tail broiled and served with Sherried Butter	24.95

Entrees are accompanied by the chef's selection of pasta or potato and
your choice of Sage's Famous Mushroom Salad, Mixed Greens or Pasta Salad

Star Top Cafe

To know it is to love it. The mostly American food, served with an off-the-wall ambiance, does not leave the taste buds wanting; the subliminal taste message here is "Season with Reason."

STAR TOP CAFE

Menu Changes Daily

shrimp & sweetbread saute w/ Chinese mustard & fresh rosemary 6.

bay scallops w/ mint, montrachet & cappellini 6.

saba w/ sushi rice, gari and wasabi 6.

bay shrimp w/ chorizo, potato, poblanos, molé & tomatillo salsa 6.

scallop & asparagus saute w/ bacon, cheddar, bitter ale mustard sauce 6.

spedino alla mozzerella 6.

baked boucheron w/ roasted garlic, fennel, tomato ragout 6.

duck confit w/ snow peas, chilies, rice stick, shiitake & szechuan peppercorn 6.

roasted acorn squash w/ duck, sundrieds, golden raisins & gruyere sherry cream 6.

roasted peppers w/ tarama, garlic toast, olive oil, anchovy & ripe olives 6.

●————————————●

Thai corn soup w/ grilled shrimp, lime leaves, lemon grass 5.

roasted garlic & pumpkin cream soup 4.50

Cuban black bean soup w/ sherry & sour cream 4.50

basil, romaine & danish blue w/ sherry hazelnut vinaigrette 4.50

cress, jicama, cherry tomato w/ walnut dijonaisse 4.50

baked montrachet w/ belgian endive, apples & bacon - honey dressing 5.

2748 North Lincoln Ave • Lincoln Park/DePaul • (312) 281-0997

skatewing saute w/ gari-wasabi beurre blanc 17.

salmon saute w/ hazelnut, cardomom, lime brown butter 16.

grilled mako shark w/ orange, chilies, cilantro, purple onion & olive oil 15.

catfish saute w/ garlic, lemon, bacon, brown butter and Lea & Perrins 15.

pike saute w/ sour plum-ginger glaze and scallion vinaigrette 16.

grilled ahi tuna, rare, w/ oshinko, scallion, sesame & sake 17.

lamb lou 17.

duck breast saute w/ lime, honey & szechuan peppercorn 17.

roasted pork loin w/ mashed potatoes, stewed hot greens & sage cream gravy 15.

grilled chicken w/ fennel sausage, manila clams, red wine & fresh thyme 15.

rapini saute w/ orchetti, olive oil, garlic, ripe olive & peccorino romano 13.

●————————————————●

eggplant saute w/ sour plum, chilies & garlic 3.

creamed spinach w/ gouda 3.

stewed hot greens w/ bacon, onion & vinegar 3.

mashed potatoes w/ sage cream gravy or butter 3.

asparagus saute w/ citrus beurre blanc 3.

DESSERTS

chocolate sambuca mousse

chocolate banana rum trifle

chocolate chip tart

white chocolate brickle charlotte

apple cranberry crisp

strawberry cobbler

chocolate truffle torte

coffee profiteroles

chocolate glazed bourbon pecan pie

passion fruit creme brule

Streeterville Grille & Bar

Tucked into a prestigous corner on the ground floor of the plush and grand new Sheraton Chicago Hotel, this clubby, comfortable restaurant and bar has made its mark in a short time with excellent dishes that are Italian but have an American frame of mind.

S T A R T E R S

Buffalo Mozzarella, Vine-Ripened Tomatoes and Basil Oil	$ 6.00
Grilled Eggplant with Zucchini, Goat Cheese and Arugula Oil	$ 4.50
Prosciutto with Warm Pears	$ 6.50
Grilled Portabello Mushrooms with Sundried Tomato Oil	$ 4.50
Chilled Jumbo Gulf Shrimp with Three Sauces	$ 7.50
Smoked Salmon with Warm Potato Pancakes	$ 7.50

S O U P S

Tuscan White Bean Soup	$ 4.00
Today's Soup	$ 4.00

S A L A D S

Spinach with Proscuitto, Mushrooms, Hard Boiled Egg, Pine Nuts and Balsamic Dressing	$ 4.50
The Streeterville Garden Greens Salad, with Bibb Lettuce, Belgian Endive, Lolla Rosa, Roasted Bell Peppers and Italian Bleu Cheese Dressing	$ 4.50
Leaves of Young Romaine with Parmesan Croutons and Garlic Anchovy Dressing	$ 4.50

M A I N C O U R S E

Grilled Porterhouse Steak with Streeterville Steak Butter	$19.50
Prime 14 oz. New York Sirloin Steak	$24.00
Center Cut Filet of Beef with Choice of Sauces	$22.00
Three Grilled Double-Cut Lamb Chops with Rosemary Butter	$23.00
Veal Chop with Lemon-Parmesan Cheese Crust and Porcini Mushroom Sauce	$24.00
Mediterranean Chicken Vesuvio	$16.00

301 East North Water St • Near North/Gold Coast • (312) 670-0788

FISH SELECTIONS

Grilled Fillet of Ivory Salmon with Zucchini Ratatouille	$22.00
Grilled Jumbo Gulf Shrimp with Roasted Bell Peppers	$21.00
Grilled Swordfish with Tomatoes and Basil	$22.00

PASTA

Orecchiette Pasta with Grilled Chicken, Fresh Spinach and Goat Cheese	$14.00
Bowtie Pasta with Jumbo Sea Scallops, Asparagus, Sundried Tomatoes and Wild Mushrooms	$14.00
Homemade Basil Pasta with Gulf Shrimp, Baby Artichokes and Italian Tomatoes	$14.00
Mostaccioli with Marinara and Buffalo Mozzarella	$12.50

FAVORITES

Vesuvio Potatoes	$ 3.00
Sauteed Leaf Spinach	$ 3.00
Fresh Fiddlehead Ferns	$ 4.00
Fresh Green Stringbeans	$ 2.00
Mashed Potatoes with Leeks	$ 3.00
Sauteed Chantrelle Mushrooms	$ 5.00
Streeterville Baked Potato	$ 3.00

DESSERTS

Twin Cannoli filled with White and Dark Chocolate Mousse, Berry Salad and Fresh Mint	$ 4.50
The Pastry Chef's Chocolate Creation	$ 4.50
Mascarpone Cheese Cake with Candied Chestnuts	$ 4.50
Selection of Homemade Ice Creams and Sorbet	$ 4.50
Tiramisu	$ 4.50
Seasonal Berries	Market Price
Creme Brulee´	$ 4.50

Plan your next event in our private dining room.

*In order to provide our guests the finest dining experience,
we reserve the right to omit menu items not meeting the highest quality.*

Twin Anchors

One of the most popular neighborhood bars in Chicago, this great 60-year-old ribs (and burgers) spot is well known to stars such as Frank Sinatra, which is why many of ol' Blue Eyes' songs are featured on the jukebox.

TWIN ANCHORS TRADITIONS

All Entrees Served with French Fried Potatoes, Our Own Special Cole Slaw, Dark Rye Bread, Crackers, Butter and Dill Pickle. Onion Rings available in lieu of French Fries. .40 additional.

OUR FAMOUS RIBS

The World Famous Twin Anchors Baby Back Ribs. Slow Cooked, Meaty and Tender, with Our Own Time Honored Barbecue Sauce. A Delicious, Zesty Barbecue Sauce is also Available.

12.95

CHICKEN

One-Half of a Tender Chicken. Fried in Pure Vegetable Oil (no cholesterol) to a Crispy Golden Brown. Served with our Regular or Zesty Barbecue Sauce on the Side. If you prefer the Chicken may be Fried, then placed on our Broiler and Quickly Basted with either Sauce.

6.50

SHRIMP

Jumbo Breaded French Fried Shrimp Served With Our Own Cocktail Sauce

9.50

NEW YORK STRIP STEAK*

We Challenge any Steak House to Serve a more Tender, Tastier Steak than our New York Strip.

10.95

FILET MIGNON*

We Proudly Offer the Choicest Steak Available, Charbroiled to your Specifications. Many People Feel it's the Best Steak value in Town.

14.95

*Grilled Onions and Garlic Butter available as an accompaniment to our Steaks. Try One or Both.

1655 North Sedgwick St • Lincoln Park/DePaul • (312) 266-1616

SALADS

CAESAR SALAD
Traditional Caesar Salad with Romaine Lettuce, Parmesan Cheese, Croutons and Anchovy Garnish. Served with Bread Basket.
5.95

DINNER SALAD
Served with your Choice of Dressing.
1.95

Creamy Garlic, French, Italian, Thousand Island, Vinegar and Oil, Low Calorie Ranch, Blue Cheese (additional .50)

SANDWICHES
Served with French Fried Potatoes, Our Own Special Cole Slaw and Dill Pickle. Onion Rings available in lieu of French Fries. .40 additional.

ANCHOR BURGER
One-Half Pound Pure Beef. Specify Grilled Onions of Slice of Raw Onion. Lettuce & Tomato also available.
4.95

ROAST PORK
Lean Loin of Pork Roasted Slowly to keep it Juicy and Tender. Then Sliced and Dipped in our Hearty Barbecue Gravy.
4.95

CHEESE ANCHOR BURGER
One-Half Pound Pure Beef Served with American or Swiss Cheese. Specify Grilled Onions or Slice of Raw Onion. Lettuce & Tomato also available.
5.25

CHICKEN BREAST
Grilled Chicken Breast Sandwich on a Sesame Seed Bun with choice of American or Swiss Cheese. Lettuce and Tomato, or BBQ Sauce.
5.95

CHEESE ANCHOR BURGER
One-Half Pound Pure Beef Served with American or Swiss Cheese. Specify Grilled Onions or Slice of Raw Onion. Lettuce & Tomato Also Available.
5.25

FISH FILET SANDWICH
Lightly Breaded, Fried Scrod Filet. Served with a side of Tartar Sauce. Lettuce & Tomato also available.
5.25

SIDE ORDERS

CHILI Cup 1.95 Bowl 2.95
Topped with either American Cheese, Chopped Onion or Sour Cream.
If more than one item, add .30 per item.

SOUP DU JOUR Cup 1.50 Bowl 2.50
Made Fresh Daily

ONION RINGS 2.00

FRENCH FRIES 1.75

DESSERT

CHEESE CAKE
Selection Changes Daily
3.00

One Guest Check per party.
A 15% Gratuity will be added to your Check for Parties of Six or More People.

Minimum Food Charge 3.50 per person
NOTE: For Carry-Outs please add .50 per item.

Dinner: Mon - Thurs 5 - 11:30, Fri 5 - 12:30, Sat until 12:30, Sun until 10:45

119

Wishbone

With the opening of the second Wishbone, some of the strain and pain have left this one and only original that everybody loves. Funky decor, delicious food and low prices will do it every time.

Menu Changes Daily

OPENERS

Blackbean Soup (w/Meat) 1.75 2.25
Soup of the Day 1.75 2.25
Seafood Chowder 2.00 2.50

SHRIMP FRICASSEE
Served with roasted sweet red peppers, mushrooms, tomatoes and cream
4.75

MAIN DISHES

YARDBIRD
Large chicken marinated and grilled, served with sweet red pepper sauce
and a choice of TWO SIDES.
Whole Leg 5.50
Breast 6.50

HOPPIN' JOHN (Vegetarian) or HOPPIN' JACK (with Black Beans - Meat Stock)
Black-eyed peas served on rice topped with cheddar cheese, scallion and tomato
4.95
with salad 5.50 with ham or grilled chicken 6.25
with salad, ham or chicken 6.75

LOUISIANA CHICKEN SALAD
Blackened Chicken breast served warm and spicy on lettuce with choice of dressing and
corn bread.
6.95

CRAB CAKES
Spicy Carolina-style crab with slaw, rice and black beans or choice of TWO SIDES
9.25

1001 West Washington • River North • (312) 850-2663 • Call for Additional Locations

BACKYARD BURGER

VERY LEAN beef with mixed spices served on Kaiser roll or black bread. 6 oz. 4.75
With cheddar cheese 5.00 With potato or SIDE 5.50

HOUSE SALAD

small 1.95
large 2.50

SIDES

(ordered separately)
Rice Pilaf 1.25   Cole Slaw 1.25   Sauteed Spinach 2.00   Cornbread .85
Brown Rice 1.25   Black Beans 1.75   Potato of the Day 1.50   Black Eyed Peas 1.50

WISHBONE DINNER SPECIALS

Blackened Bluefish	*9.25
Blackened or Grilled Mahi Mahi	*10.25
Blackened or Grilled Marlin	*10.25
Blackened or Grilled Striped Bass	*9.25
Blackened or Grilled Tuna	*11.25
Rolled Stuffed Sole	*10.25
Salmon Papillote	**10.25
Scallops	*10.25
Cray Fish Cakes	*8.75
Shrimp & Grits	**8.50
Corn Cakes with Shrimp	7.25
Salmon Cakes	**9.25
Pan Fried Chicken Leg	*5.75
Breast	*6.75
Chicken Etoufee	7.75
Chicken & Shrimp Etoufee	8.75
Jambalaya with Shrimp	8.95

* Choice of TWO Sides
** Choice of ONE Side

DINNER SIDES - Special (Additional to Menu)
Ratatouille Succotash Collard Greens
Mashed Rutabaga Acorn Squash Glazed Carrots
String Beans Turnips Okra & Tomato
Sweet Potato Corn on the Cob Zucchini & Onions
Mashed Celery Root Cauliflower & Broccoli (w/Hollandaise)
Brussel Sprouts with nuts

Yvette

A bistro atmosphere is one-third of the appeal at this popular North Side spot. A lively crowd and basic bistro food at reasonable prices complete the equation.

"CHICAGO'S NEWEST TRADITION"

FIRST COURSE

CHARRED BEEF SIRLOIN CARPACCIO $5.50
served with watercress and mustard sauce

WILD MUSHROOM STRUDEL $5.95
served with chive cream

CHEF'S HOME MADE PATE $5.95

SALMON GRAVLAX $5.50
salmon cured with fresh dill and peppercorn served with dill sauce

POLENTA TIMBALE AND GRILLED EGGPLANT $5.50
served with marinara sauce

GRILLED SHRIMP $6.95
served with tomatoes, cucumbers and fried capers

SOUP OF THE DAY $1.95

CLASSIC LOBSTER BISQUE $2.95

HOUSE SALAD $2.50

CAESAR SALAD $4.95

1206 North State Pkwy • Near North/Gold Coast • (312) 280-1700

SECOND COURSE

VEGETARIAN ENTREE OF THE DAY   MARKET VALUE

SAUTEED SEA SCALLOPS WITH CITRUS BUERRE BLANC $12.50
served with mushrooms and rice

GRILLED CHICKEN BREAST $11.50
served over field greens with apples, walnuts and grapes

GRILLED PORK TENDERLOIN $12.95
served with a spicy pear sauce and herbed spaetzle

ROASTED WHITEFISH $13.50
served with finely diced vegetables

TENDERLOIN TIPS OF BEEF $12.50
sauteed with bacon, mushroom, onion and red wine sauce

ROASTED LAMB AU JUS $13.95
served with ratatouille and roasted potatoes

ROASTED BREAST OF CHICKEN $12.50
served with wild mushroom mouse and natural jus

SAUTEED TOURNEDOS OF BEEF $14.95
served with sweet and sour onions in a red wine sauce

YVETTE'S HOME SMOKED SALMON $14.95

FRESHLY BAKED DESSERTS OF THE DAY $3.00

COFFEE/TEA $1.00   ESPRESSO $2.00   CAPPUCINO $2.50

PLEASE INQUIRE ABOUT OUR PRIVATE PARTY FACILITIES
CALL CATERING AT 408-1247

Dinner: Mon - Thurs 5 - 12, Fri - Sat 5 - 1, Sun 5 - 11

Yvette Wintergarden

An excellent choice for dinner before the opera. The open-air decor floats into a more intimate dining scene where live music harmonizes with the carefully prepared cuisine.

Menu Changes Seasonally

PRE-THEATER MENU

$19.50 per person

Served from 5 to 7 p.m. Monday-Saturday

PRELUDE	*INTERMEZZO*
Chef's paté selection or Soup of the Day	Boston Hydro Lettuce with Creamy Dijon Vinaigrette

ENTRÉE SELECTIONS

Grilled Salmon with Mustard Glaze served with angel hair pasta, julienne vegetables and soy buerre	Grilled Sirloin served with potato gratin and caramelized tomatoes

FINALE

Pastry Selection
Coffee

DINNER MENU
FIRST COURSE

SALMON GRAVLAX $5.95
cured salmon with creme fraiche and croutons

PROSCIUTTO OF DUCK AND VEGETABLE RAGOUT $6.50
served over lobster Risotto

SHRIMP PROVENCAL $6.50
served with tomatoes, onions and herbs

SALMON TARTARE $5.50
served with cucumber and caviar

311 South Wacker Dr • Downtown/Loop • (312) 408-1242

SECOND COURSE

PASTA OF THE DAY   MARKET VALUE

GRILLED VEGETABLES OF THE SEASON $10.95
served with a crispy pasta cake

CALF'S LIVER AND POTATO GRATIN $12.95
served with baby greens and balsamic vinegar

ROASTED CHICKEN PROVENCAL $13.50
served with roasted shallots, tomatoes, onions and fine herbs

ROASTED WHITEFISH WITH CRISPY VEGETABLES $13.95
served in ratatouille vinaigrette

SCALLOPS AND PRAWNS $14.50
served with julienne of vegetables in puff pastry

ROASTED PORK LOIN AND PEAR ONION CAKES $14.50
served with gingered bacon and spinach

GRILLED SALMON WITH MUSTARD GLAZE $15.95
served with angel hair pasta, julienne vegetables and soy beurre

GRILLED SIRLOIN $17.50
served with potato gratin and caramelized tomatoes

SEARED VEAL CHOP $18.95
served with an herb crust and wild mushrooms

FRESHLY MADE DESSERTS OF THE DAY $4.00
COFFEE/TEA $1.25   ESPRESSO $2.50   CAPPUCCINO $2.95

PARTIES FOR 10 TO 1500! CALL CATERING AT (312)408-1247

Dinner: Mon - Thurs 5 - 9:30, Fri - Sat 5 - 10:30

The bazaarlike atmosphere—flying carpets, murals of the Middle East, music—sets the mood for some wonderful couscous, hummus and shish kebab. And the romantic panache is firmly enhanced by the excellent service.

Appetizers and Salads

CHEESE BOEREK   **2.00**
Seasoned cheese baked in phylo.

SPINACH BOEREK   **2.00**
Spiced spinach baked in phylo.

CASBA PIZZA   **5.00**
Baked lamb and spices on pita.

IMAM BAYELDI   **5.00**
Braised eggplant. tomatoes, onions, peppers.

TABBULÉH   **4.50**
Tomatoes, parsley. cracked wheat. olive oil. lemon juice.

MUHAMMARA   **5.50**
Walnut, peppers, olive oil. spices.

KIBBÉE NAYYEH   **8.50**
Raw lamb blended with cracked wheat.

NEEVICK   **4.00**
Seasoned spinach and chick peas.

COMBINATION APPETIZER   **8.50**
YALANCI SARMA, NEEVICK, HOMMOS, MUHAMMARA.

Entrees
Include
SOUP AND TOSSED SALAD

SHISH TAOUCK	**13.95**
Chicken breast kabob, garlic sauce.	
TUSS KABOB	**15.95**
Lamb cubes served over eggplant, Bechamel sauce.	

COUSCOUS

TANGIER LAMB	**14.95**
VEGETARIAN	**12.95**
LAMB MARRAKESH	**14.95**
Stewed tender lamb in onions, raisins, almonds and herbs.	
KIBBÉH	**13.95**
Cracked wheat shells stuffed with ground meat, onions and walnuts.	
SARMA-KHASHLAMA	**13.95**
Stuffed grape leaves, simmered with tender lamb. Served with Yogurt.	
STEAK MADAGASCAR	**17.95**
Sautéed tenderloin of beef with green peppercorn in cream and brandy.	
VEAL MT. OLIVE	**16.95**
Tenderloin of veal, sauteed with olives and onions in cream-brandy sauce.	
CHICKEN PÉSTO	**14.95**
Grilled chicken breast in pesto, sour cherry sauce.	
LAMB OR BEEF SHISH-KABAB	**15.95**
Grilled marinated lamb or beef, served with a medley of vegetables and pilaff.	
YOGURTLY KABOB	**12.95**
Grilled ground meat with yogurt & tomato coulis.	
COMBINATION PLATE	**16.95**
Sarma, Kibbeh, Imam Bayeldi.	
FISH OF THE DAY	

Sayat Nova

It just keeps going and going and going. A favorite downtown haunt with its own brand of romantic attraction. The lamb dishes are lavish, the tabbouleh is terrific, and the value is hard to beat.

Menu Changes Seasonally

Appetizers

Cheese or Spinach Beoreg $2.00

Taboule $3.00
Cracked wheat salad.

Hummos $3.00
Chick pea & sesame seed dip.

Baba Ghannouj $3.50
Egg plant dip.

Raw Kibbee $9.00
Armenian Steak Tartar.

Sarma $2.50
Grape leaves stuffed with meat, rice & spices, served with yogurt sauce.

Jajekh $2.00
Cucumber & yogurt with mint.

Armenian Spinach $2.50
Cooked in olive oil & served cold.

Red Cabbage Salad $2.00
Crisp red cabbage in oil & vinegar dressing.

Stuffed Eggplant $2.50
Tomato, green pepper & ground lamb stuffed into eggplant.

Plaki $2.50
White beans in olive oil, onions & spices.

House Specialties

All Entrées include soup or green salad & hot Armenian bread.

Kebab Combo $11.95
Combination of Shish Kebab, Lulla Kebab & Chicken Kebab served with rice pilaf, broiled green pepper & onion.

Vegetarian Combination Dinner $10.90
Spinach beoreg, taboule salad, rice pilaf, plaki bean dish & Armenian spinach.

Shrimp Kebab $14.95
Fresh jumbo shrimp marinated then broiled to taste, served with rice pilaf, green pepper & onion.

157 East Ohio • Near North/Gold Coast • (312) 644-9159

128

Sautéed Scallops   **$12.95**
Fresh scallops lightly sautéed with green peppers & onion.

Cous Cous, Lamb or Vegetarian   **$10.95**
*A traditional North African dish of steamed semolina and assorted
fresh vegetables, cooked in a light red sauce with or without lamb.*

Trout with Herbs   **$12.95**
*Fresh trout stuffed with scallions, parsely, cilantro and dill,
charcoal broiled, deboned and topped with lemon juice,
olive oil & herbs, served with rice pilaf.*

Shish Kebab   **$11.95**
*Leg of lamb cubed & charcoal broiled, served with rice pilaf,
broiled green pepper & onion.*

Dinner Entrées

All entrées include soup or green salad & hot Armenian bread.

Lulla Kebab   **$10.95**
*Lean ground beef & lamb charcoal broiled, served with
rice pilaf, broiled green pepper & onion.*

Chicken Kebab   **$10.95**
*Marinated breast of chicken, charcoal broiled, served
with rice pilaf, broiled green pepper & onion.*

Lamb Chops   **$16.95**
*Charcoal broiled, to your taste served with rice pilaf,
broiled green pepper & onion.*

Sarma   **$9.90**
*Grape leaves stuffed with diced meat, rice & spices,
served with madzoun sauce.*

Kufta   **$10.75**
*Ground meat mixed with cracked wheat, skillfully turned into balls and
stuffed with diced meat, nuts & spices, served with madzoun sauce.*

Sautéed Chicken   **$10.75**
Specially marinated breast of chicken sautéed with green pepper & onions.

New York Strip Steak   **$12.50**
*Charcoal broiled to your taste, served with rice pilaf,
broiled green pepper & onion.*

Stuffed Breast of Chicken   **$10.95**
*Charcoal broiled breast of chicken stuffed with spinach and cheese,
served with rice pilaf, broiled green pepper & onion.*

Robinson's No. 1 Ribs

The leader of the rib pack in Chicago, Robinson's ribs have a straight-to-the-bone flavor that is at once tangy and smoky, sweet and delicious. And the barbecue chicken is straight up and fine eating too.

Appetizers

All Appetizers are Breaded and Deep Fried, except Rib Tips. Deep Fried only in 100% Pure Vegetable Oil.

RIB TIPS 3.95

BEER BATTERED ONION RINGS 2.95

BUFFALO CHICKEN WINGS 3.95

BEER BATTERED
MUSHROOMS 3.95

CHEESE STICKS 3.95

BREADED ZUCCHINI 2.95

BREADED OKRA 2.95

Vegetarian Entrees

VEGETABLE LASAGNA
  Meatless 3.95

MACARONI & CHEDDAR
  CHEESE 3.95

PASTA SALAD 2.95

TURNIP GREENS &
  CORN BREAD 2.95

BLACK-EYED PEAS &
  CORN BREAD 2.95

Seafood

All Seafood Served with Robinson's Famous BBQ Sauce on the Side. (Cocktail or Tartar Sauce upon request.)

OCEAN PERCH 5.95
  Battered & Deep Fried

JACK FISH TRAY .... (8 oz.) 4.95

Chicken

1/2 BBQ CHICKEN DINNER 4.95
  Half Chicken served with our Famous
  Sauce.

WHOLE BBQ CHICKEN DINNER 8.95
  Same Chicken, but lots more of it.

BONELESS BREAST OF
  CHICKEN DINNER 5.95
  8 oz. Breast, Smoked in a Pit
  and Covered with Sauce.

BUFFALO CHICKEN
  WINGS DINNER 4.95
  Breaded and Deep Fried in
  100% Vegetable Oil.

CAJUN TURKEY BREAST
  DINNER 4.50
  (5 ounce) (98% Fat Free)

940 Madison St • Oak Park • (708) 383-8452

Super Sandwiches

Served with Celery-Seed Cole Slaw and
Choice of Hickory Smoked Baked
Beans or Natural Cut Steak Fries or
Corn on the Cob or Potato Salad.

BBQ PORK 4.50
*Tender Chunks of Center Cut Loin
Smothered with our Famous Sauce.*

BBQ BEEF 4.25
*Hickory Smoked Beef Sliced Thinly
with Robinson's No. 1 Sauce.*

**BBQ BONELESS RIB
SANDWICH** 6.50

**ROBINSON'S HALF POUND
BURGER (8 oz.)** 4.25
Choice of American or Swiss Cheese

Ribs

Our Ribs are Seasoned with BBQ Seasonings, then Smoked to perfection and
Smothered with our #1 BBQ Sauce.

**BBQ BABY BACK RIBS
Full Slab Dinner** 11.95

**BBQ BABY RACK RIBS
Half Slab Dinner** 6.50

BBQ BEEF RIBS DINNER 6.50

Combos

RIBS & SHRIMP COMBO 12.95

RIB & HALF CHICKEN COMBO ... 10.95
The Best of Both Worlds.

ROBINSON'S SUPER COMBO 9.95
*Rib Tips, One Hot Link
& Chicken Wings.*

BBQ Specialties

BBQ RIB TIP DINNER
*Hickory Smoked Spare-Rib Tips
Covered with Robinson's No. 1 Sauce.*
Small 4.95 .... Large 6.50

BBQ HOT LINKS
*Two Perfectly Seasoned Links
Broiled to Perfection and topped
with our Special Sauce.* 4.25

Side Orders

**HICKORY SMOKED
BAKED BEANS** .... .95

NATURAL CUT STEAK FRIES .... .90

COLE SLAW .... .80

CORN ON THE COB .... .99

POTATO SALAD .... .85

FRESH BAKED CORN BREAD
(Two Pieces) .... .85

TURNIP GREENS .... .85

BLACK-EYED PEAS .... .85

PINTO BEANS .... .85

Desserts

ELI'S CHEESE CAKE 2.00

SWEET POTATO PIE .... Slice 1.50
Whole Pie 5.00

FRESH MADE POUND CAKE 1.50

**HAAGEN DAZS
ICE CREAM** .... (Pint) 2.50
(3 1/2 oz. Cup) .95

GERMAN CHOCOLATE CAKE 1.50

Ben Moy has quite a restaurant—not your run-of-the-mill Chinese by any means, as the menu is slim and trimmed down to a manageable number of dishes. I can make a meal on an appetizer called Wings of the Bird (barbequed chicken wings) and the exceptionally good fried rice.

THE BIRD RESTAURANT

Menu Changes Weekly

DINNER MENU

Appetizers

Wings of the Bird	Each 5.00
B-B-Q Pork	5.50 order
Specials:	
Egg Rolls	2.50 each
Quails (2)	6.50 order
Spicy Eggplant w/Goose	7.50 order

Entrees

Poultry:

Boneless Crispy-Skin Chicken over Romaine seasoned with Ben's Special Dressing	12.50 order
Specials:	
Roast Duck (1/2)	13.50 order

1119 North 25th Ave • Melrose Park • (708) 681-0414

132

Seafoods:

    Drunken Mermaids-Shrimp cooked in Wine and

        Ginger Sauce   20.50 order

    Specials:

        Whitefish steamed w/Black Bean & Garlic Sauce   15.50 order

        Spicy Shrimp   19.50 order

        Seafood Suprema   19.50 order

        Mock Sharksfin w/Fresh Dungeness Crabmeat   21.50 order

        Filet of Sole poached   17.50 order

        Shrimp w/Garlic Sauce   20.50 order

Red Meats:

    Steak with Peapods and Fresh Mushrooms   18.50 order

    Specials:

        Fresh Pork Tenderloin w/vegetables   16.50 order

        Rack of Lamb (8 chops) grilled   29.50 order

Vegetables:

    Vegetable Kow - A combo of the Finest Chinese

        Vegetables   8.50 order

Rice and Noodles:

    Ben's Special Fried Rice   12.50 order

        Rice   Tea   Cookies

A storefront jewel with some of the best seafood and Cantonese food in Chinatown. Service matches the food for quality and care. The Emperor would be pleased.

EMPEROR'S CHOICE
RESTAURANT

Menu Changes Seasonally

EMPEROR'S CHOICE SPECIALS OF THE DAY

Stuffed Scallops with Vegetable   **$12.95**

百花釀帶子

Steamed Scallop on the Half Shell   **$2.50 each**

蒜茸蒸鮮帶子

Stuffed Chinese Melon   **$ 8.95**

釀節瓜

Soft Shell Crabs with Spicy Salt and Pepper
    $12.95

椒鹽軟殼蟹

Braised Grouper with Bean Curd   **$9.95**

斑球豆腐煲

Mushroom Delight   **$10.95**

三菇扒菜胆

Five Spice Crispy Duck   **$9.95**

香酥鴨

White Fish Steamed in Black Bean Sauce   **$8.95**

豉汁蒸白魚

Short Ribs with Black Pepper   **$8.95**

黑椒牛仔骨

DINNER FOR TWO   **$38.00**
1. SOUP OF THE DAY
   OR HOT AND SOUR SOUP
2. POACHED SHRIMP
3. PEAPOD SPROUTS WITH
   CRABMEAT SAUCE
4. FILLET OF SOLE WITH
   BLACK BEAN SAUCE

DINNER FOR FOUR   **$68.00**
1. SOUP OF THE DAY
   OR HOT AND SOUR SOUP
2. POACHED SHRIMP
3. LOBSTER WITH GINGER
   AND ONION
4. EMPEROR'S SHREDDED
   CHICKEN
5. PEAPOD SPROUTS WITH
   CRABMEAT SAUCE
6. FILLET OF PIKE WITH
   VEGETABLES

DINNER FOR SIX   **$88.00**
1. SOUP OF THE DAY
   OR HOT AND SOUR SOUP
2. CLAMS WITH BLACK BEAN
   SAUCE
3. POACHED SHRIMP
4. SEAFOOD COMBO WITH
   VEGETABLES
5. LOBSTER WITH GINGER
   AND ONION
6. CRISPY SKIN CHICKEN
7. EMPRESS BEEF
8. STEAMED FISH OF THE DAY

2238 South Wentworth Ave • Chinatown • (312) 225-8800

1. POACHED SHRIMPS $9.95

白灼中虾

2. STEAMED OYSTERS WITH
   BLACK BEAN SAUCE $9.95

豉汁蒸生蚝

3. PEAPOD SPROUTS WITH
   CRABMEAT SAUCE $12.95

蟹肉扒豆苗

4. PEASANT'S ABALONE
   W/BLACK MUSHROOMS $12.95

北菇扒珍珠鲍

5. FILLET OF PIKE WITH
   VEGETABLES $10.95

時菜炒魚片

6. CLAMS WITH BLACK BEAN
   SAUCE $10.95

豉汁炒花蜆

7. GENERAL'S CHICKEN $8.95

左公鸡

8. FILLET OF SOLE WITH
   YELLOW CHIVES $16.95

韭皇龍利球

9. SCALLOP & SHRIMP WITH
   WALNUTS $9.50

合桃虾球带子

10. KUNG PAO SQUID (SPICY) $8.95

宮寶鮮尤

11. EGGPLANT (SPICY) $6.50

魚香茄子煲

12. FOUR SEASONS IN A
    BASKET (SPICY) $10.95

雀巢四季球

13. MAINE LOBSTER
    PEKING STYLE (SPICY) $19.95

北京炒龍虾

14. STRING BEANS WITH
    MINCED PORK (SPICY) $6.50

干烧四季豆

15. BEEF WITH ORANGE
    PEEL (SPICY) $9.25

陳皮牛

16. BEEF & CHICKEN IN A
    BIRD'S NEST $9.95

雀巢金銀柳

17. SEAFOOD COMBO WITH
    VEGETABLES $8.50

時菜炒三鮮

18. DUNGENESS CRAB
    PEKING STYLE (SPICY) $19.95

北京炒大蟹

19. VERMICELLI NOODLES
    WITH SHRIMP $9.95

虾球燴粉絲

20. SHITAKI MUSHROOMS
    W/PEAPOD SPROUTS $14.95

香菇扒豆苗

21. SEAFOOD COMBO WITH
    BEAN CAKE $8.50

海鮮豆腐煲

22. BEEF BRISKET $7.50

牛筋牛腩煲

Dinner: Mon - Sat until 1, Sun until 12

Seafood is the star attraction (steamed lobster is excellent) on the vast menu at this spartan Chinatown spot, but the dim sum lunch, and the great selection of authentic Cantonese dishes are just as appealing.

HONG MIN RESTAURANT

Menu Changes Seasonally

SPECIAL FAMILY SOUP

	Small	Medium	Large
Servings for...(2-4)	(5-7)	(8-10)	
HOT AND SOUR SOUP (with pork)	$3.95	$4.95	$6.95
SEAWEED SOUP	$3.95	$4.95	$6.95

SPECIAL DUCK & CHICKEN DISHES

CHINESE FRIED CHICKEN — $7.25
HALF OF CRISPY SKIN CHICKEN FRIED CHINESE STYLE

SHREDDED BONELESS CHICKEN — $8.95
HALF OF A CHICKEN STIR-FRIED WITH GREEN ONIONS AND
PICKLED VEGETABLES SERVED ON A BED OF CRISPY NOODLES

PHOENIX CHICKEN — $7.95
DEEP FRIED WHITE MEAT CHICKEN WITH HAM SERVED
ON TOP OF SHREDDED PORK AND VEGETABLES

KUNG PO CHICKEN — $6.95
DICED CHICKEN STIR-FRIED WITH GREEN PEPPER
AND ROASTED PEANUTS IN A SPICY HOT SAUCE

SPECIAL SEAFOOD DISHES

DEEP FRIED OYSTERS — $7.95
DEEP FRIED OYSTERS (BREADED) SERVED WITH A SPECIAL SALT

STIR-FRIED CRABS — $6.95
HARD SHELL CRABS STIR-FRIED WITH BLACK BEANS
AND GARLIC SAUCE

---

221 West Cermak Road • Downtown/Loop • (312) 842-5026 • Call for Additional Locations

CLAMS (HALF SHELL) $7.95
FRESH STEAMED CLAMS TOPPED WITH BLACK BEANS,
GARLICS AND MEAT SAUCE

KUNG PO SHRIMP $8.95
SHRIMP STIR-FRIED WITH GREEN PEPPERS, BAMBOO
SHOOTS AND ROASTED PEANUTS IN A CHILLI SAUCE

STUFFED GREEN PEPPERS $8.50
GREEN PEPPERS STUFFED WITH GROUND SHRIMP
IN A BLACK BEAN AND GARLIC SAUCE

BEEF DISHES

BEEF AND PICKLED GINGERS $8.25
BEEF STIR-FRIED WITH PICKLED GINGERS

BEEF AND STRAW MUSHROOMS $8.25
BEEF STIR-FRIED WITH STRAW MUSHROOMS
IN A LIGHT OYSTER SAUCE

BEEF AND SOUR CABBAGE $6.25
BEEF STIR-FRIED WITH HOMEMADE PICKLED CABBAGE

MONGOLIAN BEEF (HOT) $8.95
BEEF STIR-FRIED WITH GREEN ONIONS SERVED
ON TOP A BED OF CRISPY NOODLES

SPECIAL PORK DISHES

MA-PO TOFU $6.50
BEANCAKES STIR-FRIED WITH GROUND PORK
IN A SPICY HOT SAUCE

PORK AND TARO ROOTS $5.95
SLICED PORK BELLIES STEAMED WITH TARO ROOTS
IN A BEAN SAUCE

SPECIAL VEGETABLE DISHES

VEGETABLE DELIGHT $6.95
STIR-FRIED ASSORTED CHINESE GREENS - BROCCOLI, LILY BUDS,
CHINESE CUCUMBERS, FUGUS, ONIONS, PEAPODS & LOTUS ROOTS

EGG PLANTS IN HOT SAUCE $6.95

Dinner: 7 Days a Week until 2am

137

Serene and well-appointed, lavish actually, with some of the best duck and vegetables to be had. Also, the mu shu dishes are exceptionally good.

House of **Hunan**
Michigan Avenue

Menu Changes Seasonally

House Specialties

HSIEN KAO SU FONG — Mock Peking Duck *(Hunan)* 12.95
Shredded ham and tiny minced bits of dried shrimp baked between crisp layers of soybean skin, served wrapped in a delicate pastry

YU LONG SHEE FUNG — Shrimp and Chicken *(Hunan)* 14.95
Delectable combination of shrimp and chicken, stir-fried with vegetables

TSO TSONG TANG CHEE — General Tso's Chicken *(Hunan)* 12.95
HOT! *Chunks of chicken with red peppers, ginger and garlic*

NING MENG TSU CHEE — Tender Lemon Chicken *(Canton)* 12.95
Batter-coated deep fried chicken served in a tangy lemon sauce

YÜ HSIANG NIU JOU CHUAN — Stuffed Beef Roll *(Szechwan)* 13.95
Beef roll filled with shredded golden mushrooms and bamboo shoots

LONG FUNG HU PEI — Dragon and Phoenix *(Hunan)* .... Market Price
Special combination of lobster (the dragon) and chicken (the phoenix)

Mu Shu Specialties

Tasty mu shu fillings are wrapped in a Mandarin pancake with scallions

MU SHU BAO YÜ — Mu Shu Abalone 15.95
MU SHU JOU — Mu Shu Pork 8.95
MU SHU NIU JOU — Mu Shu Beef 8.95
MU SHU CHEE — Mu Shu Chicken............................ 8.95
MU SHU HSIA PIEN — Mu Shu Shrimp........................ 9.50
CHA HO TSAI — Vegetarian Mu Shu with Noodles 8.95

Vegetables

YU HSIANG CH'IEH TZU — Egg Plant Szechwan *(Szechwan)*.......8.50
HOT! *Satisfying combination of egg plant, mushrooms and peppers in garlic sauce*

HUNAN SU HWAY — Hunan Mixed Vegetables *(Hunan)*...........8.50
Fresh seasonal vegetables stir-fried in a delicate sauce

TS'AO KU TS'AI HSIN — Straw Mushrooms and Cabbage Hearts . 8.95
Straw mushrooms braised with cabbage hearts in wine sauce

SU CH'AO SIU-EH TOU — Snow Pea Pods *(Mandarin)*..............8.50
Lightly stir-fried snow pea pods and water chestnuts

Pork

GOO LAO JOU — Sweet and Sour Pork *(Canton)*..................8.95
Deep-fried pork sauteed with vegetables in sweet and sour sauce

HUNAN LA JOU — Smoked Pork *(Hunan)*.......................10.50
HOT! *Slices of preserved pork butt, sauteed with cabbage, leek and red peppers*

Beef

KUNG BAO NIU JOU — Szechwan Beef *(Szechwan)*................10.95
HOT! *Sliced beef stir fried with peanuts in hot pepper sauce*

HUNAN NIU LI'O — Hunan Beef *(Hunan)*........................10.95
HOT! *Thin slices of beef sauteed with baby corn and bell peppers*

TS'UNG PAO NIU JOU — Mongolian Beef *(Peking)*................10.95
Sliced tenderloin, sauteed with green onion

Seafood

KUNG BAO HSIA JEN — Kung Bao Shrimp *(Szechwan)*.............12.50
HOT! *Whole shrimp, shelled and sauteed with peanuts and red peppers*

SUNG TZU HSIA JEN — Shrimp with Pine Nuts *(Shanghai)*.........12.50
Stir-fried shrimp with pine nuts in a light delicate sauce

YÜ HSIANG GAN BAY — Scallops in Garlic Sauce *(Szechwan)*.......12.95
HOT! *Scallops sauteed with water chestnuts and cloud ears in garlic sauce*

Dinner: 7 Days a Week until 10:30

One of Chinatown's most elegant restaurants, and a jewel of a place for excellent seafood and Cantonese creations.

MANDAR-INN RESTAURANT

Menu Changes Seasonally

APPETIZERS

HOT

Kwoh-Te (6) **4.25**
Pan fried dumplings filled with ground pork and vegetables.

Chicken Sate (3) **4.25**
Tasty, marinated in Chinese spices, grilled in skewers.

COLD

Szechuan Chicken Pasta (Hot!) **4.95**
Shredded chicken and noodles topped with spicy creamy sesame-peanut sauce.

Three Delicacies **14.95**
Jelly fish, bon bon chicken and sweet & sour cucumber combination.

Drunk Chicken **4.95**
Steamed sliced chicken chilled in wine sauce.

Shrimp Pasta **4.95**
Noodles tossed in shrimp and veggies.

SEAFOOD

Lobster and Scallops Volcano **28.00**
Dramatic! This dish erupts with a flavor like nothing else you've ever
tasted. Lobster and scallop chunks smothered with pea pods and mushrooms
in a rich wine and oyster sauce and served on a sizzling hot platter.

Scallops in Hot Sauce (Hot!) **10.55**
Scallops sauteed in a spicy hot sauce.

Seafood in a Nest **10.55**
Scallops, shrimp sauteed with veggies in light sauce nested
in a golden potato basket.

POULTRY

Szechuan Diced Chicken (Hot!) 8.25
Diced chicken sauteed with hot pepper and peanuts.

Empress Chicken 8.25
Tender pieces of chicken dipped in egg batter, lightly fried, sauteed with broccoli in a delicious mildly spicy sweet sauce.

BEEF

Mongolian Beef 8.25
Sliced beef, bean sprouts, bamboo shoots, mushrooms in brown sauce.

Orange Beef 10.95
Tender slices of steak dipped in egg batter, lightly fried, sauteed in a delicate spicy orange sauce.

Curry Beef 8.25

Shredded Beef Country Style(Hot!) 8.25
Shredded beef, carrots, celery in a hot pepper sauce.

Beef with Baby Corn 8.25

Da Chien Beef (Spicy Hot) 8.25
Chunks of beef sauteed with celery, green peppers, bamboo shoots, red bell peppers in brown sauce.

PORK

Mu Shu Pork 7.95
Shredded pork with bamboo shoots, cloud mushrooms, served with Mandarin pancakes.

Sweet and Sour Pork 7.95

Shredded Pork in Peking Sauce 7.95
Shredded pork sauteed in a sweet brown sauce.

PASTA

Singapore Rice Noodles 7.95
Shrimp, barbecued pork, onions, peppers, thin rice noodles sauteed with curry.

Yang Chow Chow Mein or Lo Mein 8.95
Shrimp, pork, chicken stir-fried with vegetables, topped on a bed of noodles.

Chicken Chow Fun 8.25
Chicken slices sauteed with green peppers, onions in a black bean sauce.

Dinner: Sun, Tues - Thurs until 9:30, Fri - Sat until 10:30

Pine Yard Chinese Restaurant

An unpretentious no-frills atmosphere, expert and no-nonsense service, and a menu that focuses on quality instead of quantity are the strong points here. Duck dishes are first-rate, as are pot stickers and egg rolls.

Pine Yard
Chinese Restaurant

APPETIZERS

Pine Yard Egg Roll — House Special (1)	1.65
Fried Dumpling (Koo-Teigh) (6)	4.25
Hong Kong Fried Shrimp (4)	4.25
Shrimp Toast	3.95
Barbequed Pork	3.75
Fried Won Ton	2.75

SOUPS

Mandarin Sour Hot Soup	4.25
Won Ton Soup with Barbequed Pork	3.95
San-sze Soup with Shredded Chicken, Baboo Shoots and Black Mushrooms	3.95
Egg Drop Soup with Vegetables	3.75
Bean Cake Soup with Szechuan Mustard Pickles, Pork	3.95

BEEF

Mongolian Beef with Green Onions & Crisp Bean Threads	8.95
Szechuan Beef with Broccoli	8.95
Szechuan Spicy Beef	8.95
Beef with Snow Peapods	8.95
Mandarin Curry Beef with Onion	8.95
Shrimp, Chicken and Scallops Beef with Special Pekinese Sauce	8.75
Beef with Ginger	8.95
Beef with Black Mushroom and Bamboo Shoot	8.75
Tomato Pepper Steak in Black Bean Sauce	8.25
Beef with Bean Cake and Black Mushrooms in Oyster Sauce	8.95
Beef with Assorted Vegetables	8.25

CHICKEN

Szechuan Hot Diced Chicken	8.75
Diced Chicken with Cashew Nuts	8.75
Chan Pow Chicken with Special Pekinese Sauce	8.45
Chicken with Mushroom and Assorted Vegetables	8.45

SEAFOOD

Shrimp with Lobster Sauce 9.95
Szechuan Spicy Shrimp with Garlic Flavor Sauce 9.95
Sweet Sour Shrimp (Shrimp and Sauce Separate) 9.75
Shrimp with Cashew Nuts 9.95
Mandarin Shrimp with Chinese Vegetables 9.95
Mandarin Shrimp with Green Peas 9.75
Shrimp with Snow Peapods 9.75
Szechuan Spicy Shrimp with Peanuts 9.95
Szechuan Spicy Scallops with Garlic Flavored Sauce 10.95
— Served With Steamed Rice —

PORK

Moo Shu Pork (Comes with 4 Pan Cakes, Extra (1) 50¢) 9.25
Szechuan Spicy Pork with Wood Ears & Water Chestnuts 8.45
Szechuan Spicy Pork with Brocolli 8.75
Sweet Sour Pork (Pork and Sauce Separate) 8.25
Twice Cooked Pork 8.75
Mandarin Hot Green Pepper Pork 8.25
Barbequed Pork with Snow Peapods 8.25
Szechuan Ma-Po's Bean Cake 7.95
— Served with Steamed Rice —

VEGETABLES

Sauteed Snow Peapods 6.25
Sauteed Szechuan Spicy Broccoli 6.95
Moo Shoo Vegetables (Comes with 4 Pan Cakes) 8.95
Bean Cake with Black Mushrooms 7.25
Mandarin Mixed Vegetables 7.45
Vegetable Chow Mein (Mandarin Style) 7.45
Vegetable Fried Rice 6.95
— Served with Steamed Rice —

NOODLES AND FRIED RICE

Pork Chow Mein (Mandarin Style) 7.45
Beef Chow Mein (Mandarin Style) 7.75
Shrimp Chow Mein (Mandarin Style) 7.75
Chicken Chow Mein (Mandarin Style) 7.75
Ten Ingredient Chow Mein (Mandarin Style) 7.75
Pork Fried Rice 6.95
Beef Fried Rice 6.95
Shrimp Fried Rice 7.25
Chicken Fried Rice 6.95
Ten Ingredient Fried Rice 7.25
Extra Order of Steamed Rice — 1 Pint $.75   1 Quart $1.50

Dinner: Mon - Thurs 4:30 - 9:30, Fri - Sat 4:30 - 10, Sun 4:30 - 9

The location alone makes this a popular downtown spot, but even more impressive is the wonderfully comfortable atmosphere and pristine decor.

SZECHWAN HOUSE

Menu Changes Seasonally

Appetizers

STEAMED DUMPLING (6) - 4.95
*Seared dumpling filled with chicken,
cabbage steamed in bamboo container.*

♪ **SZECHWAN WON TON - 4.95**
Meat dumplings in a spicy hot sauce.

POT STICKERS (6) - 4.95
*Seared dumplings filled with ground
chicken and vegetables.*

STUFFED CRAB CLAWS (4) - 5.95
*Delicious fried croquettes of minced shrimp
and crab served on crab claws.*

FRIED WON TON (6) - 3.95
Crab meat and cream cheese won ton.

FIRE POT BEEF (4) - 4.95
*Tasty slices of tender beef
on a skewer served over a mini fire pot grill.*

Soup

WON TON SOUP - 2.25
*Tender meat dumplings
with vegetables in a delicate clear broth.*

♪ **HOT AND SOUR SOUP - 2.25**
*Spicy blend of chicken, mushrooms
and Tofu in a rich egg-flower broth.*

Chef's Specialties

CORAL CHICKEN - 11.95
*Elaborate recipe of many seasonings
and savory sauces which lend unique flavor
and texture to delectable twice-cooked chicken.*

LEMON CHICKEN - 10.95
*Succulent pieces of chicken first deep fried
then sauteed in smooth lemon flavored sauce.*

BLACK BEAN CHICKEN - 11.95
*Choice white chicken tenderloin sauteed
in light black bean sauce.*

HONEY GARLIC CHICKEN - 10.95
*White meat chicken dipped in light batter,
deep fried, and then sauteed
with honey garlic sauce and sesame seeds.*

THREE IN A NEST - 13.95
*Beef, prawns, and scallops sauteed
with vegetables served in a potato bird's nest.*

♪ **GOVERNOR'S CHICKEN - 10.95**
*Meaty chunks of chicken sauteed with
sliced bell peppers, minced ginger and garlic.*

HOUSE SPECIAL RIB EYE STEAK - 14.95
*Choice rib eye steak marinated in fresh garlic,
black pepper and sesame seed oil then Chinese grilled
with a special plum wine sauce to perfection, garnished
with colorful vegetables. We'll put our reputation on this one.*

Seafood

♪ GOVERNOR'S PRAWNS - 13.95
*Prawns stir-fried with bell peppers,
blackened hot peppers, ginger and garlic.*

♪ SZECHWAN PRAWNS - 13.95
*Prawns sauteed with minced vegetables
in a fiery hot red ginger sauce.*

♪ CRISPY FISH - 14.95
*Deep fried, batter dipped fish filets sauteed
in spicy red ginger garlic sauce.
EXCELLENT!*

SALMON A LA TAIWAN - 14.95
*Pan fried salmon lightly seasoned
with ginger, served in caramel soy sauce.*

♪ KUNG BAO SHRIMP - 12.95
*Shrimp stir-fried with peanuts,
blackened red peppers, minced ginger and garlic.*

Chicken

♪ KUNG BAO CHICKEN - 10.95
*Diced chicken sauteed in spicy hot sauce
with peanuts and scorched red peppers.*

CHICKEN TWO DELIGHTS - 10.95
*Tender slices of chicken with black mushrooms
and bamboo shoots.*

CHICKEN WITH VEGETABLES - 10.95
*Sliced chicken sauteed with fresh mushrooms,
bamboo shoots, water chestnuts, and pea pods.*

Beef

PEPPER BEEF - 11.95
*Tender slices of beef marinated then sauteed
with light black bean sauce.*

BEEF TWO DELIGHTS - 11.95
*Sliced beef tenderloin lightly sauteed
with black mushrooms and bamboo shoots.*

♪ KUNG BAO BEEF - 11.95
*The famous kung bao dish with marinated
sliced beef stir fried with peanuts
and scorched hot peppers.*

MONGOLIAN BEEF - 11.95
*Sliced beef stir-fried with mushrooms
in wine sauce served
on a bed of fried rice noodles.*

Entree

SNOW PEA PODS - 8.50
*Snow pea pods delicately sauteed
with mushrooms and water chestnuts.*

FESTIVAL OF MUSHROOMS - 8.50
Four types of mushrooms with light brown sauce.

SZECHWAN STRING BEANS - 8.50
*Fresh string beans stir-fried
with minces pork, dried shrimp bits and Szechwan pickles.*

SZECHWAN MIXED VEGETABLES - 8.50
*Bok choy stir-fried with straw mushrooms,
lotus root bamboo shoots and gingko nuts.*

Dinner: 7 Days a Week until 10:30

One of the most elegant and comfortable Chinese restaurants in Chicago, and the food isn't far behind. Seafood dishes are particularly well-crafted, and the presentations are most appealing.

T'ang Dynasty

Menu Changes Seasonally

Cold Delicacies

JELLYFISH   8.95
Crunchy strands of jellyfish
in sesame oil

*SZECHWAN SESAME CHICKEN   5.50
Shredded chicken tossed in
spicy sesame sauce with ginger
and hot peppers

*SZECHWAN NOODLE SALAD   5.50
Noodles tossed with shredded
chicken, carrots and cucumbers in
sesame dressing

SMOKED SALMON   7.95
Salmon glazed with honey sauce and
smoked over smoldering tea leaves

Hot Appetizers

FLORAL CRAB CLAWS (4)   4.95
Delicious fried croquettes of
minced shrimp and crab served on
crab claws

TAIWAN CHICKEN ROLL   4.95
Tasty chicken in bean curd wrapper

VEGETABLE DUMPLINGS (6)   4.95
Light and healthy steamed dumplings

HOT APPETIZER
MEDLEY   5.95 per person
Sparerib, Won Ton, Spring
Roll, Beef Roll and Prawn Finger

House Specialties

BEGGAR'S HEN (LIMITED)   18.95
Our chef's version of Vagabond
Chicken is a stuffed Rock Cornish
Hen baked in clay, served in an
aromatic tableside presentation

JADE PRAWNS IN BIRDS' NEST   13.95
Prawns sauteed with pineapple
and vegetables, served
in a woven nest made
of potato

T'ANG DYNASTY SCALLOPS   13.95
Lovely crepe-skin packages filled with
an exquisite mixture of scallops,
minced bamboo shoots and black
mushrooms

*GLAZED ORANGE BEEF   12.95
Beef tenderloin marinated with orange zest, sauteed with hot peppers
then glazed to a satisfying crisp in a
sweet hot orange sauce

100 East Walton St • Near North/Gold Coast • (312) 664-8688

Seafood

**GENERAL TSO'S PRAWNS   12.95
Prawns stir-fried with bell peppers,
blackened hot peppers, ginger
and garlic

MU SHU SHRIMP   11.95
Shrimp sauteed with shredded
vegetables, wrapped in Mandarin
pancake

VELVET SHRIMP   12.95
Marinated shrimp sauteed with green
vegetable, minced water chestnuts
and mushrooms in egg-flower sauce

**KUNG BAO SHRIMP   12.95
Shrimp stir-fried with peanuts,
blackened red peppers, minced
ginger and garlic

Poultry

*YU HSIANG CHICKEN   10.50
Chicken with black mushrooms, bell
peppers, water chestnuts and ginger
in garlic sauce

**GENERAL TSO'S CHICKEN   10.95
Meaty chunks of chicken stir-fried
with bell peppers, minced ginger
and garlic

SWEET AND SOUR CHICKEN   10.50
Batter-dipped fried chicken
sauteed with green peppers
and pineapple in pungent sweet
and sour sauce

SMOKED TEA DUCK   13.50
Half a duck, marinated in five spices
and slowly smoked over tea and
camphor wood, then crisply
deep-fried just before serving

Meat

FOUR COLOR SIZZLING STEAK   12.95
Steak with sweet red peppers,
bamboo shoots and mushrooms
served on a sizzling platter

*HUNAN LAMB IN SATAY   11.50
Sliced lamb cooked with spinach
in a peppery Chinese barbecue
sauce with five spices

PINEAPPLE BEEF   11.50
Marinated slices of beef sauteed with
pineapple, served in pineapple crust

KUNG BAO BEEF   11.50
Sliced beef stir-fried with peanuts
and blackened red peppers

Vegetables

SZECHWAN STRING BEANS   8.50
Fresh string beans stir-fried
with minced pork, dried
shrimp bits and
Szechuan pickles

*STUFFED EGG PLANT   8.50
Egg plant stuffed with minced water
chestnuts and black mushrooms
cooked in spicy hot chili paste with
garlic sauce

* Indicates spicy hot dish

Dinner: Sun - Thurs 3 - 10:30, Sat 3 - 11

Biggs

The many dining rooms in this lavish mansion are most pleasing to the eye, and the atmosphere and appointments, seemingly from another era, offer diners a serene and intimate place to dine and relax.

Biggs

Menu Changes Daily And Seasonally

Appetizers

GULF SHRIMP COCKTAIL, SEAFOOD SAUCE   6.75

CHILLED SEASONAL MELON WITH PORT WINE   4.95

SMOKED SLICED NORWEGIAN SALMON, CAVIAR DRESSING   8.25

CHILLED LOBSTER AND SHRIMP SALAD, TRUFFLED ORANGE VINAIGRETTE   11.50

CAPON AND DUCK BALLONTINE WITH PISTACHIOS,
CORNICHON-AVOCADO PUREE   6.50

RUSSIAN BELUGA CAVIAR WITH CHILLED STOLICHNAYA CRYSTAL VODKA   35.00

OYSTERS ON THE HALF-SHELL, COCKTAIL SAUCE   6.75

PEPPERED, CHARRED SIRLOIN CARPACCIO,
ARUGULA AND ROASTED BELL PEPPER   6.95

SLICED, SMOKED NORWEGIAN POIVRE-LACHS, CUCUMBER GARNISH   7.50

ESCARGOTS, BAKED WITH GARLIC, JULIENNE OF PROSCIUTTO,
HERBS DE PROVENCE, EN COCOTTE   6.75

GRILLED JUMBO SHRIMP, PINEAPPLE-AVOCADO-PAPAYA SALSA   8.50

SLICES OF GRILLED EGGPLANT WITH GOAT CHEESE AND ROASTED TOMATO   7.00

LOBSTER GRATINEE WITH SHIITAKE MUSHROOMS AND LEEKS,
CHABLIS-SABAYON SAUCE   11.50

1150 North Dearborn St • Near North/Gold Coast • (312) 787-0900

BEEFSTEAK TOMATO SALAD, MOZZARELLA CHEESE, BALSAMIC VINAIGRETTE   4.50

BELGIAN ENDIVE AND WATERCRESS, STILTON-SOUR CREAM DRESSING   4.50

TOSSED CAESAR SALAD   4.25

Entrees

ENTREES ARE ACCOMPANIED BY THE CHEF'S GARNITURE

GRILLED DOUBLE BREAST OF CHICKEN, HONEY-YOGURT SAUCE,
TOASTED SESAME SEEDS   10.95

SAUTEED PORK CHOP, CHARRED ANDOUILLE SAUSAGE, ROESTI POTATOES   13.75

ROASTED HALF DUCKLING, GRILLED SWEET POTATO,
GREEN PEPPERCORN SAUCE   15.75

FISH DU JOUR, TODAY'S FRESH FISH SELECTION AND PREPARATION   Market Price

SAUTEED VEAL SCALOPPINE MILANAISE, PASTA, TOMATO BASIL SAUCE   15.95

PASTA DU JOUR, OUR CHEF'S PASTA SELECTION OF THE DAY

BROILED, LIME-SEASONED SWORDFISH, TRI-COLOR PASTA, ORIENTAL SAUCE   18.75

AMISH FARM-RAISED PHEASANT, PREPARATION OF THE DAY   Market Price

SAUTEED SALMON ON A BED OF FRESH SPINACH, CHAMPAGNE SAUCE   17.75

WHITEFISH, SAUTEED IN A POTATO CRUST, LEMON-MUSTARD JUS   16.00

CLASSIC BEEF TENDERLOIN WELLINGTON, MEDIUM RARE, TRUFFLE SAUCE   22.50

GRILLED VEAL RIB CHOP, ASSORTED WILD MUSHROOMS, THYME-MERLOT SAUCE 23.00

ROASTED RACK OF LAMB, RATATOUILLE, NATURAL
ROSEMARY JUS (25 - 30 MINUTES)   24.00

GRILLED NEW YORK STRIP STEAK, AU JUS, POTATO, FRESH HORSERADISH   21.50

FRESHLY PREPARED PASTRIES AND CHEESE, SORBET, TORTES OR FRUITS   4.00

BREWED COLOMBIAN COFFEE, DECAFFEINATED COLOMBIAN
COFFEE, ENGLISH TEA   1.50

Dinner: 7 Days a Week 5 - 11

Boulevard Restaurant, The

A spirited combination of French and Continental cuisine served in a handsome and luxurious ambiance. The service is nothing short of excellent, and the kitchen knows how to make the food eye appealing.

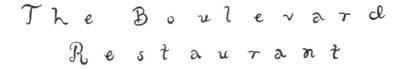

The Boulevard Restaurant

Menu Changes Weekly And Seasonally

The Boulevard invites you to experience Mediterranean dining,
a mixture of Southern French, Italian, Spanish and Moroccan cookery.

Starters

Tuna & Beef Carpaccio
with Vinaigrette of Preserved Lemon, Ginger & Lime
$6.00

Grilled Portabella Mushrooms
with Arugula and Aged Balsamic Vinegar
$5.00

Goat Cheese Napoleon
slivers of Goat Cheese between layers of Crispy Potatoes
with Pine Nuts, Mint and Tomato Fondue
$4.00

Grilled Spinach and Wild Mushroom Pizza
with Sundried Tomatoes, Mozzarella and Asiago Cheese
$5.00

Seasonal Greens
Garnished with Pancetta Roasted Potatoes Balsamic Vinaigrette
$4.00

Boulevard Caesar Salad
with Oven Roasted Tomatoes, Asiago and Anchovy Croutons
$5.25

Entrees

Lemon Angel Hair Pasta & Sauteed Shrimp
with a Sauce of Tomatoes, Almonds, Roasted Peppers and Pernod
$8.00/17.00

Roasted Lobster
with Wild Mushroom Risotto
$24.00

Grilled Veal Chop
on a Zingara Ragout of Mushroom, Prosciutto and Red Onion
served with Tomato Dumplings
$21.00

Paella
Seafood, Chicken, Beef, Veal and Merquez Sausage
baked with Saffron Rice, Artichokes and Peas
$21.00

Roast Pheasant
with Barbaresco Wine Risotto and Baby Root Vegetables
$18.00

Bouillabaisse
Mediterranean Fish and Seafood Stew with Saffron Aioli and Rouille
$22.00

Roast Rack of Lamb
with a Ratatouille Tart
$22.00

Seared Salmon, Spinach & Crispy Potatoes
served layered with Sherried Tomato Sauce
$18.00

Medallions of Beef Pamplona
with Mashed Red Bliss Potatoes, Garlic Chips and
Green Peppercorn Sauce with Port and Cream
$20.00

Dinner: Mon - Sat 6 - 10

O'Briens

It was good to see the rebirth and remodeling of this Old Town restuarant, which has been around since 1979. The new ambiance is plush yet casual, and if you enjoy tableside preparation of classic dishes like Dover Sole, Steak Diane and Caesar Salad, you'll like this place a lot.

Appetizers

OYSTERS ON THE HALF SHELL 6.50

OYSTERS ROCKEFELLER 7.50

ESCARGOT 6.25

CALAMARI FRITTI
Marinara sauce and lemon wedges 6.75

BAKED CLAMS 6.75

FRESH CLAMS 6.25

Poultry

SOUTHERN FRIED CHICKEN
O'Brien's special recipe, crisp, tender and succulent 9.50

♥ **PLAIN BROILED CHICKEN** Crisp and juicy 9.75

CHICKEN VESUVIO Half chicken baked in white wine
with special herbs with vesuvio potatoes 12.50

BONELESS CHICKEN BREAST Sauteed in a lemon
butter white wine sauce with fresh bell peppers
and mushrooms 11.95

Sea Food

LAKE SUPERIOR WHITEFISH Plain broiled with
almondine butter and lemon wedges 13.95

ATLANTIC SWORDFISH Plain broiled with
almondine butter 17.95

SEA SCALLOPS Sauteed in lemon butter and white wine 15.50

STUFFED RAINBOW TROUT Stuffed with seafood 13.95

♥ **DOVER SOLE** Sauteed in olive oil served with almondine butter
and boned at your table 20.95

LOBSTER TAIL Drawn butter .... Market Price

1528 North Wells St • River North • (312) 787-3131

Veal

♥ **MEDALLIONS OF WHITE VEAL** Baked with butter,
lemon, fresh herbs and capers 14.50

VEAL SCALOPPINE Medallions of white veal sauteed
with Marsala wine, fresh mushrooms and spices 14.25

Chicago's Finest Prime Beef

♥ **FILET MIGNON** The most tender of all cuts, broiled to
perfection, served on toast and crowned with bearnaise
sauce or mushroom caps 15.75

NEW YORK PRIME STRIP Our Specialty! Charcrust or
plain broiled. Served with french fried onions
or mushroom caps 18.50

O'BRIEN'S PRIME CHOPPED STEAK Blended with green
peppers, onions and fresh garlic - broiled to perfection,
served with toast points 9.95

LAMB CHOPS (Triple Cut) Widely Proclaimed To Be
The Tastiest In Chicago! Broiled to your taste on toast
points, accompanied by mint jelly or bearnaise sauce 21.95

Entrees may be prepared in a ♥ "Heart Healthy" manner.
Please request when ordering.

Pasta

ROTELLE ARLECCHINO Shrimp, scallops and clams sauteed
in extra virgin olive oil, fresh garlic, cherry tomatoes,
herbs and topped with fresh parmesan cheese 14.75

LINGUINE PRIMAVERA Sauteed fresh vegetables in
extra virgin olive oil tossed with linguine and fresh
parmesan cheese 9.95

Pasta Available in Half Portions

Sides

COTTAGE FRIES 2.50

FRENCH FRIES 1.95

GRILLED ONIONS 2.50

FRENCH FRIED ONION RINGS 3.00

O'BRIEN POTATOES 2.50

Dinner: Mon - Thurs until 10:30, Fri until 12:30, Sat 5 - 12:30, Sun 4 - 10

Zaven's

An oasis of civility that often goes unnoticed. Zaven's features crisp napery, plush carpeting, walls paneled in lustrous, rich wood, polished and attentive service. A selection of continental food, expertly prepared, compliments this pleasant scene.

Menu Changes Seasonally

Hors D'oeuvres

Hot

Millefeuille of Sea Scallops and Basil 8.00

Escargots Farcis Bourguignonne 8.00
Snails in pastry shells baked with a bouquet of herbs and garlic butter.

Oysters Rockefeller 8.00
Baked oysters with a layer of spinach covered with cheese morney.

Crabmeat Strudels 8.00
Alaskan crabmeat seasoned and wrapped in Phyllo dough.

Spinach and Feta-Beureg 7.50
Fresh spinach and feta cheese Phyllo dough turnovers.

Cold

Caviar From The Caspian Sea .... Market

Oysters on the Half Shell 7.50

Shrimp Cocktail 8.50

Prosciutto and Melon 7.50

Hearts of Palm Wrapped in Prosciutto 7.50

---

260 East Chestnut St • Near North/Gold Coast • (312) 787-8260

From the Grill

Prime New York Cut Sirloin Steak	23.00
Filet Mignon Bearnaise	23.00
Calfs Liver (Thin Sliced)	17.50

Cooked at your chosen temperature and served with onions and bacon.

From the Fish Market

Lobster Tail	Market
Shrimp Toulon	Market

White vermouth, garlic, fresh tomatoes and basil.

Frog Legs Provencale	Market

Sauteed in garlic, shallots, parsley and dry sherry wine.

Chef's Tour Around the World

Chicken Jerusalem 17.50
Segments of skinless chicken, white wine, whipping cream, artichoke hearts, celery and mushrooms.

Veal Picante 21.00
Medallions of veal, lemon butter, capers, served with house special zucchini.

Brochette Balkan 21.00
Cubes of beef tenderloin seasoned and marinated, then skewered with selected vegetables and broiled.

Steak Armagnac 24.00
New York Steak sauteed in black cracked pepper, with Poivrade Sauce.

Kufta Kebab (Armenian Style) 18.00
Ground lamb kneaded with finely chopped parsley, onions, tomatoe and herbs, then broiled.

Duck Maison 19.50
Crisp roasted duck, with sauce du jour.

Roast Rack of Lamb 25.00
A delectable experience at Zaven's.

Tania's

Part nightclub, part restaurant, all pizzazz. Adding to the allure is the food (seafood dishes are excellent) and the spirited crowd.

Menu Changes Seasonally

ENTREMESES - APPETIZERS

EMPANADILLAS VEGETARIANAS
Vegetarian Foldovers filled
with Ricotta Cheese and Spinach
$3.95

PICO DE GALLO JAROCHO
Minced Tomatoes, Onions
and Cilantro
$6.95

CROQUET DE JAMON
Ham Croquettes
$1.80

GAMBAS A LA PLANCHA
Authentic Grilled Whole Shrimp
in Lemon, Garlic,
and Olive Oil
$7.95

CALAMARES A LA ESPANOLA
Fried Squid Spanish Style
$6.95

COCKTAIL DE CAMARONES
Shrimp Cocktail
$7.95

PLATOS ADICIONALES DEL CARIBE
SIDE DISHES FROM THE CARIBBEAN

PLATANOS TOSTONES
Fried Green Plantains
$1.95

MARQUITAS O CHICHARRITAS
Fried Green Plantation Chips
$1.95

YUCA CON MOJO
Yucca with Garlic and Olive Oil
$1.95

PAPAS FRITAS
French Fries
$1.75

SOPAS - SOUPS

SOPA DE FRIJOLES NEGROS
Black Bean Soup
$2.75

SOPA DE POLLO
Chicken Soup (Homemade)
$2.50

CARNES Y AVES
MEAT AND POULTRY

PECHUGAS DE POLLO
RELLENAS A LA RIOJANA
Chicken Breast Stuffed with Ricotta Cheese,
Prosciutto and Spinach in Wine Sauce served
with White Rice and Ripe Plantains
$15.95

POLLO CON CAMORONES
Slices of Chicken Breast with Shrimp
cooked in a light sauce served with
White Rice*
$15.95
*Tania's own authentic recipe

PESCADOS Y MARISCOS FRESCOS
FRESH FISH AND SEAFOOD

CAMARONES EMPANIZADOS
Breaded Shrimps served with
French Fries
$14.95

ENCHILADO DE CAMERONES
Shrimps cooked in Creole Sauce
served with White Rice
$14.95

CAMERONES AL AJILLO
Scampi in Garlic
Sauce served with
White Rice
$14.95

LANGOSTA A LA PARRILA
Broiled Lobster Tail
Market Price

ESPECIALADADES CUBANAS
CUBAN SPECIALS

ARROZ CON POLLO (55 minutos)
Chicken and rice (55 minutes)
(for two persons)
$22.95

BOLICE MECHADO
Slice of Pot Roast stuffed with
Chorizo (Spanish Sausage) served
with White Rice and Ripe Plantains
$9.95

ROPA VIEJA
(Old Clothes) Spanish Shredded Beef in
Tomato and Garlic Sauce served with
White Rice and Fried Rice Plantains
$9.95

LECHON ASADO
Slices of Roast Pork served with White Rice
and Black Beans, cooked together and Yucca
$9.95

COMIDAS MEXICANAS
MEXICAN FAVORITES

BISTECK A LA MEXICANA
Steak (Morsels) Mexican Style served
with White Rice and Refried Beans
$11.95

BISTECK A LA MILANZEA
Spanish Style Breaded Steak
served with French Fries
$11.95

Dinner: 7 Days a Week until 3:30am

The sandwich combinations are amazing, the surroundings fun, and on the weekends when Water Tower Place is packed, so is this place. I go for the chicken soup and the pastrami sandwiches.

The Wild Bunch

If they don't make them like they used to it's because we're doing it instead. Every one of our sandwiches is made with the finest deli ingredients available anywhere in the universe (alright, at least on planets that have delis).

All sandwiches include pickle and your choice of potato salad, cole slaw or potato chips.

THE CALIFORNIAN – Do you know the way to Monterey Jack? Open-faced sandwich of melted monterey jack and cheddar cheese over turkey, sliced tomatoes, avocados, and toasted almonds on wheat toast _____ $6.29

LE LAI – Turkey salad mixed with crushed pineapple, topped with leaf lettuce and served on a croissant. _____ $6.29

AVA-CADA DEAL FOR YOU? – Avocado, tomato slices, lettuce, and monterey jack cheese on wheat bread. _____ $6.29

Say Ah...Wider, Wider
Triple Deckers

Like good art (which sandwiches building is) we wanted these items to work on many levels. How does three sound? Open wide for towering Triple Deckers.

THE MICHIGAN AVENUE – More to it than window dressing! Roast beef, breast of turkey, topped with muenster cheese, shredded lettuce, bermuda onions and russian dressing on rye. _____ $6.49

DAVID LIVERMAN – with Paul Shraeded lettuce. Vienna corned beef, chipped liver, swiss cheese, shredded lettuce, tomato slices and M & M on rye toast. _____ $6.49

GOT-HAM CITY – Ask your waiter Alfred about this one! Breast of turkey, baked ham, shredded lettuce, tomato slices and mayo on an onion roll. _____ $6.49

IKE AND TINA TUNA – Hold the Ike! White meat tuna salad, hickory-smoked bacon, monterey jack cheese, shredded lettuce and tomato slices, served piping HOT on an onion roll. _____ $6.49

THE CHICAGO CLUBS – Guaranteed to make you choke in September! Breast of turkey, hickory-smoked bacon, lettuce, tomato slices, mayo and russian dressing on three pieces of wheat toast. _____ $6.49

Amalgamated Sandwiches, Inc.

Or simply, combinations. We picked universally favorite ingredients and incorporated them in new and utterly stupendous ways. Try merging with one of these.

THE SAN DIEGO CHICKEN – Mounds of chunky chicken breast salad, leaf lettuce and tomato, all packed away nicely in fresh pita bread. _____ $6.29

THE SWALLOWS OF CAPASTRAMI – N.Y. style pastrami, Vienna corned beef, swiss cheese, onions, and dusseldorf mustard, served HOT on an onion roll. _____ $6.29

SYLVESTER STALAMI – Hard salami, danish ham, shredded lettuce, sliced tomatoes, onions, and mozzarella cheese with dusseldorf mustatd, served HOT on an onion roll. _____ $6.29

JOHNNY B.L.T. – The Leisure Suits go crazy in Chicago for this one. Hickory-smoked and canadian bacon, american cheese, shredded lettuce, tomato slices and mayo, served HOT on wheat toast. _____ $6.29

Grill and Bear It

REUBEN, REUBIN – Vienna corned beef or N.Y. style pastrami, swiss cheese, sauerkraut, and russian dressing on pumpernickel bread. _____ $6.99

GRILL COSBY – Sliced american cheese, tomato slices, and hickory-smoked bacon between three slices of Rosen's jewish cholly, and grilled until golden brown. $5.99

Topless

Why leave anything to the imagination? You can see all the delicious layers perfectly perched on perky English muffins.

LITTLE MISS MUFFIN – Sit down beside her. White meat tuna salad, sliced tomatoes, and cheddar cheese, served HOT on a toasted english muffin. _____ $5.99

PLAY IT AGAIN, HAM – Danish ham, alfalfa sprouts, artichoke hearts with V & O dressing, served on a toasted english muffin. A-Classic! _____ 5.99

Souper Market

Mama Kaplan's Magic Elixer-keeps you healthy, wealthy and a wise-guy. Homemade chicken noodle soup with noodles and crackers served plain or with your choice of matzoh ball or kreplach.

cup _____ $1.79   bowl _____ $2.29

Soup D.B. _____ cup _____ $1.79   bowl _____ $2.29

Mish Mosh Soup – Go ahead; Eat, Eat! Our homemade chicken noodle soup with both matzoh ball and kreplach. _____ bowl $2.49

Enjoy Mama Kaplan's homemade soups even more with two ends of rye bread and butter for dipping. Delicious! _____ 79¢ extra

Or for a change of pace try Mama Kaplan's Chili.

cup _____ $2.59   bowl _____ $3.79

Dinner: Sun - Thurs until 9, Fri - Sat until 10

Run by the D.B. Kaplan people, this deli draws big at lunchtime. Nice place to fuel up after going to the top of the Sears Tower.

Old Fashioned Chicken Noodle
with Matzoh Ball or Kreplach $.39 each
Mushroom Barley
Cold Beet Borscht (In-season)

♦ MRS. LEVY'S DELI SALADS ♦

ALBACORE WHITE MEAT TUNA
Whole tomato stuffed with Albacore tuna on a bed of leaf
lettuce with sliced cucumber, carrots, Bermuda onion
and a choice of potato salad or cole slaw. $5.99

FRESH FRUIT SALAD (IN SEASON)
Cantaloupe, honeydew, watermelon, oranges and grapes
with cottage cheese. $6.49

MRS. LEVY'S COBB SALAD
Fresh chopped carrots, cucumbers, celery with turkey,
ham and cheese. $6.49

♦ MRS. LEVY'S DELI PLATES ♦

STUFFED CABBAGE
Two cabbage rolls with seasoned beef brisket
and gravy. $5.99

HOT BRISKET PLATE
Tender slices of beef brisket,
served with au jus. $6.99

MEAT BLINTZES
Thin crepes with seasoned beef brisket
filling, topped with gravy. $6.49

MRS. LEVY'S FRIED CHICKEN
Crispy chicken, fried 'til golden brown. $5.99

Above served with Vegetable of the Day and
choice of Mashed Potato with Grivenes (chicken
cracklings), Kasha Varnishkes (toasted
buckwheat with pasta shells), or Potato Pancakes
and bread & butter.

♦ SPECIAL GRILLED ♦
SANDWICHES

TUNA MELT
White meat tuna salad with hickory
smoked bacon and cheddar cheese on grilled
rye bread. $6.49

MY FAMOUS REUBEN
Corned beef or N.Y. pastrami with
sauerkraut, Russian dressing and Swiss
cheese on grilled black bread. $6.49

GRILLED RACHAEL
N.Y. pastrami with sauerkraut, Russian
dressing and Swiss cheese on rye
bread. $6.49

MRS. LEVY'S SPECIAL PATTY MELT
1/3 Pound Hamburger patty, American
Cheese, Russian dressing, and sauteed
onions on grilled rye bread. $6.49

◆ HIGHER-THAN-SKY ◆
TRIPLE DECKER SANDWICHES

Served with Potato Salad, Cole Slaw or
Potato Chips.

#1—THE JOY JEFFERSON
Corned beef, roast beef, cole slaw,
Swiss cheese and Russian dressing on
black bread. $6.79

#2—THE ROGER SHIFFMAN
Roast beef, breast of turkey, topped with
muenster cheese, lettuce, Bermuda onions
and Russian dressing on rye. $6.79

#3—THE ROBERT SHAMBERG
Roast beef, hickory smoked bacon, muenster
cheese, lettuce, Russian dressing, served hot
on rye toast. $6.79

#4—THE SONNENSCHEIN
Breast of turkey, hickory smoked bacon,
colby longhorn cheese, cole slaw and Russian
dressing on chale bread. $6.79

#5—THE NORMIE FINKEL
Beef brisket, N.Y. pastrami, monterey jack
cheese and Dusseldorf mustard served hot
on an onion roll. $6.79

#6—THE J. PARSONS SPECIAL
Breast of turkey, hickory smoked bacon,
lettuce, tomato slices, mayo and Russian
dressing on three pieces of wheat toast. $6.79

#7—THE A.T. BERNSTEIN
N.Y. pastrami, corned beef, Swiss cheese,
onions and Dusseldorf mustard served hot
on an onion roll. $6.79

#8—THE WM. E. ETHINGTON
Avocado and tomato slices, alfalfa sprouts
and lettuce served with yogurt cucumber
dressing between slices of Swiss cheese. $5.99

#9—THE J. IRA HARRIS
Breast of turkey, alfalfa sprouts, cucumbers,
tomatoes and green onions tossed with low
calorie mustard-yogurt dressing and served
inside pita bread. $6.79

#10—THE RON BLIWAS
Breast of turkey, baked ham, Swiss cheese
and Dusseldorf mustard. Served hot on an
onion roll. $6.79

#11—THE HOLLY DURAN
Breast of turkey, alfalfa sprouts, avocado,
sliced tomatoes and low fat low cholesterol
ranch dressing between slices of Monterey
Jack and cheddar cheese. $6.79

🥤 FOUNTAIN FAVORITES 🥤

MRS. LEVY'S MILK SHAKES $2.49
MRS. LEVY'S MALTED MILK SHAKES $2.49
ICE CREAM FLOATS $1.99
Our shakes, malts and floats are served the old fashioned
way in your favorite flavor
EGG CREAM . . . . $ .99
Seltzer, chocolate syrup and milk
CHOCOLATE PHOSPHATE . . . . $ .99
BOVINE BLASTS $1.99
    BLACK COW . . . vanilla ice cream and root beer
    BROWN COW . . . French silk ice cream and coke
    WHITE COW . . . vanilla ice cream and cream soda
    JUAN'S BURRO . . . coffee toffee fudge ice cream and Coke

Lunch: Mon - Fri 6:30am - 3pm

Bossa Nova

Global tapas is the tour de food of this Clybourn Corridor spot that has become wildly popular within a matter of months. The pulsing beat of live music with the tapas late at night feeds the mood, but the food would make it even without the music.

Soups

Seafood Chili (Shrimp and Calamari) 2.95/5.95
Black Bean Soup with Lime Sour Cream 1.95/3.95
Tom Ka Kai (Spicy Chicken and Coconut Milk) 1.95/3.95 **

Tower Salads

Oriental Chicken Salad 4.95/8.95
Crackling Calamari Caesar Salad 4.95/8.95
Salad Nicoise with Fresh Grilled Tuna 8.95
Mixed Field Lettuces with a Remoulade Dressing and Olive Salad 2.95
Baked Goat Cheese on Baby Lettuces with a Balsamic Vinaigrette 5.95
Beefsteak Tomatoes, Fresh Mozzarella, Fresh Basil and Extra
    Virgin Olive Oil 5.95
Indonesian Grilled Shrimp, Romaine and a Cilantro Roast
    Cashew Vinaigrette 5.95/9.95

Hot Tapas

Grilled Chicken Fingers on Black Beans with Guacamole and Lime Sour
    Cream 3.95
Chillied Shrimp and Corn Pancakes with a Sour Cream Salsa 4.95
Eggplant, Tomato and Goat Cheese Big Mak 4.95
Sweet Potato Fries 3.95
Grilled Jamaican Jerk Chicken 3.95/8.95 *
Sesame Crusted Tuna Medallion with a Mirin Soy Butter 5.95
Garlic Mashed Potatoes with Olive Oil and Green Onions 1.95
Mashed Potato Pie with Shredded Chicken and Chilies 3.95

Cold Tapas

Veracruz Style Shrimp Cocktail 5.95 *
Baba Ghannouj (Eggplant Caviar) served with Pita 3.95
Hummus 3.95
Trio: Hummus, Baba Ghannouj and Feta with Olives 5.95
Asparagus with a Seven Herb Vinaigrette and Shaved Parmesan 3.95

Charred Raw Peppercorn Crusted Beef Tenderloin with Spicy Aioli 3.95
Yellowfin Tuna Tartare with Wonton Crackers 5.95
Grilled, Chilled and Thrilled Swordfish 4.95 **
Iced Caviar 35.00 per ounce
Oyster Shooters 1.50 each
Baby Chicken Tostadas Torillios 3.95 *
Sesame Spinach 3.95
Smoked Salmon Roll 5.95
Hung Tao Dragon Noodles 3.95 ***
Som Tom (Raw Papaya Salad) 3.95
Three Olive and Sweet Pepper Salad 3.95
Very Spicy Scallop Cerveche 4.95 ***

Skewers

Shrimp, Chorizo and Sweet Peppers Grilled with a Cumin Aioli 4.95
Fresh Vegetable Spiedini with Sundried Tomato Tapanade 3.95
Grilled Tenderloin Beef Brochette with Horseradish Cream 5.95
Mixed Grill with Three Pestos: Cilantro, Ginger and Basil 6.95
Grilled Cumin Chicken with Cous Cous, Fez Style 3.95

Entrees

Chicken and Chillies Stir-Fry in a Box 4.95/9.95 *
Cowboy Style Sirloin Steak 11.95
Blackened Rib Eye 12.95 *
Mongolian Porkchop 10.95
Ginger-Scallion Grouper 12.95
Sesame Crusted Tuna with Somen Noodles and Soy Butter 14.95

Pasta

Pasta from Hell 4.95/9.95 ***
Spaghettini with Skewered Meatballs 4.95/8.95
Linguini with Roasted Peppers, Tomatoes, Pine Nuts and Chili Oil 4.95/9.95
Angel Hair with Sesame Oil, Grilled Chicken, Green Onion
    and Ginger 4.95/9.95
Cold Spicy Chicken Cannelloni with Tomato Vinaigrette 4.95/9.95

Pizza

Margarita (Tomato, Basil, Pine Nuts and Mozzarella) 8.95
Barbecued Chicken 8.95
Thai Shrimp 8.95 *
Mexican 8.95 *

Jalapeno Scale
*Spicy
**Very Spicy
***Seriously Hot

Dinner: Sun - Fri 5 - 2am, Sat 5 - 3am

Suburban restaurants often give new life to old homes, and The Greenery has done just that, which means a mix of style and grace to go along with the Cajun-Creole offerings that are right on the mark.

SPRING 1993 DINNER MENU

REGIONAL AMERICAN CUISINE

Menu Changes Seasonally

APPETIZER:

Saute of Wild Mushrooms...Garlic Crouton $ 5.75
Maryland Blue Crab Cakes...Three Citrus Sauce $ 6.75
Herb Coated Indiana Goat Cheese, Fried in Olive Oil,
Radicchio Custard $ 6.75
Seared Venison Loin...Spring Vidalia Onion Relish $ 8.95
Confit of Michigan Duck...Fried Tortilla Strips, Spring Sweet Corn-Ancho Chili Salsa $ 5.95

SOUP:

Asparagus and Asiago Cheese with Proscuitto $ 4.50

SALAD:

Spring Salad...Warm Illinois Brie Cheese, Raspberries, Assorted Greens, Pecans and
a Raspberry Vinaigrette $ 7.25
Baby Red New Potatoes with Wild Boar Bacon...Yogurt-Mustard Dressing $ 6.50
Asparagus, Georgia Sweet Vidalia Onion and Smoked Salmon with
a Balsamic Vinaigrette $ 8.95
House Salad...Tossed Greens, Sprouts, Cucumbers, Grated Swiss Cheese,
Creamy Herb Vinaigrette $ 2.50

ENTREE:

Jumbo Gulf Shrimp and Sausage...Grilled and Served with a Creole Mustard Sauce $ 18.25
Grilled Lake Superior Whitefish...Seasoned and Served with a Julienne of Vegetables $ 16.95 *
Grilled Hawaiian Mahi Mahi, Wrapped in Napa Cabbage, Seafood Broth $ 19.95 *
Saute of Louisiana Gulf Shrimp, Crawfish, Andouille Sausage and Fettucine $ 19.75
Grilled Breast of Chicken, Grilled Spring Vegetables and a Sweet Pepper Sauce $ 17.95 *
Roasted Loin of American Lamb, Coated with Grits and Potatoes,
Herb Reduction Sauce $ 22.50
Roasted Eggplant, Sweet Peppers, Wild Mushrooms, Fiddlehead Ferns, Fresh Wisconsin
Mozzarella and Bow Tie Pasta $ 16.95 *
Veal Rib Chop...Michigan Morel Mushroom Sauce $ 24.95
Beef Tenderloin, Fried Potatoes, Artichoke Hearts and Roasted Vegetables,
Tarragon-Artichoke Sauce $ 23.50

All Entrees are served with the House Salad
* These Entrees have been prepared using low levels of fat and cholesterol
Please refrain from smoking pipes and cigars

Dinner: Mon - Thurs 5:30 - 9, Fri - Sat 5:30 - 10

It used to be called Senkowski Home Bakery, so don't get confused. But the slight name change has not altered the low, low prices and the well prepared food.

HOME BAKERY
Delicatessen and Restaurant

Menu Changes Seasonally

FISH DINNERS

Served with potato, rice, or dumplings, hot vegetables and choice of polish style cold salad. Dinner includes soup and dessert.

BREADED FISH DISHES

	A la Carte	Dinner
BREADED WHITE FISH Biala Ryba Smazona	4.99	5.99
BREADED PERCH Karmazyn Smazony	4.79	5.79

BROILED FISH DISHES

	A la Carte	Dinner
BROILED RED SNAPER Red Snaper Duszony	5.69	6.69

FISH SOUTE DISHES

	A la Carte	Dinner
WHITE FISH SOUTE Biala Ryba Soute	4.99	5.99
PERCH SOUTE Karmazyn Soute	4.79	5.79
TRAUT SOUTE Pstrag Soute	4.99	5.99
ORANGE RAFI SOUTE Rafi Soute	4.99	5.99

EVERYDAY SPECIALS

Served with potato, rice, or dumplings, hot vegetables and choice of polish style cold salad. Dinner includes soup and dessert.

	A la Carte	Dinner		A la Carte	Dinner
SHISHLEEK Szaszlyk	5.99	6.99	**POLISH PLATE** Polski Talerz	7.99	8.99
VIENNAR SCHNITZEL Sznycel Widenski	6.59	7.59	**BRISKET OF BEEF** Sztuka Miesa w Sosie Chrzanowym	4.99	5.99
BRISOL W/ MUSHROOMS Bryzol z Pieczarkami	5.99	6.99	**ROAST PORK** Pieczen Wieprzowa	4.79	5.79
BEEF STROGONOFF Wolowina Strogonoff	5.59	6.59	**ROAST BEEF** Pieczen Wolowa	4.79	5.79

EVERYDAY SPECIALS cont'd

	A la Carte	Dinner
PORK LOIN WITH PLUMS	5.59	6.59
Schab ze Sliwkami		
ROAST CHICKEN	3.99	4.99
Kurczak Pieczony		
BEEF GOULASH	4.49	5.49
Gulasz Wolowy		

	A la Carte	Dinner
BLINTZES w/CHEESE AND APPLE	3.99	4.99
Nalesniki z serem i jablkami		
STUFFED DUMPLINGS WITH PLUMS, STRAWBERRY, OR BLUEBERRY	3.99	4.99
Pierogi z jagodami, sliwkami lub truskawkami		

SATURDAY

RED BEET SOUP		1.39
Barszcz Czerwony		
RED BEET SOUP WITH PATTY		1.79
Barszcz Czerwony z Pasztecikiem		
BEEF BARLEY SOUP		1.39
Krupnik		
PICKLE SOUP		1.39
Zupa Ogorkowa		
SWISS STEAK WITH VEGETABLES	5.59	6.59
Kotlet Mielony		
PORK LOIN WITH PLUMS	5.59	6.59
Schab ze Sliwkami		
STUFFED DUCK WITH RICE	7.99	8.99
Kaczka Nadziewana z Ryzem		
HUNGARIAN GOULASH	5.49	6.49
Gulasz Wegierski		
SHORT RIBS WITH VEGETABLES	5.49	6.49
Zeberka Wolowe w Jarzynach		

SUNDAY

RED BEET SOUP		1.39
Barszcz Czerwony		
RED BEET SOUP WITH PATTY		1.79
Barszcz Czerwony z Pasztecikiem		
MUSHROOM SOUP		1.39
Zupa Grzybowa		
VEGETABLE SOUP		1.39
Zupa Jarzynowa		
ROAST VEAL	5.99	6.99
Pieczen Cieleca		
PORK LOIN WITH PLUMS	5.59	6.59
Schab ze Sliwkami		
STUFFED DUCK WITH RICE	7.99	8.99
Kaczka Nadziewana z Ryzem		
CHICKEN KJEW	5.39	6.39
Kurczak po Kijowsku		
BEEF STROGONOFF	5.59	6.59
Wolowina Strogonoff		
NEW YORK STEAK	4.99	5.99
New York Steak		

Dinner: 7 Days a Week until 9

Even if you're not totally up on Romanian food, this is the place for lots of it at low prices. Check it out before or after a Cubs game or anytime you're in the neighborhood—I think you'll like it.

Little Bucharest

Menu Changes Seasonally

Veal, Sausage & Pork

Veal "Tournedous"
Fresh tender veal, stuffed with Swiss cheese and ham, breaded and served with natural veal sauce, vegetables and homemade spaetzele **$12.50**

Shnitzel Ala Bucharest
Fresh breaded veal, served with natural sauce, vegetables and homemade spaetzele **$11.95**

Veal Rouladen and Beef Rouladen
Stuffed with fresh ground beef or veal, onions, vegetables, homemade spaetzele and natural sauce **$10.75**

Special Veal Rolls
Fresh veal rolls cooked with white wine, onions, red sweet peppers, pickles, mushrooms, black olives, served with natural wine sauce, potatoes, vegetables and homemade spaetzele **$10.75**

Veal Scampi Tournedous-Breaded
Fresh veal stuffed with Swiss cheese and fresh scampi, served with natural beef sauce, vegetable and homemade spaetzele **$12.75**

Homemade Sausage
Our own smoked sausage, served with homemade spaetzele, fresh mamaliga, sauerkraut and vegetables **$8.95**

Romanian Style Sauerbraten
Marinated beef with red wine, black olives, onions, tomatoes, served with natural sauce, vegetables, fresh homemade red cabbage and spaetzele **$8.59**

Romanian Style "Mititei"
Small sausages (no skin) served with vegetables and spaetzele **$8.59**

3001 North Ashland • Uptown/Lincolnwood • (312) 929-8640

Beef, Pork & Lamb

Butt Steak with Alaskan King Crab Legs or Scampi Shrimp

A smaller steak served with fresh vegetables, spaetzele, lemon and hot butter sauce **$13.95**

Beef Goulash

Fresh tender beef, cooked with natural sauce, vegetables, and homemade spaetzele **$8.95**

Romanian Baked and Stuffed Fresh Pork Chops

(2) stuffed with fresh shrimps, eggs, onions, baked with white wine, served with fresh broiled red cabbage, vegetables and spaetzele **$10.95**

Special Pork Chops Ala Bucharest

(2) fresh baked pork chops stuffed with smoked sausage, served with special wine sauce, carrots, vegetables, and spaetzele **$10.95**

Romanian Special Style "Baked Boneless Lamb Leg"

Baked with onion, tomatoes, lemon, red wine, served with vegetables and a special salad made of: onions, black olives, eggs, celery, carrot, potato, apple. **$10.95**

Stuffed Vegetables

Stuffed Cabbage

(2) cabbages stuffed with fresh ground beef, onions, vegetables, natural sauce, homemade spaetzele and corn meal **$8.95**

Fowl

Chicken Paprikash

One half chicken, baked with homemade paprika sauce, served with vegetables, homemade spaetzele, paprika and sour cream sauce **$8.95**

Roast Duckling

One half of a duckling baked with orange sauce, served with homemade potato pancake, vegetables and spaetzele **$10.25**

Dinner: 7 Days a Week 4 - 12

Meals that are most pleasing, at prices most attractive (the prix fixe dinner is an excellent value), have made this Highwood French restaurant a favorite for many years.

Alouette

Menu Changes Monthly

~~ *Hors d'Oeuvres* ~~

Escargots à l'Ail en Chemise $6.00
One-half dozen plump Snails baked with Garlic Butter and Parsley, Spanish Onion, fresh squeezed Lemon juice and covered with a puff pastry to keep in the aroma.

Saumon Fumé de Norvege $7.00
Thinly sliced cold-smoked fjord Norwegian Salmon garnished with Spanish Capers and Bermuda Onion and served with toasted rounds of French Bread.

Vol au Vent aux Champignons Sauvages et aux Asperges $6.00
Light, warm pastry filled with wild Mushrooms and Asparagus.

Limaude ála Vapeur, Sauce Champagne $5.00
Lemon Sole with Champagne Sauce.

Crevettes Grillee's au Mange et Airelles $8.00
Grilled Shrimp with a Mango, Cranberry Sauce.

Assortiment de Patés et Fromages $6.00
Three different Pates (Duck & Orange, Venison, and wild Mushroom)
and fine Cheeses (Vermont goat and Illinois brie) served with a dollop of
Dijon Mustard, miniature Pickles, toast points and fresh Fruit.

Gateau de Crabe à la Ciboulette $8.00
Two delicate Maryland-style Crab cakes with Shitake Mushrooms
and green Onion set atop a white Wine sauce.

~~ *Poissons* ~~

Crevettes Sautées au Citron et á l'Ail $16.00
One dozen peeled and headless gulf Shrimp sauteed with Garlic and Lemon, served
atop a bed of Wild Rice.

* Le Poisson Frais du Jour $16.00
Fresh fish flown in daily from Alaska, California, Florida, Hawaii or Europe.

* * Saumon Sauté au Citron Sur Son Lit d´ Epinards $16.00
Fresh Fillet of Atlantic Salmon, sauteed and served on a Bed of Spinich.

Sole de Douvre Sautée Almondine ou Meuniere $23.00
Sauteed Dover Sole served Meunière style (with clarified Butter) or
Almondine (with Butter and Almond slivers), filleted tableside.

~~ *Viandes* ~~

Carré d'Agneau roti à la Crème d'Ail $24.00
Whole rack of open-range New-Zealand Lamb roasted with a Garlic,
Honey, Mustard breading, served with a green Peppercorn sauce.

Boeuf Wellington $19.00
Beef Wellington baked with Mushrooms Duxelle and Onions
wrapped in Puff Pastry.

Filet Mignon, Côte d'Agneau et Escalope de Veau $23.00
Trio of Lamb chop, Provimi Veal medallion & tender filets of Beef
sauteed served with three different sauces.

Entrecôte de Boeuf sautée au Porto $22.00
Lean, large center cut New York strip Steak " 12oz " sauteed with
Mushrooms served with Port Wine sauce.

Poitrine de Poulet Rôtie au Artichaut et Sauce Béarnaise $10.25
Roasted Breast of Chicken served with Artichoke Hearts and Champignon
Mushrooms with a Béarnaise sauce.

Canard roti à l'Orange $16.00
Fresh Duck slowly roasted served with a delicate Orange sauce.

Dinner: 7 Days a Week 5 - 10

Ambria

It doesn't get much better than this. A special restaurant for that special occasion. The service is impeccable, the atmosphere elegant without being puffy, the wine list outstanding, and the food, created by owner Gabino Sotelino, is an experience not to be missed.

Menu Changes Seasonally

HORS-D'OEVRE

Terrines Saisonnières Assorties　　　　　　　　　　**$8.50**
　ASSORTED TERRINES

**Raviolis aux Epinards et Tomates Farcis de Faisandeau et
Foie Gras, Flan au Chèvre; Coulis de Poivrons Jaunes**　**$9.25**
　SPINACH AND TOMATO RAVIOLI OF BABY PHEASANT AND FOIE GRAS,
　GOAT CHEESE FLAN; YELLOW PEPPER COULIS

**Mille-Feuille au Homard, Morue et Pomme de
Terre Croquante à la Basque**　　　　　　　　　　**$11.95**
　NAPOLEAN OF LOBSTER, BACALAO AND CRISPY POTATO BASQUE STYLE

SALADES

Salade du Marché　　　　　　　　　　　　　**$7.00**
　SUMMER SALAD

**Carpaccio de Thon et Sériole avec Pâte de Blé Noir;
Vinaigrette Orientale**　　　　　　　　　　　　**$10.95**
　CARPACCIO OF TUNA AND YELLOWTAIL WITH BUCKWHEAT
　PASTA; ORIENTAL VINAIGRETTE

Salade de Pigeon Tiède au Chou Rouge, Frisée aux Lardons　**$11.95**
　SQAUB, RED CABBAGE, ENDIVE AND BACON

**Légumes Verts de la Saison avec Ecrevisses, Ris de
Veau et Foie Gras; Vinagrette à la Framboise**　　　　**$11.95**
　SEASONAL GREENS WITH CRAYFISH, SWEETBREADS AND FOIE
　GRAS; RASPBERRY VINAIGRETTE

VIANDES ET VOLAILLES

Feuilleté au Ris de Veau avec Céleri et Poireaux Croquants;
Coulis de Tomates au Basilic Frit   **$23.50**
  FEUILLETÉ OF SWEETBREADS WITH CRISP CELERY AND LEEKS;
  COULIS OF TOMATO WITH FRIED BASIL

Aloyau Carbonisé, Pommes de Terre Soufflées,
Haricots Verts et Tomate; Sauce au Zinfandel   **$27.50**
  CHARRED PRIME SIRLOIN, SOUFFLÉ POTATOES, GREEN BEANS
  AND TOMATO; ZINANDEL SAUCE

Suprême de Canard avec sa Garniture de la Saison;
Jus Naturels   **$27.50**
  BREAST OF MUSCOVY DUCK WITH SEASONAL GARNITURE;
  NATURAL JUICES

Carré d'Agneau aux Petites Aubergines Farcies, Couscous et
Lamelles d'Artichaut; Jus aux Fines Herbes   **$28.50**
  ROASTED RACK OF LAMB WITH STUFFED BABY EGGPLANT,
  COUSCOUS AND ARTICHOKE CHIPS; FINE HERB JUICES

Médallions de Selle de Chevreuil Rôtis avec leur Galette de Riz
Sauvage, Rhubarbe Caramélisée et Légumes à Racine;
Sauce aux Mûres
  ROASTED MEDALLIONS OF VENISON WITH WILD RICE PANCAKE, CARMELIZED
  RHUBARB AND ROOT VEGETABLES; BLACKBERRY SAUCE

FROMAGES AU CHOIX

Choix d'un Assortiment de Fromages
CHOICE OF ASSORTED CHEESES
$9.50

DESSERTS

Sorbets et Glaces Bouquet de Nature   **$7.00**
  SHERBETS AND ICE CREAM FLAVORED WITH FRUITS AND NUTS

Baies Fraîches de la Saison   **$9.00**
  FRESH BERRIES OF THE SEASON

Dinner: Mon - Thurs 6 - 9:30, Fri - Sat 6 - 10:30

173

Its convenient location near Water Tower Place makes this a favorite stop for shoppers, but they often have to elbow it out with the loyals who live in the neighborhood. The atmosphere is cheery, and the specialties such as the oven-roasted chicken and fish specials are always excellent.

Bistro Favorites

Fillet of Salmon
Fresh North Atlantic salmon roasted
over wood and served with roasted
seasonal vegetables. $17.95

Oven-Roasted Half Chicken
Bistro 110's signature specialty prepared
with garlic, rosemary, and thyme and served
with roasted seasonal vegetables. $13.95

Veal Chop
Served with its own natural juices
with seasonal roasted vegetables. $19.95

Steak Au Poivre
New York strip steak with cracked peppercorns,
served with a light Cognac-cream sauce
and a garlic-potato cake. $17.95

Appetizers

Wood-Roasted Mushrooms
Seasonal mushrooms with garlic, rosemary,
and thyme. $6.95

Pizza de la Maison
Boursin and a special blend of cheeses
with sun-dried tomatoes on a crispy semolina crust.
$5.95

Roasted Eggplant and Mushroom Duxelles
With blue-cheese glaze. $4.95

Oven-Roasted Calamari
Baby frisée, roasted potatoes, tomatoes,
and a basil olive oil. $6.95

♪Entrees♪

Paillard of Chicken with Wild Mushrooms
Served on a bed of angel-hair pasta with spinach,
tomatoes, mushrooms, and an oven-roasted
garlic-and-rosemary sauce. $13.95

Calf's Liver Steak
Served with fried angel-hair onions
and a honeyed balsamic-vinegar sauce. $14.95

Bistro Steak 110
Grilled sirloin, our own steak sauce, and pommes frites.
$14.95

Oak-Fired Scallops
Roasted tomatoes, spinach, peppers, and garlic cream. $15.95

Panée of Veal
Lightly breaded veal sautéed in olive oil and served
with mixed baby lettuces in a light vinaigrette. $15.95

Swordfish Au Poivre
Roasted onions, new potatoes, and sour cream. $17.95

♪Light Dishes♪

Red Snapper, Roasted Whole
Wood-roasted Florida snapper seasoned with rosemary,
thyme, and garlic. Very low in cholesterol, sodium,
and saturated fats. $17.95

Angel-Hair Pasta
With wood-roasted tomatoes and pesto. $10.95

Whole-Wheat Linguine and Grilled Eggplant
Zucchini, tomatoes, basil, aged goat cheese,
and a white-wine sauce. $11.95

Cheese Filled Ravioli
Served with fresh basil, tomatoes, and feta cheese.
$12.95

Grilled Breast of Chicken Sandwich
Roasted red peppers and Pommery mustard dressing.
Served with a marinated tomato salad. $9.95

Roasted Vegetables, Bistro 110 Style
A selection of seasonal vegetables
roasted whole in our oak-fired oven. $4.95
Entrée Portion. $9.95

Dinner: Mon - Thurs until 7, Fri - Sat until 11:30, Sun until 10

175

Cafe Bernard

It hasn't changed much since the time—circa 1975—that I first ate here. One of the first true French bistros in Chicago, Cafe Bernard still draws loyalists from the neighborhood and people like me, who like the comfortable and romantic ambiance.

CAFE BERNARD

Menu Changes Seasonally

Welcome to Cafe Bernard, and we are
pleased that you have chosen to join us.

SOUP

TOMATO BASIL 3.50

FRENCH ONION AND LEEK GRATINEE 4.50

APPETIZERS

TOMATO BREAD, WILD MUSHROOM 5.75

ONION SPINACH, GOAT CHEESE 5.75

SHIITAKI MUSHROOM IN PHYLLO 5.95

FRESH FOIE GRAS SAUTE OYSTER MUSHROOM 6.95

SALMON MOUSSE PATE 5.50

GALANTINE OF DUCK 5.50

COUNTRY PATE 5.00

ENTREES

NEW YORK STEAK AU POIVRE 16.50

CASSOULET TOULOUSAIN 14.50

GRILLED SALMON/CABERNET SAUVIGNON SAUCE 15.75

STUFFED TROUT W/ SHRIMP AND SPINACH 12.50

1/2 DUCK BREAST W/ GRAND MARNIER SAUCE 13.75

ROAST LEG OF LAMB AU JUS 13.50

PORK SCALOPINI W/ SAUCE FORESTIERE 12.00

FILET OF HASSELBRING BUFFALO JUNIPER
BERRY SAUCE 25.00

GRILLED CHICKEN BREAST 12.50

BOUILLABAISSE 15.75

SOFT SHELL CRABS FRESH HERB BUTTER 16.50

BLACK ANBLUE TUNA BLUEBERRY SAUCE 16.00

STUFFED QUAIL W/ LIVER MOUSSE, THYME SAUCE 15.75

WALLEYE PIKE EN PAPILLOTTE 13.00

WISCONSIN RABBIT FRICASSEE 12.00

MEDALLION OF VENISON PORT WINE SAUCE 18.00

Cafe du Midi

A storefront restaurant with a bistro complex, this "in" spot has an agenda of its own, a positive one more often than not.

CAFÉ du MiDi

Menu Changes Seasonally

HORS D'OEUVRES

POTATO - GARLIC SOUP	3.00
MEDITERRANEAN ANTIPASTO	5.00
SAUTÉED GOAT CHEESE W/ GARLIC & OLIVE OIL	5.00
PATÉ MAISON	4.50
FAVA BEAN SALAD W/ ENDIVE & CHICKEN, CUMIN, SWEET PEPPER SAUSAGE	6.00

ENTRÉES

ROAST DUCK W/ RASPBERRY VINEGAR GLAZE AND ROASTED SHALLOTS	14.00
CHICKEN W/ LEMON, GARLIC & OLIVES	11.00
BOURRIDE du MIDI	13.00
(WHITE POTATO AND CREAM FISH STEW W/ SAFFRON AND AIOLI)	
PROVENÇAL BEEF STEW	14.00
W/ FRESH HERBS, OLIVES, TOMATOES	
BRAISED LAMB SHANK W/ THYME	13.00
RED WINE AND AROMATIC VEGETABLES	
N.Y. STRIP STEAK W/ BLACK PEPPERCORNS	15.00
COGNAC, MUSTARD, CREAM SAUCE	
GRILLED LARGE SEA SCALLOPS AND SHRIMP	15.00
W/ SUN DRIED TOMATO-BASIL PESTO	

2118 North Damen • Lincoln Park/DePaul • (312) 235-6434

VEGETARIAN PLATES, ETC.

PASTA W/ CREAM, FETA, OLIVES & BASIL	8.00
(ORECCHIETTE PASTA)	
BAKED BRIE IN PASTRY W/ FRUIT & ALMONDS	5.00
SAUTÉED VEGETABLES W/ POTATOES	7.00
VEGETARIAN COUSCOUS PLATTER	11.00
CHEESE AND FRUIT PLATE	7.00
(BRIE, CHEVRE, MORIER, BLUE)	
CAPONATA	5.00
W/ GRILLED EGGPLANT	
LA CRIQUE	5.00
(PROVENÇAL POTATO PANCAKES)	

SALADS AND CREPES

HOUSE SALAD	2.50
CAESAR SALAD	3.50
MIXED FIELD SALAD	3.50
SALADE NIÇOISE W/ FRESH GRILLED TUNA	8.00
SMOKED CHICKEN SAUSAGE SALAD W/ APPLES	7.00
BLUE CHEESE AND PEAR SALAD W/ WALNUTS	7.00
GRILLED CHICKEN BREAST W/ CAESAR SALAD	7.00
SPINACH AND CHEESE CREPE W/ POTATOES	6.00
RATATOUILLE & CHEESE CREPE W/ RICE	6.00

SPECIALS

LENTIL SOUP W/ SMOKED BUTT	3.00
HUMMUS/TAPENADE W/ PITA	5.00
ARUGULA BLACK BEAN SALAD	4.00
GRILLED BABY EGGPLANT W/ CAPONATA	5.00
MUSSELS PROVENÇALE	5.00
GRILLED ATLANTIC SALMON W/ SORREL SAUCE	15.00
CASSOULET W/ DUCK, SAUSAGE AND ROAST PORK	13.00
GRILLED MAHI-MAHI W/ RED PEPPER SAUCE & BLACK BEANS	14.00
SAUTÉED SKATEWING W/ CAPERS	14.00
GRILLED LAMB SIRLOIN W/ OYSTER MUSHROOMS,	
FRESH ROSEMARY, MUSTARD & CREAM	15.00
CASSIS/LEMON CHEESECAKE	3.50
RASPBERRIES "ROMANOFF"	4.50
BRANDIED CHERRIES W/ ICE CREAM AND CHOCOLATE SAUCE	4.00

Dinner: Sun - Thurs 5:30 - 10:30, Fri - Sat 5:30 - 11:30

It's expensive, but it's worth it. Luxury does not come cheap. Two cliches, certainly, but when all has been served and eaten, you will be sated and satisfied and know that you have dined first class.

CARLOS
RESTAURANT

Hot Appetizers

Raviolis de gibier a l'ail	$13.00
Raviolis of wild game with garlic sauce	
Ragout d'escargots aux parfums du jardin	$11.00
Snails with lemon thyme, tomatoes and chives	

Potages & Salades

Soupe du jour	$ 7.50
Chef's selection of the day	
Salade gourmande au stilton	$ 8.50
Petite salad of baby red romaine, braised endive and stilton	

Entrees

Caneton grille sauce au foie gras et truffes	$27.50
Grilled duckling and braised cabbage with perigord sauce	
Petits tournedos au vieux vinaigre	$26.50
Filet of beef with balsamic vinegar and parsley foie gras sauce	
Veal medallions with wild mushrooms and rosemary sauce	
Whitefish grille sur couronne du courgettes	$25.50
Grilled whitefish on a wreath of zuchinnis	
Saumon marinee aux epices japanaise et jus de miso	$26.50
Salmon marinated in Asian spices on a bed of Udon noodles, miso jus	
Ris de veau sautes aux champignons	$25.50
Sweetbreads sauteed with wild mushrooms	

Degustation

****

**Beluga Caviar with Assorted Garnishes
With Degustation $35.00   A La Carte $55.00**

or

"Sashimi" of Salmon, Haricot Vert, Cardamom Flavored Daikon,
Sauce Ponzu

or

Hot Cream of Potato with Fresh Thyme and Garlic

***

Prince Edward Island Mussels Mariniere

***

Wild Game Andouille, Cornbread and Flageolet Ragout with
Onion Sprouts, Poblano Oil

***

Choice of Sorbet

***

Pan Fried Halibut, Basil Glaze, Root Vegetable and Herb Coulis,
Roasted Tomato Oil

or

"Bouillabaisse" with Corn Saffron Broth, Wilted Spinach,
and Sweet Potato Flans

or

Sauteed New Zealand Venison Saddle with Dungeness Crabmeat,
Mango Coulis, White Truffle Oil

or

Combination of Wisconsin Black Bear and Squab, Spicy Couscous,
Three Mustard Red Wine Reduction

***

Symphony of Desserts

****

$70.00 Wine Included $90.00

Dinner: Wed - Mon 5:30 - 10

A culinary bastion that regular visitors to Chicago return to time and again. The mansion-like setting, candlelight, crisp napery and polished service are always appealing. Better still is the food, which has improved dramatically over the past year.

CHEZ PAUL

Menu Changes Seasonally

Pour Vous Ouvrir l'Appetit

Tatin de St. Jacques Infusées à l'Huile de Homard *$7.00*
> *Scallop tart with lobster essence*

Echantillons de Saumon : Mariné au Cognac, Fumé, et en Tatar à l'Avocat *$6.75*
> *Salmon sampler : marinated in Cognac, smoked, and tatar with avocado*

Strudel d'Escargots au Chêvre et Epinards avec Coulis de Poivrons Rouges *$8.50*
> *Strudel of escargots, goat cheese, spinach and red pepper coulis*

Les Potages

Bisque de Crabe et Asperges *$5.00*
> *Crab and asparagus cream soup*

La Gratinée des Halles *$4.75*
> *Baked French onion soup*

Potage du Jour *$4.00*
> *Today's soup*

Les Salades

Salade Jules César *$5.00*
> *Classic Caesar salad*

Salade de Saumon et Cresson à la Vinaigrette de Tomate *$5.50*
> *Salmon and watercress salad with warm tomato vinaigrette*

Petites Laitues au Fromage de Chêvre et à la Ciboulette *$5.25*
> *Baby lettuces with warm goat cheese-croutons and chives*

Les Plats De Resistance

Sôle de la Manche Meuniere *$27.00*
Dover sole pan-fried with browned butter and lemon

Espadon Grillé et Crabe de Maryland aux Trois Poivres *$19.95*
Grilled swordfish steak with Maryland crabmeat and peppercorn trio

Médaillons de Homard aux Champignons et Crème de Caviar *$26.00*
Lobster medallions with champagne cream and caviar

Navarin de Homard aux Poivrons Rouges et Haricots Verts *$30.50*
Steamed Maine lobster navarin with roasted red peppers and green beans

Suprème de Volaille Fermière aux Pommes, Cidre et Calvados *$19.00*
Breast of free range chicken grilled with apples and cider jus

Magret de Canard à la Mangue et la sa Cuisse Confite aux Pommes Anna *$19.00*
Sauteed duck breast with mango and duckleg confit with Anna potatoes

Filet d'Agneau Rôti au Miel et à la Lavande *$24.50*
Roasted lamb loin with honey-lavender jus and tart of eggplant, zucchini and tomato

Coeur de Filet au Brie et Champignons des Bois au Porto *$24.50*
Grilled beef tenderloin with Brie cheese and wild mushrooms in Port

Filet Mignon Poelé à la Sauce Foyot $24.00
Sauteed beef tenderloin with meat-glaze flavored Bearnaise sauce

Selle de Veau aux Morilles et au Jus d'Asperges *$25.75*
Saddle of veal with morels and asparagus jus

Medaillons de Veau à la Chez Paul *$25.50*
Veal and lobster medallions with Cabernet and Bearnaise sauces

Les Plats de Resistance

Pâtes Fraiches au Saumon Poivré et Fumé et Sauce au Noilly Prat *$12.50*
Fresh pasta with smoked peppered salmon, mushrooms, vermouth sauce

Filet de Fera du lac à la Julienne de Poireaux et Ciboulettes *$12.75*
Crispy baked filet of whitefish with julienned leek and chives

Noisette d'Espadon et Crabe aux Trois Poivres *$14.50*
Grilled swordfish with crabmeat and three peppercorn sauce

Saumon à la Nage au Thym Frais et Bouquetière de Légumes en Saison *$12.75*
Poached salmon in fresh thyme broth with seasonal vegetables

Many hotel dining rooms are elegant, but this one stands out as being rather special. There isn't a bad seat in the house, thanks to the unique arrangement of the banquettes and tables, but that comfort level is exceeded by the creativity and quality of the food as well as the efficient and refreshing service.

THE RITZ-CARLTON
CHICAGO
A Four Seasons Hotel

The Dining Room

MENU CHANGES DAILY

Chef Sarah Stegner's suggestions:

Appetizers

Soup and sandwich $9.00

Sautéed duck liver with quince purée
toasted brioche laced with white truffle oil $18.00

Maine crab cakes scented with lemon, gazpacho sauce
and cucumber-lemon relish $10.00

White and green asparagus strudel with
Vermont goat cheese and hazelnuts $8.75

Main Courses

Sautéed veal chop with French lentils,
crisp sweetbread and leeks braised with saffron $27.00

*Amish chicken with roasted beets and poached pear in red wine,
wild rice and corn pancake $22.00

Ritz-Carlton Hotel • 160 East Pearson • Near North/Gold Coast • (312) 227-5866

A la Carte Selections

Appetizers

Saddle of rabbit filled with braised rabbit
and oven roasted tomatoes, portobello mushrooms $10.00

Duck confit and root vegetables with poached quail egg,
baby corn salad $9.75

Apple wood smoked salmon prepared in house
with beluga and salmon caviars $12.50

*Mixed greens with tomatoes, baby red romaine, red oak leaf,
mâche, endive and chervil lettuces, sherry vinaigrette $8.00

Main Courses

Atlantic salmon wrapped in potato crust, baby spinach and red onions
braised in balsamic vinegar, tomato-herb glaze $26.00

Maine lobster with eggplant, roasted peppers and citrus,
sautéed shrimp $30.00

*Lightly smoked farm raised sturgeon with fresh morel, hedgehog
and black trumpet mushrooms, red wine sauce $25.00

Sirloin steak with porcini mushrooms, bacon and purple pearl onions
in the Burgundy style $27.00

Rack of lamb, braised lamb shank and spicy couscous,
stuffed zucchini blossoms $29.00

Medallion of venison with
caramelized onion-squash ravioli $22.00

Dinner: Mon - Sat 6 - 11, Sun 6 - 10

Everest

Jean Joho, chef and managing partner, has turned this elegant room, with its sweeping views of the city and beyond, into a culinary shrine, one that knowledgeable diners pay homage to on a regular basis. The idea is to see what creative and delicious surprise the chef is cooking up this week. Excellent service and a bargain pre-theater dinner only add fuel to the culinary fire that blazes here.

Menu Changes Seasonally

J. Joho, vous Propose
Son Menu Degustation

Les Ouvertures de la Soiree

Le Consomme d'Agneau de Lait aux Raviolis de Romans
Double Lamb Consomme, Fresh Goat Cheese Ravioli

Le Foie de Canard des Hudson Valley Roti Eutier au Suri Rueuve
New York State Foie Gras Roasted with Suri Rueve Colmar Style

La Coquille Saint Jacques du Rhode Island aux Flageolets et Champignons
Hand Harvested Rhode Island Sea Scallops, Flageolets and Wild Chanterelles

Le Medaillon de Cabillaud de L'Atlantic Fume Maison en Vinaigrette
Home Smoked Atlantic Finan Haddie Alsace Style

Le Filet de Veau du Wisconsin Roti, Sabayon de Moutarde, Oignons Frits
Roasted Wisconsin Veal Rib Eye, Mustard Sabayonne

La Pomme de Teure Rotic au Munster Chaud et Cumin
Warm Baked Potatoes and Alsace Munster

Le Sachet a'l'ananas au Romarin et au Miel D'Accacia
Crispy Pineapple Sachet, Rosemary and Wisconsin Honey

All items are available in full-sized a la carte portions

Everest Breads from J. Joho's Corner Bakery

$69.00 per person
Minimum for Two

---

440 South LaSalle • Downtown/Loop • (312) 663-8920

LES HORS d'OEURVES FROIDS

Les Joues de Porc Sautees aux Lentilles vertes et Foie de Canard
Sauteed Pork Cheek, Green Lentils, Warm and Cold Frois Gras

La Terrine de Pomme de Terre et Hareng du Maine Marine, Creme au Caviar
Terrine of Potato and Marinated Maine Herring with Cucumbers

Crabe du Maryland en Cocktail au Concombre et Coeur de Palmier
Maryland Crab Cocktail, Cucumber and Fresh Hearts of Palm

Le Saumon Fume Maison aux Blinis de Flocons d'Avoine
Home Smoked Salmon served with Warm Oatmeal Blinis

LES HORS d'OEUVRES CHAUDS

Le Risotto Carnaroli a la Courgette et Feuille D'or 24 Carats
Carnaroli Risotto, Zucchini and 24 Karat Gold

L'Oeuf Brouille au Caviar et Marc de Gewurztraminer
Shirred Egg, Golden Beluga Caviar, Marc de Gewurztraminer

La Coquille Saint Jacques du Rhode Island aux Flageolets et Champignons Sauvages
Hand Harvested Rhode Island Sea Scallops, Flageolets and Wild Chanterelles

Les Langoustines British Columbia au Macaroni et au Fromage
British Columbia Langoustines, Macaroni and Gruyere

LES PLATS PRINCIPAUX

Le Filet de Fletan Roti dans sa Croute de Pomme de Terre au Thym
Filet of Maine Halibut Wrapped and Roasted in Potato with Thyme

Le Steak de Saumon Sauvage Pique au Lard aux Lentilles
Roasted Wild Atlantic Salmon, Green Lentils

Le Homard du Maine Roti au Gewurztraminer D'Alsace et Gingembre Doux
Maine Lobster with Alsace Gewurztraminer and Ginger

La Composition d'Agneau des Pres de Latrobe Roti a L'Ail Doux
Composition of Pennsylvania Farm Raised Lamb

Le Pigeon Roti au Chou Vert, Foie Gras et Truffe
Roasted Squab, Savoy Cabbage and Truffles

Le Filet de Boeuf Poche en Pot au Feu au Raifort et Legumes
Poached Tenderloin of Beef, Pot au Feu Style, Horseradish Sauce

Le Rable de Lievre Sauvage Pare au Poivre Noir au Wassertrivualle
Wild Hare Saddle, Breaded with Black Peppercorn and Wassertrivualle

Le Canard Muscovy roti au Pain D'Epices et au Miel a la Mode de Gertwiller
Roasted Muscovy Duck with Virginia Honey and Alsace Spice Cake

Dinner: Tues - Thurs 5:30 - 8:30, Fri - Sat 5:30 - 10

Froggy's

It seems to get busier each year, proving that good food at a fair price is all that customers want. The atmosphere is plain, and the tables are too close together, but, hey, you can't have everything.

Menu Changes Seasonally

SOUPE OU CREME DU JOUR, CHAUDE OU FROIDE 2.95
Hot or cold soup of the day

"COLD APPETIZERS"
4.95

CAILLE SUR CONFIT D'OIGNONS AU VINAIGRE DE FRAMBOISES
Baby quail filled with a mousse of veal served cold with onions marinated in raspberry vinegar

TERRINE D'ARTICHAUTS AU POIVRE VERT ET ROSE
Cold terrine of artichokes with a green and pink peppercorn sauce

"HOT APPETIZERS"
4.95

FEUILLETE D'ESCARGOTS A LA CREME DE ROQUEFORT
Flaky pastry shell filled with snails and served with a roquefort cheese sauce

MOULES EN 'CASSEROLE A LA CREME DE POIVRONS
Fresh mussels served with a bell pepper cream sauce

"SALADS"

SALADE D'ENDIVES AUX CREVETTES 12.95
Imported Belgian Endive salad with baby shrimp

SALADE PLEINE MER 12.95
Fresh seafood salad

SALADE DE HOMARD A L'EFFILOCHE DE LEGUMES Market Price
Fresh cold lobster salad garnished with fresh vegetables and served with an herb sauce

---

306 Greenbay Rd • Highwood • (708) 433-7080

"GOURMET MENU"
24.95

Choice of cold appetizer
Choice of hot appetizer
Sorbet du jour
Choice of meat or fish entree
Salade
Choice of dessert

ENTREES

POITRINE DE POULET BRAISE A L'ESTRAGON 11.95 ET AUX CREVETTES
Breast of chicken braised in a tarragon cream sauce with baby shrimps

TOURNEDOS SAUTE GRAND MERE 15.95
Tournedos of beef sauteed with red wine, bacon, mushrooms, and onions

CONFIT DE CANARD AUX OIGNONS 13.95
Duck braised with sweet onions

RIS DE VEAU BRAISE FORESTIERE 14.95
Sweetbreads braised in white wine with fresh mushrooms

CARRE D'AGNEAU ROTI A LA GRAINE DE MOUTARDE 15.95
Roast rack of lamb with a mustard seed sauce

PAUPIETTE DE SAUMON A LA CIBOULETTE 14.95
Filet of salmon filled with a mousse of seafood served with a chive sauce

WHITEFISH PROVENCALE 11.95
Fresh whitefish grilled with tomatoes, onions, herbs, and a touch of garlic

HOMARD A LA VANILLE ET AUX POIREAUX Market Price
Fresh lobster served out of the shell on a bed of leeks with a vanilla sauce

ASSIETTE DE LEGUMES DU MARCHE 10.95
Fresh vegetable plate

"SOME OLD FAVORITES"

TRIPES A LA MODE DE CAEN 11.95
Tripes basted in white wine with celery and carrots

ASSIETTE DE FROMAGES 9.95
Cheese plate

Dinner: Mon - Thurs 5 - 10 Fri - Sat 5 - 11

Jackie's Restaurant

Jackie Shen cooks, sticks her head out of the kitchen to check the dining room, counsels with her service staff, attends to myriad details, and still manages to create and add sizzle to one fine dish after another. The once tiny restaurant has grown some, but there is still a pleasant intimacy to go along with the beguiling food.

APPETIZERS

Chicken Liver Pate $5.25

Hot Seafood Terrine $5.95
served with lemon butter sauce

ENTREES

POACHED SALMON WITH LINGUINI NOODLES $18.95
with Beluga Caviar with white wine chive sauce

ROASTED BREAST OF DUCK, CONFIT OF LEG $17.95
with black peppercorn sauce

SAUTEED CALVES LIVER $17.00
with fried potatoes, raspberry sauce

TOURNEDOS OF BEEF $19.95
with sauce perigourdine

RACK OF LAMB, ROSEMARY SAUCE $24.50

SCALLOPINE VEAL, SWEET BREADS,
GOOSELIVER MOUSSE $23.00
morel mushroom sauce

ABOVE ENTREES SERVED WITH SALAD AND VEGETABLE

DESSERTS

ASSORTED PASTRIES AND TORTES $5.00

CAPPUCINO $2.50   ESPRESSO $2.25

2478 North Lincoln • Lincoln Park/DePaul • (312) 880-0003

Seasonal Menu

APPETIZERS

TRI-COLOR WONTON - Half filled with crabmeat, ginger, goat cheese and sundried tomato. Half filled with snails, goat cheese, garlic, basil and sundried tomato. Served with Napa cabbage and shiitaki mushrooms in a ginger butter sauce. $12.95

ASPARAGUS WITH PROSCIUTTO HAM - Served with marinated mozzarella cheese. $10.95

BEEF CARPACCIO - With crumbled blue cheese with Julienne of bamboo shoots, heart of palm and tossed with extra virgin olive oil. $10.95

SALMON CARPACCIO - With marinated ginger tomato, yellow and green zucchini noodle, garnished with Belgian endive drizzled with white truffle oil. $10.95

ENTREES

FRESH FISH PYRAMID OF TRILOGY - Tower of crab cake, fish of the day and fresh shrimp combination, surrounded by red chili pepper fettucine, diced tomato, fresh peas, feta cheese, Greek olive, and Szechwan pepper butter sauce. $26.00

FRESH TUNA WITH RISOTTO AND FLAGEOLLETS - Tuna marinated with soya and ginger sauteed to medium rare, garnished with raspberry, snails and blue cheese with raspberry demiglace butter sauce. $26.00

BROCHETTE OF SHRIMP AND SWORDFISH - Marinated in olive oil and coriander, sauteed on a skewer with tomato, figs and shiitaki mushrooms, served on a bed of Chinese ratatouille with orzo. $25.00

SCALLOPINE OF VEAL MEDALLIONS - Veal medallions with layers of mousse of foie gras, duxelle mushroom and spinach, served on a bed of fettuccine with garnishment of French green beans with truffle sauce. $27.50

NEW YORK STRIP STEAK WITH LOIN OF LAMB - On a bed of pepperoni spaghetti cake with exotic mushroom, green peppercorn sauce. $27.00

SPICY LOIN OF RABBIT AND SWEETBREAD - Served on a bed of risotto with shiitaki mushroom with green peppercorn sauce. $25.00

HONEY GLACED SQUAB - With cornmeal ginger scallion waffle, served with raspberry demiglace. $25.00

Jimmy's Place

Most of the time, owner Jimmy Rohr is on hand to handle this detail or that in the front of the house while chef Kevin Shikami is creating and doing some fussing of his own in the kitchen. That combo creates a wonderful dining experience in this opera-oriented restaurant (great opera posters and delicious background opera renditions) that never seems to falter or waver.

WARM CHARTREUSE OF WILD MUSHROOMS & GOAT CHEESE WONTONS WITH
MUSTARD POTATO SALAD IN BING CHERRY VINAIGRETTE   12.00

SAUTEED SHRIMP PACKED IN MEDITERRANEAN SPICES WITH
SAFFRON JUS, TOMATO, LEEKS, CHILI, ARTICHOKES AND
GARLIC ATOP OLIVE OIL-FOCACCIA CRUST   12.50

BRAISED SNAILS IN RED WINE SAUCE WITH CANNELLINI BEANS,
MUSHROOMS, AIOLI AND A ROMANO CROUTON   12.00

CHILLED JAPANESE SOMEN NOODLES IN GINGER-DUCK CONSOMME
WITH PRESSED SESAME CHICKEN, SCALLIONS,
ENOKIS AND APPLE SLICES   12.00

ASSORTMENT OF OUR HOUSE PATES AND TERRINES   12.50

CREAM OF POTATO SOUP WITH SMOKED SALMON & STURGEON,
BELUGA CAVIAR, CHIVES AND CROUTONS   12.00

3420 North Elston Ave • Lincoln Park/DePaul • (312) 539-2999

MIXED GREEN SALAD WITH HOUSE DRESSING
(INCLUDED WITH YOUR MAIN COURSE)

"JIMMY'S PLACE" SALAD + 5.50
(WATERCRESS, HEARTS OF PALM, FRENCH GREEN BEANS & TOMATO
IN BALSAMIC VINAIGRETTE WITH ANCHOVIES, CAPERS,
NICOISE OLIVES, CHOPPED EGG AND CROUTONS)

xxxxx

TODAY'S FRESH FISH SELECTION 28.00-29.00

FRIED SWEETBREADS BREADED IN PANKO ON A BED OF MIZUNA -
LIGHT SAKE SAUCE WITH GINGER, SCALLIONS, LEMON GRASS,
TOASTED SESAME SEEDS AND JAPANESE EGGPLANT 29.50

GRILLED MEDALLIONS OF VEAL ON CREAMY RISOTTO
WITH PARMESAN AND WHITE TRUFFLE OIL -
PORT SAUCE WITH SHIITAKES & LIMA BEANS 32.50

ROAST SADDLE OF LAMB WITH HONEY-MUSTARD GLAZE, SPICY
PEANUT SAUCE AND MOROCCAN-STYLE COUSCOUS 32.50

RAGOUT OF VEAL KIDNEYS IN MADEIRA SAUCE WITH PEARL ONIONS,
PANCETTA AND MUSHROOMS ON SAUTEED SPINACH 28.50

SAUTEED FILET OF BEEF WITH ROASTED NEW POTATOES AND GRILLED
MUSHROOMS - RED WINE SAUCE & A CURRANT-ONION COMPOTE 30.50

+ CHEF SHIKAMI'S MANY DAILY SPECIALS

xxxxx

YOUR SERVER WILL TELL YOU ABOUT TODAY'S SELECTION OF
OUR HOUSEMADE DESSERTS AND PASTRIES 5.50-6.50

COFFEE, TEA AND BREWED DECAFFEINATED 1.50
ITALIAN ESPRESSO 2.25 A CUP

OUR KITCHEN WILL MAKE EVERY POSSIBLE EFFORT TO
ACCOMMODATE ANY SPECIAL DIETARY REQUIREMENTS.

Dinner: Mon - Sat 5 - 9:30

193

Kiki's Bistro

A bistro true and through, one that offers value and wonderfully crafted French food in a casual, country French setting. High marks, too, for its never less than pristine ambiance.

APPETIZERS:

(Froid - Cold)

Saumon Fumé
  Smoked Atlantic Salmon, traditional garnish   6.95

Paté de Canard
  Duck Pate with pistachio   5.75

(Chaud - Hot)

Escargots de Bourgogne
  Snails with Pernod and Garlic Butter   5.95

Grilled Lamb Sausage
  Potato Salad with Lemon Confit and Rosemary   5.95

Tarte de Provence
  Rotatouille with goat cheese in a light
  pastry, tomato coulis   6.25

Fricassée de Coquille St. Jacques
  Sea scallops sauteed with roasted red pepper,
  scallions & fresh basil   7.50

Ragout of Assorted Mushrooms
  A mixture of wild and domestic mushrooms with
  shallots & garlic madeira wine   6.95

LES VIANDES

Poulet Roti
> Roast chicken marinated in olive oil, garlic
> and herbs of Provence - natural juice
> mashed potatoes   13.75

Poitrine de Canard avec son Confit
> Sauteed breast of duck with leg confit, wild
> rice & green pepper corn sauce   15.50

Foie de Veau
> Sauteed calf's liver, pearl onions, red cabbage,
> wine vinegar sauce   12.75

Steak au Poivre
> Steak rolled in cracked pepper corn, cognac,
> cream sauce and vegetable   15.95

Steak Pommes Frites
> French style steak grilled with French fries   13.95

Gigot d'Agneau
> Sliced leg of lamb, roasted eggplant compote
> jus au natural   13.95

LES POISSONS: (Fish & Seafood)

See Daily Fish and Seafood Specials

LES PATES

See Daily Pasta Specials

LA PIZZA DU JOUR

See Daily Pizza Specials

L'Escargot

There have been a few facelifts (one triggered by an unfortunate fire) since it first opened in 1968, but the finely crafted French food has remained consistently great. Ratatouille, cassoulet, rack of lamb, delicious desserts...slowly but surely the "snail" carried on.

L'ESCARGOT

Menu Changes Daily & Seasonally

*Dinner prices include entree, ratatouille, soup, appetizer, and dessert.
Additional price items are indicated by a plus (+) sign.*

LES POTAGES et HORS d'OUVRES
(Soup and appetizer included with dinner)

Soup du Jour

Chilled Gazpacho soup

Soup a l'oignon gratinee (authentic baked French onion soup)   +$3.25

****

Fresh broccoli with lemon dressing

Poireaux braises aux vinaigrette balsamique (braised leeks with balsamic vinaigrette)

Champignons a la grecque (cold mushrooms marinated in white
wine and fresh herbs)

Feuillete d'oignons (onions in puff pastry with port wine sauce)

Souffle tiede de legume et fromage (warm vegetable and cheese souffle)   +$3.25

Escargots Bourguignonne (six snails in shell with butter and garlic sauce)   +$4.25

Plus chef's daily special appetizer

LES SALADES

Salade verte vinaigrette   +$3.75

Frisse avec frommage   +$4.75

(curly endive with goat cheese and Sherry vinaigrette)

2925 North Halsted St • Lincoln Park/DePaul • (312) 525-5522

LES ENTREES

Chef's hot market-fresh vegetable entree selection $21.50

Pasta aioli with shells $21.50

Crevette et coquille grillee avec linguine $28.50
(grilled shrimp and scallops with linguine and fresh basil sauce)

Delice d'escargot (chef's selected preparation) $28.50

Supreme de volailles avec Moutarde de Pommery $24.50
(grilled chicken breast, Pommery mustard, and diablo sauce)

Canard roti avec fruits de saissons $28.50
(roast duckling with seasonal fruits, orange sauce, and wild rice)

Epinard au langue fume $24.50
(warm spinach with smoked tongue, French green beans,
and garlic sherry vinaigrette)

Veau Nicoise $26.50
(fricasee of veal in white wine and tomato sauce, mushrooms,
and Nicoise olives on spinach pasta)

Navarin French lamb stew $24.50

Gigot d'agneau avec mousse a l'ail (roast leg of lamb au jus with garlic custard)
$28.50

Entrecote grillee forrestierre (grilled 8 oz. center cut sirloin with wild mushrooms)
$29.50

Pork medallions with port and prune sauce $22.50

L'Escargot's traditional Cassoulet Toulousain $29.50
(lamb, duck, pork, and sausage with white beans)

Plus Chef's daily special entrees

LES DESSERTS au CHOIX

ACCOMPAGNEMENTS

Garlic custard   +$3.25

Wild rice medley   +$3.25

Imported French haricots verts   +$3.75

Pomme frites (French french fries)   +$3.25

Sauteed shitake and oyster mushrooms   +$3.75

Dinner: Tues - Sat 4:30 - 10:30

The decor is striking, the atmosphere chic, the food first-rate. All of this and a view through a wall of windows that takes in the old Water Tower and bustling Michigan Avenue. In the winter, when the snow is on the ground, the scene is quite surreal.

LA TOUR DINNER MENU

Menu Changes Seasonally

APPETIZERS

Truffle Parmentier, Essence of Cepes	$11
Petrossian Smoked Salmon, Potato Tart and Chive Oil	$12
Brandade of Salt Cod with Small Sweet Peppers	$7
Daily Pate Selection with Marinated Mushrooms	$9
Chicken Liver Terrine, Tart Cherry Conserve and Green Bean Salad	$6
Malpeque Oysters on the Half Shell with Beet-Horseradish Vinaigrette	$8

SALADS

Smoked Fresh Buffalo Mozzarella and Coppa Ham Wrapped in Romaine, Grilled and Served on a Roast Pepper Relish	$7
Dungeness Crab, Oriental Salad and Soy Emulsion	$8

INTERMEZZO

Tart Fruit Sorbet	$3

ENTREES

SEAFOOD

Atlantic Salmon Braised with Morels and Chicory, $25
Pan Jus with Creme Friache and Tarragon-Mustard

Sauteed Red Snapper with Beurre Noisette and Essence of Leek $23

Roast Monkfish with Artichoke Tortellini in a Saffron-Garlic Broth $24

Rare Grilled Yellowfin Tuna with Basil Whipped Potatoes, $23
Aged Balsamic Vinaigrette

MEATS AND GAME

Veal Medallions with Mushroom Duxelle and Truffle Glacage $26

Beef Tenderloin Roasted in an Herb Crust, Bordelaise $25
Sauce

Roast Rack of Lamb with Crisp Polenta, Basil and a Natural $27
Jus

Roast Barbarie Duck Breast with Basil Gnocchi, Tomatoes, $23
Roasted Garlic and Olives

CHEESE

Selection of French Farm Cheeses with Toasted Walnut $9
Bread

A Four Course Prix-Fixe Dinner $44
Including Wine $70

Dinner: Sun - Fri 6 - 10, Sat 6 - 10:30

Le Français

Roland and Mary Beth Liccioni have not missed a beat since they bought this suburban French jewel from the estimable Jean Banchet. Unparalleled care in food preparation and food quality of impeccable provenance combine to create some of the most delicious and perfectly arranged dishes that one could ask for. And, of course, the food is perfectly complemented by an outstanding wine list and service.

Le Français

Menu Changes Seasonally

Les Hors d'oeuvres

Fantaisie de caviar Beluga sur glace   60.00

Pâtés et terrines de saison
Homemade pâtés and terrines of the season   13.75

Assiette de thon frais et saumon mariné avec saumon fumé
Marinated tuna and salmon with smoked salmon   14.25

Duo de savarin de homard et galette de crabe aux deux sauces
Duo of crab cake and lobster mousse with two sauces   14.25

Surprise d'escargots
Today's preparation of fresh snails   13.75

Raviole de canard, jus a l'ail
Duck ravioli accompanied by natural juice lightly scented with garlic   13.75

Assiette aux deux foie gras
Two preparations of foie gras   15.50

∽

Les Salades

Salade de chicorée frisée aux lardons et Crottin de Chavignol tïede
White curly endive with warm goat cheese and bacon   8.00

Les Poissons et Les Crustacés

Sole sautée á l'infusion de basilic
Dover sole sauteed and served with an infusion of basil   28.50

Pavé de saumon rôti aux oignons doux
Roasted Norwegian salmon served with compote of sweet onions   28.50

Bass grillé avec son jus naturel aux herbes fraîches
Grilled bass accompanied by natural juices flavored with fresh herbs   27.50

Nage de homard et snapper
au jus de homard parfumé a l'huile de noisettes
Lobster and snapper in a broth lightly scented with hazelnut oil   30.50

ℭ

Les Viandes et Les Volailles

Magret de canard du jour
Today's preparation of duck   27.50

Tian de boeuf avec son jus naturel
Center cut prime filet served with natural juices   27.50

Médaillons de veau poêlé au romarin et champignons sauvages
Veal medallions with wild mushrooms and rosemary   28.50

Salmis de pigeon aux choux confits
Roasted squab with cabbage accompanied by red wine sauce   28.50

Duo d'agneau au fumet de chou-fleur
Combination of rack of lamb and lamb tenderloin served with vegetable essence 28.50

Ris de veau du jour
Today's preparation of veal sweetbreads   28.50

Chef Roland Liccioni

Dinner: Mon - Thurs 5 - 9:30, Fri - Sat 5 - 10

Le Mikado

The location is choice, and the ambiance—a multi-level, modern-appointed dining room with cozy booths and carefully placed tables—is most pleasant. French food with Asian influences rewards patrons with some very appealing choices. New owners are holding the quality line.

Menu Changes Seasonally

PRIX FIXE MENU
$16.75 Excluding Tax and Tip (Dessert Included)

STARTERS: (choice of one)

Soupe du jour

Assorted Seasonal Greens: w/Red Onion and Cherry Tomato, Red Wine Vinaigrette.

Cold Spicy Szechuan Sesame Noodles: w/Peanuts and Scallions.

Fondus au Parmesan: Fried Parmesan and Gruyere Croquettes.

ENTREES: (choice of one)

Chicken Breast Skinless: Charcoal Grilled w/Black Vinegar, and Soy Sauce.

Grilled Sausages: Served w/Mashed Potatoes and Port Wine Sauce.

Fettucine: Cancalaise w/Sweet Chinese Sausage, Topped w/Cheese.

Grilled Pork Chops: w/Chinese Five Spices & Shitake Mushrooms.

Fish of the Day: Pan Fried w/Black Bean, Ginger and Scallion Sauce, Celery and Potatoes Pancake and Vegetables.

21 West Goethe St • Near North/Gold Coast • (312) 280-8611

STARTERS

<u>Eggrolls</u>: filed w/vegetable and baby shrimps served w/Pesto Aïoli, and sweet and sour Cabbage.	$550
<u>Cold Soba Noodles</u> w/Alaskan Baby Shrimps, wild Mushrooms and Wasabi spicy dipping sauce.	$600
<u>Crab Dumplings Steamed</u>, Light Curried Crayfish Sauce and Mushrooms.	$525
<u>Coquilles Saint Jacques Grillees</u> Scallops Wrapped in Bacon and Grilled.	$650
<u>Gyoza of Pheasant</u> w/Stir Fried Shiitake Mushrooms and Chinese Oyster Sauce.	$550
<u>Calamari Crispy Fried</u> w/Sweet and Spicy Chili Sauce, Yellow Pepper and Sesame Aïoli.	$575
<u>Truite Au Raifort</u>: Smoked Trout w/Horseradish Sauce.	$600

ENTREES

<u>Poitrine D'oie à la Moutarde</u>, Roasted Goose Breast in a mustard sauce	$1595
<u>Free Range Chicken Roasted</u> w/A Honey and Herb Glaze, Lemon and Parsley Butter.	$1295
<u>Catfish Filets Crispy Fried</u> w/Tamarind Sauce, Tempura Vegetables.	$1295
<u>Lamb</u> Roasted w/Japanese Tonkatzu Sauce & Cracked Black Peppercorn	$1695
<u>Sea Bass Filet Grilled</u>, Potato Pancake, Shallot and Rosemary Sauce, Tomato Provencale and Vegetables.	$1395
<u>Peking Duck Breast</u> w/Pink Peppercorn Sauce.	$1495
<u>Poissons du jour Cuit au Fumoir</u> Fish of the Day Cooked in a smoker and Served w/Cumin Butter Sauce.	$1495
<u>Thai Style Sauteed Shrimps</u> w/Basil, Cilantro, Garlic & Curry.	$1695

Dinner: Mon - Thurs 5 - 10, Fri - Sat 5 - 11, Sun 5 - 9

Le Perroquet

Michael Foley, slowly and surely, is breathing life back into "the parrot," one of the original fine dining French restaurants in the city. The cool and classy style of the restaurant evokes a special place in time.

Menu Changes Seasonally

LES SURPRISES

CURED SALMON WITH PARSNIP CREAM

POTAGE DU JOUR

AN ASSORTMENT OF PATES AND TERRINES

CHILLED OYSTERS, SHALLOT VINAIGRETTE

LEG OF LAMB PROSCUITTO STYLE, FIG COMPOTE

TOMATO GLAZED FROG LEGS, POTATO COULIS

MUSSELS LE PERROQUET

ESCARGOTS SIMMERED WITH TRADITIONAL GARLIC BUTTER

MUSHROOMS SIMMERED WITH BRANDY AND CREAM

MOSAIC OF ARTICHOKE AND VEGETABLE, ONION FRITES

FILET OF VEAL, GRATIN OF MACARONI

70 East Walton, Third Floor • Near North/Gold Coast • (312) 944-7990

LES POISSONS FRAIS

ROAST PHEASANT, SALAD OF HARICOT VERT AND HAZELNUTS
SWEETBREADS WITH TARRAGON

NOS PLATS DU JOUR

GRILLED PETIT PIGEON ON THE BONE, SPRING GREEN CABBAGE
NOISETTE OF LAMB, SHOULDER CRISP, SWEET CORN PESTO
TOURNEDOS OF BEEF WITH SHALLOTS
SYMPHONY OF RABBIT, OLIVE OIL VINAIGRETTE
CHICKEN, HERBED AND GRILLED, ROASTED GARLIC JUS
CHEESE ($4.00 PER PERSON)
CHOCOLATE AND MOCHA MOUSSE
CHOICE OF PASTRY

SORBETS ET GLACES MAISON

FRESH FRUIT
SOUFFLES (FOR TWO OR MORE, $5.00 PER PERSON)
LEMON
GRAND MARNIER
BANANA RUM
CHOCOLATE
SEASONAL FRUIT

COFFEE   DEMI-TASSE   ESPRESSO   TEA

LE DINER $38.50

Dinner: Mon - Thurs 5:30 - 10, Fri - Sat 5:30 - 11

Le Titi de Paris

Pierre Pollin's marvelous nearby country restaurant is worth a drive any day or night of the week. Classic French dishes are beautifully interpreted but do not hold M. Pollin back from exploring new culinary frontiers. The restaurant is a charmer that bristles with subdued sophistication.

Le Titi De Paris

Menu Changes Daily & Seasonally

Hors d'oeuvres

Grilled Boneless Quail with Homemade
Sauerkraut and Jicama Orange Relish   8.50

Hot and Cold Foie Gras of Duck, with
Toasted Brioche and Kumquat Preserves   13.00

Mushroom Barigoule with Portabello Ravioli
in Mushroom Herb Broth   6.25

Cold Maine Lobster and Dungeness Crab Meat
Taboule, Cranberry Vinaigrette   9.50

Crispy Potato Basket with Duck Confit, Mushrooms,
Proscuitto and Black Bean Vinaigrette   5.75

Tartare of Hawaiian Ahi Tuna with Caviar   7.50

Chilled Smoked Salmon and Mascarpone Cheese
Terrine, Horseradish Cream   6.75

Salades

Warm Goat Cheese with Watercress, Poached
Pear, Bacon and Raspberry Vinaigrette   6.00

Belgium Endive, Avocado, Green Beans and
Tomatoes, Balsamic Vinaigrette 6.00

Cold Asparagus Salad with Cider Vinaigrette 6.00

Poissons
(Cholesterol Free Sauce is Available)

Pan Roasted Red Snapper,
Three Mustard Vinaigrette 21.50

Potato Crusted Sturgeon, with Squid Ink Pasta
and Lobster Consomme 22.00

Sauteed Rain Forest Golden Tilapia, with
Grilled Scallops, Ginger Sauce 22.50

Viandes

Medallions of Venison Loin,
Sauce Grand Veneur 24.50

Breast of Duck and Loin of Veal,
Fresh Cilantro Sauce 22.50

Filet of Beef with Roquefort Cheese Sauce 22.00

Roasted Baby Pheasant, Morel Mushrooms,
Forestiere Sauce 22.50

Desserts

Hot Apple Tart with Prune Ice Cream
(Please Allow 20 Minutes) 6.00

Almond Tulipe Cookie with Homemade
Ice Cream Assortment 5.00

Citrus Creme Napolean with Berries 6.00

Creme Brulee Assortment 6.00

Profiteroles with Banana Nut Ice Cream
and Warm Chocolate 6.00

Dinner: Tues - Thurs 5:30 - 9:30, Fri - Sat 5:30 - 10

Le Vichyssois

It's quite a hike from downtown Chicago, but Bernard Cretier's lovely country French restaurant continues to attract urbanites—like moths drawn to a flame—looking for fine food that is prepared á la Francaise.

Menu Changes Daily

APPETIZERS

Quail Pate	$4.25
Duck Pate	$4.25
Warm Pike & Salmon Terrine, Basil Sauce	$5.50
Warm Sweetbread & Morrel Pate, Bercy Sauce	$6.00
Duck Pate en Croute, Green Peppercorn Sauce	$6.00
Feuillete of Asparagus, Vermouth Sauce	$6.00
Galette of Crab, Two Sauces	$6.00
Mussels Mariniere	$6.50
Assortment of Cold Pates	$6.50
Escargots Bourguignonne	$6.50
Warm Salmon Crepes with Salmon Caviar	$7.00

SOUPS

Asparagus Soup	$3.50
Corn & Crab Chowder	$3.75
Cream of Asparagus & Shiitake Mushroom Soup	$3.75
Crayfish Soup	$3.95
Vichyssoise (hot or cold)	$3.50

220 West Route 120 • Suburbs Northwest (McHenry) • (815) 385-8221

SALADS

French Greenbeans, Mushrooms, Walnut Oil Dressing	$4.25
Spinach, Mushrooms, Bacon, Egg Dressing	$4.25

FISH

Mahi Mahi, Sweet & Spicy Shiitake Mushroom Sauce	$15.95
Sea Scallops, Spinach Flan, Lobster Sauce	$15.95
Walleye Pike, Red Wine Sauce & Mushroom Gateau	$17.95
Halibut, Champagne Sauce & Spinach	$17.95
Salmon en Croute, White Wine Sauce	$17.95
Dover Sole, Vermouth Sauce with Chives	$25.95

ENTREES

Chicken, Cream Sauce, Julienne Vegetables	$14.95
Veal Kidneys Dijonaise	$15.75
Roast Duck, Sherry Wine Sauce	$15.95
Pintelle with Morrels & Black Trumpet Mushroom Sauce	$18.95
Peppercorn Steak	$20.00
Sirloin Steak, Bercy Sauce	$20.00
Tournedos Bordelaise	$20.00
Rack of Lamb, Porcini Sauce	$21.00
Noisettes of Venison, Green Peppercorn Sauce	$23.95
Veal Loin Steak, Black Trumpet Mushroom Sauce	$25.00

LE VICHYSSOIS VOUS SOUHAITE UN BON APPETIT!

Set in an old warehouse building, this is without a doubt one of the best French restaurants in the western suburbs. The ambiance plays to the patrons, who applaud the food and the gentle aura. It's all quite nice.

MONTPARNASSE

Menu Changes Daily

Lunch

Soup

Black Bean with cilantro creme fraiche 3.50

Appetizers

French Ham and Belgian Endive Salad 3.75

Entrees

Crisp Whitefish with chive butter 9.50

Seared salmon with seasame seeds and garlic 9.50
   with ginger lime butter

Grilled Halibut with spicy corn compote 9.50

Sauteed Sea Scallops on basil lemon linguini 9.50

Grilled Noisettes of Venison on couscous 14.00
   with smoked apple chutney and apple cider sauce

Sandwich of Grilled marinated Portabello mushrooms, ... 8.00
   goat cheese, french ham and arrugula pesto

Dessert

Pineapple Macadamia Nut Tart 5.00

---

200 East Fifth Ave • Naperville • (708) 961-8203

Dinner

Soup

Asparagus and Fennel with grilled shrimp 5.00

Appetizers

Grilled quail salad, avacado, goat cheese, ... 7.50
   croutons and smoked bacon vinaigrette

Palette of fresh lump crabmeat, herbed 9.25
   mustard sauce

Grilled foie gras with crayfish, spicy blackbean oil 12.00

Belgian endive, jambou français and white rose 8.50
   asparagus salad

Entrees

Charteuse of asparagus, grilled shrimps and 27.00
   snapper, preserved Meyer lemon oil

Sauteéd John Dory on a bed of braised swiss 27.00
   chard, warm ginger rhubarb emulsion

Grilled halibut on blackbean potato cake, java 24.00
   bean salad, cilantro creme fraîche

Grilled noisettes of Nenaison on sweet potato 29.00
   hay, arrugula pesto

Desserts

Milk chocolate and Mas Carpone cheese tart, ... 6.00
   passion fruit

Pineapple and Macadamia nut tart, coconut 6.00
   ice cream

Dinner: Mon - Sat 6 - 9:30

Oo-La-La

It's a bistro with an unusual mix of Italian and French food, so I suppose Mediterranean would best describe the food. The Halsted Street location attracts a crowd that is as eclectic as the food.

MENU CHANGES SEASONALLY

APPETIZERS....

CALAMARI ALLA GRIGLIA... GRILLED BABY SQUID W/BLACK OLIVE RELISH	5.95
VEGETALE MARINATE... GRILLED SEASONAL VEGETABLES, OLIVE OIL & LEMON	4.25
CALAMARI D'ORATI... DEEP FRIED SQUID W/BRANDY MARINARA	5.95
CAPRESE ALLA GORGONZOLA... TOMATO, ONION, BLACK PEPPER & OIL W/BASIL	4.95
CARPACCIO... POUNDED BEEF TENDERLOIN W/OIL, BLACK PEPPER & PARMESAN	5.95
MELANZANE BRUSHETTA... ROASTED EGGPLANT SALAD W/GRILLED BREAD	3.95

SALADS....

INSALATA DI CASA... MIXED GREENS W/LEMON OIL, TOMATO & CUCUMBER	3.95
CAESAR SALAD... ROMAINE, CROUTONS & OUR SPECIAL CAESAR DRESSING	5.95
LATTUGA ROMANA... ROMAINE, RADDICCIO, APPLE, WALNUT & GORGONZOLA	4.95

SIDE DISHES....

POLENTA... LIGHTLY CRISP POLENTA W/ROAST TOMATO	2.95
VEGETABLE ARROSTO... ROASTED POTATOES, CARROTS, RED PEPPERS, OLIVES & GARLIC	2.95

3335 North Halsted • Lincoln Park/DePaul • (312) 935-7708

ENTREES....

PIATTONE DI VERDURE...
ASSORTMENT OF GRILLED AND ROASTED VEGETABLES & POLENTA 12.95

POULET PAILLARD...
SAUTEED BREAST OF CHICKEN W/LEMON, SHALLOTS, SPINACH & ROASTED TOMATO 9.95

POLLO SICILIANA...
½ CHICKEN MARINATED W/ORANGE & SERVED W/ROASTED GARLIC, POTATO,
PEPPERS, CARROTS & OLIVES 10.95

BIFTEE BISTRO...
BEEF TENDERLOIN W/MADIERA & MUSHROOMS 14.95

SALSICCIA ANGELINA...
ITALIAN SAUSAGE GRILLED W/RAISINS, PINE NUTS, ROSEMARY & BALSAMIC VINEGAR 11.95

PAN ROASTED PORK TENDERLOIN...
IN CARAWAY & MUSTARD GLAZE W/SWEET & SOUR CABBAGE & NEW POTATOES 14.95

PASTAS....

PASTA CON POMODORO...
YOUR CHOICE OF PASTA W/POMODORO 8.95

FUSILLI CON POLLO...
CHICKEN, SPINACH & TOMATO CREAM 10.95

LINGUINE CON COZZE...
BLACK MUSSELS, GARLIC & CAPERS. RED OR WHITE SAUCE 9.95

SPAGHETTI CON POLPETTI...
VEAL MEATBALLS & POMODORO 9.95

FETTUCCINE AL SAPORI FORTI...
RAISINS, PINE NUTS, GARLIC & BREAD CRUMBS, OLIVES 9.95

PENNE CON MELANZANE...
SMOKED EGGPLANT, GOAT CHEESE & POMODORO 9.95

FETTUCCINE ALLA BARIGOULE...
CHICKEN TENDERS & ARTICHOKE HEARTS, IN CREAM & PARMESAN 10.95

GRATUITY FEE FOR PARTIES OF SIX OR MORE... 18%

CORKAGE FEE... 5.00

Dinner: 7 Days a Week 5:30 - 11

213

Sweeping booths, mirrors, candlelight, and piano bar give this cozy restaurant a "name" for being romantic. But there is a consistency to the food that dazzles as well.

Menu Changes Seasonally

HORS D'OEUVRES

DUCK PATE $7.00
Pate du Canard

MARINATED SALMON SALAD $7.00
Salade du Saumon

SNAILS WITH WILD MUSHROOM SAUCE $7.00
Escargots a la Forestiere

CRAB CAKES, MUSTARD SAUCE $7.50
Galette de Crabe

FRESH SEAFOOD ASSORTMENT $7.50
Assiette de Fruits de Mer

"BEST ONION SOUP IN TOWN" $4.00
"Chicago Tribune"
Soupe a l'oignon

SALADS

TOULOUSE SALAD $3.50
Salade Toulouse

LEEK SALAD WITH ROQUEFORT TERRINE $4.50
Salade de Poireaux au Roquefort

---

49 West Division • Near North/Gold Coast • (312) 944-2606

ENTREES

PASTA OF THE DAY   PRICE QUOTED
Pasta du Jour

ROAST DUCK, GREEN PEPPER CORN SAUCE $14.50
Canard Roti

ROASTED RACK OF LAMB WITH COUSCOUS $19.50
Carre d'Agneau Roti Aux Couscous

SALMON WITH PEPPERCORNS, TOMATO CAPER BUTTER SAUCE $16.50
Saumon Au Poivre

SPECIAL LOW SODIUM, LOW CHOLESTEROL ENTREE OF THE DAY
MARKET VALUE
Cuisine Alternative

ROASTED RED SNAPPER WITH ORIENTAL VEGETABLES, GINGER BUTTER SAUCE
$17.00
Poisson Roti

ROASTED FILET MIGNON, ROASTED GREEN AND RED PEPPER SAUCE $18.00
Tournedos Roti

VEAL SAUTEED, LEMON AND CAPER BUTTER $18.50
Veau Granbolais

CHEF'S SELECTION OF THE DAY   PRICE QUOTED
Special du Chef

DESSERTS

$3.00 - $4.00

ALSATIAN CHEESECAKE

PEAR ALMON TART

LEMON TART

Dinner: Tues - Thurs 5:30 - 1:30am, Fri - Sat 5:30 - 3am

Un Grand Cafe

The personification of bistro in appearance and menu, this is the place to try marvelously wrought bistro fare like steak frites, onion soup, roast chicken and mousse au chocolat. The waitstaff handle matters with aplomb and finesse, and now that reservations are accepted, the cafe is more popular than ever.

Menu Changes Seasonally

HORS-D'ŒUVRE

Assortiment de Pâtés du Chef
Assorted Pâtés of the Chef $5.95
Tarte du Pêcheur Provençale
Seafood Tarte Provençale $6.95
Pommes de Terre Nouvelles Farcies aux Escargots
New Potatoes Stuffed with Snails; Garlic Butter $5.95
Soupe à l'Oignon Gratinée
Onion Soup with Gruyère Cheese $3.50
Soupe du Jour
Soup of the Day $3.25
Moules à la Crème
Mussels with Cream, Leeks and Fennel $6.95
Saucisse de Canard

SALADES

Salade Maison
Selected Greens with Tomato, Avocado and Niçoises Olives,
Red Wine Dressing $3.95
Salade Frisée
Frisée with Garlic Croûtons, Anchovy and Parmesan Vinaigrette $5.75

ŒUFS ET ENTRÉES LÉGÈRES

Omelette Grand Café
Omelette with Spinach, Potato and Onion $7.50
Hamburger de Thon
Tuna Burger on Ciabatta with French Fries $8.95
Suprême de Canard avec sa Galette de Légumes
Breast of Duck with Galette of Vegetables $11.95

ENTRÉES

Steak Frites $16.95
Steak Grand Café
Medallions of Tenderloin with Green and Red Peppers, Shallots,
Mushrooms, Onions and French Fries $17.95
Jarret d'Agneau Braisé
Braised Lamb Shank with Couscous, Flageolets and Ratatouille $15.95
Carré de Porc Rôti
Roast Pork Loin Stuffed with Prunes; Mashed Potatoes $14.95
Poulet Rôti
Roast Chicken and French Fries $11.95
Faisandeau Grillé
Grilled Baby Pheasant on Grilled Vegetables; Mustard Vinaigrette $17.95
Bouillabaisse $15.95

POISSONS
Fresh Fish Selected Daily

PLATS DU JOUR

Spécialités Régionales du Chef
Chef's Regional Specialties

DESSERTS AU CHOCOLAT

Mousse au Chocolat
Chocolate Mousse $4.50
Sorbet au Chocolat
Chocolate Sherbet $4.50
Petits Choux Farcis au Chocolat
Profiteroles with Hot Fudge Sauce $4.50

AUTRES DESSERTS

Desserts Assortis
Puddings, Custards $4.50
Gâteaux, Tartes
Cakes, Pies $4.50
Glaces, Sorbets
Ice Creams, Sherbets $4.50
Fruits de la Saison
Fresh Seasonal Fruits $4.50

BOISSONS

Café, Décaf, Thé
Coffee, Decaf, Tea $1.50

Perrier $1.75
Orangina $1.75

Dinner: Mon - Thurs 5 - 11, Fri - Sat 5 - 12, Sun 4 - 9

217

It's worth the drive just to take in the elegant mansion setting of this classy restaurant, one of the most romantic spots in this part of Chicagoland.

THE

WAYSIDE MANOR

RESTAURANT

Menu Changes Seasonally

WELCOME to the WAYSIDE MANOR !
It is our aim to present to you traditional French Cuisine served in an elegant Victorian setting. We take pride in using the finest of products available. All of our entrees are prepared in the original European style of cooking "A la Minute" which means made to your order. So please sit back, relax, and enjoy your evening with us while we prepare your dinner. We sincerely hope your evening with us is leisurely, relaxing, and satisfying.

Sincerely,
The Howard Family

APPETIZERS:

SPICY SALMON CAKES *with Tartare Peppercorn Sauce*
         & garnished with Fresh Vegetables.......$4.95

ESCARGOT *in shell with Garlic Butter* $4.95

SHRIMP & SCALLOPS *served in a puff pastry shell*
         & laced with Lime Creme Sauce...........$6.95

GRAVLAX & CRAB *on French Toast with Lite Mustard*
         Dill Sauce.............................$5.95
         With a shot of Iced Vodka.............$6.95

SMOKED GAME SAUSAGE PLATE *(Duck, Venison, Buffalo)*
         Served cold with pickled vegetables.....$5.95

SEARED RED SNAPPER *with Garlic Vegetables*........$5.95

SOUP:

SOUP *of the DAY* ......(*choice of with entree*)...$3.00

ENTREES:

GULF WHITE SHRIMP *braised in brandy, garnished with pasta and fresh Ginger Butter* *$18.95*

ATLANTIC SALMON *pan broiled with Hoisin Sauce and Lotus Root* *$18.95*

SAUTEED JUMBO SEA SCALLOPS *with Lime Creme Sauce & garnished with Caviar* *$19.95*

ROAST DUCK A LA GRIOTTINE *half duck glazed with Brandied Cherry Sauce(14 oz.)* *$16.95*

ROAST QUAIL *semi boneless, (2 - 5 oz.)served with Cumberland Sauce* *$17.95*

SUPREME of PHEASANT *(double skinless boneless breast) with Scotch Sauce* *$19.95*

FILLET of BEEF TENDERLOIN *(8 oz.) with Mushroom Red Wine Sauce or Blue Cheese Sauce* *$18.95*

SPRING LAMB *Eye of the Loin Roasted with Rosemary & Peppercorns served with Mint Infused Chardonnay Sauce* *$18.95*

BEVERAGES:

COFFEE or TEA *$1.00*
SPARKLING MINERAL WATER *Appia from Italy(14 oz.).* *$2.50*

FRENCH ELEGANCE, FRENCH EXCELLENCE, *without* FRENCH EXTRAVAGANCE

There will be times when all entrees will not be available due to quality. There is a corking fee of $5.00 for your wine and a $1.50 extra plate charge when requested. Minimum service charge $5.00/ person. For parties of six or more a service charge of 17% will be added.
Please do not smoke Cigars or Pipes.

Dinner: Tues - Thurs, Sat 5:30 - 10

Yoshi's Cafe

Small, intimate, comfortable and with its own particular brand of charm. Owner/chef Yoshi Katsumura has a knack for the innovative and a flair for the creative, which is to say he never runs out of tempting ideas to savor and enjoy.

Menu Changes Daily And Seasonally

- HOR D'OEUVRE -

Fresh sea scallops in lobster sauce with buckwheat pasta
8.00
Steamed whited asparagus and artichoke bottom served chilled, in Italian dressing
6.50
Squid salad with rice wine vinegar, soy, and daikon, and scallop escabéche
7.00
Crepe filled with snow crab meat, smoked salmon, shittake mushrooms, domestic caviar and sour cream
9.50
Tuna tartare with guacamole and toast
7.00
Saffron ravioli filled with crab meat, with red and yellow pepper sauces
7.00
Sauteed softshell crab with horseradish sauce and herb sauce
9.00

- SALAD -

Braised shiitake and oyster mushroom salad, in oriental dressing
7.00
Sauteed goat cheese salad with red bell pepper mousse
6.00
Steamed spinach with sesame seed dressing and oven dried tomato wrapped in cucumber, balsamic vinaigrette
6.00
Mixed greens, champage vinegar-olive oil dressing
5.00

3257 North Halsted Street • Lincoln Park/DePaul • (312) 248-6160

-ENTREE-

Mixed Grill:
Striped bass, au poivre
Spanish mackerel, with sweet miso sauce
Fluke, with motoyaki sauce
22.50
Braised red snapper with canadian prawns,
lobster saffron au jus
22.00
Tuna, grilled medium rare,
in oriental sauce with papaya, and oriental garden salad
19.00
Sauteed medallions of veal, with candied apple,
in yogurt sauce with raisin couscous
20.00
Grilled lamb in garlic au jus and
grilled medallion of beef in red zinfandel sauce with mango
25.00
Gourmet salad:
Shrimp, caviar, sauteed sweetbreads, confit of duck
and pate of foie gras with balsamic vinaigrette
25.00
Grilled vegetable plate with shrimp,
sesame seed oil and soy on the side
19.00

-DESSERT-

Selection of homemade desserts
from 6.00

Ice cream or sorbet   Combination platter
5.00   12.00

Coffee or tea
1.50
Espresso 2.50   Cappuccino 3.00

Chef Yoshi Katsumura is using less butter, salt,
and heavy cream for healthier, lighter sauces

Berghoff Restaurant

A must-go-to for visitors to Chicago, for the food, the sometimes frenzy, and just to say you've been there. Excellent soups, pot roast and other home-comfort foods such as buttered noodles, creamed spinach and strudel, and the private label Berghoff beer is a fine beer in its own right.

Menu Changes Seasonally

LUNCHEON SUGGESTIONS

Sauerbraten
with potato pancake
and creamed spinach. 7.75

Wiener Schnitzel
(breaded veal cutlet) german fried potatoes,
and creamed spinach. 8.70

Smoked Thuringer Sausage
with sauerkraut and boiled new potatoes. 6.50

Boiled Brisket of Corned Beef
with new cabbage
and boiled new potatoes. 7.50

Roast Leg of Lamb
mashed potatoes, mint jelly
and fresh fruit compote. 7.95

**"House" Smoked Bar-B-Que
Baby Back Ribs**
served with french fries and cole slaw.
½ rack 8.95

Boiled Pork Shank
with boiled new potatoes
and sauerkraut. 6.95

Schlacht-Platte
combination of bratwurst, "Kasseler Rippchen"
(tender smoked pork loin), smoked thuringer
with sauerkraut and tossed salad. 7.75

Knockwurst
with sauerkraut and boiled new potatoes. 6.50

Roast Top Round of Beef au jus
with mashed potatoes and tossed salad. . . 7.25

German Pot Roast
(sirloin of beef) served with mashed potatoes
and tossed salad. 7.25

Chicken Dijon
broiled boneless breast of chicken,
served with mushroom Dijon cream sauce
on a bed of pasta and tossed salad. 7.75

Geschnetzeltes
veal with sauteed mushrooms in wine sauce,
served with mashed potatoes
and fresh fruit compote. 8.75

FISH AND SEAFOOD SELECTIONS

Chef recommends cooking fish medium unless otherwise requested.

French Fried Sea Scallops
with tartar sauce, choice of potato,
and cole slaw. 8.50

Broiled Halibut Steak*
served with seasonal vegetables
and boiled new potatoes. 9.95

Broiled Fresh Filet of Salmon*
served with seasonal vegetables
and boiled new potatoes. 9.50

French Fried Shrimp
with cocktail sauce, choice of potato,
and cole slaw. 8.50

Fresh Farm Raised Catfish
(lightly coated with corn meal)
served with stewed tomatoes, onions,
basil and tossed salad. 8.50

Filet of Sole
served with toasted almonds, lemon
beurre blanc, sauteed vegetables and
rice pilaf. 8.95

Broiled Fresh Lake Superior Whitefish
with lemon parsley butter,
boiled new potatoes and tossed salad. . . 8.25

*Choice of salsa relish, lemon parsley butter, tomato garlic beurre blanc, caper beurre blanc, citrus beurre blanc. (on the side)

17 West Adams St • Downtown/Loop • (312) 427-3170

CHEF'S CHOICE

Stir Fry Chicken and Vegetables
sauteed sliced breast of chicken with zucchini,
yellow squash, mushrooms, peppers and
pea pods, served with rice pilaf. 7.75

Broiled Seafood Brochette
shrimps, scallops, swordfish,
peppers, onions, mushrooms, tomatoes
on a bed of rice, served with
tomato garlic beurre blanc on the side
and tossed salad. 9.95

Southwestern Style Chicken Breast
marinated chicken breast topped with sauteed
red and green peppers, melted Jalapeño
pepper cheese, served with rice and
tossed salad. 7.75

Chicken Schnitzel
(breaded chicken breast with herbs)
served on a bed of stewed tomatoes,
fresh garlic, basil and tossed salad. 7.75

Rähm Schnitzel
(breaded pork cutlet) with sauteed mushrooms
in a wine sauce, served with spaetzels
and fresh fruit compote. 7.75

Grilled Marinated Breast of Chicken
mesquite seasoned chicken
served with sauteed seasonal vegetables
and fresh fruit compote. 7.75

Fresh Roast Young Tom Turkey
with dressing, cranberry sauce,
mashed potatoes and tossed salad. 7.50
(all white meat . . . . add .75)

SALADS AND LIGHT ENTREES

Berghoff Caesar Salad
served with grilled-marinated
sliced chicken breast. 7.50
served with blackened swordfish. 7.95

Blackened Swordfish Sandwich
with roasted red peppers, tomatoes,
bibb letuce, monterey cheese on brewers bread,
served with curly fries. 7.50

"House" Smoked Chicken Salad with Pasta
with sun-dried tomatoes, broccoli,
mushrooms, peppers, onions, tossed with
pommery mustard vinaigrette. 7.95

Penne Pasta with Marinara
tomatoes, garlic, fresh basil, fresh parmesan
cheese, served with tossed salad. 6.95

Fajita Chicken Sandwich
marinated strips of chicken with peppers,
grated cheddar cheese, shredded lettuce,
onions, black olives, sour cream, salsa, on
flour tortillas served with curly fries. 7.00

Grilled Marinated Breast of Chicken Sandwich
served with curly fries and cole slaw. . . . 5.95

Fresh Garden Salad
romaine, iceberg lettuce, broccoli, cauliflower,
carrots, mushrooms, red cabbage, peppers,
tomatoes and choice of dressing. 5.95
(Maytag Bleu Cheese . . . . add .60)

Cobb Salad
mixed greens with sliced breast of chicken,
avocado, bacon, bleu cheese, and
chopped eggs. 7.95
(Maytag Bleu Cheese . . . . add .60)

Berghoff Tenderloin Steak Salad
garnished with tomato and seasonal fruit. . . 7.50

Broiled Fresh Vegetable Brochette
broccoli, cauliflower, peppers, mushrooms,
onions, tomatoes on a bed of rice,
served with tomato garlic beurre blanc
on the side and cole slaw. 6.50

Fresh Fruit Plate
seasonal fruits served with fruit
flavored yogurt. 6.95

Salad dressings: house, italian, sour cream and garlic, low-cal yogurt dill, sweet and sour,
*ranch, thousand island, french, **Maytag Bleu Cheese—add .60 extra.***

STEAKS
The Berghoff does not recommend well-done steaks.

Broiled Filet Mignon
with fresh mushrooms, choice of potato
served with tossed salad. 12.95

Broiled Chopped Sirloin (8 oz.)
with french fried onion rings, choice of potato
served with tossed salad. 6.95

Dinner: Mon - Thurs until 9:30, Fri - Sat until 10

Grand portions and hearty fare are the signatures of this north-side landmark. Though suddenly surrounded by gentrification, it still has an Old World ambiance that is pleasing and comforting.

The Golden Ox Restaurant

Specials Change Daily

Appetizers

Westfälien Ham on Pumpernickel	**Jumbo Shrimp Cocktail**
4.95	7.95
French Fried Mushrooms	**Jumbo Shrimps, French Fried**
2.95	7.95
Fresh Chopped Chicken Livers	**Onion Rings**
3.50	2.95

German Specialties

BEEF STROGANOFF
Special Mushroom Sauce,
Butter Noodles
16.95

PEPPER STEAK
Prime Beef Tenderloin Sauteed with
Green Peppers Mushrooms and
Onions, Butter Noodles
16.50

SAUERBRATEN
Prime Beef Marinated in Wine and Vinegar
with its Own Flavorful Gravy. Potato Dumpling Red Cabbage
16.50

GENUINE VEAL SWEETBREADS
Sauteed in Butter, Mushrooms
and Slivered Green Onions
17.95

**CRISP ROASTED YOUNG
DUCKLING (half)**
Red Cabbage or Sauerkraut,
Potato Dumpling
15.95

WIENER SCHNITZEL
A Tender Veal Steak dipped in Egg Batter,
Flaked with Special Breading Mushroom
Sauce, Spätzle
17.50

1578 North Clybourn • River North • (312) 664-0780

From Our Broiler

U.S. PRIME FILET MIGNON
Sauteed Mushrooms
21.50

U.S. PRIME FILET MIGNON PETITE
Sauteed Mushrooms
17.50

U.S. PRIME RIB OF BEEF
Natural Juice
18.95

VEAL CHOPS WITH KIDNEY
Gourmet Cut! Breaded or Sauteed,
a Delicacy
21.95

Fish

FRESH LAKE PERCH*
Boneless Fried or Sauteed in Butter
16.50

**BROILED FRESH LAKE SUPERIOR
WHITE FISH**
Almondine Sauce
14.95

GENUINE FRESH LEMON-SOLE*
Sauteed or Bavarian style
13.95

**IMPORTED ENGLISH DOVER
SOLE (whole)**
Almondine Sauce
21.95

On The Lighter Side

HACKEPETER STEAK (Steak Tartar)
Garnish Anchovies, Caper, Onions, Tomato
13.95

HOT SEAFOOD PLATTER
Baby Lobster Tail, Shrimp, Perch, Snapper -
Boiled Potato
19.95

JULIENNE SALAD, BIBB LETTUCE
Our House Specialty. Choice of Dressing.
10.95

FRES FRUIT PLATTER (in season)
10.95

FREDERICK'S SPECIAL SALAD
Bibb Lettuce, Asparagus, Artichoke
Heart Mushrooms, Tomatoes, Eggs,
Hearts of Palm
11.95

BROILED CHOPPED SIRLOIN
Cottage Cheese and Tomato Garnish
12.95

Desserts

**Triple Chocolate and our
Cheesecake of the week**
2.95

Fresh Homemade Strudel
Apple, Cherry, Plum
2.75

Fresh Fruit in Season
2.75

**Rum Torte, German Chocolate Torte,
Black Forest Cake, Special
Chocolate Mousse Cake**
2.95

The coziness is enhanced by the Bavarian lodge look, complete with beamed ceilings, beer steins and cuckoo clocks. The ladies on waiting still sport spotless dirndls as well as shining smiles while dispensing one delicious hearty dish after another.

Menu Changes Seasonally

Appetizers

MARINATED HERRING IN WINE SAUCE   4.95
FRESH GULF SHRIMP COCKTAIL SUPREME   5.50

Soups

SOUP OF THE DAY   1.75
FRENCH ONION SOUP   3.50
LIVER DUMPLING   1.95

Complete Dinners

Your Dinner Includes:
Choice of our soup of the day or
tomato juice, papaya juice, or grapefruit juice.
Choice of the daily vegetables
Choice of potatoes: German or french fried, mashed,
potato dumpling homemade spaetzle
Garden fresh salad with choice of our homemade dressings:
German, French, garlic or 1000 Island (Roquefort 95¢ extra)
Assorted bread basket and butter

HEIDELBERGER PLATTER - A combination of Kassler Rib, Bratwurst and
Thueringer on Sauerkraut **12.75**

*SAUERBRATEN - Top Choice Beef, Marinated in Wine Vinegar and Spices **10.95**

WIENER SCHNITZEL - A Tender Veal Steak, Pan Fried in Butter and topped
with a Lemon Wedge **11.95**

4300 North Lincoln Ave • Uptown/Lincolnwood • (312) 478-2486

A LA HOLSTEIN - Fried Egg, Lox, Anchovie and Caviar Canapes .... **Extra 1.25**

*DEUTSCHE BRATWURST - A finely ground Veal Sausage with a touch of Pork to add to its flavor. Broiled or Pan Fried to your order **9.50**

SeaFood

RAINBOW TROUT, BLUE - A whole Trout Poached, served
with Drawn Butter **11.75**

RAINBOW TROUT "MEUNIERE" - A whole Trout, Pan Fried in Butter **11.75**

IMPORTED ENGLISH DOVER SOLE "MEUNIERE" - A whole imported
English Dover Sole **18.50**

IMPORTED NORDSEE HALIBUT STEAK - Parsley Butter **12.50**

Ask for our Special of the Day

OUR POPULAR SPECIAL GERMAN BEEF STEAK - A Delicious Chopped Beef
Steak with German Fried Potatoes; Garnished with a Fried Egg,
in a Casserole **10.50**

BROILED FILET MIGNON - Beef Tenderloin Broiled, Garnished with
Sliced Mushrooms **13.95**

BROILED SIRLOIN STEAK - Topped with Sliced Mushrooms **13.75**

WIENER ROASTBRATEN - Pan Fried with Fried Onions **13.95**

BROILED AFRICAN LOBSTER TAIL - Served with Drawn
Lemon Butter .... **Market Price**

Late Evening Suggestions

HACKEPETER SANDWICH **7.95**

HACKEPETER STEAK **9.75**

GERMAN STYLE ROLLED PANCAKE - Served with Strawberry Jelly
or Applesauce **6.75**

TURKEY SANDWICH **6.50**

CLUB SANDWICH - Sliced Bacon, Turkey, Tomato and Lettuce **5.95**

BAKED HAM & CHEESE SANDWICH **6.95**

LIVER SAUSAGE SANDWICH **5.75**

BEEF TENDERLOIN STEAK SANDWICH **8.95**

Desserts

GERMAN APPLE STRUDEL **2.75**	**CHEESE CAKE** **2.75**
WITH WHIPPED CREAM **2.85**	**BAVARIAN CREAM** **2.75**

Dinner: Wed - Mon 4 - 10

227

Go for the goulash and stay for the schnitzel or whatever piques your taste buds—the hearty fare here makes it difficult to decide, but it's hard to go wrong.

Menu Changes Bi-Annually

Speisekarte

Dinners include choice of Soup or Salad or Tomato Juice

"Appetizers"

Herring in Wine Sauce.	$3.50	Our Own Sülze.	$3.50
Hackepeter on Ryebread.	$3.50	Nova Lox & Caviar on Toast.	$4.50
Fried Mushrooms.	$3.50	Fried Onion Rings.	$3.00
Mozzarella Cheese Sticks.	$3.75	Fried Chicken Nuggets.	$3.50

"Old World Classics"

Hungarian Style Beef Goulasch $11.95
　　Spätzle and Red Cabbage

"Sauerbraten" $12.95
　　Red Cabbage and Dumpling Marinated Beef in Sweet & Sauer Sauce

"Braised Beef in Burgundy" $11.95
　　Homemade Red Cabbage and Dumpling

"Beef Rouladen" $12.95
　　Spätzle and Red Cabbage

Schweinebraten - Roast Loin of Pork $11.95
　　Red Cabbage and Dumpling

The German Schnitzel Bank

Original Wiener Schnitzel $11.95
　　Pan Fried - Breaded - with Spätzle and Sc. Burgundy

Pariser Schnitzel $12.95
　　Folded in Eggs and sauteed in Butter - Spätzle Sc. Burgundy

---

3454 West Addison • Uptown/Lincolnwood • (312) 463-1962

Wurst

Bratwurst .... ala carte $8.95   dinner $9.95
  Sauerkraut and Mashed Potatoes

Smoked Thuringer.................................... ala carte $8.95   dinner $9.95
Knackwurst... ala carte $8.95   dinner $9.95
  Sauerkraut and Mashed Potatoes

"Chef Werners Veal Primaforte"

"Original Zuricher Kalbsgeschnetzeltes" $13.95
  Tender veal tips sauteed in fresh mushroom, white wine sauce

"Kalbsteak Mirabell"...$14.95
  Natural Veal sauteed in Butter on Top of fresh leaf spinach - Ham and Cheese - Topped with
  Creamy fresh Mushroom Sauce- Served with Homemade Spätzle

"Fowl"

Chicken Breast sauteed $10.95
  in fresh Mushroom sauce - Rice and fresh vegetables

Chicken Breast Tips Mirabell $10.95
  Sauteed with Fresh Mushrooms - Onion - Pepper - Tomato - Peas and Rice

Wiener Backhend'l...$9.95
  Breaded - Fried Chicken 1/2 - Tartar Sauce - Cole Slaw - French Fries

Chicken Paprikash Hungarian Style $10.95
  Pan Fried with Sweet Paprika - Red Wine Sauce - Spätzle

"Steaks"

X-Thick Cut N.Y. Sirloin "Pepper Steak" $16.95
  Dipped in Crushed Black Peppercorn - laced with Cognac Simmered with Fresh Whipping
  Cream

N. Y. Sirloin Tips - Pepperbeef $13.95
  Sauteed with fresh mushrooms - Green Pepper - Onions - Bacon -Tomatoes - Sc Burgundy -
  Served with Risi-Bisi Rice

Seafood

Seafood Platter $11.95
  Breaded Shrimp - Perch - Scallops - Filet of Sole, French Fries and Cole Slaw and Tartar Sauce

Boned Rainbow Trout Almondine...$11.95
  sauteed - Parsley Potatoes and fresh Vegetables - Tartar Sauce

Fried Ocean Perch Filet $10.95
  French Fries - Cole Slaw - Tartar Sauce

Islandic Cod Fish - Loin Cut $11.95
  Poached in Rhine Wine - Parsley Potatoes and fresh Vegetables

Dinner: Mon - Thurs 5 - 10, Fri - Sun 5 - 11

Zum Deutschen Eck

The massive chalet-style building takes up a city block, and inside you can cut the gemutlichkeit with a knife. It's a spirited restaurant with a big menu and even bigger German specialties such as schnitzel or pig's knuckles. The active bar is fun too.

Zum Deutschen Eck

Menu Changes Daily

FEATURED DINNERS

APPETIZERS: (CHOICE OF ONE)

Ochsenmaul (Meat Salad)   Chilled Tomato Juice   Homemade Suelze (Headcheese)
Pork in Aspic   Chicken Liver Pate   Fresh Fruit Cup
Soup Du Jour   Herring Salad   Deutsche Art

TEUFEL SALAD (Devil Salad) Julienne of Beef Tongue, Ham, Corned Beef, Pickles, Green Spanish Olives, Green Peppers, Onions, Shallots and Mixed with a Tangy Cocktail Sauce

---

ORIGINAL BAKED FRENCH ONION SOUP
SERVED BUBBLY HOT WITH MELTED CHEESE . . . 3.50

BEEF TENDERLOIN A LA DEUTSCH and Buttered Noodles (Slices of Beef Tenderloin cooked in a Red Wine Sauce with fresh Mushrooms, Green Peppers, Onions, Shallots and Tomatoes) 14.95

WIENER SCHNITZEL and Hot Potato Salad "The Pride of Vienna" 14.95

WIENER SCHNITZEL A LA HOLSTEIN (Sauteed Breaded Veal Cutlet garnished with a Fried Egg, Anchovies and Capers) served with German Potato Salad 15.95

SCHNITZEL DIJON (Tender Cutlets Sauteed with Shallots and Fresh Mushrooms, simmered in a light Dijon Mustard Cream Sauce) served with Buttered Noodles 15.95

RAHMSCHNITZEL (Tender Cutlet Sauteed with Bacon, Shallots and Fresh Mushrooms in a White Wine Sauce and Sour Cream) mit Buttered Noodles 14.95

SCHNITZEL A LA JAEGER (Tender Cutlet Sauteed in Red Wine with a Savory Sauce of Green Peppers, Onions, Fresh Mushrooms and Red Peppers) mit Buttered Noodles 14.95

SCHWEINS HAZEN (Giant Pork Shank) with Sauerkraut and Parsley Potato 14.95

2924 North Southport Ave • Lincoln Park/DePaul • (312) 525-8121

HASENPFEFFER (Marinated Rabbit) and Dumpling 15.95

HALF ROAST DUCKLING with Dumpling and Bavarian Red Cabbage 15.95

HUNGARIAN BEEF GOULASH and Buttered Noodles 13.95

SAUERBRATEN (Marinated Beef) and Spaetzles "Germany's
Most Famous Delicacy" 14.95

FRESH THUERINGER (Bratwurst) and Hot Potato Salad 13.95

SMOKED RIESEN (Giant) Thueringer Sausage with Sauerkraut, and
Whipped Potato 13.95

KNACKWURST with Sauerkraut and Whipped Potato 13.95

KOENIGSBERGER KLOPS German Meat Balls (Fluffy Meat Balls made of Veal,
Port and Beef) with Caper Sauce, Sauerkraut and Whipped Potato 13.50

DELUXE RIBS in Barbecue Sauce (Meaty Juicy Ribs with Just the right sauce)
with French Fries 16.95

BEEF ROULADEN Pig in a Blanket (Braised Rolled Beef Steak stuffed with Bacon,
Onion and Pickle and our Special Seasoning) with Buttered Noodles 14.95

WIENER ROSTBRATEN MIT POMMES FRITS (Sirloin Steak sauteed in a rich
Red Wine Sauce with Shallots and Onions) served with French Fries 17.95

FILET MIGNON with Mushrooms and French Fries 18.95

LADY'S CUT NEW YORK STRIP SIRLOIN STEAK with French Fried Onion
Rings and French Fries 15.95

*Included are: (Choose One) Tossed Garden Salad, Cucumber Salad,
or Kidney Bean Salad Assorted Rolls and Butter*

TRY ONE OF OUR SPECIAL DESSERTS:

OUR HOUSE SPECIALTY: DIE ZUGSPITZE (CHERRIES JUBILEE) 5.95
*Cherries sauteed in a Special Cherry Sauce with the essence of Cherry
Brandy and Dark, Sweet, Pitted Bing Cherries served Hot over Vanilla Ice Cream.
"Keep the glass as a Souvenir"*

GERMAN APPLE STRUDEL 2.75

RASPBERRY CHEESECAKE 2.95

PECAN CARMEL CHEESECAKE 2.95

CHOCOLATE MOUSSE (Delightful) 2.95

SCHWARTZWALDER KIRSCH TORTE (Black Forest) 2.95

DELUXE ICE CREAM SUNDAE with Whipped Cream
Chocolate, Strawberry or Butterscotch 2.96

Ice Cream or Whipped Cream with Any Dessert 1.25

Dinner: 7 Days a Week 4 - 10:30

Courtyards of Plaka

The Greek salad is great, the fresh fish specials are excellent and, like every other restaurant in Greektown, the flames from the saganaki rise high. This is a comfortable and easy-to-like place that seems to get better with age.

THE COURTYARDS OF

Plaka
RESTAURANT

APPETIZERS

COLD   **TIROSALATA** A blend of Feta and Kaseri cheeses whipped together with sweet red peppers and herbs. 3.50

MELIZZANOSALATA A tasty spread of eggplant and garlic. 3.25

TARAMOSALATA Delicate dip of whipped fish roe. 3.25

SKORDALIA A chilled purée of garlic and potatoes. 2.95

TZATZIKI Thin slices of cucumber in yogurt seasoned with garlic. 3.25

MEZEDES

Uniquely Greek, Mezedes refers to certain dishes that can be ordered as a starter course, entrée or late-supper selection.

GYROS Barbecued layers of specially seasoned lamb and beef on a bed of parsleyed onions, served with Tzatziki. Small 4.95 Full 7.95

KALAMARI PLAKIOTIKO Baby squid sautéed with fresh tomato, Feta cheese and herbs. Small 4.25 Full 7.95

SMALL SHRIMP SHISHKEBOB Served with grilled tomato and onion. 5.95

LOUKANIKA (Grilled) Our chef's own recipe for Greek sausage. Small 4.25 Full 8.25

SALADS

GREEK SALAD Hearts of lettuce, tomatoes, cucumbers, Feta cheese, olives, peppers and anchovies in olive oil, vinegar and oregano dressing. 3.25

HORIATIKI SALATA Tomatoes, cucumbers, Feta cheese, peppers, olives, onions and anchovies, in olive oil, vinegar and oregano dressing. 3.50

PASCHALINI SALATA Greek lettuce, fresh onions, dill, tomatoes, Feta cheese and Kalamata olives in olive oil and fresh lemon dressing. 3.50

AEGEAN SALAD Platter of diced shrimp, tomato, lettuce, celery, cucumber and Feta cheese tossed in a light cream dressing. 4.95

340 South Halsted St • Greektown • (312) 263-0767

232

ENTREES

MEATLESS DISHES

VEGETARIAN MOUSSAKA Layered slices of eggplant, potato and squash covered in a béchamel sauce and baked individually in a ceramic pot. 8.50

MELIZZANOPITA Lightly sautéed eggplant and fresh onion tossed with Kefalotiri cheese, wrapped in phyllo and baked. 7.95

LAMB DISHES

ARNI ATOMIKO Prime lamb simmered in tomato sauce and baked with spaghetti in a ceramic pot. 9.25

ARNI KAPAMA Braised lamb with rice pilafi, potatoes or vegetable. 9.25

ARNI PSITO Slices of roast prime leg of lamb served in natural juice with roast potatoes and vegetable. 9.95

ARNI NEFRAMIA Roast prime loin of lamb in natural juice. Served with vegetable and rice pilafi or roast potatoes. 10.95

LAMB SHISHKEBOB Marinated chunks of prime lamb broiled on a skewer with onion, tomato and green pepper. Served with rice pilafi. 11.95

BEEF DISHES

KREATOPITA Lightly seasoned beef in a savory sauce wrapped in phyllo and baked. Served with vegetable. 9.25

MOSCHARI STAMNAS Beef and potatoes simmered in a flavorful combination of tomatoes, herbs and wine and baked in a ceramic pot. Served with vegetable. 9.25

MOSCHARI KAPAMA Braised beef with rice pilafi or vegetable. 9.25

CHICKEN DISHES

KOTOPITA Boned, skinless chicken in light cream sauce wrapped in phyllo and baked. Served with vegetable. 8.50

CHICKEN SPANAKI Skinless breast of chicken, baked with spinach and Feta cheese. Served with rice pilafi. 8.25

CHICKEN KAPAMA Skinless breast of chicken simmered in fresh tomato and herbs. Served with rice pilafi. 8.25

SKINLESS BREAST OF CHICKEN Broiled with fresh lemon and oregano. Served with rice pilafi or vegetable. 8.50

SEA FOOD

KAKAVIA This version of Bouillabaisse was one of the most popular dishes of the ancient Greeks. Fillets of grouper, red snapper, shrimp, scallops, mussels and fresh vegetables are simmered in fresh tomatoes and served in a ceramic pot. 15.95

SWORDFISH SHISHKEBOB Served with rice pilafi. 11.95

SHRIMP SHISHKEBOB Large shrimp broiled on a skewer with onion and tomato, flamed in brandy. Served with rice pilafi. 14.95

SCALLOPS FLAMBE Sautéed in butter and flamed in brandy. Served with vegetable and rice pilafi or pan-fried potatoes. 14.25

BROILED FRESH WHOLE SEA BASS or RED SNAPPER Cooked to a turn and served with our special dressing. Served with rice pilafi or pan-fried potatoes. (Based on availability) Market price $17.95

Dinner: 7 Days a Week until 12

Greek Islands

This Greektown institution packs them in, and there's plenty of packing space. The pace and the seemingly frantic waiters (it's part of the show) make this place a favorite for families. The expertly prepared food—saganaki, lamb, chicken, Greek sausage, gyros—disappears as fast as it arrives, but one thing is certain: you won't leave hungry.

Greek Islands
RESTAURANT

Appetizers
Hot & Cold

Anchovies	1.75	**Cold Kalamari & Shrimp Salad**	
Green Peppers & Olives	1.00	in wine sauce	7.50
Spinach Cheese Pie	5.50	**Feta Cheese**	2.65
Tzatziki		**Kefalotiri**	2.65
(yogurt, cucumbers & garlic)	2.50	**Scordalia** (garlic sauce)	1.95
Melitzanosalata (egg plant)	2.25	**Keftedakia** (4 meatballs	
Cold Octopus Salad in wine sauce	7.50	in tomato sauce)	2.85

Sandwiches

Gyros served on Greek bread 4.95

Roast Lamb au jus on Greek bread 5.75

Meat Ball Sandwich 4.75

Greek Sausage 4.95

Fresh Vegetables - Potatoes - Side Orders

Fresh Artichoke (1) 1.95

Fasolakia (string beans) 1.50

Potatoes 1.00

Mpamies (okra) 1.50

Mpriami (mixed vegetables) 1.50

Spanacorizo spinach-rice 1.50

---

200 South Halsted St • Greektown • (312) 782-9855

Greek Island Specials

Gyros Plate slices of ground lamb & beef with special
seasoning served with onion 5.95
Combination Plate roast lamb, mousaka, meatballs,
dolmades, mixed vegetables & potato 6.75

Mousaka 5.75	**Rice & Yogurt** 3.95
Dolmades (stuffed vine leaves) 5.75	**Baked Lima Beans** 2.95
Kokkinisto braised lamb w/ tomato sauce & choice of rice, potato or vegetable 6.50	**Spaghetti Grecian Style** .... 3.95 **Meatballs** plain or with tomato sauce 5.75

From the Oceans

Porgie broiled fresh whole sea bass with
oil, lemon & oregano .... **market price**

Broiled Fresh Red Snapper oil,
lemon & oregano .... **market price**

Pan Fried Smelts 6.25

**Broiled Fresh Lake Superior
White Fish Tail** 7.95

Hot Octopus in Greek Islands
tomato sauce with onions 6.95

Kalamari pan fried squid 6.25

Bakalao pan fried cod fish
with garlic sauce 6.50

Fresh Swordfish Shish-Ke-Bob 7.95

Roast Lamb

Roast Loin of Lamb .... 7.25   **Roast Leg of Lamb** 6.95

From the Broiler

Special Greek Sausage 5.95

Center Cut Pork Chops (2) 7.95

New York Sirloin Steak
broiled to order 11.25

Lamb Chops
Athenian style, thick & juicy (2) ... **12.95**

Shish-Ke-Bob
tender chunks of meat on a skewer **6.95**

It's Greek to Me

Whitewashed walls, sea blue color accents, green plants, hardwood floor...this is one of the niftiest looking Greek restaurants in Greektown. Broiled whole snapper and sea bass are always excellent. Greek salad and gyros are first-rate too.

Menu Changes Seasonally

APPETIZERS

HOT

FRIED ZUCCHINI	3.95
SAGANAKI FLAMBE	2.95
GYROS PLATE	5.25
SPANAKOTIROPITA	4.95
Spinach Cheese Pie	
KALAMARAKIA KRASATA	4.25
Baby Squid in Wine Sauce	
MELITZANES EMAM	3.50
Stuffed Egg Plant with Raisins, Onions and Tomato Sauce	
STUFFED MUSHROOMS	
with Crabmeat	4.45

COLD

TARAMOSALATA	2.95
Grecian Caviar Spread	
MELITZANOSALATA	3.50
Egg Plant Salad	
OCTAPODI KRASATO	6.75
Octopus in Wine Sauce	
TZATZIKI	3.25
Thin Slices of Cucumber in Yogurt with a Touch of Garlic	
SKORDALIA	3.25
Garlic Potato Puree	
LIMA BEANS	2.95

> The **GREEK CONNECTION**
> **COMBO PLATTER OF HOT & COLD**
> **APPETIZERS (for Two or More)**
> **3.95 per person**

IT'S GREEK TO ME HOUSE SPECIALTIES

ARNI EXOHIKO with Rice only 9.95
Baby Lamb Stuffed with Artichokes, Pine Nuts, Feta Cheese, Peas and Tomatoes wrapped in Fillo

PASSA DAVA with Rice only 9.95
Baby Lamb in Layers of Fried Egg Plant Topped with Parmesan Cheese Gradine

KOTOPOULO GEMISTO 8.95
Deep Fried Breast of Chicken Stuffed with Feta Cheese, Pine Nuts, Butter and Topped with Creamy Mediterranean Sauce

---

306 South Halsted St • Greektown • (312) 977-0022

ENTRÉES

ARNI GEMISTO Boneless Breast of Baby Lamb Stuffed with Ground Beef, ... 8.25
Raisins, Pine Nuts. Cooked with Wine

ARNI YOUVETSI Lamb with Rosa Marina 6.75

ARNI FASOLAKIA Lamb with Fresh Green Beans 6.75

NEFRAMIA Roast Loin of Lamb 8.95

ARNI KAPAMA Braised Lamb in Tomato Sauce and Spices 6.75

ROAST LEG OF LAMB Rice and Potato 7.95

B.B.Q. LAMB 8.95

MOUSAKA Layers of Eggplant & Ground Beef Topped with 6.50
Bechamel Sauce and Cheese

PASTICHIO Layers of Macaroni & Ground Beef Topped with 6.50
Bechamel Sauce and Cheese

DOLMADES Stuffed Vine Leaves 6.50

SPANAKOTIROPITA Spinach Cheese Pie 6.25

GYROS PLATE Served with Onions, Sliced Tomato and Tzatziki Sauce 6.25

FILET MIGNON MEDALLIONS MEDEIRA Medeira Wine and Mushrooms 13.95

FILET MIGNON MEDALLIONS ORGANATA 13.95

SEAFOOD-THALASSINA

WHOLE BROILED RED SNAPPER .... (Market Price)

WHOLE BROILED SEA BASS .... (Market Price)

SWORDFISH KEBOB With Tomato, Onion and Green Pepper 11.25

SWORDFISH STEAK 11.25

FLOUNDER FILET Stuffed with Spinach & Feta Cheese 9.25
Stuffed with Crabmeat 11.25

BROILED STUFFED TROUT with Spinach & Feta Cheese 9.25
with Crabmeat 11.25

PAN FRIED CODFISH Served with Skordalia 7.50

FRIED KALAMARI (Baby Squid) 6.50

SHRIMP CORFU with Rice only 12.25
Jumbo Shrimp Sauteed with Feta Cheese, Creole wine Sauce

SHRIMP STUFFED WITH CRABMEAT 13.25

SHRIMP ALA MEDITERRANEAN Chef's Special Creamy Mediterranean Sauce 12.25

SHRIMP SAGANAKI 11.25

Dinner: Mon - Sat until 1, Sun until 12

Papagus Greek Taverna

A Lettuce Entertain You re-creation of a Greek taverna that is so authentic—in a kitschy sort of way—that the very thought of it brings a smile to my face. It's fun, the food is most pleasing, and the outdoor cafe is great for people watching.

Ζεστοί Μεζέδες
Hot Appetizers

Μουσακάς / Moussakas
Moussakas – Ground Beef layered with Lamb, Eggplant, Squash . **3.95 7.75**

Σπανακόπιτα Θείας Λένας/Spanakopita Theas Lenas
Spinach and Greek Feta Pie in Phyllo **3.95 7.75**

Γύρος "Papagus" / Gyros "Papagus"
Gyros – Sliced Homemade Lamb and Pork Made the Authentic Way **4.25 7.95**

Γύρος Κοτόπουλο / Gyros Kotopoulo
Chicken Gyros. **4.25 7.95**

Πίτα Σπιτική μέ Τομάτα, Ἐλνές, Μελιτζάνα καί Φέτα / Pita
Baked Pita topped with Tomato, Olives, Eggplant and Feta. . . **4.50**

Ἀρνάκι Φέτα Ρολό Γεμιστό μέ Κρεμύδια / Arnaki Rolo Yemisto
Braised Lamb with Sweet Onions. **4.25**

Κρύοι Μεζέδες
Cold Appetizers

Τυροσαλάτα / Tyrosalata
Whipped Feta Cheese **3.75**

Μελιτζανοσαλάτα / Melitzanosalata
Roasted Eggplant Spread **3.95**

Τζατζίκι / Tzatziki
Creamy Yogurt Cucumber and Garlic **3.95**

Σούπα/Σαλάτες
Soup/Salads

Σούπα Αὐγολέμονο / Soupa Avgolemono
Traditional Egg and Lemon Soup. . . . . cup 1.95 bowl 2.50

Σούπα τῆς Ἡμέρας /Soupa tis Imeras
Soup of the Day. 1.95   2.50

Ἑλληνική Σαλάτα / Greek Salata
Greek Salad of Romaine Lettuce, Tomatoes, Onions, Olives, Feta . . 3.75

Χωριάτικη Σαλάτα /Horiatiki Salata
Peasant Salad of Tomato, Cucumber, Feta, Olives 4.25

Σαλάτα μέ Ἐλιόψωμο καί Πιπεριές/Salata me Eliopsomo
Olive Bread Salad with Roasted Peppers and Chicory Lettuce 4.50

Χόρτα Βραστά / Horta Vrasta
Horta - Boiled Dandelion Greens, Virgin Olive Oil, Lemon 3.25

Μεγάλα Πιάτα
Large Courses

Ἀρνάκι Κοκκινιστό μέ Μανέστρα /Arnaki Kokkinisto me Manestra
Braised Lamb with Orzo, Grated Kefalotyri Cheese 8.95

Χοιρινό Σουβλάκι / Hirino Souvlaki
Char Grilled Marinated Pork Shish Kebob. 9.95

Κοτόπουλο στόν Φοῦρνο /Kotopoulo ston Fourno
Greek Roast Chicken . . . . Half 9.95 Whole 13.95

Κοτόπουλο Σουβλάκι / Kotopoulo Souvlaki
Char Grilled Marinated Chicken Breast on a Skewer. 10.75

Φιλέτο ἀπό Μοσχάρι στήν Σχάρα/Fileto apo Moschari
Broiled Filet of Beef Tenderloin, Fried Onions 17.95

Ψάρι Τσιπούρα Ψητό / Psari Tsipoura Psito
Broiled Whole Striped Bass . . . . Market

Ψάρι Ξιφίας Σουβλάκι / Psari Xifias Souvlaki
Char Grilled Skewer of Swordfish 15.50

Παϊδάκια ἀπό Ἀρνί Ψητά / Paidakia apo Arni Psita
Broiled Marinated Lamb Chops (Additional Chops 6.25 each). 18.95

Μακαρόνια μέ Ἀγκινάρες σέ Κρέμα /Makaronia me Aginares
Macaroni Pasta, Baby Artichokes and Spinach and Lemon Cream. 8.95

Λευκόψαρο τῆς Σχάρας / Lefkopsaro tis Scharas
Charred Fillet of Whitefish, Lemon Vinaigrette. 9.95

Λεπτά Μακαρόνια μέ Κυμά / Lepta Makaronia me Kyma
Spaghetti with Ground Lamb and Beef, Tomato Sauce. 8.25

Σπανακόρυζο, Μπριάμι καί ἄλλα Λαχανικά /Spanakorizo, Briami
Spinach Rice, Briami, Grilled Vegetable Plate. 7.50

Κώτσι ἀπό Ἀρνί μέ Ἀγκινάρες /Kotsi apo Arni me Aginares
Braised Lamb Shank with Artichokes. 8.75

Dinner: Sun - Thurs until 10, Fri - Sat until 12

Parthenon

One of the original Greektown spots is also one of the most spirited. Waiters waltz like ballet dancers (well, almost) with plates of food through the three large dining rooms. Excellent lamb dishes, and fish dishes such as cod with skordalia are outstanding.

The Parthenon

Menu Changes Seasonally

HOT APPETIZERS - ΟΡΕΚΤΙΚΑ ΖΕΣΤΑ

SAGANAKI - ΣΑΓΑΝΑΚΙ 3.10
    Kaseri cheese flamed in brandy - a creation of the Parthenon.
    Saganaki made from either Kefalograviera or Kefalotiri (salty) also available
SMALL SPINACH-CHEESE PIES (2) - ΣΠΑΝΑΚΟΤΥΡΟΠΙΙΤΑΚΙΑ 2.75
CHEESE PIES - ΤΥΡΟΠΙΤΤΑΚΙΑ 3.75
    Special mixture of feta cheese wrapped in phyllo
TRIGONA - ΤΡΙΓΩΝΑ 3.95
    Baked delicacy of ground beef and feta cheese wrapped in phyllo

COLD APPETIZERS - ΟΡΕΚΤΙΚΑ ΚΡΥΑ

EGGPLANT SALAD - ΜΕΛΙΤΖΑΝΟΣΑΛΑΤΑ 2.75
    A tasty spread of eggplant flavored with garlic
FISH ROE SALAD - ΤΑΡΑΜΟΣΑΛΑΤΑ 2.60
    Delicate dip of whipped fish roe
BEAN SALAD - ΦΑΣΟΛΙΑ ΜΠΙΑΖΙ 2.35
    Great Northern beans vinaigrette, served chilled

FRESH GARDEN VEGETABLES - ΦΡΕΣΚΑ ΛΑΧΑΝΙΚΑ

GRILLED VEGETABLES - ΛΑΧΑΝΙΚΑ ΣΧΑΡΑΣ ....regular 3.25, large 4.25
    Cauliflower, broccoli, zucchini and carrots grilled with olive oil
BRIAMI - ΜΠΡΙΑΜΙ ....regular 2.75, large 3.95

---

314 South Halsted St • Greektown • (312) 726-2407

DINNER SELECTIONS - ΦΑΓΗΤΑ ΔΕΙΠΝΟΥ

AMNOPITA - ΑΜΝΟΠΙΤΤΑ **7.25**
Lean pieces of Leg of Lamb with vegetables and feta cheese
wrapped in phyllo and baked individually. Served with rice pilafi
ROAST LEG OF LAMB - ΑΡΝΙ ΨΗΤΟ, ΜΠΟΥΤΙ **7.25**
Served with rice pilafi and roast potatoes
ROAST LOIN OF LAMB - ΑΡΝΙ ΨΗΤΟ, ΝΕΦΡΑΜΙΑ **7.75**
Served with rice pilafi and roast potatoes
BARBECUED LAMB - ΑΡΝΙ ΣΟΥΒΛΑΣ **7.50**
Served with rice pilafi and roast potatoes
BAKED LAMB'S HEAD - ΚΕΦΑΛΑΚΙ ΦΟΥΡΝΟΥ **4.25**
Served with roast potatoes
LAMB WITH ARTICHOKES - ΑΡΝΙ ΑΓΚΙΝΑΡΕΣ .... **market price**
Served with fresh hearts of artichokes in Avgolemono sauce

CHICKEN KAPAMA - ΚΟΤΟΠΟΥΛΟ ΚΑΠΑΜΑ 4.25
Simmered in tomatoes, herbs and wine, and served with either rice pilafi,
potatoes or okra
CHICKEN RIGANATI - ΚΟΤΑ ΡΙΓΑΝΑΤΗ 5.95
Baked in fresh lemon and oregano. Served with rice pilafi and roast potatoes
SKINLESS BREAST OF CHICKEN - ΣΤΗΘΟΣ ΚΟΤΑΣ 6.50
Broiled with fresh lemon and oregano. Served with rice pilafi or vegetable
BARBECUED CHICKEN - ΚΟΤΟΠΟΥΛΟ ΣΟΥΒΛΑΣ 5.95
Served with rice pilafi and roast potatoes
TIGANIA - ΤΙΓΑΝΙΑ...7.50
Marinated pieces of pork tenderloin, sauteed in wine sauce
and served with rice pilafi and okra
ROAST YOUNG PIG - ΧΟΙΡΙΔΙΟΝ ΦΟΥΡΝΟΥ 6.95
Served with rice pilafi and roast potatoes

SEA FOOD - ΨΑΡΙΑ ΘΑΛΑΣΣΙΝΑ

FRESH WHOLE RED SNAPPER or SEA BASS (based on availability)..................market price
FRESH FILLET OF GROUPER - ΦΙΛΕΤΟ ΑΠΟ ΡΟΦΟ ....market price
Served with rice pilafi
SHRIMP FLAMBE - ΓΑΡΙΔΕΣ ΦΛΑΜΠΕ 12.50
SCALLOPS FLAMBE - ΣΚΑΛΛΟΠΣ ΦΛΑΜΠΕ 11.95
SWORDFISH SHISHKEBOB - ΣΟΥΒΛΑΚΙ ΑΠΟ ΞΙΦΙΑ 9.25
Broiled in lemon-butter sauce. Served with rice pilafi
PAN-FRIED SQUID - ΚΑΛΑΜΑΡΙΑ ΤΗΓΑΝΙΤΑ 6.25
Crisp and meaty - an unusual taste treat. Served with rice pilafi
BAKED SQUID - ΚΑΛΑΜΑΡΙΑ ΓΙΑΧΝΙ 5.95
Simmered in tomatoes, herbs and wine
SHRIMP and SCALLOPS FLAMBÈ - ΓΑΡΙΔΕΣ και ΣΚΑΛΛΟΠΣ ΦΛΑΜΠΕ......................12.50
Presented in a sizzling platter, flamed in brandy and served with rice pilafi

Dinner: 7 Days a Week until 1

241

Wide open, bright, and very comfortable, this "winged horse," as the menu clearly shows, doesn't miss a Greek dish. I particularly favor the pan-fried cod, the moussaka, and the roast leg of lamb.

PEGASUS SPECIALTIES

Yiayias Fry Pan (Greek Style Fajitas) Tender
Marinated Strips of Chicken Breast presented to you
Sizzling in a Skillet with Onions, Green Peppers,
Tomatoes and Mushrooms. Pita Bread is Served
on the Side **7.50**

Yiayias Fry Pan (Greek Style Fajitas)
with Shrimp **8.75**

Briami Fresh Assorted Cooked Vegetables
for the Vegetarian in you **3.95**

GREEK SPECIALTIES

Gyros Plate (yee-ros) Served with Onions,
Tzatziki and Pita Bread **5.75**

Arni Kokkinisto Braised Lamb Served
with your Choice of Cooked Vegetables,
Rice or Potato **6.95**

Arni Psito Roast Leg of Lamb, Natural Au Jus
Served with your Choice of Cooked Vegetables,
Rice or Potato **7.95**

Neframia Broiled Loin of Lamb, Natural Au Jus,
Served with your Choice of Cooked Vegetables,
Rice or Potato **9.25**

Combination Greek Specialty Plate
Slices of Leg of Lamb, Gyros, Pastitso, Mousaka,
Dolma, Potato and Rice **8.25**

130 South Halsted St • Greektown • (312) 226-3377

FROM THE BROILER

Grecian Style Broiled Chicken
Just the way the Spartans liked it. 1/2 Chicken
Broiled Slowly with Greek Spices. (please
allow 30 minutes) **7.50**

Lamb Chops (3) Tender and Juicy **14.95**

Pork Chops (2) Center Cut Pork Chops
Broiled, may we suggest Well Done **8.95**

Beeftekia Sharas (beef-TAY-kya-sha-RAHS)
Broiled Lean Ground Beef, Artfully Spiced with
Onion, Oregano and Choice Seasonings,
Hamburger Greek Style! **6.50**

New York Strip Steak Topped with
Mushrooms....................................... **14.25**

Filet Mignon Topped with Mushrooms...... **16.25**

Steak Mediterranean The other way to eat
a Filet Mignon. Sauteed in our Special Way **16.25**

FISH

Sinagrida (whole Red Snapper)
Fresh Daily .... **Market Price**

Octopus on Charcoal........................ **8.50**

Kalamarakia (Squid) Pan Fried............... **7.25**

Swordfish Ke-Bob **10.75**

Bakalaos (Cod Fish) Pan Fried
Served with Scordalia............................. **7.95**

Marides (Smelt) Pan Fried **6.25**

Combination Fish Platter
(Bakalaos, Marides, Kalamarakia)
Served with Scordalia............................. **10.25**

Dinner: 7 Days a Week until 12

Santorini Restaurant

A comfortable and gracious atmosphere, complete with an Aegean fireplace, makes this place one of my favorites. The grilled octopus and grilled fresh fish dishes are outstanding, as are the Greek salads. The service gets equally high marks.

Appetizers

TZATZIKI *Thin slices of cucumber in yogurt with essence of garlic.*	2.75
RAW CLAMS	4.95
MELITZANOSALATA *(Eggplant Spread)*	3.00
TIROKAFTERI *(Spicy Feta Cheese Spread)*	3.00
BAKED OYSTERS	5.25
BAKED CLAMS	5.25
OCTOPUS *Charcoal grilled.*	6.75
GREEK SAUSAGES *Charcoal grilled.*	6.75

Steaks

NEW YORK SIRLOIN *USDA choice grilled to order.*	12.95
FILET MIGNON *USDA choice grilled to order.*	13.95
CHOPPED STEAK *One pound 100% beef charcoal grilled, and topped with brown mushroom sauce.*	7.25

Oceanic Fish *(THALASSINA)*

WHOLE RED SNAPPER   *Market Price*
Prepared Greek Style. (Occasionally unavailable).

WHOLE BLACK BASS   *Market Price*
Prepared Greek Style. (Occasionally unavailable).

FLORIDA RED SNAPPER   9.95
A boneless, skinless filet lightly broiled and topped with Santorini sauce.

Fish From The Shell

BAY SCALLOPS   7.95
Lightly sauteed and finished with wine sauce.

SHRIMP TOURKOLIMANO   9.95
Oven baked, butterflied jumbo gulf shrimp in tomato and feta cheese sauce.

Fresh Water Fish

LAKE SUPERIOR WHITEFISH TAIL   8.95
Finest cut available, broiled to your liking.

CANADIAN WALLEYED PIKE   8.95
Sauteed or broiled and served with Santorini sauce.

Fine Chicken Dishes

AUTHENTIC GREEK STYLE CHICKEN   7.25
Please allow 30 minutes.

CHICKEN ALA SANTORINI   6.95
Introducing the newest style of chicken in Greek Town. If it bears our name, it has to be the best.

Chops

LAMB PAIDAKIA *(Pound)*   9.75
Thin cut lamb chops prepared in the original Greek way. Order by the pound.

CENTER CUT LAMB CHOPS   *Two* 14.25

Dinner: Sun - Mon until 12, Fri - Sat until 1

Bukhara

One of the premier Indian restaurants in the city, in both atmosphere and food,
Bukhara continues to impress me, especially when I'm in a vegetarian state of
mind and lusting for the taste of delicious Indian breads.

BUKHARA

Menu Changes Seasonally

APPETIZERS -- "Shuruat"

MANTY beef brochette with mushrooms **3.95**
pineapple and spinach marinated in malt
vinegar and sauteed, served with yogurt-mint
dip.

CHOOZA KANDHARI tandoori   **3.25**
chicken, soaked in pomegranate juice,
served with black peppercorn yogurt
dressing.

KHOOLE MOONG KI CHAAT   **2.95**
protein rich sprouted beans
flavored with royal cummin.

SALAD-E-KHAS our special tandoori **2.95**
salad from the best pick of greens,
served hot with pineapples and tomatoes.

ENTREES -- "Tosha-E-Khas"

MURGH MALAI KABOB creamy   **13.95**
chicken supremes marinated in ginger,
garlic and green corriander, roasted in
the clay oven.

PESHAWARI BOTI leg of lamb   **13.95**
cubed and seasoned with aromatic herbs,
marinated in a mixture of yogurt, ginger,
and malt vinegar, roasted in the clay oven.

KHYBER TIKKA succulent boneless **11.95**
pieces of chicken leg marinated in ginger,
garlic, spiced with pounded black
peppercorns, coated with egg yolk and
grilled over live charcoal.

PASLION KE PANJE the popular   **11.95**
pork spare ribs now from tandoor.

TANDOORI MURGH BUKHARA **9.95**
the "king of kabob" -- the tastiest way to
barbecue chicken.

BARAH KABOB choicest chunks of **10.95**
tenderized lamb marinated in yogurt flavored
with cummin, cooked in the tandoor.

SEEKH KABOB tender rolls of   **10.95**
succulent minced lamb with royal cummin
and aromatic hot spices, skewered and grilled
over charcoal.

MACHHLI-AFGHANI fish filet   **12.95**
flavored with ramarind and cooked in tandoor.

KARARE QUAILS quails cooked to **17.95**
perfection in clay oven; ideal finger food.

2 East Ontario St • Near North/Gold Coast • (312) 943-0188

246

OUR SPECIALTIES -- "Tohfe"

TIGER PRAWN BUKHARA　19.95
jumbo shrimp marinated in caraway seed
flavored yogurt, blended with oriental
spices, and baked in the shell.

SIKANDARI RAAN (Serves 2)　24.95
whole leg of spring lamb marinated in
dark rum, braised in the oven, then
cooked to perfection in tandoor.

KADAK RESHMI KABOB　12.95
tender rolls of minced chicken enriched with
cashews, spiced with royal cummin, blended
with cheddar cheese and cooked to perfection.

BEEF TENDERLOIN AFGHANI　17.95
choicest cuts of tenderloin
marinated and flavored with caraway
seeds, grilled to your taste in the
clay oven.

VEGETARIAN - "Subz Tandoor"

SHIMLA MIRCH TANDOORI　6.95
bell peppers stuffed with piquantly spiced
vegetables, nuts and dried fruits, roasted in
tandoor.

ALOO BHARWAN scooped potatoes　6.45
with a rich stuffing of raisins, cashews,
green chillies, coriander, garam marsala
and royal cummin grilled in tandoor.

TANDOORI PHOOL　6.45
whole cauliflower seasoned in exotic spices,
dipped in an aromatic batter and glazed in
the clay oven.

MATAR PANEER PATHANI　6.95
a popular north Indian delicacy - cubes
of homemade cottage cheese and fresh green
peas cooked in an aromatic tomato sauce.

**DAL BUKHARA-HOUSE
SPECIALTY**　6.95
black lentils harmoniously combined with
tomatoes and ginger, simmered overnight on
a charcoal fire.

RAITA lightly churned yogurt spiced　2.95
with broiled and pounded royal cummin, red
chillies and cummin powder, with your choice
of pineapple, onion, tomato or cucumber
garnish.

DESSERTS -- "Mithai"

KULFI NARANGI famous frozen　3.75
dessert made from pista enriched
reduced milk, now served in fresh
orange shell. Our chefs specialty.

GULAB JAMUN golden brown　2.75
dumplings made from milk solids, served in
hot syrup, gently flavored with saffron.

RAS MALAI fresh cottage cheese patties **3.75**
laced with pistachio-enriched milk. An
East Indian specialty.

KHAJOOR KI KHEER exotic　2.75
pudding made from slivered dates and
condensed milk, flavored with saffron
and served chilled.

Dinner: Sun - Thurs 5:30 - 10, Fri - Sat 5:30 - 11

Gandhi India Restaurant

This place is small enough that you can hear the bread being slapped against the side of the tandoor. Many aficionados of Indian food, me included, say the Indian food here is as authentic as it gets outside Bombay.

GANDHI INDIA RESTAURANT

SHURUAT KIJIYE
(START WITH THE APPETIZER)

PAKORA 1.50
Assorted Vegetable Fritters with Chick-Pea Flour

SAMOSA 1.50
Deep Fried Potato Pastries - Two Pieces

APPETIZER PLATTER 5.95
Samosa-Pakora-Chicken Tikka-Siekh Kabob-Papad and Kachumber Salad

"TANDOORI NAMUNE"
(OUR PRESENTATION FROM THE CLAYOVEN)

CHICKEN TANDOORI
Whole Chicken 7.95
Half Chicken 4.00

CHICKEN TIKKA 4.75
Charcoal Grilled Boneless Chicken Pieces

SIEKH KABAB *(4 pieces)* 5.25
Soft Skewed Rolls of Spiced Minced Lamb

BOTI KABAB 5.25
Spring Lamb Pieces Marinated in Spices, Yogurt, Garlic, Ginger and Roasted in the Tandoor

TANDOORI JHEENGHA 6.95
Shrimp Marinated and Toasted in Tandoor

FISH TIKKA 5.25
Succulent Pieces of Fish Marinated in Spices, Yogurt, Garlic Ginger and Roasted in the Tandoor

"MURG KI RASOI"
(CHICKEN DELIGHTS)

CHICKEN TIKKA MASALA 6.50
Boneless Chicken Pieces Cooked with our Special Sauce

CHICKEN MUGHLAI 5.50
Chicken Curry Cooked with Eggs

DAL CHICKEN 5.25
Chicken with Cream Lentil(Beans)

SAAG CHICKEN 5.50
Flavorful Combination of Spinach and Tender Chicken

CHICKEN CURRY 5.25
Chicken Cooked with Onions, Tomatoes and Freshly Ground Herbs and Spices

---

2601 West Devon • Uptown/Lincolnwood • (312) 761-8714

"GOSHT KI RASOI"
(LAMB PREPARATION)

LAMB DO PIAZA 5.50	ROGAH JOSH 5.50
Lamb Curry with Onions	Lamb Curry Prepared with Rich Spices - A Special Treat

"SAMUNDER SEY"
(FROM THE SEA)

FISH TIKKA MASALA 7.45	JHEENGHA CURRY 7.45
Succulent Pieces of Fish Cooked in our Spicy Blend of Onions, Tomatoes and Cream	Shrimp Cooked in Tomatoes, Spices, Cream

"VAISHNU BHOJAN BHANDAAR"
(VEGETARIAN SPECIALTY)

ALU GOBHI 4.75	MALAI KOFTA 4.95
Cauliflower with Potato, Tomato and Spices	Homemade Cheese Balls Cooked with Secret Sauce
MATTER PANNEER 4.75	BHARTA 4.75
Homemade Cheese Cooked with Green Peas	Mashed Eggplant with Spices

"CHAWAL KI SARGOSHI"
(RICE SPECIALTY)

LAMB BIRYANI 5.95	VEGETABLE BIRYANI 3.95
Lamb Cooked with Rice	Rice Cooked with Fresh Vegetables and Spices
CHICKEN BIRYANI 5.25	PEAS PULAO 2.50
Chicken Cooked in a Richly Flavored Rice	Fried Rice with Peas
SHRIMP BIRYANI 6.95	PLAIN RICE 2.00
Shrimp Cooked with Rice	Steamed Rice

"SAATH MEY LIJIYE'
(BREAD FROM TANDOOR)

NAAN 1.20	PARATHA 1.35
Unleaved Bread Tandoori baked	Whole Wheat Butter Layered Bread
ROTI 1.00	ALU PARATHA 1.85
Round Bread of Whole Wheat Flour	Stuffed with Potatoes

GOBHI PARATHA 1.85
Stuffed with Cauliflower (in Season)

"DESSERT"

RASMALAI .... 1.25   KULFI 1.25

Kanval Palace

Serene and fanciful, the menu at this smart-looking Indian spot misses nothing. Especially good are the vegetarian dishes and the great selection of special breads.

KANVAL PALACE

RESTAURANT

Ibteda-E-Khana (Appetizers)

Vegetable Samosa 1.50
Crisp Patties filled with Potatoes, Green Peas, Fresh Coriander Leaves and Spiced Fried in Vegetable Oil

Assorted Appetizer 5.50
Assortment of Vegetable Fritters, Seekh Kabab, Samosa, Chicken Tikka and Papadum

Masala Dosa 3.95
Crispy Creper filled with Mild Spiced Potatoes, Onions and Herbs

"Shorba" (Soups)

Mulligatawny Soup 2.50
Traditional Chicken Soup, Mildly Spiced

Lentil and Vegetable Soup 2.25
Fresh Vegetable and Lentils with Mild Spices

Jheel Ki Saugaath (Traditional Seafood)

Shrimps Curry 10.95
Shrimps Cooked with Onions and Mild Spiced

Fish Curry 8.95
Fresh Fish Cooked with Butter, Onion and Tomato Sauce

Tandoori Saugaath (Barbecue Items)

Murgh Tandoori .... Half 5.50
.... Full 9.95
Chicken Marinated in Yogurt, Lemon Juice, Garlic, Ginger and Spices

Tandoori Lobster .... Market Price
Lobster Tail Marinated in Yogurt and Special Spices

Boti Kabab 6.95
Boneless Lamb Marinated in Yogurt and Spiced

"Kanval Palace Specials"

Charga Chicken 12.95
Whole Chicken Marinated in Fresh Lemon Juice, Paprika, Deep Fried in Vegetable Oil, Garnished with Dry Mango Powder, Fresh Cilantro. Served with Salad

Sabzi Ki Thali
(Vegetarian Platter) 10.95
Combination of Three Vegetables with Soup, Peas Pullau, Raita, Papadum, Salad. Served with a Choice of Rôti or Naan and Kheer

Mughlai Thali
(Non-Vegetable Platter) 13.95
Starting with Soup Served with Tanduri Chicken, Seekh Kabab, Chicken Tikka, Fish Tikka, Lamb Curry or Murgh Makhani. Peas Pullau, Navratan Korma, Naan or Rôti, and Kheer.

Traditional Murgh Dishes (Chicken Specialties)

Murgh Curry 6.50
Chicken Cooked with Onions, and Tomato Gravy

Murgh Makhani 6.50
Tandori Boneless Chicken, Sauteed in Butter, Cooked with Onion, Tomato Sauce and Cream

Murgh Saag 6.50
Chicken cooked with Spinach and Spiced

Gosht Ki Lazat (Lamb Specials)

Karhai Gosht 7.50
Boneless Lamb Cooked with Fresh Tomatoes, Onion, Garlic and Mild Spices. Garnished with Fresh Cilantro and Ginger

Bhuna Gosht 7.50
Boneless Lamb Cooked with Tomatoes, Onion, Bell Pepper in a Spiced Gravy

Sabzi Ki Bahaar (Traditional Vegetarian Dishes)

Saag Paneer 5.50
Homemade Cheese Cubes Cooked with Spinach, Tomatoes, Onions and Spiced

Mattar Paneer 5.50
Homemade Cheese Cubes Cooked with Fresh Green Peas, Onion Gravy and Cream

"Mithai Ki Mithaas" (Indian Special Desserts)

Kheer 2.25
Special Dessert made of Rice, Milk and Sugar. Served Cold with an Assortment of Nuts

Pista Kulfi 2.95
Homemade Ice Cream Flavored with Saffron and Pistachios

Dinner: Sun - Thurs 5 - 10, Fri - Sat 5 - 11

The atmosphere of this fine restaurant has set a new standard for Indian restaurants in Chicago, and you'll find no better service anywhere. The food keeps pace with those superlatives. Tandoori chicken and tandoor-baked breads are first-rate.

appetizers

jheenga til tinka 7.95
Prawns marinated in yogurt, lemon juice, paprika, coated with sesame
seed and fried on bamboo skewer

reshmi kebab 6.95
Ground chicken, spiced with cumin, cloves, cinnamon, rolled and
cooked on a skewer in the clay oven

sabzi pakoras 4.95
Chick-pea flour coated, golden fritters from an assortment of fresh
seasonal vegetables

salads

piaz ka salat 3.95
Sliced red onions, green chili, fresh lemon juice and green mint leaves

kachoombar 4.95
Diced onions, tomatoes and cucumber tossed in a tangy lemon dressing

breads

Wholesome breads are freshly baked in our clay ovens.

nan 2.00
Leaf-shaped, whole wheat, soft yogurt bread

piaza kulcha 2.50
Flat whole wheat bread with spiced onion filling

414 North Orleans • River North • (312) 527-3999

from the klay oven

All food is prepared fresh to order. Please allow 30 minutes preparation time.

tandoori lobster . . . . market price
Lobster tail marinated in yogurt, ground black pepper, fresh lemon juice, garlic butter

jheenga bemisaal 24.95
Tiger prawns marinated in yogurt, ginger and paprika, flavored
with royal ground cumin, fresh coriander leaves, garlic butter

machchli ke tikke 17.95
Mahi-mahi fillets marinated in lemon juice, ground cumin
seeds, black pepper, and paprika

tandoori machchi 16.95
Whole trout marinated in lime juice, dried mango powder,
ground coriander and cumin seeds

tandoori murg 12.95
One half chicken marinated in yogurt and tandoori spices

murgh malai tikka 13.95
Tender cubes of boneless chicken breast marinated in garlic,
cheddar cheese, and fresh coriander leaves

sikandari champa 24.95
Rack of lamb, marinated in lemon juice, garlic, black pepper, cumin

from the karhai

*Karhai is an Indian cast iron wok. Dishes prepared in the Karhai are stir-fried and
are very low in fat and cholestrol.*

jheenga lajawab 17.95
Shrimps cooked in onions, fresh tomatoes, ginger and garlic

chooza tikka masala 16.95
Boneless cubes of chicken marinated in yogurt, lemon juice, roasted
in clay oven, sauteed in fresh tomatoes, ginger, green chili and onion

aloo jeera 5.95
New potatoes with cumin, crushed peppercorn, turmeric, all-spice and
chopped fresh coriander leaves

palek paneer 7.95
Home made cheese cubes cooked with spinach, tomatoes, onions and green chili

baingan piaz masala 7.95
Eggplant roasted in clay oven and sauteed in fresh tomatoes, onions,
green chili, ginger root and fresh coriander leaves

Dinner: Sun - Thurs 5 - 10:30, Fri - Sat 5 - 11:30

Standard India

The setting is plain, but there is solidly good Indian food here, food that has just the right flair and flavor and is truly representative of classic Indian cooking. Check out the buffet—it's a bargain.

Menu Changes Seasonally

Appetizers
(IBT-DA-E-DAWAT)

SAMOSA *(Vegetables)*	2 pcs - Golden brown fried patties filled with mild spiced potatoes and peas 1.25
ALOO TIKKI	(2pcs) Crisp patties made of mashed potatoes, filled with spiced lentils, peas, & herbs. (Highly Recommended) 1.95
VEGETABLE PAKORAS	Mixed vegetable fritters dipped into a batter of garbanzo beans 2.75

Seafood Delicacies
(SUMUNDRI SUGGAT)

SHRIMPS MASALA	Shrimps cooked with green pepper, spices and herbs in a curry sauce 8.95
FISH CURRY	A speciality of Goa, fish made with ground coconut, and an array of masterfully blended spices 7.95

Clay Oven Specialties
(TANDOORI KHAZANA)

CHICKEN TANDOORI	Chicken marinated in yogurt, lemon juice, ginger, garlic and herbs, cooked over charcoal in a clay oven Half 4.95 Full 8.95
CHICKEN TIKKA	Charcoal grilled pre-marinated boneless chicken pieces 5.95
TANDOORI MIX GRILL	(A must for every barbeque lover) Assorted tandoori delicacies served on grilled onions on a sizzler along with Nan 9.95

917 West Belmont Ave • Lincoln Park/DePaul • (312) 929-1123

Lamb Specialties

(GOSHT LAJAWAB)

LAMB VINDALOO A specialty of Goa, Lamb pieces and potatoes cooked in a thick and spicy hot curry sauce made with fresh coconut 5.95

BOTI KABAB MASALA Pre-marinated and roasted lamb pieces cooked with mild gravy and herbs 6.50

SAAG LAMB Mildly spiced lamb cooked with creamed spinach (OUR BEST) 5.95

Chicken Specialties

(MURGH-E-BENAZIR)

CHICKEN JALFRAZIE Tender pieces of chicken marinated in fresh spices and herbs and sauteed with fresh tomatoes, onions and capsicums 6.95

CHICKEN TIKKA MASALA Pre-marinated and roasted chicken pieces cooked in mild gravy and herbs 6.95

Rice Specialties

(TARIF-E-BIRYANI)

(We only use the best of
"BASMATI RICE" in each and every rice dish)

LAMB BIRYANI Fried rice flavored with saffron, and cooked with tender pieces of lamb, nuts, eggs and fresh herbs 5.95

CHICKEN BIRYANI Fried rice flavored with tender pieces of boneless chicken, sauteed with nuts, eggs, and onions along with exotic spices and herbs 5.95

SHRIMPS BIRYANI Fried rice flavored with saffron, and sauteed with shrimps, nuts, egg and green onions along with special herbs 8.95

Vegetable Specialties

(SOGGAT-E-CHAMAN)

MUTTER PANEER Famous Punjabi dish of homemade cheese and peas 4.50

ALOO GOBI MASALA Cauliflower and potatoes cooked with mild spices and herbs 4.50

BENGAN BHARTHA Baked eggplant mashed and cooked with onion, tomatoes and herbs 4.50

NAVRATTAN CURRY Farm fresh mixed vegetables cooked exclusively in a cream base, mildly spiced curry sauce 4.50

SAG PANEER Homemade cheese cooked with spiced creamed spinach 4.50

Dinner: Sun - Thurs 5 - 10, Fri - Sat 5 - 11

Avanzare

It's not Milan, but if this restaurant were plunked down near La Scala it would fit right in. Stylish Italian dishes mix with more traditional Italian fare and are very pleasing. Service is friendly and aware of how the kitchen prepares various dishes. Located just off Michigan Avenue, in the heart of the city, the crowd is always hip and upbeat.

Menu Changes Seasonally

ANTIPASTI
♥ **Cappesante En Cartoccio**
(fresh sea scallops baked in foil with capellini, vegetable saffron broth) .... $ 6.75

Insalata Di Gamberetti E Asparagi
(baby shrimp, asparagus, red oak leaf, enoki mushrooms, lemon-basil dressing) .... $ 6.75

Gamberi Alla Griglia
(grilled shrimp wrapped with prosciutto, melon, sambuca) $7.50

Polenta Al Forno Con Formaggio Di Capra
(baked polenta, Italian sausage, goat cheese and tomato sauce) ...... $ 6.75

Risotto Del Giorno
(Arborio rice, preparation varies daily) .... Market Price

ZUPPE
Zuppe Alla Fantasia Del Cuoco
(soups according to the chef's fancy) .... $ 3.75

INSALATE
♥ **Insalata Mista Della Casa**
(small salad of mixed greens, tomato, olives)............................ $ 3.75

Insalata Romagnola
(romaine, radicchio, cucumbers, plum tomato, white anchovy, romano, garlic croutons).. $4.75

Insalata Caprino
(goat cheese marinated with garlic, basil and red chiles, roasted peppers, baby frisee, olive oil) .... $ 5.25

PASTE
Agnolotti Verdi Ai Tre Formaggi
(spinach pasta filled with ricotta, parmigiano, romano cheeses, Alfredo sauce) .... $ 7.25/$10.75

♥ **Farfalle Con Pollo E Limone**
(bowtie pasta, grilled chicken, broccoli, garlic, lemon-black pepper broth) .... $7.25/$10.75

---

161 East Huron • Gold Coast • (312) 337-8056

Tortelloni Di Pollo Affumicato
(smoked chicken filled pasta, spinach, grilled chicken,
provolone sauce) .... $ 7.75/$11.25

Cavatappi Sorrentini
(corkscrew pasta, eggplant, mozzarella, tomato basil sauce) .. $6.75/$10.25

Ravioli Della Casa
(homemade ravioli, preparation varies daily) .... $ 7.75/$11.25

Capellini Con Astice E Zafferano
(angel hair pasta, lobster, saffron,
orange-fennel butter sauce) .... $11.75/$15.25

Spaghettini Con Aglio Arrostito
(thin spaghetti, roasted garlic, basil, sun dried tomatoes,
parmigiano, olive oil) .... $ 6.75/$10.25

Lasagnetti Con Funghi E Prosciutto
(wide ribbon pasta, prosciutto di Parma, Porcini mushrooms,
butter, parmigiano).. $ 11.25/$14.75

PIETANZE   ### ♥ Grigliata Di Pollo Con Pomodori Secchi
(grilled breast of chicken, oven dried tomatoes, arugula,
potatoes, rosemary broth) $13.25

Anatra Al Porto
(sauteed duck breast, red cabbage, fennel, pancetta,
port wine sauce) $18.75

Costolette Di Abbacchio Con Carciofi
(roasted baby lamb chops with garlic and herbs,
artichokes, potatoes, natural juices) $22.25

Vitello Alla Saltimbocca
(sautéed scaloppine of veal with prosciutto and sage,
white polenta, marsala wine).. $18.25

Costoletta Di Vitello Suprema
(grilled prime veal chop, roasted potatoes, seasonal vegetables) $23.50

Tonno Al Tramanto
(grilled tuna marinated in soy and Cinzano, gnocchi,
enoki mushrooms, prezzemolo sauce).................................... $16.75

Filetto Di Bue Tartufati
(grilled filet of beef, seasonal mushrooms, spinach,
white truffle butter) $23.75

♥ *These items are prepared from recipes that meet the fat and*
cholesterol guidelines of the American Heart Association of
Metropolitan Chicago for Healthy Adults

Storefront and bare bones, but very comfortable. The Italian food is very well made, and the service is perky. Many enjoy lunch, as the place isn't as crowded.

The Baba Luci

ITALIAN EATERY

Menu Changes Weekly

Zuppa

Pasta E Fagiolo   2.50
    pasta, beans, prosciutto, tomato broth

Antipasti

Roasted Goat Cheese   2.50
    with spicy marinara & garlic bread

Calamari, grilled & fried   2.75
    with olive oil & fresh lemon

Italian Rope Sausage (mild)   2.75
    grilled with melrose peppers

Grilled Shrimp   3.50
    with artichoke hearts, prosciutto & fresh herbs

Insalata

Panzanella Salad   5.00
    tomatoes, red onions, cucumbers, basil leaves, black olives, frezelle

Fresh Spinach Salad   5.75
    pinenuts, mushrooms, tomatoes, egg, pancetta, honey mustard dressing

Calamari & Scungilli Salad   6.25
    marinated with lemon, olive oil, garlic & Italian spices

Dinner Salad   2.00
    of fresh greens with vinaigrette dressing

Pasta

Penne alla Crodolia   6.00
fresh basil, oregano, plum tomatoes, imported ricotta & pecorino cheese

Tricolor Rotini   6.50
with 4 cheeses; pecornio, gorgonzola, fontina, parmesan

Angel Hair Pasta Arrabiata   6.75
with prosciutto, red hot chili peppers & marinara

Tortellini alla pesto   6.75
veal stuffed pasta, fresh basil, pine nuts, pecorino cheese

Linguini Primavera   6.50
tomatoes, carrots, red peppers, olives, spinach, mushrooms, garlic

Spaghetti ala Puttanesta   6.75
imported red & black olives, capers, anchovies & eggplant

Linguini with grilled chicken   6.75
with pesto and sun-dried tomatoes

Specialita' della Cana

Chicken Vesuvio   7.00
garlic, white wine, lemon, oregano

Sicilian Steak Milanese   7.75
fresh herbs breaded, hot giardinera garlic, olive oil & grilled tomatoes

Sausage & Chicken Scarpetti 7.00
grilled with sweet peppers, garlic, rosemary, potatoes

Oven Roasted Orange Roughy 6.95
with fresh herbs in a light lemon butter sauce

Veal Amanti   8.50
sauteed veal, marsella wine peppers, mushrooms, carrots, zucchini

All of the above served with fresh vegetables & pasta or risotto

Desserts

homemade cheesecake	3.00
assorted Italian cookies	2.00
cannoli...whipped ricotta & chocolate chip pistachios	3.00
ciocolato, chocolate, piu - ciacolato	3.25

Bella Vista

It's in a converted bank building, but the atmosphere is definitely Italian opera house. Beautiful hand-painted frescoes, expensive tile work and two wood-burning pizza ovens are only half the decor story. And the upscale Italian creations are a notch above the ordinary.

Menu Changes Weekly

Appetizers

Crisp parmesan polenta with wood roasted portobello mushrooms, carmelized pearl onions and rosemary 5.75

Grilled marinated asparagus with herbed goat cheese and basil cured tomato 5.95

Beef carpaccio with oak-roasted portobello mushrooms, arugula salad & warm parmesan bread 6.50

Grilled marinated shrimp, artichoke risotto, roast garlic and basil 6.95

Salads

Caesar - crisp romaine lettuce with Reggiano Parmesan croutons, fresh parmesan cheese and Caesar dressing 5.25

Gorgonzola salad with endive, watercress, pears and peppered pecans tossed in a red wine vinaigrette 5.50

Wood-fired Pizzas

Homemade fennel sausage with grilled onions, wild mushrooms, roasted tomato and mozzarella 7.50

Roasted baby artichokes, grilled portobello mushrooms, mixed peppers, smoked mozzarella 6.95

Fresh basil pesto, tomatoes, pine nuts and fresh mozzarella 6.95

1001 West Belmont Ave • Lincoln Park/DePaul • (312) 404-0111

Pastas

Risotto Del Giorno 8.50

Veal agnolottis with spinach, proscuitto, roasted shallots, in a fresh oregano &
veal broth   8.50/10.95

Black pepper linguini with shiitake & portobello mushrooms, baby artichokes & a
mushroom-rosemary broth 7.25/10.50

Angel hair pasta with sauteed chicken, whole roasted garlic, green beans, tomato,
pancetta and basil   7.95/11.95

* Penne pasta with grilled asparagus, roasted tomatoes and arugula in a creamy
tomato sauce   6.75/9.25

*Cavatappi noodles in a light alfredo sauce with fresh spinach and
grilled chicken 7.95/11.50

Pasta with shrimp, clams, mussels and calamari with zucchini and roasted
tomatoes served in a saffron-tomato broth   14.95

*Fresh fettuccini in a creamy parmesan alfredo sauce 6.50/8.75

Angel hair pasta with traditional marinara sauce 6.25/8.50

*From our wood burning ovens

Rotisseries, Pan Roasts &Grills

Pan-roasted herbed red snapper with potato gnocchi, corn, roasted
peppers and tomato 15.95

Grilled salmon served with crisp angel hair pasta and braised artichokes in a
tomato vinaigrette 14.95

Pan-roasted halibut with fava beans, grilled asparagus, pearl onions and
soft polenta 15.50

Spit roasted chicken with eggplant-goat cheese cannellonis and
herbed cannalini beans 13.50

Spit roasted loin of pork served with garlic whipped potatoes, mixed peppers and
escarole 12.95

Grilled tenderloin of beef with a potato-parmesan torte and
wild mushroom-onion ragout 16.95

Bice Ristorante

A real Milanese transplant (the first Bice was in Milan), there is nothing shy about this place. The beautiful people love to congregate here, and amid the sleek decor they pounce on the perfectly prepared pasta creations, veal that is excellent and desserts that can be devastatingly good.

Menu Changes Daily

ANTIPASTI

CARPACCIO DI CARNE CON SALSA MOSTARDA E CAPPERI
Beef carpaccio with a mustard sauce and capers   11.--
BRODETTO D'ARAGOSTA CON CARCIOFINI
Lobster in it's own juice with baby artichokes   15.--
PROSCIUTTO DI PARMA E MELONE
Imported Parma prosciutto with melon   11.--

GUAZZETTO DI FRUTTI DI MARE
Mixed seafood in a spicy tomato and basil broth   12.--

INSALATA DI LATTUGHINE NANE ALL'ACETO BALSAMICO
Mixed baby greens with a balsamic vinaigrette   6.--
INSALATA DI CUORI DI ROMANA DEI CESARI
Hearts of romaine lettuce with a cesar dressing   6.--
INSALATA TRICOLORE CON SCAGLIE DI PARMIGIANO
Belgian endive, radicchio and arrugola with
shaved parmesan   7.--
INSALATA RUGANTINO CON MOZZARELLA FRESCA
Onions, tomatoes and cucumber salad with oregano,
croutons and fresh mozzarella   8.--

CIGARS AND PIPES ARE WELCOME AT THE BAR
ITALIAN MINERAL WATER 4.50 PER BOTTLE

PRIMI PIATTI

*FETTUCCINE CON PROSCIUTTO PISELLI E CREMA
Fettuccine with prosciutto, peas and cream   15.--
*MACCHERONI AL PETTINE CON GRANCEOLA E PEPERONI ARROSTITI
Homemade macaroni with lump crabmeat and roasted
peppers   17.--
*TORTELLONI DI MAGRO AL BURRO E SALVIA
Ricotta and spinach filled tortelloni with butter
and sage   15.--
*GNOCCHETTI DI PATATE AL PESTO E MASCARPONE
Potato gnocchi with pesto and mascarpone cheese   15.--
*RAVIOLI DELLA MASSAIA AI FUNGHI MISTI
Veal filled ravioli with mixed wild mushrooms   17.--
*TAGLIOLINI CON GAMBERI,ASPARAGI E POMODORO FRESCO
Tagliolini with shrimp, asparagus and tomatoes   17.--
PENNE ALL'ARRABBIATA
Penne with a spicy tomato sauce   13.--
RISOTTO CON GAMBERI E CHAMPAGNE
Risotto with shrimp and champagne   17.--
RISOTTO ALLA CREMA DI TARTUFO
Risotto with cream of white truffles   17.--
TORTELLONI IN BRODO DI CAPPONE
Capon tortelloni in its own broth   6.--
PASTA E FAGIOLI ALLA VENETA
Venetian pasta and beans soup   6.--

* WE MAKE OUR FRESH PASTA DAILY

PIATTI DEL GIORNO

SELLA DI CAPRIOLO ARROSTO CON SALSA AL GINEPRO
Roasted venison saddle with a juniper berry sauce   23.--
PETTO DI FAGIANO IN CASSERUOLA CON PORCINI E VERZA
Breast of pheasant in casserole with Porcini and
cabbage   22.--
BRACIOLA DI VITELLO PROFUMATA ALLA SALVIA,
CON FUNGHI E PEPERONI   Roasted veal chop with sage,
mushrooms and mixed peppers   22.--
FILETTO DI BUE AL RUBESCO
Filet of beef with a Rubesco wine sauce   21.--
COSTOLETTA DI VITELLO ALLA MILANESE
Classic breaded veal chop, pounded thin
Milanese style   21.--
TAGLIATA DI BUE CON INSALATINA DI RUCOLA
Grilled sliced New York steak over arrugola salad   20.--

Dinner: Mon - Thurs 5:30 - 10:30, Fri - Sat 5:30 - 11:30, Sun 5:30 - 10:30

Bruna's Ristorante

Located in Chicago's other "Little Italy," there is no mistaking what the food is all about here; it's Old World Italian. The no-frills atmosphere and no-nonsense service add even more authenticity to the scene.

Appetizers

ANTIPASTO ITALIANO
6.95

PROSCIUTTO E MELONE
6.95

ESCARGOT
5.95

BAKED CLAMS
5.95

FRIED CALAMARI
7.95

FRIED ZUCCHINI
4.95

Soups

MINESTRONE
1.95

STRACCIATELLA
1.95

Salads

FRESH MOZZARELLA & TOMATO
6.95

MIXED SALAD
2.95

INSALATA TRE COLORI
Endive, Radicchio, and Romaine
with Pignoli Nuts and Mushrooms
4.95

Meats
(We use only Provimi Veal)

CHICKEN VESUVIO
12.95

CHICKEN SALTIMBOCCA
13.95

BROILED NEW YORK STRIP
STEAK
19.95

BRUNA'S VEAL SCALOPPINE
16.95

VEAL MARSALA
16.95

VEAL SALTIMBOCCA ALLA
ROMANO
17.95

2424 South Oakley Ave • City South • (312) 254-5550

A la Carte Pasta

"No man is lonely while eating spaghetti - it requires too much attention."
—Christopher Morley

PENNE ALLA BOLOGNESE
With Meat Sauce
8.95

PENNE ALL' AMATRICIANA
Tomato Sauce with Pancetta
8.95

SPAGHETTI ALLA BOLOGNESE
With Meat Sauce
8.95

CAPELLINI AL POMODORO
7.95

SPAGHETTI AL POMODORO
With Tomato Sauce
7.95

SPAGHETTI ALLA CARBONARA
With Pancetta and Egg
8.95

**LINGUINE PESTO ALLA
GENOVESE**
Basil and Pine Nut Sauce
8.95

Selections of the Chef

PENNE ALLA PUTTANESCA
Spicy Tomato Sauce
with Onions
and Black Olives
8.95

LUCIANO'S FUSILLI
Cork Screw Noodles with Tomato
Cream Sauce and Mushrooms
8.95

PAGLIA E FIENO
White and Green Noodles with
Mushrooms and Peas
in a Cream Sauce
8.95

PORCINI RAVIOLI
Mushroom-Filled in Light
Cream Sauce
9.95

Seafood

SHRIMP VESUVIO
16.95

SHRIMP FRA DIAVOLA
16.95

FISH OF THE DAY
Market Price

Dessert

SPUMONE
2.95

TIRAMI-SU
4.25

CAPUCCINO ICE CREAM
3.95

VANILLA ICE CREAM
2.95

Dinner: Mon - Thurs 3 - 10, Fri - Sat 3 - 11, Sun 1:30 - 10

Cafe Angelo

This is one of the most authentic Italian restaurants in Chicago. The food always gets the personal blessing of owner Angelo Nicelli, and with his name on the door you can bet there will be few mistakes. Pleasant and comfortable surroundings, a very complete wine selection and attractive prices make this place a favorite of many Chicagoans.

CAFÉ Angelo

MENU CHANGES SEASONALLY

Antipasti e Spuntini

Grigliata Di Pesce ☀️   7.25
GRILLED SHRIMP, SCALLOPS, CALAMARI AND BABY OCTOPUS AL SALMORILLIO (ITEMS MAY BE ORDERED INDIVIDUALLY)

Involtini Di Melanzane   4.95
EGGPLANT SLICES GRILLED AND FILLED TRE FORMAGGI

Antipasto Fantasia   7.00
OUR MOST POPULAR VARIETY OF HOT APPETIZERS

Antipasto Misto   6.50
IMPORTED CURED MEATS, CHEESES, ROASTED PEPPERS, CAPUNATA AND OTHER ITALIAN SAVORIES

Funghi Alla Griglia ☀️   5.50
GIANT PORTOBELLO MUSHROOMS GRILLED WITH OLIVE OIL AND FRESH HERBS

Bruschetta ☀️   2.95
GRILLED BREAD WITH GARLIC AND OLIVE OIL OR TOPPED WITH GARLIC AND CHOPPED TOMATOES

Paste Regionali

Penne Con Carciofi Fricassea ☀️ ★   11.00
CHEF ANGELO'S NATIONAL AWARD WINNING LOW CALORIE, LOW FAT SAUCE WITH FRESH ARTICHOKES AND SUN DRIED TOMATOES

Ravioli di Mama   10.25
FILLED WITH RICOTTA AND SPINACH, TOSSED WITH YOUR CHOICE OF SAGE BUTTER, TOMATO OR PESTO SAUCE

Lasagna Casalinga ★   9.75
HOMEMADE EGG PASTA LAYERED WITH THREE CHEESES, GROUND BEEF AND EGGPLANT BAKED WITH BOLOGNESE MEAT SAUCE

Spaghetti Il Giardino ☀️   10.75
SERVED WITH FRESH GARDEN VEGETABLES AND OLIVE OIL

Linguine Alla Vongole ☀️   11.95
WITH FRESH CLAMS, GARLIC AND OLIVE OIL

Bucatini Alla Matriciana   10.95
TUBE SPAGHETTI WITH PANCETTA AND ONIONS IN A FRESH TOMATO SAUCE WITH BASIL

Combinazone dello Angelo   12.95
CHEF ANGELO'S CHOICE OF THREE PASTAS

---

225 North Wabash • Downtown/Loop • (312) 332-3370

Frutti di Mare

Salmone Dello Chef — 16.50
FRESH SCOTCH SALMON, CHEF'S WHIM

Griglitata di Pesce Misto ☀ — 15.95
CHARGRILLED SHRIMP, SCALLOPS, TINY OCTOPUS,
CALAMARI AND TROUT WITH BALSAMIC VINEGAR, OLIVE
OIL AND FRESH HERBS

Trotta ☀ ★ — 13.50
WHOLE FRESH RAINBOW TROUT SIMPLY GRILLED

Gamberi Ammudicati — 16.50
LARGE SHRIMP BAKED WITH BREAD CRUMBS, GARLIC,
OLIVE OIL AND FRESH HERBS

Cioppino ☀ — 17.75
A ZUPPA - STEW OF SEAFOOD IN A TOMATO FISH STOCK
INCLUDING SHRIMP, CONCH, CALAMARI, OCTOPUS AND
MAHI - MAHI OVER LINGUINE

Arragosta Porto Vecchio — 17.95
WHOLE 1¼ LB. LOBSTER TAKEN OUT OF THE SHELL
AND PRESENTED OVER LINGUINE IN A CREAMY
LOBSTER TOMATO TINTED SAUCE

Secondi

Pollo Sorrentino — 12.75
CHICKEN BREAST LAYERED WITH EGGPLANT,
MOZZARELLA DI LATTE AND PROSCIUTTO SERVED
WITH ORANGE SAUCE

Petti di Polo Empolese ☀ ★ — 12.75
GRILLED SKINLESS BREAST OF CHICKEN WITH
ARTICHOKES, SUN DRIED TOMATOES AND
BLACK OLIVES

Filetto di Maiale al Pepe Verde ★ — 13.50
GRILLED PORK TENDERLOIN WITH GREEN
PEPPERCORN SAUCE DIAVOLO

Filetto di Manzo Gorgonzola ★ — 15.50
TWO MEDALLIONS OF BEEF TENDERLOIN GRILLED
WITH GORGONZOLA BRANDY SAUCE

Filetto di Manzo — 17.75
CENTER CUT BEEF FILET CHARGRILLED

Costatini di Agnelo — 18.95
RACK OF LAMB TRIMMED, WITH
ROSEMARY WINE SAUCE

Salsiccia Luganega Rustica ★ — 12.95
OUR ACCLAIMED HOMEMADE SAUSAGE SERVED WITH
SAUTEED GREENS, PEPPERS AND POTATOES

Scaloppine Al Piacere — 16.50
VEAL SCALLOPS WITH YOUR CHOICE OF PORCINI MUSHROOM,
MARSALA WINE OR PICANTE LEMON SAUCE

Costata di Vitello Al Ferri — 23.50
LARGE THICK VEAL CHOP TRIMMED, SERVED WITH
POLENTA AND ARTICHOKES

Bistecca Al Ferri — 19.50
SELECT TOP QUALITY CENTER CUT N.Y. STRIP STEAK
CHARGRILLED, WITH BORDELAISE SAUCE OR CRACKED BLACK
PEPPERCORNS

★ **Speciale prima del Teatro** (Before Theatre speciale 4:30 TO 6:30 PM) — 17.95
BUON APPETITO! START WITH OUR GRAND ANTIPASTO TABLE (A CULINARY TOUR OF ITALY)
SELECT ONE OF THE ★ ENTREES SERVED WITH ZUPPA DEL GIORNO OR
INSALATA MISTA, AND YOUR CHOICE OF VANILLA GELATO OR CASSATTA CAKE.

🌀 CUCINA DEL SOLE. CUT CALORIES AND CHOLESTEROL WITH OUR MEDITERRANEAN CUISINE.
COOKED WITH ONLY OLIVE OIL AND FRESH HERBS. DELIZIOSO!

Dinner: 7 Days a Week 5 - 10

267

Cafe Spiaggia

The windows in this casual and likable cafe overlook Michigan Avenue, but the design of the room makes it a trattoria hideaway serving first-rate pizza, pasta and salads.

ZUPPE

ZUPPA DEL GIORNO
Soup of the day $3.50

PASTA E FAGIOLI
Pasta and bean soup $3.50

ANTIPASTI

CALAMARI ALLA GRIGLIA
Tender grilled calamari and potatoes with
olive oil and lemon juice $4.95

POLLO AL PESTO
Chicken salad with pesto, raisins,
and pine nuts $5.50

CALAMARI ALLA GRIGLIA
Tender grilled calamari and potatoes with
olive oil and lemon juice $4.95

BRUSCHETTA
Grilled Italian bread with garlic and olive oil,
topped with a tomato-basil salad $4.50

ANTIPASTI DELL'ORTO
Assorted marinated vegetable antipasti.
Today's selection $4.95/8.95

INSALATE

INSALATA ALLA CAPRESE
Vine-ripened tomatoes with fresh
mozzarella and basil $4.95

INSALATA DI FUNGHI, RUCOLA E PARMIGIANO
Delicate, nutty arugula with sliced mushrooms,
Parmesan shavings, and tangy lemon dressing
$5.50

INSALATA ALLA CICERONE
Romaine lettuce with light anchovy-garlic
dressing $4.50

VERDURE CON MOZZARELLA
Grilled seasonal vegetables with fresh
mozzarella $5.95/10.95

INSALATA CON FORMAGGIO DI CAPRA
Radicchio and arugula salad with baked
goat cheese $4.95/8.95

---

980 North Michigan Ave, Second Level • Near North/Gold Coast • (312) 280-2764

PIZZE

SENZA FORMAGGI
Cheeseless pizza with grilled zucchini, garlic, sun-dried tomatoes, and a spicy chili oil

QUATTRO FORMAGGI
Four-cheese pizza with sun-dried tomatoes

MARGHERITA
Tomatoes, basil, and provolone

SALSICCIA D'ANITRA
Duck sausage, sage, and goat cheese

BOSCAIOLA
Wild mushrooms, prosciutto, and provolone

CALAMARI ALL'ARRABBIATA
Spicy calamari, tomatoes, black olives, capers, garlic, basil, provolone, and Romano

$8.95

FARINACE

SPAGHETTINI AL CARTOCCIO
Spaghettini and scallops, clams, mussels, and calamari baked in parchment sack with white wine and herbs $11.95

TAGLIATELLE CON RAGU VERO BOLOGNESE
Flat noodles with authentic Bolognese sauce of beef, prosciutto, and sausage meat $9.95

RISO CON ZUCCHINE, POMODORO E BASILICO
Warm arborio rice with zucchini, tomato, and basil $7.50

GNOCCHI CON FUNGHI MISTI
Potato dumplings with a rich forest mushroom ragu $9.50

RAVIOLETTI DI MAGRO GRATINATI
Ravioli filled with ricotta and parsley, browned in a creamy sage sauce $10.50

BAVETTE CON COZZE E PORRI AL PREZZEMOLO
Linguini and fresh mussels with light sauce of leeks, parsley, and olive oil $10.95

PIATTI PRINCIPALI

SALTIMBOCCA DI POLLO
Boneless chicken breast, sage, prosciutto, white wine, and vegetables $11.95

OSSO BUCO
Braised veal shank, lemon zest, and vegetables $13.95

SALMONE AL FORNO
Wood-roasted salmon with tomato and scallion salad $16.95

SALSICCE PEPERONATA
Plump sausages with mushrooms, onions, bell peppers, and wine sauce $9.95

POLLO AL MATTONE
Cornish hen roasted golden brown under a brick in natural juices; rosemary potatoes $10.95

Dinner: Mon - Thurs 5:30 - 10, Fri - Sat 5:30 - 11, Sun 4 - 9

Capri Ristorante

It's expanded three times since I first started going here, but in no way has the quality of the food suffered. Some very interesting daily specials along with my favorite dish, linguine with clam sauce, keep me coming back for more.

Menu Changes Seasonally

ANTIPASTI

Calamari Fritti	6.25
baby fried squid	
Insalata Di Mare	8.95
assorted cold seafood salad	
Cozze Alla Capri	8.95
delicately steamed California mussels in red or white sauce	
Vongole Alla Capri	9.95
tender steamed baby clams in red or white sauce	
Calamari Alla Griglia	7.95
grilled baby calamari	
Pulppo Alla Griglia	8.95
grilled baby octopus	
Zucchini Fritti	4.50
fried zucchini	
Funghi Fritti	4.50
fried mushrooms	

VERDURA

Escorola Sauteeda	2.95
sauteed in olive oil and garlic	
Spinach Sauteeda	2.95
sauteed in olive oil and garlic	
Spinach Ala Diavolo	2.95
cold spinach with lemon	

SPECIALITA DI CASA

Piato Di Marri	13.95
shrimp, vongil squid, mussels & broccoli over linguini with choice of white or red sauce	
Linguini Con Broccoli	8.50
fresh broccoli with oil and garlic	
Cavatelli Con Broccoli	9.95
homemade small dumplings with fresh broccoli sauce	
Fettucini Alfredo Con Broccoli	10.50
our tasty cream sauce with broccoli added	
Linguini e Gamberi Ala Marinara	11.25
fresh baby shrimp in a light marinara sauce	
Linguini Con Gamberi e Broccoli	11.95
baby shrimp and tender broccoli	
Linguini Con Cozze	9.95
delicious fresh mussels served with red or white sauce	
Linguini Con Calamari	9.50
tender baby squid in red or white sauce	
Linguini Con Scallopi	11.75
fresh whole scallops in a fresh red sauce	

3126 South Oak Park Ave • Berwyn • (708) 484-6313

PASTA DI CASA

Cappolini	7.25
Ravioli (Meat or Cheese)	8.25
tortellini romano	
Tortellini Paesano	9.95
mushroom, peas & prosciutto	
in a rich Alfredo sauce	
Baked Lasagna	8.50
Fettucini Primavera	9.25
fresh vegetables Alfredo	
Pasta Carbonara	9.50
Rigatoni Arrabiato	10.00
spicy sauce with prosciutto	
Rigatoni Basilico	9.25
lightly sauteed fresh tomatoes and basil	
Gnocchi Quattro Formaggi	9.95
served with four cheese sauce	

"OUR FAVORITE"
Chosen by Pat Bruno — Chicago Sun Times

Linguine Con Vongole	11.00
served with tender whole vongole	
in white or red sauce	
Mellinzana Parmigiana	7.25
eggplant layered with marinara sauce	
and fresh mozzarella	
Pollo Ala Vesuvio	9.95
half chicken sauteed with mushrooms,	
onions and just the right seasoning,	
served with roasted potatoes	

POLLO

Pollo Calibrizala	9.50
delicious baked half of chicken	
sauteed with pepper, onions and olives,	
served with oven roasted potatoes	
Petti Di Pollo Ala Lemone	10.95
tasty breast of chicken	
with a delicate lemon sauce	
Petti Di Polla Pompei (Con Patate)	11.25
prepared with spinach,	
red and yellow marinated peppers	

PESCE DI MARE

Scampi De Cozzenzia	12.25
large shrimp, artichoke hearts	
& mushrooms sauteed in oil, garlic	
and white wine served over pasta	
Scampi Basilico	12.95
large shrimp, fresh tomatoes	
and basil over pasta	
Linguine Scampi Diavola	11.95
large shrimp, olive oil, crushed	
hot peppers and marinara sauce	
Zuppa Di Mari	21.50
seafood in a rich, red sauce	
Shrimp Florentina	12.25
shrimp with large artichoke	
hearts in Alfredo sauce over	
fresh fettucini	
Stuffed Calamari	10.95
two tender squid,	
stuffed and baked to perfection	

VITELLO

Vitello Fresco Ala Parmigiana	13.95
veal with tomato sauce	
and fresh mozzarella cheese	
Vitello Limone	13.25
veal in a light lemon sauce	
Vitello Ala Marsala	14.95
sauteed mushrooms in a	
light marsala wine	
Vitello San Giuseppe	16.95
layered and baked with eggplant	
and homemade mozzarella	
Vitello Vesuvio Con Patate	15.95
sauteed with mushrooms and onions	
in a light white wine sauce	
Vitello Pepprinata Con Patate	15.95
veal sauteed with roasted red peppers,	
olive oil and garlic	
Vitello Pompei Con Patate	14.50
prepared with spinach and red peppers	

Owner Joe Carlucci is ever watchful of the goings-on in his eponymous house of pasta and other good food. The atmosphere is very Italian and very eater-friendly, and that goes double for the food. When in season, the outdoor garden will transport you to the hills of Tuscany.

CARLUCCI

Menu Changes Seasonally

ANTIPASTI

Arlecchino vegetariano
Warm layers of spinach, fontina cheese, and roasted red peppers; tomato sauce $6.25

Mozzarella farcita
Home-made mozzarella pinwheels filled with ricotta, prosciutto, toasted pinenuts, arugula $5.95

Funghi alla griglia
Charcoal-grilled giant portobello mushroom, fresh rosemary, garlic, extra-virgin olive oil $6.95

Calamari ripièni
Grilled calamari stuffed with spinach and breadcrumbs, served on a bed of radicchio and spicy fresh tomato $5.95

Scampi grigliati alla cruda di pomodoro
Grilled prawns with garlic crostino and fresh tomato $7.95

Carpaccio montanaro
Thin sliced beef with parmesan, cremini mushrooms, truffle oil; served warm $7.50

PIZZE

Focaccia al gorgonzola
Dome shaped pizza with gorgonzola cheese, pinenuts, basil, and onions $7.95

Pizza quattro stagioni
Yellow tomato, radicchio, grilled zucchini, mushrooms, and smoked mozzarella $7.75

Pizza caprina
Grilled eggplant, goat cheese, tomato, virgin olive oil $7.75

Pizza margherita
Tomato, basil, homemade mozzarella $6.95

2215 North Halsted • Lincoln Park/DePaul • (312) 281-1220

272

INSALATE

Insalata tonnara
Marinated tuna, radicchio, arugula, endive, mustard-oil vinaigrette $5.95

Mista verde
Mixed green salad with balsamic vinegar and extra-virgin olive oil $4.25

Quattro colori
Radicchio, arugula, endive, yellow tomatoes, walnuts, lemon oil,
and gorgonzola cheese $5.50

PASTE

Gnocchetti di patate al pomodoro e basilico
Potato dumpling with basil and tomato sauce $11.75

Tagliatelle nere con gamberi
Black pasta, shrimp, spicy tomato sauce $12.95

Bucosilli alla boscaiola
Long curly pasta, artichoke, pancetta, shiitake mushrooms, and cream $11.50

Tortelloni di vitello con salsa di finocchio
Veal stuffed tortelloni with rosemary-fennel sauce $12.25

Mafaldine con funghi selvatici
Wavy pasta, porcini and cremini mushrooms, garlic $12.95

CARNE, PESCE E POLLAME

Pollo alla Pitigliano
Grilled half chicken with kalamata olives, bell pepper, sage and lemon $13.95

Costolette di maiale alla brace
Charcoal grilled porkchops, sautéed zucchini, tomato, and thyme $14.25

Spiedini di pesce
Skewer of grilled prawns, scallops, and calamari; sautéed escarole,
lemon-mint sauce $15.95

Petto di anatra alla griglia
Grilled duck breast, radicchio, black-peppercorn sauce $14.95

Paillard di vitello ai ferri
Grilled veal scaloppini with zucchini, tomatoes, mushrooms, Chianti sauce $16.95

Involtini di agnello alle olive nere
Rolled lamb stuffed with goat cheese, mint, black-olive sauce $16.50

Dinner: Sun - Thurs 5:30 -10:30, Fri - Sat 5:30 - 11:30

Club Lago

From another era, this bar-cum-restaurant is just great—real Chicago stuff. The customers, many of whom work in the neighborhood, stop by for Italian food which is very basic, very good, and very inexpensive.

Menu Changes Daily
The full "cucina Toscana" is ready for you!!

APPETIZERS*

Antipasto	6.25
Baked Clams	4.75
Fried Calamari	5.50
Fried Zucchini & Mushrooms	4.15
Pizza Bread	3.95
Prosciutto & Melon	6.60
Shrimp Cocktail	4.70

SOUPS

Barley	1.40
Clam Chowder	1.40
Chicken Broth	1.40
Minestrone*	1.40
Onion	1.40
Pea	1.40
Egg Drop	1.40

SANDWICHES*

American Cheese	3.15
Bacon, Lettuce & Tomato	3.85
Club House	5.00
Fontina Cheese	3.55
Grilled Ham & Cheese	4.15
Ham	4.00
Italian Salami	4.75

SALADS*

Dante	6.50
Lago	6.50
Executive	6.50
Marinated Calamari	6.50

PASTAS

Fettuccine - Alfredo	6.55
Fettuccine - Caruso	6.55
Green Noodles al Forna	6.10
Linguine*	
Mostaccioli*	
Spaghetti*	
Meat Sauce	5.60
Meat Balls	6.45
Sausages	6.45
Tomato Sauce	5.60
Meat & Mushroom	6.45
Clam Sauce	7.50
Marinara	5.60
Carbonara	7.50
Lasagna	6.60
Manicotti	6.60
Shells - Baked	6.70
Tortellini	6.65
Cannelloni	7.50

OMELETTES

Cheese	5.15
Denver	5.15
Ham	5.15
Mushroom	5.15
Sausage	5.15
Shrimp	6.20

VEGETABLES

Egg Plant Parmigiana	6.50
Zucchini	6.50

BEEF

Bar-B-Q Ribs	6.70
Brochette	7.95
Braciole	6.60
Calves Liver	6.50
Corned	6.45
Meat Loaf	6.45
Pot Roast	6.70
Pepper Steak	6.45
Roast - Plate*	6.70
Stew	6.70
Steak - Butt*	13.50
Steak - Sirloin*	16.00
Steak - Chopped*	6.45
Tenderloin Tips	7.00

CHICKEN

Champaigne	7.00
Meuniere	9.25
Parmigiana	6.70
Roast	6.70
Tetrazzini	6.70
Wine Sauce	6.70
Vesuvio	9.25
Cacciatore	10.25
Marsala	6.70
Bolognese	7.25

PORK

Chop	6.50
Roast	6.50
Sausage & Pepper	6.45
Shank	6.35
Smoked Butt	6.40
Thuringer	6.35

VEAL

Cacciatore	8.50
Cordon Bleu	9.00
Cutlet	8.50
Limone	8.50
Marsala	8.50
Parmigiana	8.50
Piccante	8.50
Piccata	8.50
Rusticana	8.50
Scaloppini	8.50
Saltimbocca	9.00
Stew	6.50

FISH

Perch	6.80
Sole	7.75
Smelts	6.75
Scallops	8.45
Turbot	8.45
Baccala	9.00
F. Shrimps	8.30
Red Snapper	8.45

COLD PLATES*

Beef	7.25
Salmon	8.50
Tuna	7.25
Sardine	7.25
Ham & Cheese	7.25

* Always available

Dinner: Mon - Fri 3:30 - 8

Club Lucky

A sizzling newcomer in an up-and-coming location. The bar is straight out of the '50s, and the dining room isn't far behind. Nothing fancy, nothing cute; just wonderful service and excellent food.

Club Lucky

TRADITIONAL *Italian* FOOD

House Specialties

Filet Oreganato — *Slices of beef tenderloin broiled with garlic, tomato, roasted red pepper and chives* 14.95

Giambotta — *Broiled Italian sausage with sauteed onions, mushrooms, green peppers and potatoes* 10.95

Double Cut Lamb Chops *Two chops broiled with lemon and oregano* 18.95

Italian Style Ribs *A full slab of baby backs with our own sauce* 13.95

Veal Francese *Lightly breaded and sauteed with white wine, lemon, mushrooms, and butter* 14.95

Grilled Pork Chops *A little spicy! Boneless chops topped with onions, mushrooms, pepperoncini and roasted potatoes* 12.95

Grilled Chicken Breast *Boneless breast marinated with lemon, herbs and spices* 8.95

Our Own Chicken Vesuvio *The Club Lucky favorite with roasted potatoes, peas, white wine and garlic*   Half .... 8.95 ...... Whole 15.95

Baked Chicken Oreganato *Baked with white wine, oregano and roasted potatoes (no garlic)*   Half .... 8.95 .... Whole 15.95

Traditional Scampi *Topped with bread crumbs, garlic and spices on a bed of spinach* 13.95

Seafood of the Day .... A.Q.

Homemade Eggplant Parmigiana *Layers of thinly sliced eggplant baked with mozzarella and tomato sauce* 7.95

Escarole in Broth 5.95
        With sausage and beans 8.95

1824 West Wabansia • Lincoln Park/DePaul • (312) 227-2300

Sandwiches

Italian Sausage or Meatball Sandwich 4.95

Veal Cutlet Sandwich 6.95

Filet Sandwich 6.95

Club Lucky Submarine 4.95
Genoa salami, fontinella cheese, and marinated eggplant.

Grilled Chicken Breast Sandwich 4.95

Sides

Steamed Broccoli 2.95

Sauteed Spinach 2.95

Sauteed Escarole 2.95

Veal Meatballs 2.95

Meatballs 2.95

Italian Sausage 2.95

Roasted Potatoes 1.95

New Potatoes 1.95

Roasted Peppers 1.95

Fresh Mozzarella 1.50

Marinara 1.00

Sweet Peppers 1.00

Hot Peppers 1.00

Roasted Garlic 1.00

Desserts

Tiramisu 4.25

Spumoni 2.95

Amaretto Ricotta Cheesecake 3.95

Cannoli 3.95

Fresh Fruit 3.95

All Recipes Include a Little Love!!!

A Chicago landmark with many uniquely decorated dining rooms located in this massive building. Excellent value, great place for family gatherings.

COMO INN

Menu Changes with Daily Specials

Antipasti Caldi

PIATTO DI BEPPINO - *An assortment of hot hors d'oeuvres, our best for 4 or more persons* — $9.95 p.p.

PIZZA MARGHERITA - *Pizza slices with fresh tomatoes, basil and mozzarella cheese* — 3.50

FUNGHI RIPIENI - *Whole oven-baked mushrooms stuffed with Parma ham, cheese and parsley* — 7.95

GAMBERI SALTATI - *Whole shrimp sautéed in olive oil, garlic and white wine* — 9.95

VONGOLE ALLA COMO - *Clams, finely minced and twice baked with Italian herbs and spices* — 7.95

MELANZANE ALLA PARMIGIANA - *Eggplant baked with mozzarella and tomato sauce* — 5.95

CALAMARI FRITTI - *Calamari fried till crispy golden brown and served with a tangy cocktail sauce* — 7.95

Antipasti Freddi

CARPACCIO - *Thin slices of raw filet served with shaved parmesan cheese* — $10.95
FRUTTI DI MARE ALLA VENEZIANA - *Shrimp, lobster & crab meat marinated in olive oil* — 10.95
FRUTTI DI MARE ALLA COMO - *Marinated octopus, calamari and cuddlefish* — 7.95

Insalata

INSALATA DI ARUGULA - *Arugula, radiccio and endive with fresh shaved parmesan cheese* — $8.95
INSALATA PORTOFINO - *A mixture of shrimp, lobster and crabmeat, served on bibb lettuce* — 14.95
INSALATA DI SPINACI - *Leaf spinach with bacon, mushrooms, eggs and a tangy oregano dressing* — 7.95

Our World Famous Pasta

	side order	full order
SPAGHETTI, PENNE O RAVIOLI ALLA COMO - *Pasta with Como Inn's famous meat sauce*	$5.00	$11.95
RAVIOLI DI RICOTTA O FETTUCCINE VERDE ALLA MARINARA - *Pasta with tomato sauce, anchovies, herbs and spices*	6.00	11.95
LINGUINI O RAVIOLI DI RICOTTA ALLA PESTO - *Pasta with Pesto sauce*	6.00	10.95
MAFALDA ALLA AUGIE - *Pasta with artichokes, roasted peppers, capers and black olives*	6.50	12.95
CANNELLONI DELLA CASA - *Pasta filled with ricotta cheese and baked with tomato sauce and mozzarella cheese*		11.95
PENNE ALLA SORRENTINA - *Pasta served with tomatoes, fresh basil and mozzarella cheese*		11.95

Specialita Della Casa

POLLO ARROSTO - *Half chicken, slowly roasted with chopped garlic, celery, onions, herbs and spices*	$12.95
POLLO VESUVIO - *Boneless breast of chicken in olive oil, garlic and rosemary*	13.95
POLLO ALLA CACCIATORE - *Sautéed chicken with tomatoes, mushrooms and spices in a white wine sauce, served on a bed of spaghetti*	13.95
SALTINBOCCA ALLA ROMANO - *Thin slices of veal sautéed and garnished with Parma ham*	19.95
VITELLO AL LIMONE - *Thin slices of veal sauteéed in butter and lemon*	19.95

Pesce e Frutti di Mare

BROILED LAKE SUPERIOR WHITEFISH ALMONDINE	$14.95
BROILED RED SNAPPER - *Served with Almondine sauce*	18.95
FRENCH FRIED GULF SHRIMP	16.75
SHRIMP DE JONGHE ALLA COMO	17.95
IMPERIAL SEAFOOD CASSEROLE - *Crabmeat, shrimp and scallops baked in a creamy wine sauce*	19.95
CALAMARI MARINARA - *Baby calamari sautéed with tomatoes, garlic, herbs and spices*	12.95

Dalla Nostra Griglia

BREAST OF CHICKEN BEPPINO - *Marinated in olive oil, white wine, lemon and herbs*	$13.95
BROILED PRIME FILET MIGNON - *Served with button mushrooms*	19.95
BROILED PRIME AGED T-BONE STEAK OR PORTERHOUSE	24.95
BROILED PRIME AGED SIRLOIN STEAK	19.95
BROILED LAMB CHOP - *Double-cut lamb chops served with mint jelly*	18.95

Dinner: 7 Days a Week until 11

279

Franco's Ristorante

A favorite spot for baseball fans going to Comiskey Park, Franco's excellent service staff is accustomed to getting customers to the game on time. The prices are most affordable, the homemade pasta excellent, and the veal dishes are highly recommended.

franco's
RISTORANTE
Your hosts - Frank & Jeanine

APPETIZERS

ANTIPASTO PLATE 4.25
FRIED CALAMARI . . . 5.25   MOZZARELLA STICKS . 3.50
FRIED ZUCCHINI . . . . 3.50   PIZZA BREAD 1.75
FRIED MUSHROOMS . 3.25   GARLIC BREAD 1.50

BAKED CLAMS   RAW CLAMS
½ dozen . . . 4.95   full dozen . . . 9.50   ½ dozen . . . 4.25   full dozen . . . 8.50

FRIED APPETIZER COMBINATION PLATTER 5.25
Mushrooms, zucchini and cheese sticks

POULTRY

Served with Soup or Salad and Side of Pasta

Please Allow 25 Minutes

CHICKEN VESUVIO 8.25
Sauteed in olive oil, wine, garlic and oregano, served with vesuvio potatoes

CHICKEN OREGANATO 8.25
Sauteed in butter, lemon and oregano

CHICKEN PARMIGIANA 7.95
Breaded chicken baked with cheese in a tomato sauce

CHICKEN CACCIATORE 8.25
Sauteed w/mushrooms, tomatoes and red wine

CHICKEN BREAST MARSALA 7.95
Boneless chicken breast sauteed with mushrooms and marsala wine

300 West 31st St • Downtown/Loop • (312) 225-9566

SEAFOOD

Served with Soup or Salad and a Side of Pasta

JUMBO SHRIMPS sauteed in butter and wine **10.75**

FILET OF SOLE broiled with lemon and butter **8.75**

BACALA codfish with tomatoes, black olives and capers . . . **9.00**

SWORDFISH VESUVIO **10.95**
Sauteed in olive oil, wine, garlic and oregano served with vesuvio potatoes

PASTAS OF THE HOUSE

Served with Bread and Butter

SPAGHETTI AGLIO OILIO sauteed in garlic and oil **5.25**

FETTUCINE ALFREDO **7.50**

LINGUINE E CLAMS with red or white sauce **7.25**

LINGUINE E CALAMARI fresh squid in red sauce **7.25**

LINGUINE E SHRIMP, CLAMS AND CALAMARI in red or white sauce **16.95**

LINGUINE CARBONARA cream sauce with bacon and cheese **7.50**

SPAGHETTI PUTTANESCA a tangy sauce w/black olives and capers **7.50**

LINGUINE CAPRICCIOSA with shrimp and tomato sauce **7.95**

LINGUINE E BROCCOLI sauteed in garlic and oil **6.75**

LINGUINE E BROCCOLI and SHRIMP sauteed in garlic oil **11.95**

LINGUINE PRIMAVERA served w/fresh vegetables in a secret sauce **7.95**

RIGATONI ARRABIATA a hot tomato sauce with prosciutto **7.50**

ITALIAN SAUSAGE OR MEATBALLS . . . . Extra **1.75**

VEAL

Served with Soup or Salad and Side of Pasta

VEAL PARMIGIANA breaded veal baked w/cheese in a tomato sauce **7.95**

VEAL MARSALA sauteed with mushrooms and marsala wine **9.25**

VEAL LIMONE sauteed in butter and lemon **8.95**

VEAL PICANTE sauteed in lemon with capers **8.95**

Dinner: Mon - Thurs 3 - 10, Fri - Sat 3 - 10:30

Home Run Inn

Another Chicago pizza institution (circa 1947), this mammoth restaurant has some of the best thin-crust pizza around. Because the pizza is so popular many people overlook the excellent Italian dishes such as lasagne and spaghetti and meatballs.

Home Run Inn®
Pizza

APPETIZERS

Turano Soft Bread Sticks $1.95
with garlic butter

Potato Skins $4.35
Buffalo Wings $3.85
Breaded Mushrooms $3.85
Breaded Onion Rings $3.85
Breaded Zucchini $3.85
Breaded Cheese Sticks $3.85

SOUPS

Baked French Onion $3.50
A crock of delicious onion soup, topped with Mozzarella Cheese, then baked to perfection and served with a soft bread stick

Minestrone $2.95
A blend of vegetables and paste in an unforgettable broth, served with a soft bread stick

SALADS

Small Salad $1.75
Lettuce, carrots, cabbage, onions and green peppers

Antipasto Salad $3.50
Lettuce, carrots, cabbage, onions, green peppers, eggs, pepperoncini, tomatoes, cheese, cucumbers with assortment of Italian meats

4254 West 31st St • Downtown/Loop • (312) 247-9696

282

SALAD DRESSINGS
Italian, Lite Italian, French, Garlic, Thousand Island, House or Ranch
Blue Cheese **$ .75 extra**

PIZZA

	Small 12"	Large 14"	X-large 16"
Sausage	**$8.85**	**$12.45**	**$14.75**
Cheese	**$7.25**	**$10.85**	**$13.15**

Line up of Extras on Pizzas

Spinach · Mushrooms · Peppers · Cheese · FalboLite Cheese · Sausage · Hot Peppers
Anchovies · Onions · Black Olives · Plum Tomatoes · Garlic · Pepperoni
Each Ingredient $1.60

PASTA SPECIALTIES
Includes Bread, Butter and Salad

Spaghetti & Meatballs $6.95
Long slender pasta, topped with home made meat sauce, accompanied by 2 fresh
meatballs. May substitute Italian Sausage

Mostaccioli & Meatballs $6.95
Tubular pasta, topped with home made meat sauce, accompanied by
2 fresh meatballs. May substitute Italian Sausage

Lasagna $6.95
Layers of pasta noodles with Ricotta & Mozzarella cheese filing,
topped with more cheese and then baked to perfection

SANDWICHES
Includes French Fries & Cole Slaw

Italian Sausage $3.75
Hamburger (1/3 lb.)   **$4.25**
Cheeseburger (1/3 lb.)   **$4.50**
Pizza Burger $4.95
(1/3 lb.) Mozzarella cheese, mushrooms, grilled onions & green peppers

Bacon Burger $5.95
Bacon & Cheese

Dinner: Sun - Thurs until 12, Fri - Sat until 1:30

It's a neighborhood Italian restaurant with a friendly atmosphere assured by the long open dining room. Earthy and interesting Italian dishes that please. One of my favoite dishes is the Chicken Vesuvio.

JIM N' JOHNNYS'

Menu Changes Daily

FRIED CALAMARI	6.75
GIAMBOTTA	6.00
ANTIPASTO SALAD	3.75 per
SPINACH & SCALLOP SALAD	7.50
CAESAR SALAD	6.00
TOMATO & MOZZARELLA	6.00
MAMA T'S STUFFED ARTICHOKE	6.00

PASTA

GNOCCHI	8.95
RAVIOLI	8.95
CAPELLINI	8.95
MOSTACIOLI	7.50
SPAGHETTI	7.50
LINGUINE	7.50

W/ MEATBALLS OR SAUSAGE

VEAL LIMONE	14.95
VEAL PARMIGIANO	14.50
PORK CHOPS	14.95
STEAK DI JOHNNY	15.00
FISH OF THE DAY	MARKET
CATFISH VESUVIO	11.95
SALMON LOMBARDI	12.95
SHRIMP MARSALA	13.95
LINGUINE & CLAMS RED/WHITE	12.95
SHRIMP SCAMPI	14.95
LINGUINE & CALAMARI	12.95
PASTA PRIMAVERA	9.95
FETTUCINI ALFREDO	9.50
LINGUINE TOMATO BASIL	9.50
ARTICHOKE RAVIOLINI	12.95
SHELLS AND BROCCOLI	8.50
MAMA'S EGGPLANT	9.75
CHICKEN VESUVIO	8.50/15.95
CHICKEN CHAMPAGNE	11.50
CHICKEN PARMIGIANO	10.50

DOLCI

SPUMONI	3.95
TIRAMISU	4.95
MAMA'S CHEESECAKE	3.95
LEMON ICE	3.50

Dinner: Mon - Thurs 5 - 10, Fri - Sat 5 - 11, Sun 5 - 9:30

La Bella Pasteria

In Oak Park, a short hop from the center of the city, this family-run spot serves great Italian food. In fact, a friend from New York City, after eating here a few times, declared it to be better than any Italian restaurant in the Big Apple. Quite a compliment, but I say it's accurate and well deserved.

APPETIZERS

BAKED CLAMS-LITTLE NECKS
1/2 doz. 5.95
doz. 9.95

RAW CLAMS *1/2 doz. 4.95*
doz. 8.95

SHRIMP COCKTAIL 8.95
SHRIMP SCAMPI 7.95
ARTICHOKE PATÉ 4.95
Baked hearts with garlic and bread crumbs, chilled.

FRIED CALAMARI *1/2 order 4.95*
full order 7.95

FRIED ZUCCHINI 3.95
GARLIC BREAD 2.50
BRUSCHETTA 3.95
Tomato, Green Onion, Fresh Basil, Olive oil on Garlic Bread.

ROLLED EGGPLANT WITH RICOTTA CHEESE 4.95

PASTA

FETTUCCINE ALFREDO 7.95
Pasta in a creamy saue.

FETTUCCINE ALLA CARBONARA 8.95
Cream Sauce and Prosciutto

CAVATELLI 8.95
Special cheese and Vodka sauce

LASAGNA 8.95
Imported cheese and meat sauce

CHEESE RAVIOLI, SPINACH RAVIOLI OR MEAT RAVIOLI 7.95
In Marinara or meat sauce

BAKED CAVATELLI 10.95
Romano, Parmigiano, Ricotta, Mozzarella

LINGUINE BROCCOLI 7.95
Prepared with garlic and oil.

RIGATONI FRESH MOZZARELLA BASIL SAUCE 8.85

PASTA ARRABIATA ALLA BRUNO 9.95
Spicy Jalapeño and Prosciutto.

RIGATONI ALLA ABRUZESE 10.95
Served with Ricotta cheese and sausage.

PASTA MARINARA 6.95
Linguine - Spaghetti - Rigatoni - Mostaccioli.

PASTA IN MEAT SAUCE 7.95
Linguine - Spaghetti - Rigatoni - Mostaccioli.

CHICKEN • STEAK • CHOPS

CHICKEN VESUVIO   *1/2 chicken 9.95*
full chicken 16.95
Served in a white wine sauce sauteed with
Vesuvio potatoes and peas.

CHICKEN MARSALA
(2 BONELESS BREASTS)   *10.95*
Prepared in a Marsala wine sauce with
mushrooms with a side dish of pasta.

CHICKEN CACCIATORE   *10.95*
Pepper, mushrooms, onions and fresh tomatoes
in an olive oil and white wine and marinara
sauce with a side dish of pasta.

CHICKEN PARMIGIANA
(2 BONELESS BREASTS)   *10.95*
With melted mozzarella cheese and meat sauce
with a side dish of pasta.

PEPPERCORN STEAK   *17.95*
3 Filet Tenders in a cognac sauce
with a side dish or pasta.

PEPPER STEAK   *17.95*
3 Filet Tenders sautéed with onions, peppers,
mushrooms and fresh tomatoes with a side dish
of pasta.

SEAFOOD

LINGUINE WITH CALAMARI   *12.95*
Prepared with black olives and capers in a white
wine marinara sauce.

FETTUCCINE, BROCCOLI,
AND SHRIMP ALFREDO   *14.95*
Prepared in a creamy Alfredo sauce.

LINGUINE IN CLAM SAUCE WITH
WHOLE CLAMS-LITTLE NECKS   *12.95*
Your choice of red or white sauce.

BACCALA ALLA SICILIANA   *14.95*
Sautéed with capers, olives and onions in
marinara sauce with a side of pasta.

VEAL

VEAL PICANTE   *16.95*
Sautéed with roasted pine nuts

VEAL LIMONE   *16.95*
Sautéed with capers and artichoke heart

VEAL FRANCESE   *16.95*
Egg battered with a lemon white wine sauce

VEAL MARSALA   *16.95*
Prepared with Marsala wine and mushrooms.

VEAL PARMIGIANO   *16.95*
Prepared with Mozzarella and meat sauce.

VEAL SICILIANA   *16.95*
Sautéed with special breading
and roasted red peppers.

PIZZA

LA BELLA 4 CHEESE   *10" 7.95*   *14" 11.95*
Gouda, Romano, Parmigiano, Mozzarella

FRESH TOMATO
AND GARLIC   *10" 6.95*   *14" 10.95*

RICOTTA & TOMATO   *10"6.95*   *14"10.95*

PIZZA PRIMAVERA   *10" 7.95*   *14" 11.95*
Sun dried tomatoes, green peppers, broccoli

Dinner: Mon - Thurs 4 - 11, Fri - Sat 4 - 12, Sun 3 - 10

La Cantina

Tucked away downstairs in the Italian Village restaurant complex, La Cantina offers more of an Old World atmosphere and menu than Vivere, its sister restaurant above.

Menu Changes Seasonally

Antipasti

Mussels, Marinara or Baked 6.95	**Vongole en Porchetta,** Fresh Clams in a
Frutta di Mare, Cold Seafood Antipasto 6.95	Tomato, Garlic, White Wine Sauce over Crostini **6.95**
Calamari Fritte, Fried Squid 5.95	**Antipasto alla Cantina** 5.95
Calamari Ripieni, Baked Squid	**Prosciutto and Melon** 5.95
filled with our own Seasoning 6.50	**Jumbo Shrimp Cocktail** 6.75
Vongole al Forno, Baked Clams 6.50	**Cherrystone Clams,** 1/2 Shell 5.75
Oysters Rockefeller 6.50	**Bluepoint Oysters,** 1/2 Shell 5.75
Shrimp De Jonghe 7.50	**Tomatoes Alla Toscana** 4.95

Zuppe

Tortellini in Brodo .... Cup **2.25** Bowl **2.95**	**Stracciatella,** Roman Egg Soup .... Bowl **2.95**
Minestrone .... Cup **2.25** Bowl **2.95**	**Escarole** with Chicken Broth .... Bowl **2.95**

Pasta

Lasagne al Forno, Meat Filled	9.25	10.95
Manicotti, with Tomato or Cream Sauce	9.75	11.50
Cannelloni, with Tomato or Cream Sauce	9.75	11.50
Spaghetti, with Meat Sauce	9.25	10.95
Fettuccine All'Alfredo	9.95	11.75
Ravioli, with Meat Sauce	9.75	11.50
Cappellini D'Angelo, with a Light Tomato-Basil Sauce	10.50	12.25
Tagliatelle Della Contessa, Fresh Pasta, Prosciutto, Cotto, Cognac, Cream Sauce	12.95	14.75
Agnolotti Al Pomodoro e Basilico, Cheese Filled, Tomato Basil Sauce	10.50	12.25
Rigatoni Arrabiata, Hot Spicy Sauce	9.75	11.50
Linguine Genovese, Pesto Sauce	10.50	12.25
Tortellini alla Bolognese	10.50	12.25

Carne & Pollo

	A la Carte	Dinner
Chicken alla Cacciatora	11.50	13.25
Chicken Vesuvio	12.95	14.75
Petti di Pollo Francaise, Lemon, White Wine Sauce	12.95	14.95
Petti di Pollo alla Parmigiana	12.95	14.75
Calves Liver with Bacon or Onion	12.95	14.75
Baby Back Ribs	12.95	14.95
Stuffed Veal Chop A La Cantina	22.95	24.75
Broiled Prime Filet Mignon	19.95	21.75
Broiled Prime New York Strip Steak	21.00	22.75
Broiled Prime T-Bone Steak	23.50	24.95
Broiled Double Cut Lamb Chops	19.95	21.95

Specialita' Del Mare

	A la Carte	Dinner
Vongole y Linguine con Salsa Bianco o Rosso, Linguine with Red or White Clam Sauce	11.75	13.50
Cozze y Linguine con Salsa Bianco o Rosso, Fresh Green Lipped Mussels, White Wine Garlic Broth or Red Sauce	11.75	13.50
Linguine con Gamberi e Broccoli, Large Shrimp, Broccoli, Olive Oil	13.95	15.95
Rigatoni al Pescatore, Diced Clams, Shrimp, Squid and Mussels in Tomato Sauce or Garlic, White Wine Broth	14.75	16.75
Tortelli con Fruta Del Mare, Seafood Filled Pasta with Shrimp and Scallops in a Tomato Cream Sauce	13.50	15.50
Scampi al Spiedo, Large Shrimps broiled in our Specially Seasoned Bread Crumbs, with Vegetables and Rice	14.95	16.95
Scampi Marinara, Fresh Tomatoes, Olive Oil, Parsley and Garlic	13.95	15.75
Scampi Giovanni, Garlic, Lemon, Herbs and White Wine	13.95	15.75
Scampi Fritte, Fried Shrimp	13.95	15.75
Broiled Lobster Tail, Drawn Butter	Market Price	
Spaghetti Mare e Monti, Shrimp, Scallops, Mussels, Clams, Garlic, Olive Oil, White Wine, Wild Mushrooms	15.95	17.75
Zuppa Di Pesce con Linguine, The Chef's Choice of Seafood Delicacies, in a Rich Broth, Italian Style, with Linguine	17.95	19.95

Specialita' Italiana

	A la Carte	Dinner
Eggplant alla Parmigiana	10.75	12.50
Veal Scaloppine, alla Marsala, Pizzaiola or alla Serafin	15.95	17.75
Saltimbocca all Romana, Prosciutto and Sage	16.95	18.75
Veal Cutlet alla Parmigiana, Veal Cutlet Baked with Mozzarella, Parmesan and Tomatoes	15.95	17.75
Veal Limone, sauteed with Lemon, White Wine, Butter Sauce	15.95	17.75
Contro Filetto Aceto Balsamico, Veal Steak, Balsamic Vinegar, Veal Stock	17.95	19.75
Veal Donati, Mushrooms, Capers and Sherry Wine	15.95	17.95
Veal Rusticana, Veal Cutlet Baked with Fontina Cheese, Garlic and Tomato	15.95	17.95
Beef Scaloppine alla Cantina, Marsala Wine with Eggplant	17.95	19.75
Beef Scaloppine alla Marsala with Mushrooms	17.95	19.75

Dinner: Mon - Sat 5 - 12

I like to call this place "The House of Risotto," as risotto is the signature dish of this small, no-frills casually styled place. There is much to choose from beyond risotto—pasta, chicken, seafood—all of which gets the same careful touch.

la locanda
RISTORANTE ITALIANO

Menu Changes Seasonally

ANTIPASTI

DI PESCE
Calamari Alla Griglia $6.95
Marinated in extra virgin olive oil and herbs, grilled on open charcoal
Scampi E Capesante Con Funghi E Zafferano $8.50
Jumbo shrimp and sea scallops sauteed in a mushroom, saffron sauce

DI CARNE
Carpaccio Con Parmigiano E Funghi Crudi $8.25
Thin raw beef tenderloin with parmigiano and mushrooms

CON VEGETALI
Verdure Alla Graticola $7.50
Mixed grilled vegetables marinated in wine vinegar

I NOSTRI RISOTTI

DI PESCE
Risotto Con Le Telline $15.95
Fresh clams, green and black mussels sauteed in a white wine
Risotto Giallo Con Trota E Broccoletti $14.95
Fresh trout, broccoli in a wine and saffron sauce

DI CARNE
Risotto Con Polpa Di Vitellone $16.95
Veal, parmigiano, wine, touch of tomato sauce and red bell pepper

CON VEGETALI
Risotto Con Fiori Di Zucchine $14.95
Squash blossoms & parmigiano cheese
Risotto Spinaci E Radicchio $13.95
With fresh spinach and radicchio

743 North LaSalle • River North • (312) 335-9550

PRIMI PIATTI

DI PESCE

Cappellini Con Vongole $12.95
Angel hair with fresh clams, pinot grigio sauce and fresh spinach
Tagliolini Al Nero Di Seppia Piccanti $14.95
Fresh black linguine with mixed seafood in spicy red sauce
Ravioli Ai Gamberetti Con Porcini $16.95
Rock shrimps in a porcini mushrooms sauce
Tagliolini Rossi Agli Scampi Ubriachi $16.95
Tomato pasta sauteed in champagne, fresh arugola and jumbo shrimp sauce

DI CARNE

Gnocchi Prosciutto Piselli E Porcini $14.95
Imported prosciutto, peas, porcini mushrooms in a delicate cream sauce
Tortelli Ripieni $15.95
Stuffed with veal, parmigiano cheese, mushrooms in a artichoke hearts sauce
Pappardelle Con Salsiccia Di Anatra $16.95
Duck sausage, carrots, celery, white wine, basil, tomato sauce

CON VEGETALI

Strangolapreti in Salsa Verde $13.95
Ricotta spinach dumpling with a salsa of walnut, basil, extra olive oil
Cappellini Del Vegetariano $9.95

SECONDI PIATTI

DI PESCE

Involtini Di Sogliola $M.P.
Filet of sole roulade with vegetable mousse, white wine sauce
Gran Piatto Di Pesce $M.P.
.. Mixed grilled fish in white wine, lemon sauce

DI CARNE

Ossobuco Con Verdure E Risotto Alla Milanese $15.95
Our special veal shank baked with vegetables
Agnello All'Aceto Balsamico E Funghi Gialli $21.95
Grilled lamb chops, balsamic vinegar and chanterelle mushrooms
Lombata Di Vitello Ai Porcini E Barolo $26.95
Veal chop grilled lightly, sauteed in barolo wine and wild porcini mushrooms
Scaloppine Al Gorgonzola Italiano $19.95
Veal scaloppine sauteed with imported gorgonzola cheese

Dinner: Mon - Thurs 5:30 - 11, Fri - Sat 5:30 - 11:30

La Strada Ristorante

Classic Italian food in a quiet and comfortable atmosphere with first-rate service takes this place into its 11th year of operation. Excellent variety up and down the menu, but the pasta and risotto creations are exceptionally good.

La Strada®

R I S T O R A N T E

Menu Changes Seasonally

Antipasti (Appetizers)

Caldi (Hot)

Classici Mitili Possillipo   7.00
Fresh black mussels steamed in an herbed tomato wine sauce.

Scampi Strada   9.00
Fresh Gulf shrimp sauteed with garlic, green onions, fresh porcini mushrooms and a touch of tomato.

Vongole Colorossi   7.00
Whole little neck clams, stuffed with prosciutto, sun-dried tomato, asiago cheese, light garlic and baked in an herbed wine sauce.

Arrosto di Melanzane   6.00
Roasted eggplant stuffed with fresh imported cheeses, sun-dried tomato, scallions and baked with light tomato.

Funghi Portabello   6.00
Fresh imported portabello mushroom caps seared with belpaese, thyme, garlic and a light brodo.

Freddi (Cold)

Arrosto di Peperoni con Mozzarella   7.00
Roasted bell peppers with imported mozzarella di buffalo, sun-dried tomato, capers and extra virgin olive oil.

Carpaccio della Strada   7.00
Thinly sliced raw sirloin with tricolore peppercorns, shaved reggiano with a garlic infused sweet pesto dressing.

Asparagi con Parmigiana   6.00
Steamed fresh asparagus with shaved reggiano, pimento with a balsamic vinaigrette.

Mozzarella Fresca con Pomodoro.   6.00
Imported buffalo mozzarella with fresh Italian plum tomatoes, extra virgin olive oil and balsamic vinegar

Insalate (Salads)

Insalata alla Bordichera   6.00
Fresh lollo rossa, artichoke, goat cheese, sun-dried tomatoes, gaeta olives with a light tarragon flavored olive oil.

Insalata alla Caprese   5.00
Fresh imported buffalo mozzarella with fresh plum tomatoes, arrugula, endive, basil with a balsamic vinaigrette.

Insalata di Caesar   6.00
Traditional Roman recipe combining lemon, oil, dijon, garlic, anchovies, romaine and garlic crostini at your tableside.

Paste *(Pasta)*

Fettuccine con Porcini   *14.00*
Homemade wide noodles with fresh porcini mushrooms, asiago cheese, cream and a touch of tomato.

Spaghetti Puttanesca   *10.00*
Spaghetti with spicy tomato, gaeta olives, capers and anchovies.

Penne con Arrugula   *10.00*
Tube pasta with fresh tomato and arrugula.

Cappellini alla Caprese   *11.00*
Angel hair pasta with fresh tomato, basil and imported buffalo mozzarella.

Penne Amatriciana   *11.00*
Tube pasta with fresh tomato, onions, smoked pancetta, prosciutto and basil.

Agnollotti di Noce   *11.00*
Ricotta and spinach stuffed half moon pasta with a walnut cream sauce.

Tagliatelle Tricolore con Pesto   *12.00*
Spinach, egg and tomato pasta with fresh basil.

Fettuccine Alfredo   *10.00*
Classic Roman style wide egg noodles in a rich cream sauce with fresh reggiano.

Risotto *(Italian Rice)*

Risotto Frutta di Mare   *14.00*
Italian rice with fresh clams, mussels, shrimp, calamari and a touch of tomato.

Risotto con Porcini   *14.00*
Italian rice with fresh porcini, reggiano cheese and herbs.

Specialita' della Strada *(Specialties of La Strada)*

Scalloppine of Veal Strada   *20.00*
Thinly sliced veal with prosciutto, fontina, roasted shallots in a madeira wine sauce.

Arrosto di Pollo alla Piemontese   *18.00*
Oven roasted chicken breast stuffed with roasted peppers and fontina with a white truffle laced sauce.

Pollo val D'Aosta   *18.00*
Roasted free range baby hen with chestnut laced rissoto and a sun-dried cherry sauce.

New York Prime Strip Steak

   Regular cut, *broiled with bearanise.*   *24.00*

   Double cut, *broiled with bearnaise.*   *42.00*

   Piemontese style, *stuffed with spinach and fontina cheese.*   *25.00*

Maiale Con Balsalmico   *17.00*
Sauteed pork medallions with balsamic vinegar peppers.

Lobster Fra Diavolo   *Market*
Sweet whole Maine lobster steamed in a spicy tomato sauce with fresh clams, mussels and herbs over linguine.

Prime Provimi Veal Chops

   Broiled *naturally with vegetables.*   *28.00*

   Milanese Style *with a tomato relish.*   *26.00*

Pollo Saltimbocca   *19.00*
Boneless breast of chicken sauteed with white wine and sage, crowned with prosciutto.

New Zealand Prime Lamb Chops
   Carciofi Style   *25.00*
Grilled Baby Lamb chops with artichoke hearts, wild mushrooms, shallots and a amatillado sherry wine sauce.

   Arrosto di Agnello *(Serves 2 people)*   *48.00*
Roasted rack of lamb served with roasted new potatoes, cippolina onions, baby eggplant and carrots.

Prime Tenderloin of Beef

   Filetto di Bue al Barolo   *26.00*
Prime tenderloins with cracked peppercorn in a Barolo wine sauce.

   Broiled *naturally with bearnaise.*   *24.00*

Salmone alla Griglia   *24.00*
Fresh grilled salmon served with a porcini laced cream sauce.

Dinner: Mon - Thurs 5 - 10, Fri - Sat 5 - 11

Maggiano's

Abbondanza is only the half of it here. Huge portions of food are served in an atmosphere that is tuned to replicate something you might find in Little Italy in New York City. Meatballs as big as softballs, lasagna almost as big as a desk, pasta that fills plates forever—it's not for the faint of stomach. The best part is that the food seems to improve daily.

MAGGIANŌ'S
— LITTLE ITALY™ —

Menu Changes Seasonally

Appetizers

Bruschetta	3.95
Roasted Peppers	3.95
Zuppa di Mussels	7.95
Stuffed Mushrooms	5.95

Soups & Small Salads

Minestrone	Cup 1.95	Bowl 2.95
Soup of the Day	Cup 1.95	Bowl 2.95
Sliced Tomato, Onion		3.95
Sliced Tomato, Onion, Anchovy		4.25
Lettuce and Tomato Salad		2.95
Caesar Salad		3.95

Large Salads

Chopped Salad	8.95
Caesar Salad	7.95
Italian Salad	8.95
Maggiano Salad	8.95
Maggiano Salad w/Chicken	9.95

All salads served with a choice of Italian, Blue Cheese or Maggiano's House Dressing

Sandwiches

Veal Parmesan Sandwich	6.95
PLT, charred proscuitto, lettuce, tomato	6.95
Chicken & Roasted Peppers	5.95

Parmesan Potato Chips Served with Sandwiches

Pasta & Italian Specialities

Spaghetti Marinara	7.50	Spaghetti Aglio Olio	7.95
Spaghetti Meatball or Sausage	7.95	Mostaccioli, Eggplant Marinara	7.95
Spaghetti Meat Ragu	7.95	Corkscrew Pasta, vegetables, ricotta sauce	8.50
Spaghetti Meat Sauce	7.95	**Country Style Rigatoni**	8.50
Lingiuni fini, peas, butter, parmesan . .	7.95	Linguine, Red Clam Sauce	8.95
Fettucini Alfredo w/Broccoli	8.25	Linguine, White Clam Sauce	8.95
Shells and Vegetables, Tomato broth . . .	7.95	Garlic Shrimp w/Shells	9.50

Eggplant Parmesan. . . 7.95

Ask about our oil free tomato sauce

Chicken & Veal

Chicken Parmesan	9.95
Chicken Cutlets, wine, tomato, basil	9.95
Chicken Cammarrari	8.75
1/2 Roast Chicken, rosemary, garlic	8.95
Veal Parmesan	12.95
Veal Scallopine	12.95

Seafood

Fresh Fish of the Day	AQ
Tuna "Steak Style"	13.95
Swordfish "Steak Style"	13.95
Shrimp Oreganata	10.95

Family Style Dining Available for Large Parties
Steaks Available Upon Request at Lunch
16% gratuity added to parties of 8 or more

Dinner: Mon - Thurs 5 - 1, Fri - Sat 5 - 12, Sun 4:30 - 9

Pizzeria Uno

Credit this place for putting pizza on the map in Chicago and points beyond. Celebrating its 50th anniversary this year, Uno's and delicious deep-dish pizza are a match made in pizza heaven. And the delightful barroom atmosphere remains virtually the same as the day it opened.

APPETIZERS

FLORENCE'S SOUP 2.05
Ike's wife makes a minestrone with cheese too good to be called just minestrone.
So we named it after her.

VEGGIE DIP 4.35
A medley of chilled fresh vegetables and a tasty dip.

GARLIC BREAD 2.15
A perennial favorite done particularly well.

WINGS OF FIRE 4.95
Not for the timid! Hot and spicy chicken wings with celery
sticks and a tasty dip. (15 minutes)

SALADS

SPINACH SALAD 4.15
The freshest spinach, mushrooms, chopped bacon, and house dressing.

Our Famous Italian
SALAD BOWL 2.25
Deliciously dressed with wine vinegar and olive oil blend. Topped with tomatoes and
onions.

DEEP DISH PIZZA

CHEESE
Individual 3.75   Small 6.95   Medium 9.75   Large 11.85

---

29 East Ohio • Gold Coast • (312) 321-1000

"THE FOUR CHEESE-PESTO PIZZA"
A blend of cheeses with a pesto base, topped with fresh tomatoes.
Individual 4.95   Small 9.25   Medium 12.75   Large 15.75

"THE UNO"
Our first choice for the most delectable pizza! Our own inimitable crust filled with cheese,
an abundance of fresh sausage, just the right amount of pepperoni...and
topped with outrageous quantities of fresh mushrooms, onions
and green peppers. Highly recommended.
Individual 5.95   Small 11.25   Medium 14.85   Large 17.85

"THE SPINACH PIZZA"
Our own inimitable crust, filled with 3 blends of cheese and an abundance of delicately
seasoned fresh spinach. Try it with mushrooms, you'll love it! (Additional charge).
Individual 5.25   Small 9.75   Medium 12.95   Large 15.95

"THE VEGGIE"
Our delicious crust filled with lots of cheese and the freshest mushrooms,
onions, and green peppers. A vegetarian delight.
Individual 4.95   Small 9.25   Medium 12.75   Large 15.75

"THE SPINOCCOLI"
Spinach, fresh Broccoli, a blend of cheeses, a little garlic and chunky tomato.
Individual 4.95   Small 9.25   Medium 12.75   Large 15.75

PASTA

CAPELLINI 4.95
(Angel Hair Pasta)
Spaghetti with our special meatless Marinara sauce and garlic bread.
(Served with Ike's Salad.)

CAPELLINI WITH MEATBALLS 5.95

SANDWICHES

ITALIAN BEEF SANDWICH 4.15
Thin slices of Italian beef au jus, with green pepper. (Served with Ike's Salad.)

ITALIAN SAUSAGE SANDWICH 3.60
With special homemade sauce.
(Served with Ike's Salad.)

MEATBALL SANDWICH 4.25
Neighborhood favorite on Italian bread with Marinara sauce. (Served with Ike's Salad.)

Dinner: Mon - Fri until 1, Sat until 2, Sun until 11:30

297

Excellent Italian food and surprisingly good service considering that the waitstaff has to sing (mostly opera) and sling food at the same time. This is the place to be if you're in a celebratory frame of mind.

PRIMAVERA
RISTORANTE · BAR
Menu Changes Seasonally

ANTIPASTI

Asparagi verde con olio di pomodori secchi
Chilled green asparagus with sun-dried tomato oil   6.25

Melanzanne alla griglia, zucchine, e formaggio di capro con olio di rugula
Grilled eggplant, zucchini and goat cheese with arugula oil   6.50

Calamari fritti con limone
Fried squid with lemon   5.75

Carpaccio alla primavera
Thinly sliced sirloin of beef, cognac, mustard sauce   6.75

Insalata mista alla romana
Italian Caesar salad   5.50

Cuori di palme con peperoni marinato al forno
Hearts of palm salad with marinated roasted bell peppers   6.25

PASTA

Risotto con limone et voncoli
Lemon risotto with asparagus and Little Neck Clams   12.50

Farfalle agli scampi e asparagi
Bow tie pasta with shrimp and asparagus in a cream sauce   14.75

Rigatoni con pomodori e mozzarella fresca
Rigatoni pasta with tomatoes and fresh mozzarella cheese   13.50

Lasagne di casa
Baked with Ricotta cheese, spinach and assorted mushrooms   13.75

Linguini con zucchine e aragosta
Linguini pasta with lobster, zucchini and bell peppers   15.50

Tortellini con radicchio et prosciutto
Meat tortellini with radicchio, prosciutto cracklings and parmesan   13.75

Cannelloni all fiorentina
Stuffed cannelloni with veal, spinach and fontina cheese   14.00

---

200 North Columbus Dr • Near North/Gold Coast • (312) 565-6655

ZUPPE

Minestrone alla genovese
Fresh vegetable and pasta soup
with pesto   4.50

Specialita del pescatore
Mussels, calamari, swordfish and shrimp
in a seafood broth   6.50

PIZZA

Pizza con frutti de mare
with spinach, jumbo shrimps,
lobster and mozzarella
cheese   13.25

Pizza Primavera
with zucchini, mushrooms,
artichokes, bell peppers and sun-dried
tomatoes   10.50

PIATTI PRINCIPALI

Served with a Bowl of Today's Pasta

Capesante alla griglia con basilico, carciofi pomodoro
Grilled jumbo sea scallops with basil oil, tomatoes and baby artichokes   17.75

Tonno alla griglia con radicchio e toscani fagioli
Grilled tuna with radicchio, tuscan beans and anchovy lemon dressing   18.25

Pesce di mare siciliano con finognio
Baked snapper with fennel, sun-dried tomato and olive oil   16.75

Scaloppine di vitello alla marsala
Sauteed veal with marsala wine sauce and mushrooms   18.75

Gamberi con aglio con salsa di burro erbe
Sauteed jumbo shrimp with garlic and herb butter   20.50

Scaloppine di vitello al limone e spinaci
Sauteed veal with lemon butter sauce and fresh spinach   17.75

Filetto di sogliola con capperi, erbe, e carciofi
Filet of lemon sole sauteed with capers, herbs and baby artichokes   16.50

Petto di pollo "Cacciatora"
Charred breast of chicken with bell peppers and olives   16.75

Saltimbocca di pollo
Breast of chicken with fresh sage, prosciutto and wine sauce   17.25

Stinco d'angello brasato con romamarina
Braised lamb shank with rosemary, cannellini beans and shallots   18.50

Dinner: 7 Days a Week 5:30 - 10:30

This Taylor Street trattoria started something wonderful quite some time ago. Stars of stage, screen and life come here to worship the food (great chicken Vesuvio, outstanding pasta dishes, captivating calamari), and soon they become part of the scene. The Old Italian ambiance just adds to the total experience.

Rosebud

DINNER MENU

APPETIZERS

Scampi Alla Carlo 8.95	Homemade Italian Sausage
Calamari (Fried) 9.95	(With Peppers) 8.95
Baked Clams (6) 6.95	Mussels Red or White Sauce 9.95
Fresh Raw Clams (6) 5.95	Fish Salad: Assorted Seafood 9.95
Mama's Homemade Stuffed Artichoke	Antipasto Tray Per Person 5.95
(In Season) 5.95	Focaccia Rosebud Style 5.95

PASTA SPECIALTIES

THE ROSEBUD

Creators of the Original Famous Homemade Country Style
Square Semolina Noodle In A Rich Marinara Sauce **13.95**

HOMEMADE EN SALAD 13.95
Fresh Tomatoes, Cappellini

FARFALLE 12.95
Vodka Sauce

LINGUINI CARBONARA 13.95
Prosciutto, Egg, Cream

**HOMEMADE DEEP DISH
LASAGNA** 12.95
Layers of Imported, Domestic Cheeses,
Rich Meat

MAMA'S PASTA FAVORITES 9.95

RAVIOLI Meat or Cheese 10.95
Meat Sauce or Marinara

BAKED MANICOTTI 12.95
Marinara Sauce, Imported Melted Cheese

BAKED CAVATELLI 13.95
Deep Dish Marinara Sauce,
Imported Melted Cheese

**"SPECIAL CAVATELLI"
Receipe Combination
(Ask Server)**

SPINACH NOODLES AL FORNO 11.95
with Dry Ricotta

AGLIO S' OLIO LINGUINI 10.95
Garlic Oil

PESCE PASTA

CLAMS PASTA 15.95
Fresh Steamed Whole Clams Over Pasta
with White Wine, Garlic Sauce or
Spicy Red Marinara

ZUPPA DE PESCE PLATTER 19.95
Olive Oil, Rich Tomato Sauce,
Special Seasoning, Simmered with a
Combination of Select Seafood

CALAMARI PASTA 15.95
Tender Baby Squid, Fresh Tomato,
Marinara Sauce

SHRIMP AND BROCCOLI 18.95
Over Linguini, Garlic, Butter

SHRIMP MARINARA 18.95
Fresh Tomato, Garlic, Oil, Sauce

1500 West Taylor • City South • (312) 942-1117

VEAL

VEAL PICANTE 17.95
Lightly Sauteed with Lemon Butter,
Roasted Pinenuts

VEAL MARSALA 17.95
Sauteed with Fresh Imported Marsala Wine,
Butter, Mushrooms

VEAL FRANCESE 17.95
Special Egg Batter, Lemon Butter Sauce

VEAL SALTIM BOCCA 17.95
Sauteed with Prosciutto Medallions
Touch of Fresh Tomato

VEAL SCALLOPINE 17.95
White Wine, Onion, Touch Fresh Tomato
and Fresh Mushrooms

VEAL PARMIGIANA 17.95
Rich Meat Sauce, Melted Imported Cheeses

VEAL DI FIORE 17.95
Sauteed White Wine Butter Zucchini,
Melted Imported Cheeses

SEAFOOD
SPECIALTIES

SHRIMP SCAMPI 17.95
Delicately Seasoned with
Whisper of Garlic

BROILED SHRIMP LEMON 17.95
BACCALA ALLA SICILIANA 14.95
Sauteed Light Fresh Tomatoes,
Black Olives, Capers and Sweet Onions

FRESH FILET OF SOLE
FRANCESE 14.95
Special Egg Batter, White Wine,
Lemon Butter Sauce

BROILED LOBSTER TAIL
. . . . (Market Price)

FROM OUR BROILER
(Aged Select Prime)

STEAK VESUVIO 25.95
New York Strip (16 oz.) Olive Oil,
Sauteed, White Wine Sauce, Roasted Potatoes

PEPPER STEAK ITALIANA 22.95
Tenderloin of Beef, Sauce,
Green Peppers, Mushrooms, Onions and
Fresh Tomatoes

ITALIAN LOIN VEAL CHOP 25.95
Served with Imported Vinegar Peppers,
Roasted Potatoes

PRIME CUT
NEW YORK SIRLOIN STEAK 25.95
Sauteed Mushrooms

PRIME FILET MIGNON 24.95
Sauteed Mushrooms

STEAK and LOBSTER . . . . (Market Price)

ITALIAN STYLE PRIME CUT
SIRLOIN STEAK 25.95
Served with Imported Vinegar Peppers,
Roasted Potatoes

POULTRY
(Please Allow Approximately 30 Minute Preparation)

FAMOUS CHICKEN VESUVIO 13.95
Olive Oil, Garlic, White Wine,
Peas and Potatoes

CHICKEN ALLA CACCIATORE 13.95
Olive Oil, White Wine, Garden Peppers,
Mushrooms, and Touch of Tomato

BROILED CHICKEN
ORIGANATO 13.95
Lemon, Oil, Special Seasoning

CHICKEN FRANCESE
(Boneless Breast) 13.95
Lemon Butter, Special Seasoning

CHICKEN PARMIGIANA
(Boneless Breast) 13.95
Special Sauce, Melted Cheeses

Dinner: Mon - Thurs 5 - 11, Fri - Sat 5 - 12, Sun 4 - 10

Scoozi

It's huge—350 seats huge—but there can be, especially on Friday and Saturday nights, a wait of an hour or more for a table. The bar area is huge, too, so have a Bellini cocktail and work up an appetite for some delicious thin-crust pizza, risotto, pasta or chicken.

APERITIVI

NEGRONI	4.50
IL GABBIANO	3.75
BELLINI SCOOZI	4.50
PORTO ROSSO	3.75
SPAZZATURA	4.50
AMERICANO	3.75

ANTIPASTI FREDDI

	PORZIONE	
	PICCOLA	GRANDE
INSALATA CAPRESE Tomato, Mozzarella, Arugula		4.95
TRE COLORE CROSTINI Marinated Goat Cheese, Walnuts, Mushrooms, Sun Dried Tomatoes on Grilled Garlic Bread		5.25
MELANZANE GRIGLIATI Grilled Eggplant, peppers, balsamic vinaigrette		4.50
CARPACCIO NOOVO MOPO Sliced raw sirloin, celery pesto		5.75
ANTIPASTI SCOOZI! An assortment of daily prepared small salads and antipasti		7.95

PIZZA

	PICCOLA	GRANDE
MARGHERITA Tomato, Pesto, Mozzarella	6.95	12.95
DEL BOSCO Roasted mushrooms, smoked mozzarella, onions	7.50	13.50
ENZO Tomato, Grilled Eggplant, Goat Cheese	7.25	13.25
FINANZIERA Spinach, onions, gorgonzola, walnuts	7.50	13.50

INSALATE

INSALATA MARCIA Field greens, pears, gorgonzola, walnuts, balsamic vinaigrette	5.50
CAESAR Caesar salad with smoked mozzarella	4.95
CALAMARI AROMATICO Caesar salad with spicy fried calamari	5.95

ZUPPE

MINESTRONE GENOVESE Vegetable soup, pesto	2.95

---

410 West Huron • River North • (312) 943-5900

PASTA

	PORZIONE	
	PICCOLA	GRANDE
MEZZALUNA BANDIERA Cheese & spinach filled, alfredo, tomato & pesto sauces	7.95	10.50
MALFADI VERDE Spinach & Ricotta gnocchi, gorgonzola cream, walnuts	8.25	10.75
CANNELLONI PIEDMONTESE Baked mushroom cannelloni, fontina, cream		9.75
RAVIOLI CHRISTINA Cheese ravioli, oven roasted tomatoes, butter	7.95	10.50
FOSILLI VERDURE Fresh tomato broth, roasted vegetables	6.95	9.50
FARFALLE CONTADINA Roast chicken, vegetables, pancetta	7.25	9.75

PIATTI DELLA CASA
PLATES OF THE HOUSE

GAMBERI SCOOZI! Oven roasted stuffed shrimp, garlic bread crumbs, tomato	14.95
ZUPPE DI PESCE Traditional Italian seafood stew	14.50

ANTIPASTI CALDI

FONGHI AL FORNO Roasted portabello mushroom, parmesan mashed potato	5.50
VERDURE AL SPIEDO Grilled vegetable skewers, herbed goat cheese	4.95
CALAMARI FRITTI Fried calamari, spicy tomato sauce	5.95
FAGIANO CON FUNGHI Smoked pheasant, mushrooms, polenta	5.50
PROSCIOTIO VAL D'ASTANO Prosciutto, parmesan glazed asparagus	6.25

ALLA GRIGLIA
FROM THE GRILL

BISTECCA BALSAMICO Balsamic glazed New York sirloin	13.95
TRIPLO ESSE Shrimp & scallop skewer, salsa verde	14.95
TONNO ALLA FINOCCHIO Tuna, fennel, orange, glazed red onion	12.95
POLLO NATURALE Grilled chicken breast, tomato & basil ragu	9.95

DOLCE

SEMIFREDDO AL CAFFÉ Vanilla gelato, espresso	2.25
GELATI Italian ice cream	3.50
PROFITEROLE Cream puffs stuffed with gelati	4.25
MILLE CALORE Mascarpone, cheesecake, apricot raisin compote	3.50
TIRAMISU	4.50
FROTTA FRECCA Fresh fruit in season	3.50

Dinner: Mon - Thurs 5 - 10:30, Fri - Sat 5 - 11:30, Sun 5 - 9

The view of Oak Street Beach from the multi-level dining room is great. Very innovative Italian food is served flawlessly in a very luxe and luxurious atmosphere. Without a doubt the classiest Italian restaurant in Chicago.

SPIAGGIA

PIZZE

AI QUATTRO FORMAGGI
Mozzarella, Romano, provolone, gorgonzola
and sun-dried tomatoes $8.95

MARGHERITA
Tomatoes, basil and provolone cheese $8.95

SALSICCIA D'ANITRA
Duck sausage, sage and goat cheese $8.95

ORTOLANO
Grilled vegetables, scamorza, provolone and basil $8.95

ANTIPASTI

CAPPESANTE CON INDIVIA BELGA
Grilled sea scallops with Belgian endive, lemon dressing
and chives $8.95

CARPACCIO DI BUE CON RADICCHIO E POMPELMO
Beef carpaccio with radicchio, grapefruit
and extra virgin olive oil $7.95

GUAZZETTO DI COZZE
Mussels steamed with white beans in an aromatic garlic
tomato broth $8.95

INSALATA SPIAGGIA
Mixed green salad with balsamic mustard dressing $6.95

ZUPPA DEL GIORNO
Soup of the day $4.95

---

980 North Michigan Ave • Near North/Gold Coast • (312) 280-2750

PASTA

FARFALLE ROSSE CON ASPARAGI
Tomato pasta butterflies with asparagus, snow peas,
cream and grana cheese — $10.95

RISOTTO CON FRUTTI DI MARE
Seafood risotto — $13.95

TORTELLI DI PATATE E PORRI AL PESTO
Potato and leek filled pasta with Parmigiano
and pesto — $11.95

STRACCI CON RAGU DI FUNGHI
Rags of fresh pasta with wild mushrooms — $12.95

GNOCCHI DI PATATE AL BURRO E ORO
Potato gnocchi with roasted tomato, butter
and Parmigiano — $8.95

RAVIOLI DI RICOTTA CON CACIOTTA TOSCANA
Ricotta filled ravioli with sweet Tuscan Pecorino — $12.95

PIATTI DEL GIORNO

SALMONE CON SPINACI E SALSA OLIVADA
Wood-roasted salmon with sauteed spinach and
black olive sauce — $17.95

SPIEDINO DI QUAGLIE ALLA SALVIA
Skewered boneless quail with mushrooms, onions and
sage in a white wine sauce — $18.95

COSTOLETTE D'AGNELLO ALLA MILANESE
Sauteed breaded lamb chops on a bed of mixed greens — $17.95

PESCE CON PESTO E FINOCCHIO BRASATO
Grilled fish with pesto and braised fennel in
tomato sauce — $16.95

VERDURE GRIGILIATE CON MOZZARELLA
Assorted grilled vegetables with mozzarella and
sun-dried tomato vinaigrette — $12.95

Dinner: Mon - Thurs 5:30 - 9:30, Fri - Sat 5:30 - 10:30, Sun 5:30 - 9

Topo Gigio

A longtime favorite trattoria of mine, this "little gray mouse" is so unassuming and low-key that it fools you. Once the food starts coming, there is excitement galore—culinary fireworks of the first order. I cannot remember ever having a dish here that I did not truly enjoy.

Menu Changes Seasonally

STUZZICARELLI

BRUSCHETTA $2.75
Toasted Italian Bread, with Garlic, Extra Virgin Olive Oil, Cherry Tomato, Fresh Basil and a Touch of Oregano

CALAMARI FRITTI $6.95
Golden Fried Calamari, served with Lemon Wedges & Marinara Sauce

PEPERONI ARROSTO $4.50
Green & Red Roasted Peppers, Peeled & Dressed with Garlic and Extra Virgin Olive Oil

COZZE ALLA MARINARA $6.95
Our Famous Mussels in a Marinara Sauce

ANTIPASTO FREDDO
A Presentation of Meats & Cheeses and Vegetables Including: Roasted Peppers, Artichokes, Frittata, Caponata, Roasted Eggplant, Calamari al Sugo di Pesce etc. FOR TWO OR MORE $5.00 PER PERSON

ANTIPASTO DI PESCE
A Seafood Platter of : Calamari, Mussels alla Marinara, Baked Clams, Scampi & Sea Scallops, and Bruschetta. FOR TWO OR MORE $6.50 PER PERSON

ZUPPE

TORTELLINI IN BRODO $3.75
ZUPPA DEL GIORNO $2.50

1437 North Wells • River North • (312) 266-9355

LE INSALATE

CALAMARI SALAD $6.50
Fresh Calamari Marinated in Lemon & Extra Virgin Olive Oil and a touch
of Giardiniera

INSALATA MISTA...$2.75
Romaine & Curly Endive, with Tomato, Cucumbers, Walnuts & Black
Raisins with Balsamic Vinaigrette Dressing

POMODORI E CIPOLLA ROSSA $4.95
Sliced Beefsteak Tomato and Red Onion in a Vinaigrette Dressing With
Bleu Cheese...Add $1.00

LE PASTE

RIGATONI AL FILO DI FUMO $9.95
Spicy Tomato Sauce, With Pancetta, Fresh Mozzarella, Basil,
Topped with Pecorino Cheese

ORECCHIETTE TAORMINA $9.95
Ear-Shaped Pasta, In a Fresh Tomato Sauce, Eggplant
and Dry Ricotta Cheese

FUSILLI ALLA TOPO GIGIO $9.95
Corkscrew-Shaped Pasta in Our Own Sauce

SPAGHETTI AI FRUTTI DI MARE $12.95
Spaghetti with Calamari, Mussels, Clams & Sea Scallops in
Our Marinara Sauce

I SECONDI

POLLO ARROSTO AL ROSMARINO $10.95
Half Chicken roasted with Garlic, Rosemary & Potatoes

VITELLA ALLA CARUSO $15.95
Veal Scaloppini Baked with Prosciutto, Roasted Eggplant & Mozzarella in
Wine, Sage Sauce

SPIEDINI ADRIATICA $14.95
Grilled Scampi & Sea Scallops on a Skewer, Served on a Bed of
Spinach in Garlic & Oil

WHITE FISH AL LIMONE E CAPPERI $12.95
Lake Superior White Fish, Baked in a Lemon, Wine & Caper Sauce

Dinner: 7 Days a Week until 11

One of the more comfortable and well-appointed Italian restaurants on Harlem Avenue, Trattoria Bellavia has romanced my tastebuds on many occasions. Under the watchful eye of owners Dennis and Elisa Vaccaro, nothing ever seems to go amiss. I have many favorite dishes here, but the two that thrill me the most are the braciole alla Barese and the panzarotti (the homemade cavatelli is great, too).

Trattoria Bellavia

ANTIPASTI

CALDI (HOT)

PANZEROTTI	3.25
ARANCINI *(Rice Balls)*	2.25
BAKED CLAMS	One Dozen 9.50
	Half Dozen 5.75
COZZE MARINARA *(Mussels)*	5.95
COZZE SCOPPIATE	5.95
CALAMARI FRITTI *(Fried Squid)*	5.95
STUFFED FUNGHI *(Mushrooms)*	5.25

FREDDI (COLD)

ANTIPASTO ALL'ITALIANA	7.95
INSALATA DI PESCE	8.95
RAW CLAMS	One Dozen 9.00
	Half Dozen 5.25

PASTA

ALLA INSALATA	8.25
(Tomato, Onion, Oregano)	
ALLE COZZE *(Red or White Sauce)*	9.95
ALLE CLAMS *(Red or White Sauce)*	10.25
ALLE CALAMARI	10.25
ALLA CAPRESE	12.95
(Shrimp/Clams Cozze)	
ALLA CARBONARA	9.95
GNOCCHI DI PATATA	9.25
CAVATELLI	10.95

CARNE

VITELLO *(Veal)* **13.95**
VINO BIANCO E FUNGHI
(White Wine and Mushrooms)
MARSALA E FUNGHI
(Marsala and Mushrooms)
SCALOPPINE LIMONE
(Lemon)
PICCANTE
PARMIGIANA
TOSCANA
(Breaded with White Wine, Spice)
VITELLO ALLA TRATTORIA 14.25
(Veal and Eggplant)
SPECIAL TRATTORIA BELLAVIA
ANGNELLO AL FORNO 11.25
(Oven Roasted Lamb)
POLLO *(CHICKEN)* **9.50**
VESUVIO
CACCIATORE
OREGANATO
PARMIGIANA

BEEF

BRACIOLE ALLA BARESE 11.95
STEAK PIZZAIOLA 13.95

PESCE (FISH)

CALAMARI FRITTI *(Fried Squid)*..11.25
GAMBERI STUFFED *(Stuffed Shrimp)* 14.95
ZUPPA DI PESCE *(Seafood in Red Sauce)* 19.95
CACIUCCO ALLA LIVORNESE *(Seafood in White Sauce)*......19.95

MEAT OR FISH DINNERS INCLUDE:
...SOUP ...SALAD ...SIDE ORDER OF PASTA
with SUGO OR MARINARA SAUCE

Dinner: Mon - Sat 4 - 11

Trattoria Gianni

Its location in a renovated house on the Near North Side is appropriate for this restaurant, as the food has a pronounced home-style goodness. The dining room is small, so the atmosphere is intimate. A good spot to try when going to one of the nearby theaters.

trattoria
GIANNI

Menu Changes Seasonally

Antipasti

Antipasto della Casa *Market Price* Variety of grilled vegetables, changes daily		**Antipasto Freddo** *$10.50* Salame, prosciutto, mortadella, cheeses, vegetables	
Zucchine Fritte *$3.95* Fried Zucchini		♥ **Bruschetta** *$1.95* Gianni's version of garlic bread	
Cozze alla Marinara *$5.95* Mussels in a marinara sauce		**Melanzane Arrotolate** *$4.95* Slices of eggplant, rolled with prosciutto and mozzarella, baked with tomato sauce	
Calamari Fritti *$5.95* Fried calamari		**Gamberi alla Napoletana** *$6.95* Shrimp sauteed with white wine, garlic, mushrooms, artichoke hearts, and cherry tomatoes	
Carpaccio di Manzo *$6.95* Thin slices of filet mignon, olive oil, lemon, capers, parmesan cheese		**Vongole al Forno** *$6.95* Baked Clams	

Zuppa

Zuppa del Giorno *$2.50*
Fresh seasonal soup, prepared daily

Insalate

Insalata della Casa *$2.50*
Romaine lettuce, carrots, cucumber, tomatoes, balsamic vinegar, olive oil

Pomodoro Cipolla e Gorgonzola *$4.95*
Tomatoes, red onions, blue cheese and extra virgin olive oil.

Insalata Caprese *$6.50*
Tomatoes, fresh mozzarella, basil and extra virgin olive oil

Contorni

Scarola con Salsiccia $3.95
Fresh escarole sauteed with olive oil, garlic, hot peppers and Italian sausage

Spinaci Aglio e Olio $4.25
Fresh spinach sauteed with olive oil and garlic

Patate Arrosto $3.25
Roasted potatoes with olive oil, garlic and rosemary

Primi Piatti

Spaghetti Melanzane $9.50
Olive oil, garlic, eggplant, fresh basil, and fresh tomato sauce

Rigatoni Nocerina $11.25
Sun-dried tomatoes, mushrooms, olive oil, garlic, fresh basil in a cream sauce

Rigatoni con Verdure $9.95
Carrots, eggplant, broccoli, and garlic in a fresh, ripe tomato sauce

Conchiglie del Mercante $10.95
Crumbled Italian sausage, mushrooms, fresh tomato sauce, scamorza cheese, peas, with a touch of cream

Fettuccine al Pomodoro $8.95
Fresh tomato sauce

Spaghetti Portofino $12.95
Scallops, scampi, cherry tomatoes, olive oil, garlic

Tortellini Baronessa $11.25
Prosciutto, Mushrooms, Peas, in cream sauce

Risotto   *Market Price*
Italian arborio rice, changes daily

Secondi Piatti

Lombata di Vitello ai Ferri $16.95
Grilled veal chop

Petti di Pollo alla Toscana $13.95
Boneless chicken breast, sauteed with white wine, mushrooms and pine nuts.

Vitello alla Gianni $14.50
Veal scalloppine sauteed in a brandy sauce with mushrooms, cherry tomatoes and artichoke hearts

♥ **Petti di Pollo alla Griglia agli Aromi** $12.95
Grilled boneless chicken breast marinated with fresh herbs, served with vegetables

Saltimbocca alla Sorrentina $14.50
Veal scalopine topped with prosciutto and mozzarella cheese, sauteed with white wine and tomatoes

Pollo alla Diavola $10.95
Broiled half chicken, sauteed with olive oil, garlic, rosemary, hot peppers, served with roasted potatoes

Pesce Fresco del Giorno   *Market Price*
Fresh fish of the day

Dolci

Tiramisu' $4.25
Gianni's specialty

Gelato $3.95

Cannoli $2.75

Dolce del Giorno $4.50
Changes daily

Trattoria No. 10

The grotto-like atmosphere with its arched walkways and evocative murals creates an atmosphere of subdued elegance. And the food is just as winning. A must to try is the homemade ravioli, a specialty of the house that is superb.

FORMAGGIO AL FORNO 5.25
Homemade mozzarella baked with prosciutto, crostini, sun dried tomato, spices.

COZZE ALLA MARINARA 6.95
Fresh mussels with garlic and tomato sauce.

GAMBERETTI CON LIMONE E BASILICO 7.95
Grilled lemon and basil-wrapped shrimp, roasted garlic and extra virgin olive oil.

POLPI CON ACETO E OLIO 6.50
Paper thin slices of octopus marinated with lime juice, extra virgin oil, garlic and spices.

ZUPPE

MINESTRONE ALLA MILANESE 3.50
Milanese vegetable soup

ZUPPA DEL GIORNO 3.50
Soup of the day

INSALATE

INSALATA DI POLLO CON POMPELMO 9.95
Grilled breast of chicken, green beans and grapefruit, mixed greens, grapefruit vinaigrette.

INSALATA NO. 10 .... 7.95/3.95
Special house salad with primavera vegetables, meats and cheeses.

INSALATA DI CALAMARI CON MELANZANE 9.95
Grilled marinated calamari with eggplant terrine, mixed greens, garlic-thyme vinaigrette.

---

10 North Dearborn • Downtown/Loop • (312) 984-1718

RAVIOLI

RAVIOLI CON GAMBERI E PESTO 13.50/7.50
With shrimp, pesto and carmelized pearl onions, fresh tomato relish.

RAVIOLI ZUCCA GIALLA 10.50/5.95
With a blend of butternut and acorn squash, walnut butter sauce.

RAVIOLI AI TRE FUNGHI 10.95/6.50
With wild mushroom caps, ricotta, porcini cream sauce.

RAVIOLI SALSICCIA 10.95/6.50
With homemade Italian sausage and mozzarella, tomato arrabbiata.

RAVIOLI DI VITELLO ALLA GORGONZOLA 13.95/7.95
With Provimi veal, sage and walnuts, gorgonzola cream sauce.

SPECIALITA DELLA CASA

POLLO RIPIENO CON SPINACI E FORMAGGIO 12.95
*Grilled boneless breast of chicken stuffed with spinach, goat and ricotta cheeses,
"Diavola" sauce.*

SCALOPPINE DI VITELLO CON LIMONE 15.95
Provimi veal medallions with wild mushrooms and lemon sage butter.

BRACIOLA DI VITELLO 19.95
Traditionally breaded veal chop "alla Milanese" or grilled with natural jus reduction.

AGNELLO TOSCANO 19.95
Roasted rack of lamb coated with pistachio and pine nuts, roasted shallot polenta.

PASTA

FARFALLE CON ANATRA 13.95
Bow tie pasta with duck confit, asparagus, carmelized onion and pine nuts, enriched veal stock.

LINGUINE FRUTTI DI MARE 15.95
Shrimp, scallops, calamari and clams with roasted garlic, tomato, basil, chive and olive oil.

CONCHIGLIE RIGATE CON POLLO EVEGETALI 11.95
*Shell pasta with sauteed chicken and fresh vegetables, light porcini mushroom
cream sauce, pine nuts.*

Dinner: Mon - Thurs 5:30 - 9, Fri - Sat 5:30 - 10

Tucci Benuch

Probably the most successful Italian restaurant in a high-rise shopping center anywhere in the world. The various dining rooms replicate those of an Italian home (library, kitchen, front room), including an umbrella-dotted patio. *Generous portions of down-to-earth Italian food are the gist of the gusto-inspired menu.*

© 1988

Menu Changes Seasonally

ANTIPASTI

BRUSCHETTA CAPO D'AGLIO - Garlic Bread, Tomato Sauce 2.50
BRUSCHETTA CON FORMAGGIO - Baked Cheese Bread 3.95
FUNGHI CON SPINACI - Baked Mushrooms Stuffed with Spinach 3.50
CAPRESE - Tomatoes, Fresh Mozarella, Basil, Olive Oil 3.95
ANTIPASTO DELLA CASA - Antipasti Plate - Sliced Salami, Italian Cheeses,
　　Grilled Vegetables, Olives, Tomatoes 5.95

BENUCCH'S ORIGINAL THIN CRUST PIZZAS

Our Special Pizza Dough is Rolled Wafer Thin to Keep the Pizzas Light and Crisp.
FORMAGGIO E POMODORI - Plum Tomato, Basil, Cheese 6.25
♥ **SEMPLICE** - Grilled Vegetables, Smoked Mozzarella 6.95
SALSICCIA - Italian Sausage, Cheese 6.95
PEPPERONI - Grilled Pepperoni, Cheese 6.95
FRUTTI DI MARE - Shrimp, Scallops, Calamari, Clams, Tomato Sauce,
　　Basil, Mozzarella 8.25
CAPRINI - Sundried Tomato, Olives, Goat and Mozzarella Cheese 7.75
POLLO AFFUMICATO - Smoked Chicken, Spinach, Onion, Bacon,
　　Red Peppers, Asiago Cheese 7.75
QUATTRO STAGIONI - A Quarter each of Formaggio E Pomodori,
　　Semplice, Salsiccia, and Funghi 7.75

PIZZE SENSA FORMAGGIO (Pizza Without Cheese)

PRIMAVERA - Spinach, Tomatoes, Peppers, Broccoli, Mushrooms, Italian Vinaigrette ... 6.95
FUNGHI - Mushrooms, Grilled Onions, Tomato Sauce, Spicy Vinaigrette 7.50

---

900 North Michigan • Near North/Gold Coast • (312) 266-1200

SALADS

♥**INSALATA DELLA CASA** - Mixed Greens, Italian Vinaigrette or Creamy Romano 2.75

INSALATA GIARDINIERA - Mixed Greens, Provolone, Homemade
Giardiniera, Olives, Tomatoes, Pepperoncini, Italian Dressing 6.95

INSALATA DI SPINACI - Spinach, Smoked Chicken, Mushrooms, Red Onion, Egg,
Peppers, Spicy Vinaigrette 7.95

INSALATA NUOVO CON GAMBERI - Grilled Shrimp Caesar Salad 9.50
Half Portion 5.50

INSALATA NUOVO CON POLLO - Chicken Ceasar Salad 8.75
Half Portion 4.75

HOMEMADE PASTA SPECIALTIES

SPAGHETTI TUCCI - Baked Spaghetti, Choice of Tomato or Meat Sauce, Meatball
or Sausage 8.95

RAVIOLI ALFORNO - Baked Homemade Cheese Ravioli, Alfredo, Parmesan 8.75

FUSILLI NOVECENTO - Braised Veal Shank, Corkscrew Pasta, Natural Gravy 9.95

PASTA - CLASSICS

♥**SPAGHETTINI AL POMODORO** - Tomato Sauce 6.25

SPAGHETTINI AL RAGU - Meat Sauce 7.25

PENNE CON SALSICCIA E POLPETTINI - Sausage and Meatball, Meat Sauce 8.50

LINGUINE SALUTARI - Mushrooms, Peppers, Broccoli, Green Onions, Olives,
Parmesan, Mozzarella, Olive Oil 7.50

MANICOTTI MELROSE - Spinach, Ricotta, Tomato and Alfredo Sauces 8.95

FETTUCCINI TUCCI - Mushrooms, Proscuitto, Peas, Cream Sauce 8.25

LINGUINE CLASSICO - Clam Sauce 8.95

RAVIOLI CASALINGUA - Homemade Cheese Ravioli with Tomato Sauce and Basil 8.75

FETTUCCINI DEL CACCIATORE - Chicken, Tomatoes, Mushrooms, Red Wine Sauce .. 8.95

OLD WORLD FAVORITES

POLLO AL'AGLIO - Half Roast Chicken, Garlic, Herbs, Roasted Potatoes 8.95

POLLO ALLA MILANESE - Parmesan Crusted Chicken Breast, Lemon Garlic
Butter Sauce, Pasta 9.95

POLLO ALLA PARMIGIANO - Chicken Breast, Tomato Sauce, Mozzarella, Pasta 10.50

PANINO

Each Day Tucci Will Offer A Sandwich From The Italian Countryside

♥These items are prepared from recipes that meet the fat and cholesterol guidelines of The
American Heart Association of Metropolitan Chicago for Healthy Hearts.

Tucci Milan

A sister restaurant to Tucci Benuuch with a menu that is quite different, as is the atmosphere, which is quite contemporary. The antipasto display just inside the entry door is enough to push the appetite to greater heights.

Menu Changes Seasonally

ANTIPASTI

DAL NOSTRO TAVOLO ALLA VOSTRA TAVOLA

A SELECTION OF THE DAY'S SPECIAL APPETIZERS FROM OUR ANTIPASTI TABLE. AVAILABLE INDIVIDUALLY OR AS AN ASSORTMENT.

PRIMI PIATTI

BRUSCHETTA 4.50
Grilled Tuscan Bread, Cannellini Beans, Tomato, Homemade Mozzarella, Basil
CALAMARI AL FERRI 5.50
Grilled Squid, Roasted Peppers, Garlic Spinach, Lemon, Olive Oil
CARPACCIO MILANO 5.50
Thinly Sliced Beef, Spicy Field Greens, Truffle Oil, Parmesan,
Grilled Radicchio, Pancetta, Goat Cheese, Basil Vinaigrette

PIZZE

MARGHERITA 6.95
Fresh Tomato and Pesto Sauces, Homemade Mozzarella, Provolone, Basil
♥MONTECATINI (Pizza Without Cheese) 7.25
Grilled Eggplant, Zucchini, Yellow Squash, Peppers, Onions, Tomatoes, Olive Oil
TRE FORMAGGI E SALSICCIA 7.95
Fontina, Provolone, Parmigiano, Italian Sausage, Spinach, Tomatoes
AFFUMICATA 8.75
Grilled Chicken, Red and Yellow Peppers, Smoked Mozzarella
BOSCAIOLA 8.25
Wild and Domestic Mushrooms, Fresh Herbs, Tomatoes, Teleme Cheese

INSALATE

INSALATA VERDE MISTA 3.50
Romaine, Radicchio, Belgian Endive, Frisée, Carrots, Beets, Italian Dressing
CAESAR SORRENTO 4.95
Hearts of Romaine, Caesar Dressing (no egg), Parmigiano, Crostini
ROMA 4.75
Avocado, Hearts of Palm, Roma Plum Tomatoes, Red Onion, Vinaigrette

---

6 West Hubbard • River North • (312) 222-0044

SAPORITA (al Formaggio Caprino) **4.95**
Baked Goat Cheese with Bread Crumbs, Mixed Greens,
Sun Dried Tomatoes, Balsamic Vinaigrette
INSALATA INSOLITA **8.50**
Grilled Chicken Breast, Pancetta, Mushrooms, Egg, Mixed Greens, Honey Mustard
Dressing
TAGLIATA DI TONNO **8.95**
Black Peppered Tuna (grilled medium rare), Avocado, Roasted Peppers, Capers,
Balsamic Vinaigrette

PASTE FATTE IN CASA
PASTAS MADE FRESH FROM DURUM FLOUR, SEMOLINA, EGGS AND OLIVE OIL

	MEZZA	PIETANZE

PAPPARDELLE AI FUNGHI .... **5.95** **8.95**
Wide Pasta, Wild Mushrooms, Porcini Broth
LASAGNE AGLI SPINACI **8.95**
Spinach Filled Lasagna, Alfredo and Tomato Sauces, Mozzarella, Parmigiano
RAVIOLI DEL GIORNO .... **6.25** **9.25**
Ravioli Special of the Day
FETTUCCINI BIANCHE CON POLLO .... **6.25** **9.25**
Fettuccine, Grilled Chicken, Broccoli, Parmigiano, Alfredo Sauce

DALLA ROSTICCERIA

ANITRA ALLO SPIEDO **13.95**
Half Rotisserie Duck, Balsamic Corriander Glaze, Red Swiss Chard, Grappa Soaked
Cherries, Polenta
SPECIALTA DEL SPIEDO .... **A.Q.**
Rotisserie Special of the Day

PIETANZE

PETTO DI POLLO MARINATO **10.95**
Grilled Marinated Breast of Chicken, Mediterranean Vegetables, Orzo Salad
♥POLLO SALUTE **10.95**
Grilled Chicken Breast Stuffed with Spinach and Lowfat Mozzarella, Tomato Basil,
Cannellini Beans
SALMONE ALLA GRIGLIA **13.95**
Grilled Atlantic Salmon, Rumesco Sauce, Crostini, Carmelized Leeks

CONTORNI

SCAROLA
Sauteed Escarole, Pancetta Peperoncini **2.25**
POLENTA
Black Pepper, Parmigiano **2.25**

♥THESE ITEMS ARE PREPARED FROM RECIPES THAT MEET THE FAT AND
CHOLESTEROL GUIDELINES OF THE AMERICAN HEART ASSOCIATION OF
METROPOLITAN CHICAGO FOR HEALTHY ADULTS

Tufano's Vernon Park Tap

Joey Di Buono runs a very nice Italian neighborhood restaurant. I liked it on my first visit in 1968 when it was nothing more than a bar and a backroom, and I like it today. This is an Italian's Italian restaurant, as the menu reflects (baccala and pork chops and peppers, for example), and I've never met a plate of food here that I didn't like.

Salads

Tufano's Special .... $4.00 per person
    Includes: lettuce, tomato, cucumber, salami, mozzarella cheese, onion, artichoke hearts, font. cheese, black olives, pepperincini, roasted red peppers, oil and vinegar dressing.

AntiPasto Salad .... $3.00 per person
    Includes: lettuce, tomato, cucumber, salami, mozzarella cheese, onion, black olives, pepperincini, oil and vinegar dressing.

House Salad .... $2.00 per person
    Includes: lettuce, tomato, cucumber, onion, black olives, house dressing.

Pastas Entree
All Pasta served with Grandma's Special Gravy, bread and butter.

Stuffed Shells $6.50
    Four large shells stuffed with rigotta cheese.

Lasagna $6.25
    Grandma's favorite four layer meatless recipe.

Raviolis (Sat. and Sun. only) $6.75
    Four large cheese raviolis

Tortellini Alfredo (Cheese) $7.25

Spaghetti, Oil and Garlic $6.50
    Our best spaghetti served under a blend of olive oil and chopped garlic.

Shells and Broccoli $7.00
    Pasta shells served under a blend of sauteed broccoli, chopped garlic, and seasonings.

Fish

Orange Roughy $8.00
   Broiled roughy served with broccoli and lemon wedges, broccoli
   may be substituted with your choice of pasta.

Chicken - Veal - Chops

Tufano's Lemon Chicken............................served with potatoes
   Whole Chicken $11.00
   Half Chicken $5.75
Veal Parmigiana $10.50
Chicken Parmigiana $8.25
Pork Chops and Peppers... $9.50
   Two center cut chops cooked to order served with peppers,
   peas, potatoes, bread and butter.
Sausage and Peppers $7.00

Fish Special

Linguine with Calamari $9.00
   Fresh calamari in marinara served on a bed of linguine.
Linguine with Red Devil Shrimp....................................... $9.75

Tufano's Specials
Item availability may vary.

Egg Plant Parmigiana $6.75
   Hand cut pan fried and layed to perfection with cheese, cheese
   and cheese.
Fried Calamari .... $8.25 full order .... $4.50 half order
   Fresh squid battered in our own recipe and fried to perfection.
Tripe.. $6.50
   Fresh honeycomb tripe sauteed in Grandma's best marinara.
Shells and Broccoli with Shrimp...................................... $10.25
   Pastas shells served under a blend of sauteed broccoli,
   shrimp, chopped garlic and seasonings.

Desserts

Cannoli $2.25
Cheese Cake.. $2.25
Tiramisu $3.00

Dinner: Mon - Fri until 11, Sat 4 - 11, Sun 3 - 9

Va Pensiero

Chicago is heavy on Italian restaurants whose names start with a "V," but include this one—an Evanston offshoot—in your eating plans, as the food is well-crafted, innovative and never stops being just plain tasty.

Menu Changes Seasonally Along With Daily Specials

Antipasti

Calamari Alla Griglia	5.25
Skewers of calamari and thinly sliced lemons, tossed with oregano, garlic and breadcrumbs, then grilled.	
Gamberi Con Salsa Di Pistacchi	6.25
Sauteed gulf shrimp served on a crispy onion risotto cake and topped with a pistachio pesto.	
Polenta Con Fonduta	4.95
Soft polenta topped with slowly carmelized onions and a creamy Fontina cheese sauce.	
Funghi Gratinata	5.95
Gratin of wild mushrooms, rosemary and garlic, topped with olive oil drizzled breadcrumbs and baked till crisp.	
Bresaola Piccante	6.25
Thinly sliced cured tenderloin of beef, topped with fresh artichokes, capers, tomatoes and olives.	

Insalate

Insalata Di Cucina	2.50
Mixed greens, toasted pine nuts, balsamic vinaigrette.	
Insalata Di Cesare	3.95
Romaine, croutons, roasted peppers, anchovy vinaigrette.	
Insalate Del Giorno	VARIES
Special salads reflecting the season.	

ZUPPE

LE ZUPPA SONO SECONDO ALLA STAGIONE   3.95
Soups according to the season.

PASTE

RAVIOLI DI CARCIOFI   15.00
Spinach ravioli stuffed with a creamy artichoke filling in a
buttered broth with lemon and fresh herbs.

FAZZOLETTI IMBOTTITI   12.50
Delicate white wine pasta squares filled with fresh spinach
and ricotta cheese, served with a roasted tomato sauce and a
parmesan sauce.

LINGUINE CON GAMBERETTI   13.50
Linguine tossed with fresh shrimp and a piquant sauce of green
olives, tomatoes, lemon, basil and cream.

GNOCCHI DI PATATE CON SALSA DI FUNGHI   13.00
Potato gnocchi with a sauce of wild mushrooms, pancetta,
garlic and parsley.

(First course portions of pasta are available)

PIETANZE

TORTINO DI MELANZANE   12.95
Layered dish of eggplant, tomato and parmesan cheese,
accompanied by a light tomato sauce with basil.

ARROSTA DI SALMON SENAPE   18.95
Roasted Atlantic salmon topped with a mustard mascarpone
glaze on a bed of fresh sauteed greens.

SCALOPPINE DI TACCHINO   15.95
Grilled slices of marinated turkey breast, served on a bed of soft
polenta and a saute of broccoli rabe, pancetta and garlic.

INVOLTINI DI MAIALE   16.50
Sauteed pork loin rolled with a stuffing of golden raisins, capers
and pine nuts and served with semolina gnocchi.

BRACIOLE DI AGNELLO ARROSTO   18.95
Herb and gorgonzola crusted lamb chops served with natural
juices and a potato and walnut gratin.

OSSO BUCCO CON LA CAPRIATA   20.50
Braised veal shank on a bed of sauteed escarole with a white
bean-garlic puree and a red wine rosemary sauce.

Dinner: Mon - Thurs 5:30 - 9, Fri - Sat 5:30 - 10

This little hole-in-the-wall spot is what an Italian who really knows his restaurants would call "uno dormiente," or a sleeper. Even better than the food, which is always very good, are the prices, which are sane.

VIA VENETO

ANTIPASTI

INSALATA RUSTICA assorted lettuce with grilled chicken
breast and special dressing .... Appetizer 4.95
Dinner 7.50

INSALATA DELLA CASA assorted lettuce, garnishes w/special
house dressing 3.00

CAPRESE buffala mozzarella with tomatoes, basil & olive oil 4.75

MELENZANE STUZZICANTE eggplant w/chopped tomato, garlic,
olive oil & mozzarella 3.95

GAMBERI AGLIO OLIO shrimps sauteed with garlic & olive oil 5.95

ZUPPA DEL GIORNO soup of the day .... (small bowl) 2.50

CALAMARI FRITTI fried squid 5.95

PASTE E RISOTTI

CAPPELLINI BELLA NAPOLI Angel Hair pasta w/fresh basil,
tomatoes, mozzarella & parmigiano 6.95

SPAGHETTI CRUDAIOLA w/fresh tomatoes, mushrooms & olives
sauteed in extra virgin olive oil 7.95

ORECCHIETTE CARRETTIER A sauteed w/broccoli,
garlic & parmigiano, w/touch of cream 7.95

SPAGHETTI CAPRICCIOSA shrimp sauteed w/wine, tomatoes,
parsley and garlic 8.95

TAGLIATELLE VERDI CAMPAGNOLA sauteed w/wine, tomatoes,
onions & parmigiano 7.95

TAGIATELLE BIANCHI ALLA CARBONARA white sauce/egg
noodles sauteed in butter pancetta and cream 7.95

RAVIOLI (meat, cheese, or pumpkin) in a light tomato and goat
cheese sauce 8.95

LASAGNA w/meat sauce 7.95

PENNE BOLOGNESE with rich meat sauce 6.95

RISOTTO AL FUNGHI arborio rice w/porcini mushrooms,
parmigiano & white wine 11.95

RISOTTO AL QUATTRO FORMAGGI arborio rice w/gorgonzola,
bel paese, fontina & parmigiano 10.95

LINGUINI AL CANESTRELLI tomato, herbs and fresh bay
scallops sauteed with olive oil, garlic and onions 8.95

SECONDI

PETTO DI POLLO VIA VENETO chicken breast sauteed w/fresh
mushrooms & white wine and side vegetables 9.95

VITELLO CON FAVE NOVELLE veal w/Fave beans chopped &
pureed with wine, olive oil, garlic and light tomato over pasta 10.95

VITELLO ARRABIATA veal w/spicy red sauce w/mushrooms
over pasta 10.95

VITELLO PARMIGIANA veal topped w/tomatoes & parmigiano
over pasta 10.95

CALAMARI RIPIENI squid stuffed w/parmigiano, bread crumbs,
garlic & parsley served in tomato sauce over pasta 9.95

PETTO DI POLLO ALLA VESUVIO chicken breast sauteed in olive oil,
garlic & topped w/sliced potatoes w/vegetables 9.95

ORANGE ROUGHY baked w/olive oil,
parsley & spices w/vegetables... 9.95

FISH OF THE DAY .... Market Price

MEAT OF THE DAY .... Market Price

Dinner: Mon - Thurs until 10, Fri - Sat until 11, Sun 3 - 9:30

One of the three dining venues in the Italian Village complex of restaurants, The Village (it's up the stairs) draws from the same family restaurant know-how as its sister restaurants—Vivere and La Cantina Enoteca. Excellent pasta creations are fairly priced.

the

VILLAGE

Menu Changes Seasonally

For The Gourmet

AGNOLOTTI AL POMODORO E BASILICO
Half-Moon Shaped Pasta filled with Ricotta and Spinach in a Light Tomato Basil Sauce - Salad
10.75

POLENTA CON POLLO ALLA CACCIATORA
Slices of Polenta served with Chicken Cacciatora - Salad
11.50

MANICOTTI
A Delicate Hollowed Pasta filled with Whipped Ricotta Cheese - Salad
10.25

CANNELLONI
A Delicate Hollowed Pasta with Meat Filling - Salad
10.25

POLLO ALL'ALFREDO
Disjointed Chicken and Italian Sausage seasoned with Sage, baked in Olive Oil with Mushrooms and Potatoes - Salad
13.95

LINGUINE FANTASIA
Linguine with Shrimp, Mushrooms, Zucchini in Seafood Cream Sauce - Salad
12.75

SALSICCE ALLA TOSCANA
From the original Tuscan recipe, Italian Sausages sauteed in a Savory Sauce of Black Olives - Salad
12.50

CAPELLINI D'ANGELO
Angel Hair Pasta in a Light Tomato Sauce with Ricotta Cheese and a hint of Capers - Salad
10.95

POLLO ALLA VESUVIO
Chicken deliciously seasoned with Herbs and Garlic, brought to the peak of taste - Salad
12.75

SALTIMBOCCA ALLA ROMANA
Slices of Veal with Sage, Prosciutto (Italian Ham) and cooked in Olive Oil - Salad
16.95

SCALOPPINE ALLA TOSCANINI
A symphony of flavor - Sliced Beef Tenderloin with Mushrooms, cooked in Marsala Wine - Salad
17.95

LOMBATINA DI VITELLO
Veal Chop with Sweet Red Peppers, Mushrooms and Dry Vermouth. For the discriminating diner - Salad
22.00

71 West Monroe • Downtown/Loop • (312) 332-7005

Village Dinners

Dinners on this page include Soup, Salad, Dessert and Coffee, Tea or Milk

Pasta

SPAGHETTI
With Meat Sauce or Tomato Sauce **9.95**
With Meat Balls, Mushrooms or Sausage **10.95**
MANICOTTI **10.95**
A Delicate Hollowed Pasta filled with Whipped
Ricotta Cheese
CANNELLONI **10.95**
Tetrazzini or Tomato Sauce, a Delicate
Hollowed Pasta with a Meat Filling
FETTUCCINE ALL'ALFREDO **11.75**
Fresh Egg Noodles served with Butter
and Parmesan Cheese

RAVIOLI (Meat Filled) **10.95**
With Meat Balls
GREEN NOODLES **10.95**
With Meat Sauce or Tomato Sauce
MOSTACCIOLI **10.95**
With Meat Sauce
**MOSTACCIOLI WITH
ITALIAN SAUSAGE** **11.50**
SEAFOOD RAVIOLI **11.50**
Ravioli filled with Mixed Seafood, prepared in
a Creamy Seafood Tomato Sauce

Poultry

BROILED CHICKEN **11.95**
Butter Sauce
**CHICKEN ALLA CACCIATORA
(with Mostaccioli)** **12.95**
Disjointed Chicken sauteed in Tomatoes,
Fresh Mushrooms, Olive Oil and Wine

**BONELESS CHICKEN
ALLA BOLOGNESE** **13.25**
CHICKEN ALLA ROMANA **13.25**
Disjointed Chicken sauteed in Shallots, Fresh
Mushrooms, Olive Oil and Wine
BONELESS CHICKEN SORRENTINO 14.50

Specialties

VEAL SCALOPPINE ALLA VILLAGE. **17.25**
Slices of Veal with Mushrooms cooked
in Dry White Wine
**VEAL SCALOPPINE
ALLA CACCIATORA** **17.25**
Slices of Veal with Mushrooms and
Tomatoes cooked in Dry White Wine
**VEAL SCALOPPINE
ALLA MARINARA** **17.25**
Sauteed in Spicy Sauce with Tomatoes, Garlic
and Anchovies

VEAL CUTLET ALLA BOLOGNESE .. **17.75**
Veal baked in a Sauce with a Slice of Cheese
and Prosciutto (Italian Ham)
VEAL FRANCAISE **17.95**
Veal coated with Egg, Sauteed in
Lemon Butter Sauce
VEAL SCALOPPINE PEPPERONCINI 17.95
Slices of Veal sauteed in White Wine with
Pepperoncini Peppers and Mushrooms

Seafoods

BROILED FRESH WHITEFISH **16.25**
Lemon Butter
BROILED FRESH WHITEFISH **16.95**
Gorgonzola Sauce
BROILED HALIBUT STEAK **14.95**
Lemon Butter

SHRIMP FRA DIAVOLO **16.25**
Shrimp in Spicy Tomato Sauce
FRUTTA DI MARE FRA DIAVOLO **16.95**
Seafood in a Spicy Tomato Sauce on
a bed of Linguine

Steaks & Chops

BROILED PRIME SIRLOIN STEAK ... **22.95**
With Mushroom Cap
**BROILED PRIME
SIRLOIN BUTT STEAK** **17.95**

**BROILED DOUBLE CUT
LAMB CHOPS,** with Bacon **20.95**
PORK CHOPS VESUVIO **14.95**

BROILED PRIME FILET MIGNON **21.25**
With Mushroom Cap

Dinner: Mon - Thurs until 1, Fri - Sat until 2, Sun until 12

Chef and owner, Paul LoDuca has his finger on the pulse of Italian cooking, the main reason that this restaurant throbs with excitement. The menu is such a good read that it is hard to make a choice. Daily specials are always innovative and exciting. The atmosphere is a beautiful combination of country Italian and city sleek.

Menu Changes Seasonally

ANTIPASTI

Olive Farcite all'Ascolana Fried green olives stuffed with sausage $3.95

Ricotta al Forno Baked ricotta with fresh tomato sauce and sausage $4.75

Bruschetta Toasted bread with assorted daily toppings $1.50 each

Verdure Ripiene Assortite Stuffed vegetables: eggplant, tomato, mushrooms, zucchini and onion $5.95

Carpaccio per Uno o per Due con Tre Salse Thin slices of beef for 1 or 2 with three sauces $5.95/$7.95

Polenta con Funghi Grilled polenta with portobello and cremini mushrooms $6.95

Calamari Marinati Calamari marinated with celery, olives, virgin olive oil, lemon $5.75

Melanzane a Scapece Marinated grilled eggplant with fresh mozzarella, mint, balsamic vinegar $4.95

Moscardini alla Brace Grilled baby octopus with cannellini beans, roasted peppers, virgin olive oil $6.25

INSALATE

Insalata Stagionale Mixed seasonal lettuces and tomato; virgin olive oil, balsamic vinegar $3.50

Insalata del Casolare Arugula, radicchio, black olive anchovy dressing, parmigiano $4.95

Insalata di Indivia Riccia Endive, potatoes, beets, pinenuts, honey, balsamic vinegar and virgin olive oil $4.75

PIZZE

Pizza Margherita Tomatoes, basil and mozzarella $4.95

Pizza di Verdure alla Griglia Grilled vegetables, virgin olive oil and ricotta salata $6.50

Pizza Donatello Roast chicken, escarole, raisins, pinenuts, tomato, caciotta $5.95

Pizza di Don Calogero Sausage, broccoli di rabe, garlic, olives and fontina $5.95

Pizza dell'Ortolano DOC Fontina, roasted garlic, arugula, radicchio, tomato, balsamic vineger, olive oil $6.75

PASTE

Fusilli col Buco alla Sarda Fusilli with sausage, cream and tomato sauce $5.95/$10.95

Linguine della Nonna "Grandma's Linguine" with roasted zucchini, garlic, tomato, breadcrumbs $5.95/$9.95

Spaghetti alla Molisana Spaghetti with pancetta, basil, parmigiano, caramelized onions $5.95/$10.95

Ravioli di Magro Ricotta and spinach filled ravioli with brown butter sage sauce $6.25/$11.50

Bucatini al Sugo di Mare Bucatini with shrimp, clams, mussels, calamari, tomato, basil, white wine $6.50/$11.95

Penne Rigate con Salsa Macchiata Penne rigate with tomato basil sauce and herbed ricotta $4.95/$8.95

Gnocchi Verdi con Salsa di Noci Spinach gnocchi with gorganzola, walnut cream sauce $6.25/$11.50

Rigatoni con Sugo di Anitra Rigatoni in a sauce of braised duck, beans and mushrooms $5.95/$10.95

PIATTI DA FARSI

Cuscussu' Trapanese Sicilian fish stew served with couscous $13.95

Anitra con Salsa Balsamica Grilled duck breast with balsamic vinegar sauce and roasted onions $12.95

Gallina al Mattone Marinated cornish hen grilled under a hot brick; cannellini beans and roasted artichokes $11.95

Spiedini del Duca Grilled thin beef, rolled and stuffed, skewered with bay leaves; roasted potatoes $12.95

Rosticciana Tuscan barbecued pork chops with rosemary, garlic, lemon; sauteed chickory $13.95

Dinner: Tues - Thurs 5:30 - 10:30, Fri - Sat 5:30 - 11:30, Sun 4:30 - 9:30

Vinny's

Bring your friends, bring the family; the platters of plenty are enough to feed everybody. Joe Carlucci's re-creation of an Italian neighborhood restaurant is right on the money. Red sauces reign supreme, but do not overwhelm the traditional menu. Excellent New York Style pizza is a sleeper.

Menu Changes Seasonally Along With Daily Specials

APPETIZERS

	FAMILY STYLE	REGULAR
Garlic Bread		2.50
Spicy Broccoli—*garlic, chilies*	11.25	3.95
Fried Zucchini	11.95	4.95
Marinated Mushrooms—*balsamic vinegar with gorgonzola*		5.50
Fried Calamari—*homemade cocktail sauce*	13.50	6.95
Scungilli—*ground conch, onions, garlic crostini, marinara*		5.95
Clams Posillipo—*steamed in wine with onions, garlic; marinara sauce*		6.95
Sausage Bread—*sausage, pepperoni, prosciutto, cheeses, pizza dough*		6.50
Mussels Marinara—*steamed in wine with onions, garlic; marinara sauce*		6.25
Antipasto Platter—*capicola, salami, pepperoni, mozzarella, provolone, marinated vegetables*		9.50

SPAGHETTI & MEATBALLS • ANCHOVIES

PEPPERS • BLACK OLIVES

NEW YORK STYLE PIZZA
All our pizzas are topped with cheese

8 inch....................................6.00
extra ingredients........each .60

13 inch...................................10.00
extra ingredients........each .95

MUSHROOMS • ONIONS

SAUSAGE • PEPPERONI • GREEN OLIVES

HOUSE SPECIALS

	FAMILY STYLE	REGULAR
Goombà Chicken—*chicken, sausage, peppers, onion, peas, roasted potatoes*	22.95	11.50
Chicken Vincenzo—*with lemon and wine; peas, roasted potatoes*	21.95	10.50
Chicken Marsala—*chicken breast with mushrooms in wine sauce*		12.50
Rigatoni with Holiday Meats—*braciole, sausage, ribs, meatballs, pork*	24.95	12.50
Sausage and Peppers	19.50	9.50
Steak Vesuvio—*Ribeye steak, with oil, garlic, and roasted potatoes*		14.95
Zuppa di Pesce with Linguine—*mussels, clams, calamari, shrimp, marinara sauce*		14.95
Shrimp Scampi—*garlic-lemon butter*		14.95
Fish of the Day		MARKET PRICE
Eggplant Parmigiana—*breaded with marinara sauce*		9.25
Chicken Parmigiana—*marinara sauce*		11.95
Veal Parmigiana—*breaded chop, meat sauce, steamed broccoli*		14.50
Asparagus Parmigiana—*marinara sauce*		9.50

side order of pasta with marinara sauce 4.25

MACARONI

	FAMILY STYLE	REGULAR
Spaghetti Marinara	19.95	7.95
Spaghetti and Meatballs or Sausage	20.95	9.75
Spaghetti with Oil, Garlic, & Broccoli	19.95	8.95
Spaghetti Napoletana—*plum tomatoes, roasted garlic, fresh basil*	21.95	9.50
Cheese Ravioli—*filled with ricotta, parsley, garlic, marinara sauce*		9.50
Linguine with Mussels—*spicy marinara sauce*	24.95	10.95
Linguine with Clams—*red or white sauce*	25.95	11.95
Tortellini—*meat-filled; prosciutto, onions, peas; red cream sauce,*	23.95	10.50
Pasta Fazool—*cavatappi and white beans; tomato-rosemary sauce*	19.95	8.50
Stuffed Shells—*filled with ricotta, parsley, garlic, marinara*	24.95	9.95
Baked Ziti & Sausage—*baked with mozzarella, marinara*	21.95	9.25
Fettuccine Primavera—*fresh vegetables, mushrooms, cream sauce*	22.95	9.50
Lasagna—*ricotta, parmesan, and mozzarella*		9.50
Vegetable Lasagna—*grilled zucchini, eggplant, carrots and mushrooms*		10.75
Linguine Chicken Pesto—*boneless breast of chicken with pesto sauce*		11.95

DESSERTS

Tiramisù	5.25
Cannoli	3.50
Spumoni	3.95
Lemon Ice	2.50
Aunt Tessie's Rum Cake	3.95
Chocolate-Cappuccino Cake	4.50

Dinner: Sun - Thurs 5 - 12, Fri - Sat 5 - 1

Vivere

The old Florentine Room got a complete remodeling, a new name, menu, and chef a few years ago. And when you experience the food you'll know just how lively and light Italian food can be—the kitchen really knows its stuff. Now you'll find a stylish room equipped with a classy staff and menu.

Antipasti Freddi

Insalata della Casa
Mixed Greens, Carrots, Leeks, Olive Oil, Vinegar   2.95

Insalata L'Amorosa
Tomatoes, Mozzarella, Garbanzo Beans, Olive Oil, Vinegar   5.25

Melanzane e Peperoni Arrostiti
Roasted Eggplant and Peppers, Traditional Marinate   5.50

Polpetti e Vongole al Vapore
Baby Octopus, Fresh Clams, Green Beans, Mint, Olive Oil   7.50

Antipasti Caldi

Zuppa del Giorno
Soup of the Day   3.75

Crespelle d'Anatra
Duck Filled Crepes, Tomato Marmalade, Chives   5.75

Insalata di Capesante
Sea Scallops, Arugola, Mushrooms, Tomato, Balsamic Vinegar   7.95

Trota-Salmonata con Salsa Nocciola
Salmon-Trout, Mixed Herbs, Hazelnuts, Fresh Tomatoes   6.50

Primi

Cavatappi al Petrino
Corkscrew Pasta, Tomato Sauce, Braised Lamb, Rosemary   5.75

Tortelli di Zucca
Pumpkin Filled Pasta, Butter, Almonds, Parmesan Cheese   5.50

Saccotini di Radicchio con Salsa di Scampi
Radicchio Filled Pasta Sacks, Shrimp, Vegetables, Shrimp Broth   7.50

Pappardelle di Spinaci con Scamorza
Wide Spinach Noodles, Scamorza Cheese, Pancetta , Cream   7.25

Agnolottini di Fagiano
Pheasant Filled Pasta, Butter, Sage, Parmesan Cheese   7.75

Capelli d'Angeli con Verdure alla Griglia
Angel Hair Pasta, Garlic, Grilled Vegetables, Vegetable Broth   6.50

Risotto del Giorno
Italian Rice of the Day   6.50

Secondi

Pesce del Giorno come Volete
Seafood of the Day; Charcoal Grilled, Broiled or Ai Ferri   16.75

Osso Buco in Bianco
Braised Veal Shank, White Wine, Olives, Capers, Herbs   15.50

Petto di Pollo alla Montecatini
Grilled Chicken Breast, Garlic, Sage, Red Peppers   10.75

Filetto alla Cardinale
Beef Fillet, Prosciutto di Parma, Tuscan Bread, Plum Tomato   17.25

Medaglioni di Vitello con Barolo
Veal Tenderloin, Shiitake Mushrooms, Barolo Wine Sauce   15.95

Petto D'Anatra con Salsa D'Aceto Balsamico Dolce
Duck Breast, Braised Fennel, Red Wine, Balsamic Vinegar   14.95

Bistecca alla Fiorentina
T-Bone Steak, Tuscan White Beans, Olive Oil, Black Pepper   19.95

Costoletta di Vitello alla Griglia
Grilled Veal Chop, Portobello Mushroom, Garlic, Rosemary   21.50

Dinner: Mon - Thurs 5 - 10, Fri - Sat 5 - 11

Benkay Chicago

Excellent Japanese food in a plush and lush setting overlooking the Chicago River, the four-room dining arrangement features a main dining room, a sushi bar, a teppan room, and outstanding Kaiseki dining. The service is as polished as the setting and the food.

Menu Changes Seasonally

KAISEKI 会 席

FULL-COURSE DINING

弁 慶 BENKAY $100.00

Our Chef will prepare a grand feast for your special occasion. Appetizer, Clear Soup, Sashimi, three to four seasonal entrees, Miso Soup/Rice/Pickled Vegetables and Dessert.

桜 SAKURA. $80.00

The Chef presents a unique array of Japanese dishes, served with the grace of the Sakura Cherry Blossom. Appetizer, Clear Soup, Sashimi, Stewed Dish, Grilled Item, Fried Item, Miso Soup/Rice/Pickled Vegetables and Seasonal Dessert.

All Kaiseki dinners require a 24-hour advance reservation.

NABE MONO 鍋 物

ONE-POT COOKING
Designed for a Party of Two or more.

ご注文はお二人様から承ります。

しゃぶしゃぶ SHABU SHABU . . . . $28.00 (per person)

Thin fillets of Beef with Tofu, fresh Greens, Japanese Mushrooms and other Vegetables, cooked in Broth at the table. Served with a Sesame and a Vinegared Soy Dipping Sauce, along with an Appetizer, Udon Noodles and Dessert.

しゃぶしゃぶ会席 SHABU SHABU KAISEKI . . . . $45.00 (per person)

Shabu Shabu Kaiseki is served with an Appetizer, Sashimi, Grilled fillet of Fish, Vinegar Dish, Udon Noodles and Dessert.

Hotel Nikko Chicago • 320 North Dearborn • Near North/Gold Coast • (312) 836-5490

SPECIAL DINNER SET 特別夕食膳

Available in the Kamakura Main Dining Room

すき焼膳 SUKIYAKI ZEN $21.00
Thinly sliced Beef, vegetables, Tofu and Shirataki noodles.

牛照焼 GYU TERIYAKI $23.50
Fillet of Beef glazed with Teriyaki sauce, served with lettuce, tomato and cucumber.

海老野菜天婦羅 EBI YASAI TEMPURA $25.00
Shrimp and Vegetables quickly fried, Tempura Style.

鳥照焼 TORI TERIYAKI $18.00
Broiled Chicken Breast glazed with Teriyaki Sauce.

寄せ鍋 YOSE NABE $28.00
Japanese style Stew with a variety of Seafood, Vegetables, Tofu and Chicken flavored with Sansho herbs, and finished with a beaten egg.

先附、味噌汁、サラダ、香の物、御飯、デザート付

All Dinners are served with Appetizer, Miso Soup, Salad, Japanese Pickles, Rice and Dessert

TEPPAN-YAKI DINNER 鉄板焼ディナー

メインコース
ENTREES

鉄板チキン
TEPPAN CHICKEN $19.50
Chicken grilled with Garlic Soy Sauce.

弁慶プライムディナー
BENKAY PRIME DINNER $27.00
Your choice of Prime Sirloin or Tenderloin Beef grilled with Garlic Soy Sauce.

シーフード デラックス
SEAFOOD DELUXE $42.00
A Deluxe combination of Lobster, Shrimp, Scallops and Salmon grilled with Garlic Butter and Soy Sauce.

All Teppan-Yaki Dinners are served with an Appetizer, Soup, Salad, Steamed Rice, Seasoned Grilled Vegetables, Benkay's Dipping Sauces, Dessert & Japanese Tea.

Dinner: Tues - Sat 5:30 - 10

Built from scratch, and rising level after dramatic level, this is one of the most beautiful Japanese restaurants around. Sushi bar, tatami rooms, this place has it all, and that includes the very expansive menu and excellent food.

HONDA

Menu Changes Seasonally

HOT APPETIZERS

KUSHIYAKI MORIAWASE **6.50**
Today's Assortment of Kushi Chef Selections

AIGAMO ROHSU **7.50**
Slices of Marinated Roasted Duckling

TORI TATSUTA AGUE... 4.75
Deep Fried Marinated Boneless Chicken Morsels

ASARI SAKAMUSHI **6.50**
Steamed Manila Clams in a Tasty Sake Wine Broth

COLD APPETIZERS

HORENSOH GOMAAYE **4.25**
Chilled Blanched Fresh Spinach with a Tasty Sesame Seed Sauce

NASU ORANDA NI **4.50**
Traditional Japanese Eggplant Simmered with Green Onions and Lemon Zest

SALAD

QUAIL SALAD **7.00**
Grilled Farm Raised Quail Tossed in a Fresh Ginger Orange Dressing on a Bed of Greens

SHRIMP SALAD **7.50**
Sweet Shrimp Sashimi Style with a Light Wasabi Soy Sauce on a Bed of Crisp Curly Endive

SUSHI BAR

SUSHI MORIAWASE DELUXE 22.50
California Roll and 10 Pieces of Nigiri Sushi Specially Selected by our Chef

CHIRASHI ZUSHI 22.50
An Assortment of Fresh Raw Fish and Vegetables Served on a Bed of Sweet Vinegared Rice

A LA CARTE

TEMPURA MORIAWASE 17.00
An Array of Shrimp and Vegetables in a Light Tempura Batter

LOBSTER & SCALLOPS TEMPURA 22.50
Lobster and Sea Scallops Tempura Style with Traditional Condiments

CHICKEN TERIYAKI with SHRIMP or SCALLOPS 17.00
Grilled Chicken with Teriyaki Sauce and Your Choice of Shrimp Tempura or Sauteed Sea Scallops

BEEF TERIYAKI with SHRIMP or SCALLOPS 18.50
Grilled Prime Ribeye Steak with Teriyaki Sauce and Your Choice of Shrimp Tempura or Sauteed Sea Scallops

NABEMONO

SUKIYAKI FOR TWO ... 45.00
Thinly Sliced Beef and Japanese Vegetables Cooked Tableside in a Sweetened Soy Sauce

HONDA NABE FOR TWO 45.00
A Variety of Seafood Cooked at your Table in a Bonito-Flavored Broth

SHABU SHABU FOR TWO 45.00
Prime Beef and Vegetables Simmered in a Special Broth with Dipping Sauce Cooked at your Table

KANI NABE FOR TWO 45.00
Succulent Crab and Vegetables in a Pot of Tasty Banito Broth Cooked Table Side

Dinner: Mon - Sat 5:30 - 11:30, Sun 5:30 - 10

335

Shilla Restaurant

Smartly appointed with plush carpeting and luxurious seating, Shilla is a warm and welcoming restaurant in which to enjoy some of the best Korean food in the Chicago area. Large portions make it easy for groups to share and enjoy.

Shilla

SUSHI BAR

생선회
SASHIMI

SMALL	$11.75	LARGE	$29.75
MEDIUM	$19.75	EXTRA LARGE	$39.75

초밥
SUSHI

SUSHI "A"	$13.50	TEKKA MAKI	$ 3.50
SUSHI "B"	$16.50	KAPPA MAKI	$ 3.25
		OSHINKO MAKI	$ 3.25
TEKKA HANDROLL	$ 3.50	KANPYO MAKI	$ 3.00
UNAGI HANDROLL	$ 4.00	FUTO MAKI	$ 8.50
HAMACHI HANDROLL	$ 3.50	CALIFORNIA MAKI	$ 3.50

도시락
BENTO

BROILED SALMON, CHICKEN OR BEEF TERIYAKI, SHRIMP & VEGETABLE TEMPURA, CHOICE OF CALIFORNIA MAKI OR SASHIMI $14.95

KOREAN BARBECUE

불고기 (Bul Goki) **$10.95**
Thinly sliced tender beef marinated in our special sauce and broiled.

갈비 (Kal Bi) **$12.95**
Short ribs marinated in Shilla's own sauce and broiled.

생갈비 (Saing Kal Bi) **$12.95**
Unseasoned short ribs.

닭구이 (Dalk Gui) **$10.95**
Boneless diced chicken marinated and broiled.

* **돼지 삽겹살구이 (Doeji Samkupsal Gui)** **$10.95**
Sliced fresh bacon marinated with spicy hot sauce and broiled.

곱창구이 (Gop Chang Gui) . . . . **$ 8.95**
Beef intestine seasoned with garlic and broiled.

주물럭구이 (Jumoo Leog Gui) **$13.95**
Sliced rib eye steak seasoned with garlic, black pepper, sugar, sesame seed oil and
scallion, and broiled.

CASSEROLES AND POTS

* **곱창전골 (Gopchang Jungol)** (Serve for 2 person) **$19.95**
Beef entails, vegetables, and noodle in spicy hot soup.

* **해물전골 (Haemul Jungol)** (Serve for 2 person) **$24.95**
Seafoods and vegetables cooked in spicy hot soup.

신라전골 (Shilla Jungol) (Serve for 2 person) **$29.95**
Lobster, shrimp, scallop, crab, mussel, clam, oyster, Oriental vegetables, cooked in
au jus, either in hot spicy or plain (depend on your taste).

TUIGUIM (TEMPURA)

도미튀김 (Domi Tuiguim) **$24.95**
Coated and deep fried Red Snapper topped over with our special sauce. Garnished
with green pepper, carrot, sea weed, and egg.

새우튀김 (Saewoo Tuiguim) **$12.95**
Large shimps & vegetables dip in our special batter, and deep fried to golden
brown crisp.

*Indicates Hot Dishes

Tuttaposto

Classic example of what real Mediterranean cooking is all about. Chef/owner Tony Mantuano has a firm grip on this eclectic but very flavorful and exciting "cuisine of the sun."

MEDITERRANEAN
TAVERNA

Menu Changes Weekly

SEAFOOD

Spanish style **calamari** stuffed with shrimp, salsa negra and garlic rice
$8

Woodroasted **sea scallops** with smoked tomato and arugula oil
$9

Pesce ai Ferri...Seared Alaskan halibut with roast cremini mushrooms, rosemary, polenta and white truffle oil
$19

Assorted spicy seafood baked in a copper Portuguese cataplana with tomatoes and couscous
$19

Grilled swordfish with roast sweet peppers, pesto and lobster oil
$19

STARCH

Crispy Sardinian **focaccia** with taramasalata, whipped feta and hummus
$6

Double decker **mushroom pizza** with mozzarella and white truffle oil
$12

Angelhair pasta with clams, chorizo, saffron, garlic, oranges
$13

Spaghetti with shrimp, tomato, garlic and lemon
$15

Greek chicken ravioli with charred tomato, thyme and feta cheese
$13

Pappardelle with Italian sausage and broccoli rabe
$14

---

646 North Franklin • River North • (312) 943-6262

M E A T

Smoked carpaccio with oven dried tomatoes, manchego cheese and lemon
$7

Grilled portabello mushroom with garlic almond sauce
$9

Moroccan barbequed quail with cilantro mashed potatoes and curry oil
$8

● ● ●

Spit roasted fennel and lemon marinated half chicken with fire breathing pommes frittes
$12

Porchetta from our rotisserie with Greek potato cakes and garlicky kale
$13

Charcoal grilled lamb t-bone with lemon and Greek style potatoes-order by the chop
$9 a chop

Bistecca alla Fiorentina... Grilled Tuscan style steak with rosemary, white beans and garlic spinach
$22

VEGGIES / LEGUMES

Brick oven **polenta** with smoky tomatoes and romano cheese
$5

Fiore di Zucca...Crispy tempura fried **zucchini flowers**
$5

Neevik...**Sauteed spinach,** garlic , chickpeas and lemon
$5

Greek hillbilly salad of tomatoes, onions, olives, peppers, cucumbers, feta cheese, anchovies, oregano and red wine vinaigrette
$6 - **$9**

Mediterranean **Caesar salad** with romano cheese, garlic croutons and grilled onion
$6 - **$9**

Tuttaposto's **green salad** with tahini dressing or Greek lemon dill dressing
$5 - **$8**

● ● ●

Vegetarian couscous platter with Moroccan style vegetables, toasted almonds and harrissa
$12

Abril Mexican Restaurant

This Logan Square Mexican eatery seems to get more popular each year, and with good reason. The food is authentic, the portions are big, and the prices are fair. I like the homey atmosphere, too.

Mexican Restaurant

Menu Changes Seasonally

ABRILTIZERS

NACHOS 4.50
"We rate Abril's Nachos - dripping with melted chihuahua cheese, chunky Guacamole, frijoles, onions, tomatoes, and cilantro - the best ever. The chips crunch, cheese oozes, guacamole soothes, and cilantro zings, all at first bite." -Chicago Magazine.

SHRIMPLY DELICIOUS

CAMARONES A LA MEXICANA 9.95
There's nothing shrimpy about more than 1/2 lb of succulently sweet butterflied shrimp delicately sauteed with mild onion, bell pepper and tomato blended in a complementary mild red sauce. Served on a bed of moist rice sprinkled with diced fresh bell peppers for covert crunchiness.

CALDO DE CAMARONES .... Quart 7.95
Spoon up nearly 1/2 pound of sweet succulent bite-sized shrimp prepared in a soup rich with garden fresh carrots, celery, bits of tomato, tender chayote, onions and a generous helping of seasoned rice with a wedge of lime. .... Pint 4.50

COCTEL DE CAMORONES 7.95
Served in a large soda glass, this lime festooned shrimp cocktail contains 1/2 lb of firm fresh shrimp awash in our fruity-tangy sauce dotted with diced avocado, tomatoes, onions and cilantro.

SPECIALITES

ENCHILADAS SUIZAS .... Three 7.25
This dish - the most popular on our menu - is an armada of corn tortillas oozing with 1/2 lb of juicy beef or chicken swabbed in 2/3 lbs of melted cheese with a gob of sour cream on the bridge and set adrift in 3/4 pints of gentle Suiza Sauce. Convoyed by rice, beans & salad .... Two 5.95

TACOS ABRIL .... Three 5.95
> These masterpieces compare to ordinary tacos as Mozart compares to Salieri. Your choice of juicy beef, steak or chicken on three sets of tortillas forested with fresh lettuce and tomato sprinkled with anejo cheese. Served with rice and homemade beans .... Two 4.75

THE MEXICAN BUFFET THAT COMES TO YOUR TABLE
Abril's "Do It Yourself" entrees let you compose your own meal.
We provide the basics and the flourishes - you provide the imagination and the ministrations

BISTEK A LA MEXICANA .... For One Person 8.50
> An old-world melange combining 1/2 lb of firm choice beef chunks, fresh onions, green peppers and tomatoes slowly simmered in Abril's mildly-sweet Ranchero Sauce. Served with moist rice, homemade beans and salad.

BISTEK LOS MEROS MEROS

CARNE ASADA 9.95
> We start with more than one pound of US CHOICE tender outer skirt steak carefully carved to produce a 8 Oz. filet. Next, we marinate it for taste in our secret potions and then broil it to perfection. Garnished with slice of orange and scallion. It's aphrodisiac!

BISTEK RANCHERO O ENCEBOLLADO 10.95
> 3/4" thick tender juicy 14 oz US CHOICE boneless strip steak charbroiled to your taste & presented with your choice of mild Ranchero Sauce or deliquescent sauteed onions (Encebollado).

AUTENTICOS GOURMET

> Authentic, adventuresome and tastefully presented, our Gourmet dinners are rarely matched on any menu outside Mexico. Rice, beans & crisp salad on the side. (Except for Guachinango).

POLLO POBLANO O VERDE 4.95
> We dip 3/4 lbs of tender chicken in your choice of our creamy Mole or bracing Verde Sauce and that's the true taste of rustic Mexico! Not familiar with these antique dressings? Ask for a sample before ordering.

CHILES RELLENOS .... Large 5.75
> Fresh and feisty tempting twin poblano peppers stuffed with soothing chihuahua cheese, dipped in our own fluffy egg batter and delicately golden fried. .... Small 3.95

The Kiva fireplace, adobe walls and natural wood beams give this popular Mexican restaurant a very likeable and enjoyable atmosphere. Their margaritas are special, too.

STARTERS

All of our special appetizers are great for sharing

Taste of Santa Fe Sampler
A selection of some of our favorites ... blackened shrimp with sauza tequila butter, jalapeño cheese sticks, grilled sirloin with roasted tomatillo sauce, B.B.Q. chicken wings, guacamole and chipotle salsa. Great for two. 7.25

Santa Fe Pizza
A cheese crust topped with our homemade chorizo, New Mexican green chile sauce, jalapeño cheese, and sweet red peppers. Served with pico de gallo and sour cream 5.95

Grilled Shrimp Jalapeño
Shrimp marinated in our jalapeño sauce and then carefully grilled. Spicy and flavorful 6.95

BLUE MESA CLASSICS

Enchilada del Mar
A delightful blend of shrimp, scallops, fresh fish, corn, mushrooms and leeks sauteed then simmered in a lobster chipotle sauce, placed between two blue corn tortillas and topped with chihuahua cheese 12.95

Entrees served with homemade sopaipillas and honey

BLUE MESA
SIZZLING FAJITAS

Marinated with fresh herbs and spices and carefully char-grilled. Served on a sizzler platter with tricolor peppers, onions, pinto beans and rancherito cheese. Accompanied by guacamole, sour cream, and pico de gallo. Served with warm flour tortillas

- Steak 11.95
- Chicken Breast 10.95
- Shrimp 12.95
- Vegetables and Tofu 10.95

Any combination of *two* 12.95

COMBINACIONS

The Grande Platter

A special seafood chalupa with shrimp, scallops, and fresh fish in a lobster chipotle sauce; a blue corn green chile chicken enchilada; a New Mexican chile relleno with red chile sauce; posole and fiesta salad 11.95

Tex - Mex

Blackened shrimp with sauza tequila butter; grilled B.B.Q. chicken carbon with poblano peppers, red onions; green rice and fiesta salad 11.95

This multiroom restaurant offers shoppers a quiet refuge in which to enjoy some well-prepared Mexican food. The fish dishes are especially good.

Dos Hermanos
Mexican Restaurante & Cantina

APERITIVOS

Guacamole
Served with freshly made corn tortilla chips. 4.99

Classic Nachos
Served with tomatoes, green onions, jalapenos and sour cream. 5.29

Vegetable Fundido
Topped with red peppers and cilantro. Served with fresh whole wheat tortillas. 4.79

Quesadillas
Two large flour tortillas filled with tomatoes, melted jack and cheddar cheese.
Served with both sour cream and jalapenos on the side. 4.79

Add chicken or vegetables for only a 1.00 more!

ENSALADAS AND SANDWICHES

Southwestern Chicken Caesar Salad
With strips of grilled breast of chicken, red peppers, tortilla strips,
romano cheese and Southwestern Caesar dressing. 6.99

Tostada Del Rey
A tortilla basket with your choice of steak, chicken, or refried beans, mixed greens,
monterey jack and cheddar cheese, guacamole, and sour cream. 7.29

Shrimp Salad
Romaine lettuce tossed in our house dressing mixed with peppers, onions, and tomatoes.
Topped wth fresh shrimp and parmesan cheese. 7.99

Hamburgesa
Fresh ground beef mixed with diced jalapenos, onions, topped with cheddar
cheese and guacamole. 6.29

Steak Sandwich
With mexican spices topped with monterey jack cheese and onions.
Served with french fries. 6.29

ESPECIALES RIO GRANDE GRILL

Fajitas, Fajitas, Fajitas--Choose your favorite ingredient and we will serve it on a mound of onions and green peppers. Chicken, Steak, Shrimp or Vegetables, it's your choice! Then we'll serve your fajitas on a sizzling hot platter with fresh guacamole, tomatoes, sour cream, and your choice of tortillas on the side! 8.95

Make it a combination of two ingredients for only 12.49!!

Fajitas El Grande
The ultimate fajita combination of fresh Chicken, tasty Shrimp, and strips of Steak piled high on top of garden fresh green peppers, marinated tomatoes, and mushrooms. Served with your choice of flour or whole wheat tortillas on the side! 13.49

Tamales
Pork tamales topped with salsa verde and jack cheese. Served with saffron rice and black beans. 7.59

Spinach Enchiladas
Three whole wheat tortillas stuffed with fresh spinach, onions, green and red peppers, topped with our salsa verde and monterey jack cheese. Served with saffron rice and black beans. 8.29

Rio Grande Burrito
Steak or chicken wrapped in a large tortilla with lettuce, tomatoes, monterey jack and cheddar cheese. Topped off with red chile sauce or salsa verde and melted cheese. 8.79

Chimichanga
A flour tortilla stuffed with seasoned chicken, lightly fried and topped with red chile sauce, melted montery jack cheese. Served with mexican rice and refried beans. 8.29

Chile Relleno
Jumbo poblano pepper stuffed with monterey jack cheese, dipped in egg batter and lightly fried, topped wth an ancho chili sauce. 6.99

Cancun
Chicken enchilada and a steak taco. 6.49

Acapulco
Mini steak tostada, chicken burrito, and cheese quesadilla 6.79

Baja
Chicken burrito, steak taco, and cheese enchilada. 6.79

Dinner: Sun - Thurs until 9, Fri - Sat until 11

The atmosphere is always heavy on the "Ole's" at this very popular northside eatery. The garden atmosphere adds to the appeal.

El Jardin
Restaurant

Comidas

Carne Asada "Michael"　　　　　　　　　　　　　　　13.25
Our marinated skirt steak, topped with melted cheese, in a delicious tomato sauce.

Chile Rellenos　　　　　　　　　　　　　　　　　　9.25
Spicy Mexican peppers stuffed with beef or cheese dipped in rich egg batter and fried until fluffy.

Carne De Puerco En Mole or En Chile Verde　　　　　　9.25
Tender chunks of pork in a dark tangy homemade Mexican sauce, or in our spicy green pepper sauce.

Fajitas

El Jardin's own version of this popular southwestern dish. Chicken...Shrimp...Steak served with tortillas, rice, beans, guacamole, pico de gallo (spicy relish) and salad.

De Carne-Marinated skirt steak　　　　　　　　　　13.25
De Camarones-Grilled butterfly shrimp　　　　　　　12.25
De Pollo-Boneless & skinless chicken breast　　　　　12.25
Mixed Fajitas-1/2 chicken & 1/2 steak　　　　　　　14.75
Mixed Fajitas-1/3 chicken, 1/3 steak, & 1/3 shrimp　　16.75

Pollo ala Parrilla　　　　　　　　　　　　　　　　9.25
Grilled boneless breast of chicken
(All dinners include salad, rice, beans, and your choice of flour or corn tortillas)

Variados

Tacos 3 for 6.00　　　　　　　　　　w/rice & beans 7.00
Corn tortilla delicately fried, filled, folded. Topped with lettuce and tomato.

Tostada 3 for 6.00　　　　　　　　　w/rice & beans 7.00
Crispy open tortilla, layered with beans, your choice of filling, topped with lettuce, tomato, onion, cheese and sour cream.

3333-39 North Clark St • Lincoln Park/DePaul • (312) 528-6775

Enchiladas 3 for 6.00　　　　　　　　　　　　　w/rice & beans 7.00
Corn tortilla filled your way, rolled with "El Jardin's" special sauce, topped with lettuce, tomato, onion, cheese and sour cream.

Flautas (orders of 3) 8.00　　　　　　　　　　　w/rice & beans 9.00
Crispy corn tortilla filled with your choice of beef, chicken, or pork, rolled, and topped with guacamole and sour cream.

Burritos (orders of 3) 8.25　　　　　　　　　　w/rice & beans 9.25
Flour tortillas filled with beans and your choice of filling, rolled, topped with lettuce, tomato, onion and cheese.

Carne Asada Burritos　　　　　　　　　　　　　　　11.75
Three flour tortillas, filled with marinated skirt steak. Topped with lettuce, tomato, onion, cheese and sour cream. With rice and beans.

Milanesa "Michael"　　　　　　　　　　　　　　　11.00
Generous rib-eye steak, dipped in thick egg batter, gently breaded, and grilled to a golden brown, topped with melted cheese, in a delicious tomato sauce or salsa chile verde.

Chilaquiles　　　　　　　　　　　　　　　　　　6.25
El Jardin's "special" cheese dish. Diced tortillas mixed with egg and chorizo, tomato and onion, topped with queso chihuahua. Served with beans and tortillas.

Ensalada "Popo"　　　　　　　　　　　　　　　　6.25
A mountain of lettuce, tomato, avocado, green pepper, onion and chihuahua sauce

Quesadillas　　　　　　　　　　　　　　　　　　5.50
Nachos　　　　　　　　　　　　　　　　　　　　6.25
Nachos Chorizo　　　　　　　　　　　　　　　　6.75

Sopas

Sopa de Fideo　　　　　　　　　　　　Lge. 3.25　　Sm. 2.25
Homemade noodle soup with a chicken and tomato base. Served with tortillas and fresh lemon.

Menudo　　　　　　　　　　　　　　　Lge. 4.25　　Sm. 3.25
Fresh homemade tripe soup, served with lemon, onion and tortillas.

Dessert

Bunuelos　　　　　　　　　　　　　　　　　　　1.75
Homemade Flan　　　　　　　　　　　　　　　　2.00

Dinner: Sun - Thurs until 11, Fri - Sat until 12

El Nuevo Mexicano

Its not very big, but this cozy neighborhood spot puts out some mighty impressive Mexican food in a very south-of-the-border atmosphere.

Menu Changes Seasonally

Combinaciones COMBINATION PLATES

(Served with beans and rice)

Guadalajara **$9.75**
A strip of carne asada, two cheese enchiladas, two beef tacos and guacamole.

Piñata **$10.75**
One cheese stuffed pepper, one beef taco, one cheese enchilada, one chicken flauta, one avocado tostada and one tamale.

Steak Fajitas **$11.00**
Choice of seasoned steak broiled with garlic, green onions and sliced poblano peppers. Served with pico de gallo, hot sauce, sliced avocado and tomatoes

Shrimp Fajitas **$12.00**
Same as above with camarones

Especialidades HOUSE SPECIALTIES

Biftec Gratinado **$14.00**
U.S. choice strip steak, broiled to your taste, basted with a special spiced sauce and topped with melted cheese. Just wonderful for the Continental taste.

**Carne de Puerco en
Salsa Verde** **$8.50**
Chunks of fried pork meat, simmered in green tomatillo sauce.

Chiles Rellenos **$8.00**
Stuffed poblano peppers (mild but piquant) your choice of beef or cheese, covered with our special Ranchero sauce.

Filetes de Ternera Gratinados **$10.50**
Tender veal, cut in thin slices, sauteed in spiced tomato sauce and topped with melted cheese. One of the best tasting ways to serve veal.

Antojitos Mexicanos OLD MEXICO FAVORITES

Enchiladas Veracruz **$5.50**
Dipped in mole sauce and stuffed with fried plantain bananas.

Chilaquiles **$6.50**
Fried tortilla strips with bits of chicken sauteed in our special tomato sauce, topped with melted cheese and sour cream.

2914 North Clark St • Lincoln Park/DePaul • (312) 528-2131

Carnes MEATS

(Served with salad, fried beans, rice and tortillas)

Carne Asada **$9.50**
Skirt tenderloin steak broiled to your
taste. Juicy.

Carne Asada Tampiqueña **$10.50**
Broiled skirt steak, topped with slices of
green poblano peppers and a cheese
enchilada on the side. Delicious.

Mariachis **$12.00**
Juicy chunks of choice tender beef mari-
nated with garlic and spices, broiled on
skewers with green peppers and tomatoes.

Biftec a la Milanesa **$11.50**
Sliced choice beef, seasoned and dipped
in a mixture of egg, flour and bread
crumbs, then fried to perfection. Served
with lemon wedges and sliced avocado. An
Italian influenced dish that is just great!

Biftec a la Mexicana **$10.50**
Mexican pepper steak, chunks of beef
seasoned with garlic and onions and
ranchero sauce. Served mild or hot.

Aves POULTRY

Polla a la B.B.Q. **$7.50**
Half a chicken broiled and simmered in our
special B.B.Q. sauce and served with rice
and beans. Just a bit hot. Another western
special from our friends down in Texas.

Pollo Huatusqueño **$8.00**
Half a chicken simmered in our very savory
and hot chipotle sauce. A hot and delicious recipe from the Huatusco region.

Pollo en Salsa **$7.50**
Spring chicken seasoned and simmered in
our special ranchero sauce or if you prefer,
in hot pepper and tomato or green sauce.
Either way it is a wonderfully tasty dish
from northern Mexico.

Pollo en Mole Poblano **$7.50**
Spring chicken cooked and simmered in
mole sauce. This famous dish from Puebla
de los Angeles, Mexico, is served to perfection.

Mariscos SEAFOOD

Jaibas Rellenas **$9.00**
Stuffed crabs topped with a mild cream
sauce and melted cheese. A superb tasting
treat from Hermosillo.

Pescado Veracruz **$9.00**
Filet of fish marinated in garlic and simmered in a delicate tomato sauce with
olives, capers and a bit of spice. Another
pleasing treat from the Gulf of Mexico.

Camarones Tampico **$11.50**
Shrimp Brochette Mexican Style, broiled on
Skewers with fresh mushrooms, green
peppers, onions and tomatoes.

Camarones a la Criolla **$10.00**
Chopped shrimp sauteed in tomatoes,
onions and green peppers, simmered and
served on a bed of rice. A dish inspired by
Creole cooks of New Orleans. Delicious!

Dinner: 7 Days a Week until 12

Frontera Grill

One of the most highly respected Mexican restaurants in Chicago. Frontera is more casual and offers a more basic selection of food than its sibling Topolobampo.

FRONTERA GRILL

Menu Changes Every Other Week

ENTREMES appetizers

Enchiladas Suizas—oven-baked **enchiladas** of grilled free-range chicken in creamy tomatillo sauce. Chihuahua cheese. (Central) 5.50

Camarones en Escabeche Rojo—grilled Gulf **shrimp** in cool red-chile escabeche (ancho peppers, fruit vinegar, olive oil and spices) with jícama. (Inspired by a Tamaulipas specialty) 5.95

* * * * * *

Entremés Surtido—**appetizer platter** of cheesy quesadillas, crispy chicken taquitos with sour cream, tangy seviche tostadas, and guacamole. 7.50 for 2; 9.95 for 3; 12.95 for 4.

Guacamole—fresh and chunky, served with tortilla chips. 4.95

Tostaditas—made-to-order **tortilla chips** with two salsas: garlicky three-chile (cascabel, morita, guajillo) and roasted tomatillo with serrano and cilantro. 1.95

EXTRAS sides

Arroz a la Yucateca-traditional **Mexican rice** flavored with achiote, studded with vegetables. 2.25

Arroz y Frijoles-black **beans** and Mexican **rice**. 2.95

Plátanos con Crema-sweet fried **plantains** with homemade sour cream and fresh cheese. 3.50

Verduras en Escabeche-homemade pickled **jalapeños with carrots and cauliflower.** 2.50

Crema-thick and rich **cultured cream,** a little sour, homemade. 1.50

---

445 North Clark St • River North • (312) 661-1434

ESPECIALIDADES specialties

Pollo en Escabeche—peppery grilled free-range **chicken breast** with a tangy
escabeche of sweet spices, red onion, roasted garlic, olive oil, poblano chiles and
rich broth. Roasted potatoes. 11.95

Pato al Guajillo—charcoal-grilled **duck breast** in spicy chile guajillo sauce, with sweet
grilled red onions and black beans. (Central) 14.50

Puerco con Acelgas—charcoaled **pork tenderloin** on a bed of Swiss chard, roasted
tomatoes, potatoes and serrano peppers. (Inspired by a Oaxacan specialty) 13.50

Borrego en Cascabel—charcoal-seared **lamb** simmered with chile cascabel sauce and
woodland mushrooms. Black beans. (West-Central) 11.95

Tortas de Lentejas—crusty **lentil cakes** flavored with garlic and fresh herbs, served
with roasted tomato sauce and herby white rice. 8.95

Camarones en Pipián—fresh Gulf **pink shrimp** in creamy toasted pumpkinseed sauce.
Roasted potatoes and Mexican vegetables. (Tamaulipas) 15.50

Chiles Rellenos—stuffed poblanos (one cheese, one minced-pork picadillo) with
roasted tomato-chile sauce; black beans and Mexican rice.
(Central) (limited supply) 10.95

PLATILLOS LIGEROS light entrees

Chilpachole—spicy **shrimp soup** with smoky chipotle chiles and
red-skin potatoes. 7.95

Enchiladas de Mole Rojo—homemade tortillas rolled around chicken, doused with
Oaxacan red mole; black beans. 8.95

Tacos al Carbón—beef, poultry or fish grilled over the wood fire, sliced thin and
served with roasted pepper rajas, two salsas, frijoles charros, guacamole, and homemade tortillas. With charcoaled green onions, add 75 cents.
> Coleman **skirt steak** marinated with garlic and spices. 9.95
> Free-range **chicken breast** marinated with fruit vinegar,
> spices and garlic. 9.50
> Amish **duck** marinated with red-chile adobo. 9.25

Dinner: Tues - Thurs 5:30 - 10, Fri - Sat 5:30 - 11

The decor is dynamite—movie stage-set stuff—big booths, massive murals, poly-filled palm trees...it's cool and classy.

HAT DANCE®

APPETIZERS

	PEQUENO	REGULAR
Tacos de Pollo chicken, guacamole		3.50
Chorizo Sope hand-made thick tortillas; Mexican sausage, guacamole		3.50
HAT DANCE™ Chile Relleno anaheim chile, cheese corn, salsa verde		3.95
Cheese Quesadilla		4.50
HAT DANCE™ Carnitas marinated pork; orange, garlic & ancho chile sauce		4.75
HAT DANCE™ Baked Goat Cheese Fundido black bean salad, toasted chips		4.95
Chicken Vegetable Chimichangas avacado tomatillo salsa		4.95
Guacamole	2.95	4.95

SEAFOOD APPETIZERS

Shrimp Ceviche Japanese cucumbers, avocado, roasted nuts		4.95
Sashimi of Yellowfin Tuna wasabi sauce		4.95
♥ Tuna Sashimi soy-sake vinaigreta		4.95
♥ Shrimp Mojo de Ajo grilled shrimp, orange-tomato salsa		4.95
HAT DANCE™ Cocktail de Camaron shrimp, tomato-shrimp broth, lime juice, scallions, avocado	2.75	5.25
Crabmeat Quesadilla		5.95
Tuna & Smoked Salmon Tartare combination tartare, Mexican herbs		5.95
Shrimp & Lobster Ceviche orange & lime juices, chives & tequila		5.95
HAT DANCE™ Queso Fundido with Seafood melted cheese, shrimp, scallops, flour tortillas		6.50

325 West Huron • River North • (312) 649-0066

352

SALADS

REGULAR

Caesar Salad lemon anchovy vinaigreta 4.50

Tomato & Red Onion Salad avocado, vinaigreta 4.50

Spinach Salad jalapeno peanut dressing 4.50

Heart of Palm, Avocado & Tomato
cilantro dressing 4.95

ENTREES

Rack of Tacos four crispy-shelled beef tacos,
cheese, lettuce, salsa, sour cream 7.95

♥ Salad Burrito lettuce, peppers, carrots, cucumbers,
mustard, salsa, sweet pea guacamole, served chilled 7.95

Chicken Enchiladas shredded chicken, cheese, choice of
sauce, ancho (red), salsa verde (green) or mole 8.95

Grilled Chicken Burrito black beans, green rice 8.95

HAT DANCE™ Chile Relleno de Pollo poblano pepper; chicken,
olives, raisins, onions, tomato-cinnamon broth 8.95

♥ Sonoran Chicken Vegetable Stew chicken,
potatoes, carrots, celery 8.95

Seafood Burrito shrimp, scallops, cheese 9.25

Sizzling Hat Dance Fajita Platter guacamole, salsa,
tortillas, sour cream, onions & peppers, chinoit beans
vegetables & cheese 10.25

chicken ...11.25

steak ...12.25

Relleno con Papas poblano pepper stuffed with mashed
potatoes, roasted chicken; green-chile-tomatillo sauce,
cranberry corn relish 10.95

HAT DANCE™ Denotes Specialties of the House.

♥ Denotes heart healthy items.

These items are prepared from recipes that meet the fat and
cholesterol guidelines of The American Heart Association of
Metropolitan Chicago for Healthy Adults.

Dinner: Mon - Thurs 5:30 - 10, Fri - Sat 5:30 - 11:30, Sun 5 - 9

Nuevo Leon Restaurant

Inexpensive and authentic three-meals-a-day Mexican spot that adds impressive daily specials to its already stunning menu.

Servicio a la Carta

FAJITAS NORTENAS	8.00
FILETE AL NEUVO LEON Filete Steak Nuevo Leon Style, served with Rice, Beans and Guacamole	8.00
CARNE A LA TAMPIQUENA Broiled Skirt Steak with Enchilada and Guacamole	8.50
CARNE ASADA Broiled Skirt Steak	7.50
ALAMBRES (Shis-Ke-Bob) Squares of Choice Skirt Steak, Guacamole, Rice & Beans	7.50
BISTEK A LA MEXICANA DE LOMO "Chef's Special." Chopped Rib-Eye Steak cooked with Tomato, Jalapeno Peppers and Onion "Delicious"	7.50
BISTEC A LA MEXICANA Succulent Pieces of Steak Simmered in Our Mexican Sauce	5.00
SESOS LAMPREADOS For the Gourmet Brains Dipped in Egg and Pan-Fried	5.00
GALLINA RANCHERA (Media) Chicken 1/2 smothered with Our Tasty Ranchero Sauce	5.00
GUISADO DE RES O DE PUERCO Beef or Pork Stew	5.00

1515 West 18th St • Downtown/Loop • (312) 421-1517

CALDO DE RES CON ARROZ	Chico 3.00 · Grande 4.00
Beef Soup, with Rice	

COMIDA CORRIDA 6.00
Incluye Caldo Chico y Guisado de Res o Puerco
Plate Lunch: Includes Small Soup and Beef or Pork Stew

MENUDO GRANDE 4.00
Tripe Soup, Large

MENUDO CHICO 3.00
Tripe Soup, Small

CALDO DE RES PARA LLEVAR 5.25

MENUDO PARA LLEVAR 5.25

Antojitos Mexicanos

ENCHILADAS DE QUESO 3.75
Tortillas (3) Dipped in Special Sauce, Rolled and
Covered with Cheese, Rice and Beans

ENCHILADAS DE POLLO 3.75
Tortillas (3) Dipped in Special Sauce, Rolled and Filled
with Chicken, Rice and Beans

ENCHILADAS SUIZAS DE PICADILLO O DE POLLO 4.00
Tortillas (3) Dipped in Special Sauce, Rolled and Filled with
Ground Beef or Chicken and Topped with Cheese

TOSTADAS DE CHORIZO 3.75
Corn Tortilla Crisp Fried and Covered with Mexican
Sausage, Lettuce and Tomato

TOSTADAS DE FRIJOLES 3.75
Corn Tortilla Crisp Fried and Covered with Beans, Lettuce and Tomato

TOSTADAS DE PICADILLO 3.75
Corn Tortilla Crisp Fried and Covered with Ground Beef,
Lettuce and Tomato

TOSTADAS DE AGUACATE 3.75
Corn Tortilla Crisp Fried and Covered with Avocado Lettuce and Tomato

TACOS DE CARNE ASADA 5.00
Skirt Steak Tacos

COMBINATION 5.00
1 Taco, 1 Tostada, 1 Tamale and Enchilada, Corn Tortillas,
Crisp Fried and Covered with Beans, Lettuce and Cheese

Dinner: 7 Days a Week until 12

The atmosphere is down and dizzy, but that just adds to the appeal of this very popular Mexican restaurant. The appetizer and side dish bar is great and grand.

The Original A-1

Menu Changes Seasonally

Appetizers

CHEESE QUESADILLA
large flour torilla, melted cheese, guacamole & sour cream,
pico de gallo $4.50

QUESO FUNDIDO $5.95

Soups & Salads

A-1 BLACK BEAN SOUP
served with sour cream and red onion .... cup $1.95
bowl $2.95

CAESAR SALAD $5.50

BORDER BURGERS

(Deluxe burgers served with spicy fries and cole slaw; add .50)

A-1 CHEESEBURGER $5.25

HICKORY BURGER
w/ our own hickory smoked sauce, jack cheese $5.25

DURANGO BURGER
topped w/ sliced pickles, lettuce, tomato, onions, mustard
& special seasoning, cheese and grilled onions
A Texas Favorite! $5.50

Enchiladas & Burritos

CHICKEN ENCHILADAS
3 corn tortillas, red chile sauce, sour cream, melted cheese $7.50

B B Q ENCHILADAS
hickory-smoked chicken, ancho BBQ sauce, chihuahua cheese $7.50

TEXAS BBQ SANDWICHES

BORDER CHICKEN BREAST SANDWICH
Avocado mayonnaise, cheddar cheese, grilled onion $6.50

BLACKENED CHICKEN BREAST SANDWICH
grilled onions, jalapeno mayonnaise...................................... $6.50

BBQ CHICKEN BREAST SANDWICH $6.50

TEXAS BBQ A-1 STYLE

BBQ CHICKEN
hickory smoked 1/2 bird $9.95

BABY BACK RIBS .... 1/2 slab $9.95
.... full slab $14.95

TEXAS BBQ

BBQ SHRIMP $13.95
BEEF BRISKET PLATTER $10.95
BBQ PORK LOIN PLATTER $10.95

Combination Platters

(Don't ask about substitions)

COMBO #1
RIB & CHICKEN PLATTER $13.95

COMBO #2
RIB & SHRIMP PLATTER $14.95

Fajitas

GRILLED ON REAL MESQUITE!

(All fajitas are served with salsa, guacamole, onions, peppers, warm tortillas & sour cream)

VEGETABLE & CHEESE $9.95
♥**CHICKEN (specify Heart Healthy)** $11.95
STEAK $12.95
SHRIMP $13.95

♥ Denotes Heart Healthy Items

Su Casa

Just off Michigan Avenue, Su Casa is a very popular restaurant. Cozy bar, white brick walls, high ceilings, and an expert waitstaff all add to the enjoyment of the food, which is quality through and through.

Appetizers

CHILI CON QUESO DIP
Melted cheddar with onions, fresh tomato and cilantro. $3.95

QUESO FUNDIDO
A blend of melted Mexican cheeses topped with chorizo..... $5.95

BOTANA
A variety of nachos and miniature tacos.
Small .... $3.95   *Large* $6.95

SHRIMP CHIVICHANGAS
Four fried flour tortillas filled with shrimp, onion, peppers, garlic and Mexican cheese. $8.95

CHIVICHANGA ESPECIAL
Two fried flour tortillas filled with chicken and Mexican cheese and two with chorizo and Mexican cheese $6.95

GARNACHOS
Fresh tortilla chips topped with refried beans, shredded beef or chicken and melted cheese.
Six .... $3.95   *Twelve* $6.95

CEVICHE
Fresh fish marinated in lemon and lime juice in a sauce of onions, cilantro, jalapeños and avocado. $7.95

Ensaladas

BEEF TACO SALAD
Ensalada de la casa topped with picadillo, guacamole, sour cream, cheddar and Mexican cheese. $5.95

ENSALADA CON POLLO
Fresh greens with crisp vegetables and avocado slices, topped with a sliced grilled chicken breast. $6.95

49 East Ontario St • River North • (312) 943-4041

Specialties

CARNE ASADA
A butterfly cut of prime
tenderloin steak served with
rice and refried beans. $12.95

COMBINATION PARAISO
Carne asada and camarones.
Served with rice and
a lime wedge. $12.95

PECHUGA DE POLLO
Boneless chicken breast
filled with peppers and
Mexican cheese. Served with
rice, refried beans, salsa roja,
and soft tortillas. $8.95

POLLO CON MOLE
Baked fresh cut chicken
topped with mole. Served
with rice and refried beans $8.95

POLLO POBLANO
A chicken breast grilled with
diced onions, and poblano
peppers and topped with
Mexican cheese. Served with
rice and pico de gallo. $8.95

SU CASA FRESH CATCH
Fresh fish of the day.
Ask your server.

FAJITAS

Fresh corn or flour tortillas served with strips
of marinated chicken or skirt steak and guacamole,
sour cream, pico de gallo and garnish.

Beef $10.95   *Chicken* $10.95   *Combination* $12.95

Combinationes traditional

SU CASA COMBINATION
A beef taco, a chicken
enchilada, and a tamale topped
with chili con carne. Served
with rice and refried beans. $8.95

GUANAJUATO
A steak taco, a vegetarian
burrito, a chicken chivichanga,
and a tamale. Served with rice
and refried beans. $9.95

SU CASA DELUXE COMBINATION
Carne asada, chili relleno,
a cheese taco and a chicken
enchilada. Served with rice
and refried beans. $11.50

FIESTA COMBO
An enchilada, a taco, a sope,
and a chivichanga. Served
with rice and refried beans. $8.95

Dinner: Mon - Thurs until 11, Fri - Sat until 12, Sun 4 - 9

One of my favorite stops for a great burrito. The new backroom addition had helped relieve the lunchtime congestion.

TECALITLAN RESTAURANT

Menu Changes Bi-Annually

ANTOJITOS - APPETIZERS

GUACAMOLE .... **Market Price**
Queso Fundido (Flame Cheese) **4.00**
Queso Fundido con Chorizo (Flame Cheese with Mexican Sausage) **4.50**
Cebollitas Asadas (Broiled Green Onions) **1.50**
Nachos (Tortilla Chips with Beans, Sour Cream, Guacamole and Cheese) **3.75**
Tecalitlan (2 Small Quesadillas, 1 Small Portion of Guacamole,
   1 Small Portion of Beans and 2 Small Flautas **4.85**

CALDOS - SOUPS

Caldo de Birria - Lamb Soup (Daily) **6.50**
Menudo - Tripe Soup (Weekends Only) **4.25**
            CARRY OUTS 30 CENTS EXTRA

TACOS - $1.50

Carne Asada (Steak)   Picadillo (Ground Beef)   Aguacate (Avocado)   Pollo (Chicken)
Chorizo (Mexican Sausage)   Pierna de Puerco (Pork)   Higado (Beef Liver)
Lechuga, Tomate y Cebolla (Lettuce, Tomato and Onions)
Sesos (Brains)   Lengua (Tongue)   Birria (Lamb)
Solo Cebolla y Cilantro (Onions and Cilantro Only)
Al Pastor (Beef and Pork)   Solamente la Carne (Plain)
Taco de Chile Relleno (Stuffed Peppers) **1.85**
   Cheese 30 Cents Extra   Avocado 30 Cents Extra   Sour Cream 30 Cents Extra

BURRITOS - $3.00

Vegetarian (Beans & Rice)
Carne Asada (Steak)   Al Pastor (Beef & Pork)   Pollo (Chicken)
Aguacate (Avocado)   Picadillo (Ground Beef)
Chorizo - Mexican Sausage **$3.00**
Combo Regular **3.78**
Suizo Regular - Covered with Melted Cheese **3.78**
   Cheese .75¢ Extra   Avocado .75¢ Extra   Sour Cream .40¢ Extra
All Burritos come with Beans, Lettuce, Tomatoes and Onions

1814 West Chicago Ave • Lincoln Park/DePaul • (312) 384-4285

TOSTADAS - $1.75

Carne Asada (Steak) **Pata** (Cow Feet) **Pollo** (Chicken)
Jamon (Ham) **Aguacate** (Avocado) **Picadillo** (Ground Beef)
Suizas (Melted Cheese) - **.50 Cents Extra**

TORTAS - MEXICAN SANDWICHES - $2.75

Carne Asada (Steak) **Aguacate** (Avocado) **Jamon** (Ham)
Pierna de Puerco (Pork) **Milaneza** (Breaded Steak)
Chorizo (Mexican Sausage) **Pollo** (Chicken) **Huevo** (Egg)
Torta Suiza (Melted Cheese) - **$1.00 Extra**
Queso (Cheese) **.50¢**   **Huevo** (Egg) **.50¢**

CENAS — DINNERS

All Dinners include Rice and Beans

Fajitas (Steak)	9.00
Fajitas (Chicken)	9.00
Fajitas Combo (Steak and Chicken)	9.95
Carne Asada (Steak Dinner)	8.50
Carne Asada de la Casa (Rib Eye Steak U.S. Choice)	12.95
Milaneza (Breaded Steak)	7.50
Milaneza Suiza (Breaded Steak covered with melted Cheese and Tomato Sauce)	8.50
Tampiqueña (Broiled Skirt Steak with Enchilada and Guacamole)	9.50
Tampiqueña Suiza (same as above plus with melted Cheese on top)	10.50
Enchiladas Suizas (4) Fillings: Cheese, Chicken or Ground Beef	7.00
Enchiladas Suizas (4) (with Steak)	8.00
Enchiladas Suizas Combo (4) Choice of four (4) different Fillings	8.00
Tecalitlan Combo (1 Taco, 1 Tostada, and 2 Enchiladas Fillings: Cheese, Chicken or Ground Beef	8.00
Tecalitlan Combo (2) - 2 Enchiladas, 1 Tostada, Rice and Beans	6.50
Tecalitlan Combo (3) - 1 Chile Relleno, 2 Enchiladas and 1 Tostada	7.50
Tecalitlan Combo (4) - 2 Enchiladas and 2 Flautas Covered with Guacamole and Sour Cream	7.50
Flautas (4) - Crispy Chicken Tacos (Only Chicken)	6.00
Chiles Rellenos, Stuffed Peppers (Cheese only)	6.50
Quesadillas - (Tortillas with Melted Cheese)	6.00
Lengua Ranchera (Beef Tongue with Tomato Sauce and Green Peppers)	6.50
Lengua en Salsa Verde (Beef Tongue with Green Sauce)	6.50
Higado Encebollado (Beef Liver with Grilled Onions)	6.50
Pechuga de Pollo al Carbon (Breast of Chicken - Charcoal Broiled)	7.65

Carry Outs — 30 Cents Extra

Topolobampo

One of the most highly respected Mexican restaurants in Chicago. Topolobampo has a more sophisticated ambience and its food cuts a finer, more polished edge than its sibling Frontera Grill.

Menu Changes Every Other Week

ENTREMESES

Ensalada de Flores de Calabaza--**squash blossom salad** with wood-grilled chiles, marinated red onions, fresh herbs and Mexican fresh cheese. 5.50

Morillas Rellenas--fresh wild morel mushrooms stuffed with country ham, tangy bread crumbs, fresh thyme and dry Jack cheese; served with roasted tomato-chile sauce. 5.50

Quesadillas de Hongos Asadas--rustic griddle-baked **quesadillas** of Texas Jack cheese, epazote, roasted chiles and a medley of wild mushrooms. 5

Sopa de Mariscos--rich red-chile broth filled with shrimp, mussels, bass and cilantro. 5

Burros de Faisán--spicy red-chile pheasant rolled into just-made tortillas, served with avocado-tomatillo salsa and crunchy garnishes. 5.50

Sopa Azteca--dark broth flavored with chile pasilla, garnished with chicken breast, avocado, cheese and crisp tortillas strips. 5

Ensalada Topolobampo--**Caesar salad** of young organic lettuces with cilantro, garlic croutons and dry Jack cheese, in lime dressing. 4.50

PLATILLOS FUERTES

Faisán con Fideos al Chipotle--Pluschke's free-range **pheasant** with creamy vermicelli, chipotle chiles, wild chanterelles, tomatoes and zucchini. 18.50

---

445 North Clark • River North • (312) 661-1434

Pato en Pipián de Tocino--Amish country **duck** in traditional pipián of chiles anchos, pumpkinseeds, sweet spices and bacon; with mashed Mexican pumpkin. 17.50

Puerco en Tinga Poblana--roasted **pork tenderloin** with classic tinga of roasted tomatoes, smoky chiles, chorizo, wild morels, potatoes and avocado. 18

Venado al Albañil--seared **venison loin** with a full-flavored, brothy sauce of manzano chiles, wood-grilled red onions, tomato and bacon; served with black bean torta. 21

Tortas de Papa--crusty Mexican **potato cakes** with tangy roasted tomatillos and spring vegetables (baby carrots, tiny green beans, favas, shiitakes, new potatoes). 14

Camarones Rellenos al Guajillo--roasted, crab-stuffed fresh Florida **pink shrimp** with tangy cactus, garlicky potatoes and spicy chile guajillo sauce. 19

Tilapia a la Milanesa--crunchy-coated fresh Rain Forest **tilapia**, pan-fried in olive oil, served with robust tomato-chile salsa and jícama-orange salad. 17.50

Merluza en Hoja Santa--fresh Chilean **sea bass** steamed in aromatic hoja santa, served with herby Oaxacan green mole and shoestring Mexican vegetables. 18.50

DESSERTS

Pastelito de Gran Torres--tender butter cake perfumed with Gran Torres orange liqueur, studded with bittersweet chocolate chunks; served with manzano banana ice cream. 5.50

Tartaleta de Limón--baked-to-order tangy sour cream **lime tart** with crimson prickly pear sauce and strawberries. 5.50

Niño Envuelto de Fresa--tender chocolate cake rolled around Chandler strawberry cream and strawberry-orange sauce. 5.50

Helados Caseros--homemade **ice cream sampler:** honey-apricot with brandy and double chocolate chunk. 4.50

Nieve de Mango--fresh mango ice with lime and orange. 5

Crepas con Cajeta--buttered crepes with homemade cajeta (goat milk caramel), toasted pecans and plantians. 5

Another ethnic "find" where the food outdistances the decor by a dozen miles or more. If you like kebabs, beans and lots of vegetables, this is the place.

TEHRAN RESTAURANT

HOT APPETIZERS

Dolmeh **2.75**
Vine leaves stuffed with ground beef, rice, yellow split peas and special spices, cooked in tomato sauce

Kashke Bademjan **2.95**
Baked, mashed eggplant and garlic, slowly cooked to perfection and topped with a special sauce

Mirza Ghasemi **2.95**
Baked eggplant, tomato, garlic and onion mixed with special spices

Joojeh Kabab **2.95**
Tender, specially seasoned char-broiled chicken

Quail **3.75**
One marinated, juicy, char-broiled quail

COLD APPETIZERS

Mast-va-Khiar **1.95**
Cool cucumber mixed with yogurt, mint and spices

Mast-va-Moosir **2.75**
Delicious elephant garlic, and yogurt

Borani **2.75**
Fried Spinach, onion and special spices with yogurt

SALADS AND SIDE DISHES

Persian Salad **1.75**
Mixed fresh tomato, cucumber and onion with house dressing

Season Salad **1.50**

Khiar Shoor **1.00**
We make our own. Tiny pickles steeped in garlic and dill, mmm

ENTREES

All dinners include: soup; Italian parsley with radishes;
onion and Persian cheese, and pita bread.

Changeh 8.75
Two skewers of specially seasoned filet mignon chunks, char-broiled and served
over rice with char-broiled tomatoes.

Cheloukabab Soltani 7.95
Combination of filet mignon and a strip of blended ground beef
and lamb, charbroiled, served with Pesian rice and tomatoes.

Chicken Soltani 7.95
Strip of tender chicken filet and a strip of seasoned, ground chicken
charbroiled. Served with rice and tomato.

Boneless Chicken 8.95
Two skewers of boneless chicken and skewer of greens.
Served with Persian rice.

Quail Kabab 8.95
Really special. Two whole quail, charbroiled, and
marinated in a wonderfully tasty sauce.

Shish Kabab 7.95
One skewer of six choice, chunk pieces of marinated beef, charbroiled,
and served with onion, green pepper, tomatoes, and rice.

Combination of Changeh and Shrimp 9.75
One skewer of specially seasoned filet mignon chunks and one
skewer of jumbo shrimp, charbroiled and served over rice and tomatoes.

VEGETARIAN

Kashke Bademjan 6.95
Baked mashed eggplant and garlic, slowly cooked to
perfection and topped with a special sauce.

Mirza Ghasemi 6.95
Baked eggplant, tomato, garlic and onion, mixed with special spices.

Khoresht Ghormeh Sabzi 6.95
Fresh green vegetables, special spices, dried lime and beans.
Served with rice.

Kookoo Sabzi 6.95
Herb and nut frittata baked with eggs and Persian spices.
It has a marvelous taste.

Dinner: 7 Days a Week until 11

Don't expect a lot of atmosphere or "downtown" culinary fringes at this small Peruvian restaurant. However you can expect a lot of very well prepared food at sensible prices.

MACHU - PICCHU

Menu Changes Seasonally

Centuries old, the cuisine of Perú
combines the rich culinary traditions
of the many peoples who settled the
rugged terrain of South America.
The native Incas, the Spanish con-
quistadors, the French and Italain
clergy, and the Oriental labor force
each contributed their heritage to
the Peruvian stock pot.

MACHU PICCHU (Formerly Piqueo) is the oldest Peruvian
restaurant in Chicago ... and many say the best.

ESCABECHE DE PESCADO **$4.95**
   Onion and pepper sauce are featured in this
   delightful cold filet of fish; the perfect marinade!

5427 North Clark St • Uptown/Lincolnwood • (312) 769-0455

PAPA RELLENA **$3.50**
Remember that Perú is the birthplace of the potato.
Mashed and sauteed potatoes, stuffed with ground
beef, minced onion, chopped olives and spices.

PASTEL DE LANGOSTA **$3.95**
Lobster souffle.

OCOPA DE CAMARONES **$3.95**
Broccoi pancake covered with a shrimp sauce.

POLLO ANTICUCHADO **$10.95**
Boneless chicken grilled, in special anticucho
sauce, served with potato and "huancaina" sauce.

CARNE ENCEBOLLADA **$11.95**
Beef served with fried onions, herbs and spices.

PUERCO EN SALSA DE MANI **$11.95**
Pork in peanut sauce.

PATO EN SALSA DE ALMENDRAS **$14.95**
Duck in Amaretto sauce.

Peruvian style coffee **$1.50**
Peruvian flan **$2.50**

It's always busy, but I say that the best seafood houses are the busiest, as the seafood is always the freshest. It doesn't get any fresher than this. The place is huge and noisy, but that just adds to the total experience.

Menu Changes Daily And Seasonally

BOB'S SUPER SPECIALS:

FLORIDA STONE CRAB CLAWS: THESE TENDER, MEATY MORSELS ARE FRESH FROM THE SUNSHINE STATE! SERVED CHILLED WITH OUR TANGY MUSTARD SAUCE.
- APPETIZER ... $10.95
- DINNER ... $20.95

HAWAIIAN ONAGA ... $20.95 THE CREME DE LA CREME OF THE RED SNAPPER FAMILY! TONIGHT'S "SIX-WAY" FISH — SEE SERVER FOR DETAILS.

FRESH ALASKAN KING CRAB LEGS... $22.95 20oz OF SWEET, SUCCULENT CRAB LEGS, FRESH FROM THE DEEP, COLD WATERS OF ALASKA! SERVED STEAMED WITH WARM, DRAWN BUTTER.
- 10oz KING CRAB & 8oz FILET MIGNON... $23.95

SHRIMP SCAMPI... $13.95 JUMBO SHRIMP BAKED IN THE SHELL WITH CREAMY BUTTER, FRESH GARLIC AND WHOLE PEPPERCORNS.

LARGE MAINE LOBSTER: GREAT FOR TWO!! 3lb-5lbs FOR $12.00 PER POUND. SIMPLY TELL YOUR SERVER YOUR WEIGHT PREFERENCE AND WE'LL TAKE CARE OF THE REST!!

HAWAIIAN AHI TUNA ... $17.95 A TENDER, MEATY TEXTURED FISH, BEST SERVED MEDIUM RARE! CHOOSE CHARGRILLED OR CAJUN-BLACKENED. ASK ABOUT OUR SIZZLING PLATTER WITH SPECIAL SAUTEED ONIONS.

FAMOUS FOR OUR STEAKS? YOU BET!! ALL OF OUR STEAKS ARE DRY-AGED 21 DAYS FOR MOUTH-WATERING FLAVOR AND TENDERNESS! ASK YOUR SERVER ABOUT OUR SIZZLING PLATTER WITH SPECIAL SAUTEED ONIONS.
- 16oz N.Y. STRIP STEAK.. $16.95
- 14oz FILET MIGNON ... $24.95
- 8oz FILET MIGNON & FETTUCCINE ALFREDO.. $14.95
- 22oz PRIME N.Y. STRIP STEAK.. $22.95
- 32oz PORTERHOUSE FOR TWO... $28.95

BRAZILIAN SCAMPI TAILS & ......:
6 TAILS & FETTUCCINE ALFREDO...16.95
6 TAILS "BOB'S VERSION" ON RICE...16.95
4 TAILS & ONE PORK CHOP...16.95
4 TAILS & 8oz STRIP STEAK...17.95
-WITH FETTUCCINE ALFREDO-

FROM OUR LOBSTER TANKS:
LOBSTER TAIL: 10oz...24.95 16oz...32.95
1½lb MAINE...19.95 - SERVED ONE OF FIVE WAYS:
①BOB'S VERSION ②½ LOBSTER & 8oz STRIP
③STEAMED ④ BROILED ⑤ ½ LOBSTER "ITALIANO"

★ LARGE MAINES – 3¼-5 lb ...12.00/lb

TODAY'S CATCH:
• HAWAIIAN AHI TUNA...17.95 - SERVED MED-RARE-
  - CHARGRILLED, BLACKENED, OR A SIZZLING
    PLATTER WITH SAUTÉED ONIONS...
• HOLLAND DOVER SOLE...19.95
• FLORIDA SWORDFISH...18.95
• NEW ZEALAND ORANGE ROUGHY...13.95
• FLORIDA GROUPER...13.95
• PACIFIC HALIBUT...15.95
• HAWAIIAN ONO...18.95
• ALASKAN KING SALMON...17.95

AU GRATIN:
SHRIMP...9.95 SCALLOPS...11.95
COMBO (SHRIMP, FISH, SCALLOPS)...9.95

FROM OUR CRAB POTS:
ALASKAN KING CRAB LEGS...22.95
ALASKAN SNOW CRAB LEGS...13.95
ALASKAN DUNGENESS CRAB: COLD OR GARLIC-
  · LEGS...17.95 · MEDIUM...18.95 · LARGE...21.95
BLUE CRAB CLAWS...16.95 - COLD GARLIC-
CRABMEAT VERMICELLI...13.95 -STIR FRIED-
MARYLAND CRABCAKES & FETTUCCINE...13.95
CRAB MARILYN ON FETTUCCINE NOODLES...18.95
SOFT SHELL: SAUTÉED...22.95 TEMPURA...20.95

HOW ABOUT SHRIMP? YOU PEEL 'EM!
GARLIC OR HOT-N-SPICY...10.50
SHRIMP SCAMPI...13.95
STEAMED SHRIMP IN EGGS...13.95 (WITH 2 LBS)
HEINZ 57: MEDIUM...10.95 JUMBO...13.95
SHOYU SHRIMP w/ ONIONS: (w/RICE)
  MEDIUM...10.95 JUMBO...13.95
B-B-Q SHRIMP: MEDIUM...10.95 JUMBO...13.95
SHRIMP "BOB'S VERSION" ON RICE...14.95 (PEELED)

BOB'S SUPER SPECIALS:
FLORIDA STONE CRAB CLAWS...10.95
THESE MEATY MORSELS ARE
FRESH FROM THE SUNSHINE
STATE!! SERVED CHILLED WITH A
TANGY MUSTARD SAUCE.
BRAZILIAN SCAMPI TAILS:
SUPER DELICIOUS! SPLIT UP
THE CENTER, LIGHTLY SEASONED,
AND BAKED TO PERFECTION!
SERVED w/ FETTUCCINE ALFREDO.
• SCAMPI TAILS & FETTUCCINE...7.95
• SCAMPI TAILS & 8oz STRIP STEAK
  & FETTUCCINE ALFREDO...9.95

HOW ABOUT A HEALTHIER ALTERNATIVE
TO SODA? TRY ONE OF OUR DELICIOUS
HAWAIIAN NECTARS IN A SOUVENIR
SPORTS BOTTLE?
GUAVA OR PASSION FRUIT...2.50

BOB'S NEWEST CREATION
LILIKOI, LIME and VODKA...4.50
A TANGY & REFRESHING COMBINATION OF
PASSION FRUIT NECTAR, FRESH MASHED LIME,
& SMIRNOFF VODKA IN A 16oz BEVELLED
ACRYLIC SOUVENIR GLASS.
SOFT SHELL CRAB...10.95
FLOWN IN FRESH FROM THE
GULF NEAR LOUISIANA.
SERVED TEMPURA STYLE w/
FETTUCCINE ALFREDO.

HAWAIIAN AHI TUNA...7.95
A TENDER, MEATY TEXTURED
FISH, BEST SERVED MED-
IUM RARE. CHARGRILLED
OR BLACKENED.

THANK YOU
FOR CHOOSING
BOB CHINN'S!

One of the oldest seafood restaurants in Chicago, it just keeps sailing along. Repeat customers are legendary, so you know the food is excellent, but much of that loyalty can be traced to the most able maitre d', Patrick Bredin, who keeps the room on a steady course night after night.

Cape Cod Room

Menu Changes Seasonally

Appetizers

COLD		HOT	
Smoked Salmon	10.50	Shrimp De Jonghe	9.75
Cherrystone Clams	7.50	Snails Bourguignonne	7.25
Little Neck Clams	7.50	Clams Casino	7.95
Selected Oysters	7.50	Oysters Rockefeller	8.50

Soups

The Cape Cod's Famous
Bookbinder Red Snapper Soup
with Sherry

Cup 3.50   Bowl 6.50

Seafood Gumbo

Cup 4.25   Bowl 8.00

New England Clam Chowder

Cup 3.50   Bowl 6.50

From Fresh Waters of the World

Bouillabaisse

Variety of Fresh and Salt-Water Fish
and Seafoods with Fresh Vegetable
Garniture; Seasoned with Garlic,
Thyme, Saffron and Chablis Wine,
Served with Garlic French Bread
24.75

140 East Walton • Near North/Gold Coast • (312) 787-2200

From the World's Oceans

Pompano Papillote
Fillet Enclosed in Parchment
with Lobster and Mushrooms
in Red Wine Sauce   24.75

Imported Dover Sole,
Broiled or Sautéed   Market Price

Broiled Red Snapper,
Lemon Butter   25.75

Imported Turbot, Broiled,
Maître d'Hôtel   Market Price

Swordfish, Broiled   24.75

Lobsters

Broiled or Steamed
Whole Maine Lobster
with Melted Butter
Market Price

ROMANOFF
On a Bed of Wild Rice with
Tarragon Sauce
27.50

Twin Lobster Tails
with Melted Butter
33.00

THERMIDOR
Seasoned with Shallots,
Mushrooms, Dry Mustard,
Worcestershire, Cayenne and Tabasco
27.50

Scallops

Ocean Scallops Broiled on a Skewer
21.50

Ocean Scallops, Sautéed
20.75

Cape Cod Scallops, Sautéed
23.00

Crabmeat

A la Newburg in a Light Cream Sauce,
Flavored with Sherry Wine
25.50

Crabmeat Cakes
with Mustard Sauce
23.00

Shrimp

A LA DRAKE
In a Casserole, Smothered with
Shallots in a Newburg Sauce,
Glazed with Parmesan Cheese
22.75

CREOLE
In a Casserole with Green Pepper,
Zucchini, Pimiento, Onions,
Celery and Tomato
22.75

Dinner: 7 Days a Week until 11

371

Catch 35

Catch one of the most elegant seafood restaurants in Chicago. Multi-level with comfortable and very private booths, this restaurant is a sleeper, offering some of the most innovative seafood dishes in town.

Menu Changes Daily

HALF SHELL OYSTERS	1/2 DOZ.	DOZ.
HOOD CANAL	6.95	12.95
COCKENOE	6.95	12.95
CHARLESTON POND	6.95	12.95
MALPEQUE	6.95	12.95
A SELECTION OF OUR VARIETIES	6.95	13.95

APPETIZERS

CATCH'S CRAB CAKE	7.95
SHRIMP COCKTAIL	7.95
SZECHWAN SCALLOP	7.95
DEEP FRIED POINT JUDITH CALAMARI & TOFU	5.95
COCONUT BEER BATTER SHRIMP	7.95
CHICKEN SATAY W/PEANUT SAUCE & CUCUMBER RELISH	5.95
BAKED OYSTER W/FRESH SPINACH, PANCETTA & ASIAGO CHEESE	7.95
TOMATO-BASIL LINGUINI W/GRILLED EGGPLANT & MARINARA SAUCE	7.95

SALADS

CAESAR SALAD	3.95
HOUSE MIX LETTUCE W/ASIAN PESTO SHRIMP	7.95
MARTHAS VINEYARD W/RASPBERRY HONEY DRESSING	4.95
FRESH MOZZARELLA & BEEF STEAK TOMATOES W/OPAL BASIL VINAIGRETTE	5.95

PASTA

SALMON, SCALLOP & SHRIMP W/PROVENCAL SAUCE ON PASTA	13.95
CHEESE FILLED TORTELLINI W/PINE NUT, PANCETTA MUSHROOM, TOMATO AND DELICATE CREAM SAUCE	12.95

---

35 West Wacker Dr • Downtown/Loop • (312) 346-3500

BLACKENED

BLACKENED SWORDFISH W/ROASTED RED PEPPER SAUCE	17.95
BLACKENED MAHI MAHI W/ANDOUILLE SAUSAGE ETOUFFÉE	16.95

OVEN BAKED

BAKED SALMON IN PUFF PASTRY W/BEARNAISE SAUCE	17.95
BAKED MARYLAND CRAB CAKES W/REMOULADE SAUCE	15.95
BAKED JUMBO PANAMA SHRIMP W/CRABMEAT STUFFING	16.95
BAKED LEMON SOLE W/MARYLAND BLUE CRAB STUFFING	15.95

LOBSTER

GRILLED AUSTRALIAN LOBSTER TAILS		30.95
GRILLED AUSTRALIAN LOBSTER TAIL & FILET MIGNON		31.95
STIR FRIED LOBSTER TAIL W/HUNAN SAUCE		24.95
AMERICAN MAINE LOBSTER	STEAMED	16.95/LB.
	BAKED W/CRAB MEAT STUFFING	17.95/LB.

GRILLED

GRILLED YELLOW FIN TUNA W/GINGER SESAME SAUCE	16.95
GRILLED MAHI MAHI W/STONE GROUND MUSTARD-HONEY SAUCE	16.95
BREAST OF CHICKEN W/LIME, GARLIC & FRESH TOMATO SAUCE	12.95
GRILLED FILET MIGNON W/FRESH HERB-MADEIRA WINE BUTTER	24.95
GRILLED BOSTON SEA SCALLOP W/BAY HOTEL BUTTER	15.95

WOK

STIR FRIED CRAB CLAW, SHRIMP & SCALLOP W/TOMATO SAUCE	15.95
STIR FRIED CATFISH W/THAI SPICES, FRENCH BEAN & BELL PEPPERS	14.95
STIR FRIED SHRIMP W/ASPARAGUS, MUSHROOM & RED PEPPER	14.95
STIR FRIED CHICKEN & SHRIMP W/BASIL AND GARLIC	13.95
STIR FRIED TEXAS BROWN SHRIMP & SCALLOP W/RICE NOODLE	14.95

PAN SEARED

SEARED SALMON W/CAJUN SPICES & SWEET GARLIC-CHILI SAUCE	16.95
SEARED TUNA W/SZECHWAN GLAZE & FRIED TEXAS ONION	16.95

SPECIALTIES

STEAMED SHRIMP W/BROCCOLI, CAULIFLOWER & JASMINE RICE	15.95
GRILLED KING SALMON W/WHOLE GRAIN MUSTARD SCALLION SAUCE	16.95
GRILLED FLORIDA GROUPER W/OLIVE OIL, GARLIC & THAI BASIL	16.95
SEARED SHRIMP & SCALLOP W/VEGETABLES & CAJUN GARLIC SAUCE	16.95
GRILLED SWORDFISH W/CRACKED PEPPERCORNS AND LIGHT COGNAC-AVOCADO SALSA	17.95
SWEET AND SOUR HALIBUT W/PINEAPPLE, ONION & BELL PEPPERS	16.95
GRILLED GLAZED ALASKAN HALIBUT W/ROCK SHRIMP AND STIR-FRIED VEGETABLES	16.95

CHEF: E. PRUKPITIKUL

Davis Street Fishmarket

The chalkboard menu never stops featuring the freshest of the catch. The East Coast ambiance adds to the allure, but the popularity of this place comes from the excellent preparation of first-quality seafood. The grilled salmon and pan-fried scallops are two of my favorite dishes.

BROILED

Whitefish	7.95
Lake Trout	8.95
Bluefish	8.95
Scrod	9.50
Salmon	12.95
Grouper	Market Price
Halibut	Market Price

PAN FRIED

Petite Frog Legs	10.95
Idaho Brook Trout	8.95
Bay Scallops	Market Price
Sea Scallops	11.95
Lemon Sole	Market Price
Scampi	Market Price
Walleye Pike	11.25
Lake Perch	Market Price
Monkfish	Market Price
Flounder	Market Price
Tilapia	Market Price

CAJUN/CREOLE

Blackened Redfish	Market Price
Blackened Gulf Shrimp	13.95
River Road Gumbo	5.95
New Orleans BBQ Shrimp	13.95
Red Beans & Rice	1.95
Shrimp Creole	9.95
Louisiana Chicken	7.95

501 Davis St • Evanston • (708) 869-3474

STEAMED

1# Whole Maine Lobster	14.95
1 1/2# Whole Main Lobster	18.95
1# U Peel em Shrimp - garlic, plain, spicy	13.45
Pot of Mussels	7.95
Garlic Mussels	8.95
Mussels Marinara	8.95
Maryland Blue Crabs	Market Price
Crawfish, 1#, 2#, 3#	Market Price

Pot of Linguine: Choice of

White Clam Sauce	6.95
Mussels Marinara	6.95
Shrimp Creole	6.95

GRILLED AFTER 4:30

Swordfish	Market Price
Salmon	Market Price
Tuna	Market Price
Mako Shark	Market Price
Mahi Mahi	Market Price
Amberjack	Market Price
Marlin	Market Price
Wahoo	Market Price

CALABASH STYLE DEEP FRIED

Smelts	6.45
Cod Strips	9.50
Calamari	7.95
Catfish	8.60
Oysters	9.60
Clam Strips	7.95
Shrimp	10.95
Large Shrimp	11.95
New England Fried Clams	11.95

OTHER

Cornbread	1.00
Hamburger	3.95
Dinner Salad	2.25

Dinner: Sun - Thurs 4:30 - 10, Fri - Sat 4:30 - 11

I go here just to experience the wonderful calamari dishes. But there is a certain lure to this large, comfortable, dimly lit seafood spot that hooks me. There is little question that "fresh" is the operative word for the seafood, so cast your line where you please.

Nick's Fishmarket

Specials Change Daily

Appetizers

Calamari Sarento
tomatoes, garlic & parmesan cheese
$6.00

Shrimp Scampi
in garlic butter
$6.95

Calamari Fritte
seasoned, with cocktail sauce
$6.00

Escargot Bourguignonne
garlic butter & pesto
$7.00

Mussels Marinara
garlic, basil & red wine
$7.00

Fresh Baked Clams Casino
garlic, bacon & parmesan cheese
$5.50

Filet Bits Teriyaki
tenderloin in teriyaki sauce
$5.75

Fresh Blue Point Oysters
on the half shell, 1/2 dozen
$6.95

Shellfish

Exotic California Abalone
ricci style or caper butter
$42.00

Blackened Lobster Tail
cajun butter sauce
$38.00

Broiled Lobster Tail
drawn butter
$38.00

Lobster Thermidor
classic preparation
$38.00

---

1 First National Plaza • Downtown/Loop • (312) 621-0200

Seafood

Hawaiian Favorites
availability & preparations change daily
$ Market price

Fresh Farm Raised Salmon
Broiled: lemon butter, hollandaise
Nesha: poached, shrimp, light cream sauce
$25.00

Fresh Seared Pepper Salmon
dijon, soy sauce
$25.00

Atlantic Swordfish
Livorno: olive oil, lemon, oregano
Stavros: spinach, feta cheese
$26.50

Catfish Clarence
hot & spicy
$24.50

Dover Sole Meuniere
boned tableside
$33.00

Specialite della Casa

Chicken Mediterranean
1/2 chicken, marinated & roasted
$23.50

Veal Chop
barolo wine truffle sauce
$31.00

Pepper Petite Daniel
dijon cognac sauce
$24.50

Porterhouse Plack
22 oz. prime beef
$33.00

Paella Ungaretti
Nick's version of the spanish classic
$28.95

Lamb Chops
seasoned, with mint sauce
$32.00

Pasta

Cavatappi Bolognese
corkscrew pasta with traditional
meat sauce
$16.00

Shrimp Ravioli Roberto
spicy lobster cream sauce
$17.00

Frutta di Mare
linguini & shellfish in lobster
cream sauce
$27.95

Lobster Fra Diavolo
linguini with spicy marinara sauce
$38.00

Dinner: Mon - Thurs 5:30 - 11, Fri - Sat 5:30 - 12

Billed as the "only seafood restaurant on the water," this crab house actually looks like a crab house, eats like a crab house (complete with hush puppies and greens), and pleases visitors and locals alike with its pristine seafood creations.

THE OLD CAROLINA
(CRAB HOUSE)

Menu Changes Seasonally

Appetizers

STEAMED CLAMS in Buttery Garlic Clambroth	8.95
STEAMED MUSSELS in Buttery Garlic Clambroth	6.95
STEAMED MUSSELS in our special Marinara Sauce	6.95
STEAMED MUSSELS AND CLAMS in our special Marinara Sauce	7.95
SOUTHERN FRIED CATFISH FINGERS	4.50
BLUE CRAB FINGERS	5.50
GARLIC BLUE CRAB FINGERS served hot	5.95
SHRIMP COCKTAIL (in shell)	7.50
SEAFOOD COCKTAIL PLATE	7.95
3 clams, 3 oysters, 2 shrimp, 5 blue crab fingers	
CRAB CAKE APPETIZER	7.95
FRESH STONE CRAB CLAWS	9.95
FRIED CLAMS	4.95
SOFT SHELL CRAB Sauteed or Tempura Fried	7.95

Crabs & Lobster

All Crab & Lobster Dinners served with Cole Slaw, Au Gratin Potatoes, Vegetable of the Day and a Basket of Hush Puppies.

SEAFOOD AU GRATIN with crabmeat, shrimp, fish, scalops	14.95
CRAB CAKES	15.95
ALASKAN SNOW CRAB LEGS	17.95
ALASKAN KING CRAB LEGS	24.95
FRESH STONE CRAB CLAWS (Oct.15 - May 1) Steamed or Chilled	22.95
1 1/2 LB. LOBSTER, steamed	23.95
BROILED AUSTRAILIAN LOBSTER TAILS	29.95
SURF AND TURF	27.95

---

465 East Illinois St • Gold Coast • (312) 321-8400

378

Lunch Landings

All our Grilled Fish is served with Coleslaw, Au Gratin Potatoes, Vegetable of the Day and Hush Puppies.

GRILLED TUNA   GRILLED SWORDFISH   GRILLED CATFISH   GRILLED SALMON
GRILLED GROUPER   GRILLED SHRIMP   GRILLED SCALLOPS
GRILLED WALLEYE PIKE

It's Shore Dinner Time

CAROLINA FRIED SHORE DINNER 14.95
catfish, scallops, shrimp, clams, fried okra, fried green tomatoes,
coleslaw, hush puppies
CAROLINA GRILLED SHORE DINNER 15.95
grilled fish, shrimp, scallops, fresh vegetable, coleslaw,
au gratin potatoes, hush puppies
OLD CAROLINA SEAFOOD LINGUINI.. 13.95
fresh-made pasta with clams, mussels, shrimp, and scallops, and our
fabulous Garlic Crab Sauce or our rich red Marinara Sauce, vegetable of the day,
coleslaw, hush puppies

From the Morehead City Shrimpers

Try our Shrimp! Nearly a pound! Have it the Mate's Way (U-Peel) or the Captain's Way (We Peel). Either way, you won't leave hungry! Anybody for Beer?

SHRIMP IN GARLIC BUTTER -
with vegetable of the day, au gratin potatoes, and hush puppies
Mate's Way (U-Peel) 12.95
Captain's Way (We Peel) 14.95
SPICY CRAB BOIL STYLE SHRIMP -
with vegetable of the day, au gratin potatoes, and hush puppies
Mate's Way (U-Peel) 12.95
Captain's Way (We Peel) 14.95

Desserts

After you look at these, read the table card for more fabulous
shortckaes and ice cream desserts!

CARTERET COUNTY SCHOOL APPLE BROWN BETTY 3.50
PEACH COBBLER 3.50

Dinner: Mon - Thurs until 9, Fri - Sat until 10 (Hours Change Seasonally)

Phil Smidt & Son, Inc.

A legend in the Chicago area even if it is in Indiana (but very close to the Illinois border), this 80-year-old-plus seafood house is worth the drive. The main dishes to catch here are the delicious frogs legs and the reliably great perch.

All entrees include our Five Star array of potato salad, cottage cheese, coleslaw, beets, and kidney beans; rolls and butter. Plus choice of boiled potatoes or French fries.

Our Famous Lake Perch
Our famous recipe of lightly seasoned flour, pan fried in cholesterol free shortening.

SINGLE SERVING
Whole or whole in butter 14.00
Boned or boned and buttered 15.50
ALL YOU CAN EAT 21.50

Our Unique Frog Legs
We prepare our frog legs two different ways;
Deep fried and crispy, or
Lightly floured, seasoned and sauteed for a buttery flavor.

SINGLE SERVING 15.50
ALL YOU CAN EAT 21.50

Perch 'N' Frog
A combination of our famous boned perch and
fried or sauteed frog.

SINGLE SERVING 15.50
ALL YOU CAN EAT 21.50

Perch 'N' Chix
A combination of our famous boned perch and chix
(leg & thigh) white meat $1.00 extra.
SINGLE SERVING 11.95
ALL YOU CAN EAT 21.50

Fried Chicken
1/2 chicken, lightly floured, seasoned and fried in cholesterol free shortening.
Broiled Chicken
1/2 chicken, lightly seasoned, baked until tender, then finished off under the broiler.

SINGLE SERVING 8.75
ALL YOU CAN EAT 11.95
($2.00 charge for all dark or all white meat.)

1205 North Calumet Ave • Hammond, IN • (312) 768-6686

SEAFOOD DELIGHTS

All entrees include our Five Star array of potato salad, cottage cheese, coleslaw, beets, and kidney beans; rolls and butter.
Plus choice of boiled potatoes, or French fries.

BAKED SALMON 13.50
Farm raised, sprinkled with pepper, garlic, seasonings and baked until flaky

STUFFED SNAPPER 9.95
Filled with crab meat, shrimp and topped with Monterrey Jack cheese and baked

FRIED SHRIMP 16.95
Jumbo gulf shrimp, lightly coated with a flavorful batter and deep fried to a golden brown.

WHOLE CATFISH 11.50
Farm raised, this sweet tasting delight, has a unique flavor all of its own. Lightly floured and deep fried.

STEAK ENTREES

SIRLOIN STRIP STEAK 16.95
One full pound (16 oz.) boneless cut . . . the "King" of steaks. For serious meat lovers only.

FILET MIGNON 17.95
This tender cut is for people who desire The Steak eating experience. Twelve ounces of melt-in-the-mouth flavor.

7 oz. portion 13.95
For those with a lighter appetite.

COMBINATION DINNERS

SURF 'N' TURF 30.95
Broiled 6-8 oz. Lobster Tail served with melted butter and a 7 oz. broiled filet mignon.

SHRIMP 'N' SHRIMP 16.95
A combination of our broiled shrimp and fried shrimp.

Dinner: Mon - Thurs 4 - 9, Fri - Sat 4 - 10, Sun 2:30 - 7:30 (Hours Change Seasonally)

Philander's

The comfortable booths and tables flow out from all sides of the big bar in the center of this very plush dining room on the ground floor of the venerable Carlton Hotel in Oak Park. When soft-shell crabs are in season, this is the place to go.

PHILANDER'S

O A K · P A R K

Menu Changes Seasonally Along With Weekly Specials

Fresh Oysters   Each - $1.10   Half-Dozen - $6.25   Dozen - $9.95

Blue Points – *New York*	Chincoteaques – *Virginia*	Malpeques – *Canada*
Chesapeake Bay – *Virginia*	Kumamoto – *Canada*	Chileans – *Chile*
Quilcenes – *Washington State*	Chilean – *Chiloé*	Bayou Blacks – *Louisiana*
Malapinas – *Canada*	Caraquets – *Canada*	Olympias – *Washington State*

Availability subject to market conditions

Appetizers

Port Chatham Smoked Salmon	$7.50
Shrimp Cocktail	6.75
Oysters Rockefeller, oysters topped with spinach & mornay sauce	6.25
Stuffed Mushroom Caps, stuffed with crabmeat	6.50
Snails in the Shell, in garlic butter	6.00
New Orleans' Barbeque Shrimp, spicy, in the shell	7.50
Roasted Whole Garlic, served with goat cheese and croutons	5.00
Dungeness Crab Cake, Maryland style, with spicy mustard sauce	7.25

Pastas   We use fresh hand made pastas.

Linguine with Spicy Lobster, pieces of lobster in a light cream sauce, with chopped plum tomatoes and crushed red pepper	$8.75/$15.50
Spicy Shrimp with Penne Pasta, Alfredo sauce, with crushed red pepper	7.75/13.50

1120 Pleasant St • Oak Park • (708) 848-4250

Fresh Fish & Seafood   Served with today's vegetables.

Trio of Seafood, Swordfish marinated in olive oil & garlic, grilled, Flounder in tarragon & Poached Salmon with hollandaise	$14.75
Dover Sole, sauté, meunière or amandine	23.50
Panfried Catfish, dusted in cornmeal & smothered in sauteéd onions, with our own tartar sauce	13.75
Flounder with Tarragon, broiled, with a buttery tarragon sauce	13.75
Grilled Swordfish, with herbed butter	16.50
Poached Salmon, with hollandaise	15.25
Mixed Grill, jumbo shrimp, fresh squid, zucchini, squash, plum tomatoes, eggplant & corn on the cob	12.50
Squid Steak, sauté meunière - "Abalone Taste Alike"	13.50

Shellfish   Served with today's vegetables.

New Orleans' Barbeque Shrimp, spicy, in the shell	$16.50
Dungeness Crab Cakes, Maryland style, with spicy mustard sauce	15.25
Sea Scallops, flamed in gin, served with cream sauce	14.25
Bouillabaisse, a tomato based fish and shellfish stew, with rouille (a garlicky condiment)	18.75
Lobster Tail, served with drawn butter	28.50
Alaskan King Crab Legs, 1 pound, steamed and served with drawn butter	26.50
1-1½ lb. Lobster, steamed, with drawn butter	17.50

Steaks & Chops   Served with today's vegetables.

Grilled Lamb Chops, with mint jelly	$16.75
New York Strip Steak, fresh beef cooked on a charcoal grill	16.75
Filet Mignon, fresh beef cooked on a charcoal grill	16.75
Blackened Pork Chops, coated in cajun spices, then seared	11.25
Steak au Poivre, New York Strip, sauté, with crushed black pepper	16.50
Panfried Breast of Chicken with Tarragon, Perdue free range	10.50

Dinner: Mon - Thurs 4 - 10, Fri - Sat 4 - 11:30

Shaw's Crab House

Another of my "If it's busy it's better" seafood houses. Shaw's does a wonderful job with oysters, usually offering several choice varieties. But for sheer seafood variety and perfectly prepared fish dishes, this is the place.

Menu Changes Seasonally

FRESH OYSTERS

On The Half Shell . . . . 6.95 ♥
Daily Regional Varieties, Shucked to Order
Oysters Rockefeller. 6.95
Pan Fried Pacific Oysters 6.95

SEAFOOD APPETIZER PLATTERS

–serves two–
Cold Combo—Shrimp, Oysters, Clams, & Blue Crab Fingers 14.90

Hot Combo—Mini Crab Cakes, Popcorn Shrimp, & Calamari 12.90

(additional servings available)

COLD APPETIZERS

Blue Crab Fingers. 4.95
Topneck Clams, Half-Dozen. 5.95
Charred Sashimi Tuna 6.95
Shrimp Cocktail (in shell) 7.95

HOT APPETIZERS

Escargot, Garlic Butter 5.95
Steamed Blue Mussels . . . . 4.95 ♥
French Fried Calamari 4.95
Popcorn Shrimp. 6.95
Baked Clams Casino. 6.50
Shaw's Crab Cake 7.50

SALADS

Shaw's Caesar Salad 3.95
Mixed Greens 2.95
Cole Slaw. 1.95
Iceberg Wedge 2.50
Sliced Tomato & Onion. 2.50
Boursin Cheese with Mixed Greens . 3.95

Dressings: 1000 Island, Mustard Vinaigrette, Italian, Maytag Blue Cheese, & Ranch

VEGETABLES

–serves two–
Creamed Spinach 2.50
Baked Ratatouille en Casserole 2.95
Steamed Fresh Broccoli . . . . 2.50 ♥
Steamed Green Beans . . . . 2.25 ♥
Green Beans and Mushrooms 2.50
Steamed Carrots . . . . 2.25 ♥
Carrots and Mushrooms 2.50

POTATOES & RICE

–serves two–
Hashed Browns 2.50
Hashed Browns w/Onions 2.95
Au Gratin Potatoes 2.95
Boiled Red Potatoes 1.95
Cajun Rice. 1.95
Four Grain Wild Rice . . . . 1.95 ♥
–single–
Charred Baked Potato. 2.50

SHAW'S SPECIALTIES

Planked Lake Superior Whitefish . . 14.95
Pan Fried Yellow Lake Perch 14.95
Shaw's Crab Cakes (2) 13.95
Sautéed Frog Legs 11.95
Sautéed Sea Scallops. 13.95

SHRIMP PLATTERS

Shrimp, Spinach, Tomatoes
   on Linguini. . . . . 12.95 ♥
French Fried Shrimp 13.95
N'Awlins Spicy Shrimp 13.95
Grilled Garlic Shrimp 13.95
Baked Stuffed Shrimp 14.95

SEAFOOD STEWS & COMBOS

Shaw's Seafood Platter 16.95
   Crab Cake, Sea Scallops, & Garlic Shrimp
Shaw's Seafood Stew 19.95
   Clams, Shrimp, Mussels, Crab, Lobster & Fish
New England Clam Bake. 21.95
   1 lb. Lobster, Clams, Potatoes & Sweet Corn
Filet Mignon/Lobster Tail. 29.95

CHICKEN & PRIME BEEF

Whole Roasted Chicken. 11.25
Garlic Roasted Chicken 11.50
Aged New York Sirloin. 22.95
Filet Mignon, Sauce Béarnaise 19.95

—DAILY SPECIALS—

FRESH FISH & SPECIAL SELECTIONS

— SAUTEED —

SHRIMP AND SEA SCALLOPS ON PENNE PASTA
   Marinara Sauce 14.95
WHOLE DOVER SOLE, Amandine 21.95
ICELANDIC ARCTIC CHAR ♥ 15.95
   Shiitake and Oyster Mushroom Sauce and Pea Pods

— GRILLED —

LINE CAUGHT OREGON KING SALMON 18.95
   Julienne Sweet Bell Peppers, Fried Tortillas and Mustard Dill Vinaigrette
AMERICAN RED SNAPPER ♥ 18.95
   Sauteed Mixed Vegetables and Heart Healthy Tartar Sauce
ECUADORIAN MAHI MAHI 16.95
   Herb Marinade, Fried Sweet Potato Chips & Soy Sauce
YELLOWFIN TUNA ♥ 17.95
   Roasted Corn Black Bean Relish and Bok Choy

–ALL FRESH FISH AVAILABLE PLAIN GRILLED WITH REGULAR OR HEART HEALTHY TARTAR SAUCE–

CRAB AND LOBSTER

Cold Water Lobster Tail . . . . 28.95   Live Maine Lobster (per lb) . 18.95
Fresh Alaskan King Crab Legs, 1lb . . 29.95   Live From our Tank, 1 lb to 4 lbs
Dungeness Crab . . . . 23.95   Stuffed Maine Lobster (per lb) 23.95

*♥ THESE RECIPES MEET THE FAT AND CHOLESTEROL GUIDELINES OF THE AMERICAN HEART ASSOCIATION
OF METROPOLITAN CHICAGO • QUALITY FIRST •*

Dinner: Mon - Thurs 5:30 - 10, Fri 5:30 - 11, Sat 5 - 11, Sun 5 - 10

If I had to pick a favorite meal here it would be breakfast when it's quiet and peaceful (or maybe it's the grits), but then again the homemade goodies at dinner get me too (or maybe it's the low prices).

JERRY'S KITCHEN

Menu Changes Daily

Southern Home Cooked Meal

Liver Onions, two vegetables...$5.95
Homemade Soup of the Day...Cup $1.10; Bowl $1.50
Oyster Crackers Served With Soup
Short Ribs of Beef smothered in gravy two sides..$7.25
Two Smoked Ham Hocks, two vegetables..$6.50
Two Pork Chops, two vegetables..$7.50
Fresh 1/2 Fried Chicken (Cooked To Order) two vegetables................................$6.95
Fresh 1/4 Fried Chicken (Cooked To Order) two vegetables................................$5.50
Fresh Cat Fish served with cole slaw and two vegetables....................................$7.25
Broiled Catfish served with two vegetables with lemon and butter sauce............$7.75
Fresh Perch served with cole slaw and two vegetables..$7.25
Broiled Perch served with two vegetables with lemon and butter sauce.............$7.75
Four chicken wings, two vegetables...$4.95

Served with choice of two vegetables and corn muffins or biscuits. With Soup or Salad.
Fried Corn, Greens, String Beans, Mashed Potatoes, Rice, Okra, Red Bean
Potato Salad or Cole Slaw, Black eye peas
Candied Yams $1.45, Corn on the Cob $1.25
Jerry's homemade Chow Chow .50

Vegetable Plate with 3 vegetables, onions and tomato.......................................$3.95
Extra Side Dish..$1.45
Order of Greens served with raw onion, tomato and corn muffin.......................$2.95
Breaded Shrimp Platter, served with French Fries and Cole Slaw.......................$6.95
Jerry's Seafood Platter, catfish or perch, 4 shrimp and 6 scallops, choice of two sides;
3 hush puppies, cole slaw, potato salad or fries (sorry no substitutions).............$9.95
Extra Catfish or Extra Perch.................$2.00

Salads

Salad $1.50
Salad - Julienne - Ham, cheese, tomato, green pepper, egg
lettuce, onions, carrots..$4.25
Blue Cheese Dressing - extra.. .50
Pepper Corn Dressing - extra... .50

Desserts

Sweet Potato Pie (Home Made)...$1.60   1/2 Bread Pudding (Home Made)...................$1.75
Peach Cobbler (Home Made).....$1.75   Cake (Home Made)..$1.75
Rice Pudding (Home Made)........$1.75   Cobbler with Ice cream (Home Made)..........$3.25

449 West North Ave • Lincoln Park/DePaul • (312) 280-9340

BREAKFAST MENU

Juices

Orange Juice..................Sm. .90; Large $1.50
Grapefruit.......................Sm. .90; Large $1.50
Tomato Juice.................Sm. .90; Large $1.50
Orange Pineaple Juice .... .90
Apple Juice... .90

Cereals

Grits...$1.45
Oatmeal with Milk............................$1.45
Assorted Cold Cereals with milk......... .95

Fresh Fruit

Pink Grapefruit.......(Market Price In Season)
Cantaloupe.......(Market Price In Season)

Breakfast Specials

(Egg Beaters, add .40 to Breakfast)
All Breakfasts Are Served With Grits, Rice, Or Hash Browns With Biscuits Or Toast.

Bacon or Pork Sausage with
    One Egg.......................................$2.45
    Two Eggs......................................$2.95
Ham with
    One Egg..$2.75
    Two Eggs.......................................$3.25
Hot Links Sausage with
    One Egg..$2.95
    Two Eggs.......................................$3.50
Hickory Mississippi Smoked Sausage
    One Egg..$2.95
    Two Eggs.......................................$3.45

Beef Sausage with
    One Egg...$2.65
    Two Eggs.......................................$3.15
One Egg with Grits.................................$1.65
Two Eggs with Grits...............................$1.95
Country Sausage (Home Made) with
    One Egg...$2.65
    Two Eggs.......................................$3.45
Country Sausage with
    Gravy and 3 Biscuits..................$2.75
    extra cup of gravy.....................$1.50
    extra cup of brown gravy...........$1.45

Eye Openers

Breakfast Steak, two eggs, grits, rice or hash browns, biscuit or toast......$5.75

One Pork Chop (with One Egg).............$5.25
Two Pork Chops (with One Egg)..... ......$6.40
Two Pork Chops (with Two Eggs)...........$6.90
Steak (with One Egg)...........................$5.45
Steak (with Two Eggs)..........................$6.90
1 Salmon Croquette (with One Egg)....$2.95
1 Salmon Croquette (with Two Eggs)....$3.45
2 Salmon Croquettes (with One Egg)...$5.75
2 Salmon Croquettes (with Two Eggs)..$6.25
Pancake (with Butter & Syrup).............$1.95
    (with Bacon, Sausage or Salt Pork)....$3.50
    (with Ham or Beef Sausage)..............$3.75

Three Egg Omelettes
    Served with your choice of
    Green Peppers, Onions, Mushrooms,
    Ham or Bacon......................$3.75
Denver Omelette.............................$3.75
Cheese Omelette.............................$2.95
Plain Omelette................................. $2.50
Extra Cheese.................................... .50
French Toast (with Butter & Syrup).......$1.95
    (with Bacon, Sausage or Salt Pork)..$3.95

Side Orders

1 Salmon Croquette............................$2.25
Bacon...$1.50
Hot Links...$2.25
Pork Sausage.....................................$1.50
Beef Sausage......................................$2.25

2 Salmon Croquettes...........................$4.25
Hash Browns.......................................$1.45
Alga Syrup.. .50
One Biscuit.. .45
One Corn Muffin................................... .45

Dinner: Sun - Thurs until 9, Fri - Sat until 10

Blue Iris Cafe

There are a lot of Southwestern creations on the menu in this comfortable and pleasant storefront restaurant, but there are some New Orleans and Caribbean dishes as well. Chef/Owner Alex Wohn knows how to handle his chiles, so they show up in a number of ways, always to full advantage.

Menu Changes Seasonally

APPETIZERS

Prickly Pear Cactus and Eggplant Bruschetta $3.95

Goat Cheese and Tomato Pico de Gallo $3.95

Baked Brie with Walnuts and Fresh Fruit $4.95

Fried Calamari $4.95

Roasted Red Peppers with Baby Corn (cold marinade) $4.95

Crawfish Cakes with Avocado-cocktail sauce $5.95

Anticuchas (Skewered tenderloin with grilled tortillas & Pico de Gallo) $5.95

Jalapeno Garlic Bread $3.00

Blue Iris Guacamole and Tortilla Chips $4.50

Baked Jalapeno Halves filled with minced clams & bread crumb stuffing $4.95

ENSALADAS

Dandelion Salad with Hard Boiled Eggs $3.95

Tomato, Onion, and Asparagus Salad with Vinaigrette Dressing $4.95

ENTREES

Shrimp and Prairie Fire Pasta $13.95
Fresh onion, tomato, mushrooms, cumin, shallots and charred hot chile peppers
spice up this shrimp and rotini pasta dish. Muy picante!

3216 North Sheffield Ave • Lincoln Park/DePaul • (312) 975-8383

American Indian Posole with Spareribs $12.95
This recipe is adapted from a dish made in the pueblos of New Mexican Indians to a
modern Southwest hominy stew with spareribs & corn bread. Served with chopped
jalapeno peppers and onion garnish.

Island BBQ Ribs $12.95
Tender pork ribs with a hint of orange. Served with Southwest potato salad & our
Golden Corn Bread.

Spicy Hot Southwest Linguini with Asparagus and White Clam Sauce $12.95

New Mexican Red Snapper Filet $12.50

Tumbleweed Swordfish & Southwest Stir Fry $11.95
Grilled Swordfish with a stir fry of baby carrots, cucumbers, baby corn, radishes,
asparagus, shallots & fresh tarragon. Served with Golden Corn Bread.

Blackened Swordfish $11.95
Cast iron skillet blackened Swordfish with Jalapeno-Lemon Parsley Rice & Golden
Corn Bread.

Carne Adovada with Espinacas and Chiles $10.95
Pork tenderloin marinated with chile caribe sauce, baked till fallin' apart tender and
served over rice. This dish comes with a side of fresh spinach sauteed with chiles, bacon,
onion, garlic and pinto beans.

Southwest Pork Chops $11.95
Two tender baked pork chops stuffed with Jalapeno corn bread dressing with a sauce of
onion, chipote chile, tomato and garlic. Served with a side of "Hoppin John".

Penne Pasta with Cauliflower and Chiles Aglio Oleo $10.95
Cauliflower and chiles are sauteed with olive oil and garlic then tossed with fresh spices,
pasta, parmesan cheese and grated dry Monterey Jack cheese.

Pan-fried Trout with "Hoppin John" $10.50
Our fresh trout coated with cornmeal, pan-fried and served with a smokey chipote chile
sauce and a side of "Hoppin John".

Turtle Creek Trout $9.50
Pan-seared whole trout and flambeed roasted hazelnuts with brandy butter sauce. Served
with Lemon Parsley Rice.

Drunken Chicken and BBQ Fire Roasted Onions $7.95
Chicken breast marinated in Hornitos Tequila, cilantro and spices, grilled then served
with fire roasted onions sauteed in a homemade BBQ sauce and Mango & Black Bean
Relish.

Dinner: Mon - Thurs 4:30 - 11, Fri - Sat 4:30 - 12, Sun 3 - 10

Arco de Cuchilleros

A casual and friendly tapas bar and restaurant that is easy to deal with (and not as crowded as Cafe Ba-Ba-Reeba!), as are the prices.

Menu Changes Every 2 to 3 Months

TAPAS CALIENTES (HOT TAPAS)

Habas a la Catalana: Broad beans sauteed with Spanish sausage	$4.95
Zortziko: Mixed seafood and vegetables sauteed in lemon butter with garlic	$4.95
Kokotxas a la Bilbaina: Fishcheeks sauteed with garlic, white wine and a touch of cayenne	$5.75
Chorizo con pimientos: Chorizo and sweet peppers sauteed together	$4.95
Gambas al ajillo: Shrimp sauteed with garlic, white wine and cayenne	$4.95
Tortilla Espanola: Spanish omelet	$2.95
Pisto: Combination of sauteed fresh vegetables	$2.95
Calamares a la plancha: Squid cooked on the griddle with lemon juice, oil, white wine, garlic and paprika	$4.50
Patatas a la brava: Sauteed potatos in a spicy tomato sauce	$2.95
Croquetas: Croquettes made of varying ingredients	$3.95
Berengena Formentor: Fresh eggplant slices dipped in batter, fried and served with sauteed Spanish sausage	$4.95
Pollo a la Navarra: Chicken sauteed with onions, cured ham, sweet red peppers and red wine	$4.95
Albondigas en vino tinto: meatballs cooked and served in a red wine sauce	$4.50
Gambas a la plancha: Butterflied shrimp marinated in olive oil, white wine, garlic, paprika and thyme. Cooked on the griddle.	$4.95

TAPAS FRIAS (COLD TAPAS)

Alcachofas a la vinagreta: *Artichoke hearts in a vinaigrette* $4.25

Montaditos de queso, chorizo, salchichon o jamon: *fresh tomato bread with either Spanish cheese, chorizo, Spanish salami or cured ham* $4.95

Ensalada de mariscos a la naranja: *Mixed seafood served on a bed of lettuce and juliened vegetables with an orange vinaigrette* $4.95

Ensalada de lentejas: *Lentil and vinaigrette salad* $2.95

Salpicon: *Salad of fresh vegetables and seafood in an oil and vinegar dressing* $4.95

Ensalada de aguacate: *Sliced avocado and vinaigrette salad* $3.25

Patatas ali-oli: *Boiled potatoes in a fresh garlic mayonaise* $2.95

Aguacate relleno: *Avocado shell stuffed with shrimp, rice, avocado and brandy mayonaise* $4.25

Aceitunas en adobo: *Marinated olives* $1.95

Ensalada de tomate: *Tomato and onion salad with an oil and vinegar dressing* $2.95

Ensalada Valenciana: *Salad of rice, shrimp and brandy mayonaise* $3.95

Ensalada de la casa: *House salad* $1.95

Combinacion de embutidos: *Combination of chorizo, spanish salami, and cured ham* $5.95

Pan tomate: *Fresh tomato bread* $1.95

Garbanzos con crema: *Chickpeas and roasted fresh vegetables in a sourcream sauce* $2.95

SOPAS (SOUPS)

Gazpacho: *Cold fresh vegetable soup* $2.95

Sopa de ajo: *Soup made with fresh garlic, chicken broth, bread and a poached egg* $2.50

Cafe Ba-Ba-Reeba!

This cafe is one of the first (and still the hottest) tapas spots in the city. Broad tapas selection to graze upon and the paella is still one of my favorite dishes. Great atmosphere.

CAFE BA·BA·REEBA!

Menu Changes Seasonally

Del Horno De Lena

Paella Valenciana . . . . $9.50 per person
Spanish rice dish with chicken, chorizo, pork, shrimp, mussels, squid, monkfish, green beans, tomatoes, and saffron

Arroz a Banda con Mariscos . . . . $11.95 per person
Spanish rice with fresh monkfish, squid, shrimp, mussels with alioli

Queso de Cabra al Horno $5.25
Baked goat cheese with tomato sauce and garlic bread

Zarzuela de Mariscos $7.95
A Spanish seafood stew with Angel hair pasta, julienne of vegetables and a cilantro saffron broth

Especialidades de Temporada

Mousse de Trucha Ahumada $3.95
Smoked trout mousse served with a horseradish cream

Arroz Español con Caracoles $5.25
Marinated snails and artichokes with garlic and parsley, grilled on skewers and served with Spanish rice and roasted pepper

Calamares Rellenas $4.95
Baby squid stuffed with shrimp spinach and served with a roasted red pepper vinaigrette

Salmón a la Parrilla $5.95
Grilled Salmon served with roasted mushrooms, shallots and a carrot juice alioli

Cazuela de Pescado Blanco con Hierbas Aromaticas $5.25
Lake Superior Whitefish roasted with a spicy peppered crust and served in a broth with vegetables, tarragon, and green onion

Lomo de Cerdo Asado con Lentejas $5.95
Roasted loin of pork marinated in thyme, apricot and garlic served on a bed of braised lentils with a romescue sauce

Cebolla Rellena con Ternera $6.25
Roasted Spanish onion stuffed with ground veal and pork, pine nuts, and tomato, served with a spicy tomato sauce and spinach

Plato de Mejillones al Azafrán $4.25
Steamed mussels served with a saffron vinaigrette and a medley of vegetables

Pincho de la Casa $6.95
A brochette of tomato bread, eggplant, sweet pepper, and goat cheese served with a toasted pine nut, raisin and watercress salad

2024 North Halsted St • Lincoln Park/DePaul • (312) 935-5000

Tapas Friás

Queso en Aceite $4.95
Marinated Spanish cheeses in olive oil and rosemary,
served with roasted garlic croutons

Patatas con Alioli $1.95
Potato salad with garlic mayonnaise

Pollo en Escabeche $4.25
Sautéed boneless chicken marinated with vinegar, garlic,
paprika and fresh herbs

Tortilla Española $2.25
Spanish omelet with potatoes and onion

Ensalada de Carne de Buey $4.95
Marinated and grilled steak salad with cumin, honey and mustard,
served with grilled vegetables

Ternera Asada $3.75
Cold roast veal with raspberry vinaigrette and oven dried tomatoes

Salpicón Blanco $5.95
Baby shrimp and scallops tossed with plum tomatoes, red and yellow pepper
green onion, and extra virgin olive oil

Pisto Manchego $3.95
Sautéed zucchini, peppers, eggplant, onions, garlic and tomato

Canalones Frios de Atún $4.25
Cannelloni stuffed with a tuna salad of basil, red onion, and mint
served with tomato basil sauce and white wine vinaigrette

Tapas Calientes

Pincho Moruno con Pollo y Chorizo $4.25
Chicken and chorizo brochette with sweet peppers and garlic cumin mayonnaise

Pulpo a la Gallega $4.95
Octopus served in the traditional Spanish manner with extra virgin
olive oil and paprika

Pollo en Salsa Picante $3.50
Spicy chicken wings served with a sherry mayonnaise

Pincho de Solomillo $4.75
Beef brochette with cracked pepper, horseradish cream, and a red onion relish

Empanada de Conejo $5.25
Braised rabbit baked in pastry with apples, sage, and a honey alioli

Gambas al Ajillo $6.95
Sauteed shrimp with garlic, olive oil, parsley, and spicy red pepper flakes

Setas Variadas a la Plancha con Mojo de Ajo $4.25
Mushrooms hot off the plancha with garlic, parsley, and olive oil

Pasta con Pollo y Tomate $4.95
Penne pasta tossed with boneless chicken, broccoli, oven-dried tomatoes,
capers, garlic and olive oil

Calamares a la Plancha $4.50
Fresh grilled squid with lemon, garlic and olive oil

Alcachofas con Jamón $5.95
Baby artichokes sauteed with garlic and Serano ham

Dinner: Mon - Thurs 5:30 - 11, Fri 5:30 - 12, Sat 5 - 12, Sun 3 - 10:30

Emilio Gervilla headed up the kitchen at Cafe Ba-Ba-Reeba! prior to opening his own place a few years ago, and its been wildly popular since opening day. I love the pan con tomate.

EMILIO'S
TAPAS BAR
RESTAURANT

TAPAS

ENSALADA RUSA 2.95
Spanish style potato salad with tuna

CAZUELA DE PULPO 4.95
marinated octopus with peppers, sherry vinaigrette

PATATAS CON ALIOLI 2.95
potato salad with garlic mayonnaise

ENTRADAS

POLLO A LA PARRILLA 4.95/9.95
grilled chicken breast on a bed of peppers with Spanish chorizo

PINCHO DE SOLOMILLO A LA PIMIENTA 3.95/10.95
beef brochette rolled in cracked pepper, grilled with sauteed
peppers, carmelized onions and horseradish sauce

SALMON CON SALSA DE CHAMPIÑONES 7.50/15.95
grilled salmon served with sherry vinaigrette

(PAELLA SERVED IN QUANTITIES OF TWO)
*Price is per person
THE FAMOUS SPANISH SAFFRON-RICE DISH

PAELLA A LA VALENCIANA 11.95
chicken, pork, lobster, shrimp, mussels, clams

PAELLA DE MARISCOS 12.95
lobster, shrimp, mussels, clams, scallops, and monkfish

4100 West Roosevelt Rd • Hillside • (708) 547-7177

ESPECIALIDADES

OSTRAS A LA PIMIENTA 5.95
grilled oysters rolled in cracked pepper

CAZUELA DE POLLO 4.95
chicken, mushrooms, and chorizo in garlic sauce

MORCILLA Y CHORIZO A LA PLANCHA 3.95
grilled Spanish chorizo and blood sausage

CARACOLES EMILIO 3.95
sauteed escargot served on croutons with tomato
sauce and garlic mayonnaise

CALAMARES A LA PARRILLA CON AJO Y LIMON 3.95
grilled squid with lemon garlic olive oil

QUESO DE CABRA AL HORNO 5.25
goat cheese baked in tomato sauce with olives,
served with garlic bread

SOPAS-ENSALADAS

SOPA DE ALUBIAS NEGRAS 1.95
black bean soup

SOPA DE LANGOSTA 1.95
lobster soup

ENSALADA DE APIO 2.95
mixed greens, celery, tomato, sherry vinaigrette

ENSALADA DE CASA 2.95
mixed greens, tomato, avocado, watercress, sherry vinaigrette

COCA DE SALMON 7.95
smoked salmon with toast, olives and dill sauce

POSTRES

FLAN AL CARAMELO 2.95
egg custard with caramel sauce

PLATANOS CON HELADO 2.95
sauteed banana with caramel, ice cream and pistachios

DELICIA DE CHOCOLATE 3.95
terrine of chocolate with raspberry sauce

Dinner: Mon - Thurs until 10, Fri until 11, Sat 5 - 11, Sun 4 - 9

395

This nice, friendly, welcoming Spanish restaurant serves paella which, as you can well imagine, is most excellent.

La Paella

APPETIZERS

Gambas al Ajillo $5.25
Shrimp sauteed in olive oil, white wine and garlic.

Almejas Albarino $5.75
Fresh clams sauteed and served in an Albarino wine,
onion and garlic sauce.

Mejillones en salsa verde $5.95
Fresh mussels in a white wine and cream sauce.

Aguacate relleno $4.95
Avocado shell stuffed with seafood and avocado mixed in a
brandy mayonnaise.

Calamares a la Gallega $4.95
Squid sauteed with potatoes, oil, paprika and garlic.

ENSALADAS

Ensalada de aguacate $3.50
Sliced avocado and vinaigrette salad.

Ensalada de la casa $2.25
House dinner salad.

SPECIALTIES

Paella Valenciana $14.75
Rice-based dish cooked with chicken, pork, chorizo and fresh
seafood.

Paella Marinera $17.95
Rice-based dish cooked with fresh lobster and seafood.

Zarzuela de mariscos — $17.95
Fresh lobster and seafood sauteed together, flambeed in
brandy and served with a romesco sauce.

Merluza a la Vasca — $15.95
Fresh cod cooked in an earthen casserole with white wine,
fresh cream, peas, pimentos, shrimp and clams.

Atun a la pimienta negra — $16.95
Fresh tuna fillet sauteed in a black peppercorn sauce.

Rape a la Gallega — $15.95
Fresh monkfish cooked in an earthen casserole with tomatoes,
onions, garlic, chorizo and potatoes.

SOPAS

Gazpacho — $3.25
Cold vegetable soup.

Sopa de ajo — $3.25
Chicken broth with garlic, bread and a poached egg.

CARNES Y AVES

Pechugas de pollo al whiskey — $13.95
Chicken breasts sauteed then flambeed in whiskey served with
a mixture of sauteed eggplant, green peppers and tomato.

Conejo al ama de casa — $15.95
Fresh rabbit sauteed in olive oil, white wine, garlic, fresh
tomato and artichoke hearts.

Pato asado a la Tinesfera — $14.95
Roast duck and mangoes in a brandy sauce.

Entrecote a la Madrilena — $14.95
Broiled sirloin with an herb butter.

POSTRES

Naranjas Alburferas — $3.25
Fresh oranges in a syrup made with oranges and Cointreau.

Flan — $3.25
Egg custard with caramel

Dinner: Tues - Sat 5:30 - 10:30, Sun 5 - 9

Billy Siegel's That Steak Joynt

Opened in 1964 and currently owned by Billy Siegel, this one time bakery was rebuilt after the great Chicago Fire, so the building is laden with history. The decor smacks of the Gay '90s, and customers smack their lips over the handsome steaks, ribs and awesome desserts.

Menu Changes Seasonally

APPETIZERS

BBQ Ribs	5.25	Shrimp Cocktail	8.50
Fried Mozzarella	4.75	Blue Point Oysters	5.75
Fried Calamari	6.95	Oysters Rockefeller	7.25
Onion Rings	3.25	Garlic Bread	3.75
Stuffed Mushrooms	6.25	Pizza Bread	3.75

Ask About Our Appetizer Platter

SOUPS

Soup del Giorno	2.75	Onion Soup	2.75

SALADS

HOUSE SALAD — with choice of: French, 1000, Garlic, Italian, Green Goddess	2.50
Roquefort Cheese Add	1.95
TOMATO MOZZARELLA SALAD — ripe tomato, fresh mozzarella, balsamic dressing	4.75
TOMATO AND ONION SALAD — ripe tomato, red onion, Italian vinaigrette	4.25
CAESAR FOR TWO	7.50
SPINACH SALAD	3.25
COLE SLAW	3.00

PASTA

LINGUINI, WHITE CLAM SAUCE	9.95
LINGUINI, RED CLAM SAUCE	9.95
CAPPELLINI MARINARA WITH SHRIMP	15.95
MOSTACCOLI MARINARA	8.95
LINGUINI OR MOSTACCOLI AGLIO A OLIO — garlic and oil	9.95
FETTUCINI ALFREDO	9.95
SPINACH ALFREDO	9.95

1610 North Wells St • Gold Coast • (312) 943-5091

FISH and SEAFOOD

LOBSTER TAILS — *broiled, served with drawn butter* 29.95
FRENCH FRIED SHRIMP 19.95
FRESH FISH OF THE DAY ....
VEGETABLE PLATE — *all cooked fresh vegetables* 12.95

STEAKS and CHOPS

Enjoy it your way: **Char-Broiled** *over the open flame, until rich natural juices start to burst*
Victorian Style *smothered sauteed onions in butter sauce*
Broiled with Garlic *studded with garlic, rich and robust*
Broiled with Pepper *peppercorns for those who prefer it spicy*

FILET MIGNON — *the center cut* 20.75
PETITE FILET MIGNON — *a smaller cut* 17.75
CHATEAUBRIAND — *the classic presentation...a large center cut for two*
with a fresh vegetable platter and duchess potatoes 42.95

TENDERLOIN TIPS — *mushroom sauce* 16.95
NEW YORK CUT SIRLOIN — *a hearty flavorful steak* 22.95
BILLY'S STEAK — *extra large New York cut* 27.95
PEPPER STEAK — *sauteed peppers, mushroom sauce* 18.95
THE T-BONE — *The Joynt's "King of Steaks"* 27.50

RIBEYE STEAK — *a long time Joynt favorite* 19.95
FILET & LOBSTER 27.95
PRIME RIB 19.95
TRENCHMAN'S CUT — *heavy cut prime rib* 23.95

All entrees are served with giardinera, bread and butter;
Choice of soup, salad, spinach salad, creamed spinach, cole slaw, baked potato or French fries.

RIBS and CHICKEN
Voted Chicago's #1 BBQ Ribs

RIBS — *full slab* .... 14.95   1/2 slab 11.95
BBQ RIBS &CHICKEN 15.95

BBQ RIBS & SHRIMP 18.95
BBQ RIBS & FILET 18.95
BBQ RIBS & FISH 20.95
BROILED OR BBQ CHICKEN 11.95
CHICKEN VESUVIO — *with peas and vesuvio potatoes (all white meat add 2.00)* 14.95

BONELESS CHICKEN BREAST 14.95
CHICKEN MARSALA 14.95
GRECIAN STYLE CHICKEN 14.95

Dinner: Mon - Sat 5 - 1, Sun 4 - 12

It may be called a chop house, but Henry Norton's two-floor establishment, located in a renovated brownstone, has a great array of prime, dry-aged steaks (and chops too). And don't miss the American fries or potato pancakes.

APPETIZERS

Freshly Shucked Blue Point Oysters—1/2 dozen
  Cocktail Sauce $5.95
Fresh Cherrystone Clams — 1/2 dozen ... $5.95
Smoked Irish Salmon —
  Traditionally garnished $7.95
Jumbo Louisiana Gulf Shrimp $7.95
Filet of Wine Herring $4.75
  Sour Cream on request
Baked Cherrystone Clams Casino $6.95
Baked Oysters Rockefeller $7.95

Russ's American Fries
$2.95
Baked Potato — Sliced, then Sauteed with
Garlic, Onion, White Pepper, Black Pepper,
Oregano and Parsley

Chicago Chop House Potato Pancake
$2.95
Shredded Potato Blended with Eggs, Onions,
Rysers Bros. Bread Crumbs, Salt, Black Pepper,
Served with Sour Cream & Apple Sauce.

---

60 West Ontario St • River North • (800) 229-2356

STEAKS AND CHOPS

Only U.S. Prime, Dry-Aged Minimum 3 Weeks

Chop House New York Strip (16 oz.)	$21.95
(24 oz.)	$27.95
T-Bone Steak (24 oz.)	$26.95
Porterhouse Steak (48 oz.)	**$48.00**
(64 oz.)	**$64.00**
Broiled New York Veal Porterhouse (16 oz.)	$22.95
Filet Mignon (10 oz.)	$17.95
(16 oz.)	$22.95
Butt Steak (16 oz.)	$17.95
Roast Prime Rib of Beef (14 oz.)	$17.95
Bone-In (20 oz.)	$22.95
Spring Lamb Chops (16 oz.)	$24.95
Roast Rack of Lamb (5 Chops)	$24.95
Roast Loin of Pork Chops (3 Chops)	$16.95
Applesauce	

POULTRY

Broiled Half of Spring Chicken — *Hot Sauce on Side*	$13.95
Chicken Vesuvio	$15.95
(All White Meat — $3.00 extra)	

FROM THE SEA

Broiled Lake Superior Whitefish *Lemon Butter*	$14.95
Sauteed Catfish Almondine	$16.95
Broiled Orange Roughy	$15.95
Broiled King Salmon	$18.95
Broiled New England Swordfish Steak *Sherry Butter*	$19.95
Sauteed Jumbo Gulf Shrimp De Jonghe	$17.95
French Fried Jumbo Shrimp *in extra light beer batter*	$17.95
Broiled Lobster Tail *Drawn Butter* 14 oz. or 32 oz.	Market Price

Entrees Include:
House Salad, Mashed or Baked Potatoes
Vegetable of the Day $2.95
French Fried Onion Rings $2.50
Sauteed Mushrooms $2.95
Creamed Spinach $2.95

Dinner: Sun - Thurs 5 - 11, Fri - Sat 5 - 11:30

The exterior of this old two-flat tucked under Chicago's famous el tracks has been redone, but the inside still harks back to the days of prohibition. Steaks are aged prime and always perfectly cooked. The dilemma is what to order, since the Italian specialties are very good too.

APPETIZERS

Shrimp Cocktail $8.25	Minestrone Soup $3.00
Assorted Italian Antipasto .. 6.50	Stuffed Celery 2.75
Mussels Marinara 8.00	Anchovy Canape 4.00

STEAKS AND CHOPS
We Serve Aged Prime Beef Exclusively

Broiled Filet Mignon	$25.00
Broiled Strip Loin Steak	25.00
Broiled Strip Loin Steak Bone-In	24.50
Broiled T-Bone Steak	30.00
Broiled Small Steak	22.50
Pepper Steak	21.00
Broiled Lamb Chops	31.00
Broiled Pork Chops	16.50
Veal Chops	29.50

ENTREES

Calf's Liver and Bacon	$16.00
Chopped Sirloin Steak	15.00
Half Spring Chicken (Broiled or Fried)	15.00
Beef En Brochette	20.00
Chicken Alla Joe	17.50

---

500 North Franklin St • River North • (312) 527-3718

ITALIAN SPECIALTIES

Chicken Cacciatora $17.50
Chicken Vesuvio 17.50
Veal Scallopine 17.50
Veal Sauted Green Peppers and Mushrooms 17.50
Veal Cutlet Parmigiana 17.50
Breaded Veal Cutlet 17.50

CHICKEN DISHES ORDERED WITH ALL WHITE MEAT $3.00 EXTRA.

SEA FOODS

Lobster Tail $35.00
Lobster Tail De Jonge 35.00
Lobster La Diavolo 36.00
Broiled Salmon 21.50
Whitefish 16.00
Shrimp De Jonge 21.50
French Fried Shrimp 21.50

COTTAGE FRIED POTATOES, HEAD LETTUCE AND TOMATO SALAD WITH OIL
AND VINEGAR OR FRENCH DRESSING INCLUDED WITH ABOVE.

PASTA

Spaghetti With Meat Sauce..................................$10.50
Spaghetti La Marinara 10.50
Spaghetti With Meat Sauce & Mushrooms 12.50
Linguini Mussels Marinara.................................. 15.50
Linguini White Clam Sauce 12.50
Canelloni with Meat Sauce.................................. 12.50
Tortellini Alla Panna 10.50
Ravioli With Meat Sauce 12.50

VEGETABLES

French Fried Onion Rings $5.00
Spinach or Broccoli 5.00
Sauted Spinach or Broccoli 6.00
Fresh Broiled Mushrooms 6.00
Mushrooms and Green Peppers Sauted 6.00

SALADS

Limestone Lettuce Salad .... $ 3.75
Cole Slaw 3.75
Sliced Tomatoes, Onions, Anchovies 7.25
Garbage Salad 10.00

Dinner: 7 Days a Week until 12

Eli's the Place for Steak

A local institution that attracts not just local celebrities but stars of stage and screen as well. Comfortable, subdued and convenient to Michigan Avenue shopping, Eli's steaks are excellent and so are Chicago's classic dishes such as shrimp de Jonghe and calves liver. Eli's famous cheesecake is a must for dessert, of course.

Menu Changes Annually

Appetizers

Baked Three Onion Soup	4.50
Homemade Soup of the Day	cup 3.50
	bowl 4.50
Baked Shrimp De Jonghe	9.25
Calves Liver Eli	6.50
Baby Back Ribs	7.00

Shrimp Ala Marc 8.50
Marinated with onions, capers and
Marc sauce.

Chilled Tiger Shrimp 8.50
Served with cocktail sauce.

Eli's Potato Pancakes .... half 3.75
Served with apple sauce   full 7.00
and sour cream.

Salads

Sliced Beefsteak Tomatoes & Onions 5.00
With herbed vinaigrette and crumbled nauvoo bleu cheese.

Caesar Salad 5.00
With croutons and fresh grated parmesan cheese.

Eli's Famous Garbage Salad 5.00

Seafood & Fish

Lake Superior Whitefish 19.95
Served with julienne of vegetables and lemon butter.

Salmon Fillet 21.95
Broiled with pesto sauce.

Pacific Swordfish... 23.95
Red bell pepper - tarragon vinaigrette.

Shrimp De Jonghe 22.95
Tiger shrimp baked with garlic and seasoned bread crumbs.
"Chicago's #1 Shrimp De Jonghe" - Chicago Tribune

---

215 East Chicago Ave • Near North/Gold Coast • (312) 642-1393

404

Poultry

Chicken Vesuvio **20.95**
Crisp pieces of chicken and potatoes seasoned with garlic, Italian herbs and lemon.

Grilled Boneless Breast of Chicken **18.95**
With roasted garlic potatoes and green onion - basil dip.

Sauteéd Boneless Breast of Chicken **20.95**
With spinach, mushrooms, shallots and plum tomatoes.

Entrees of Distinction

Eli's Special Sirloin Steak **26.95**
Broiled and seasoned with crushed black peppercorns.

Calves Liver Eli **19.95**
Sauteéd with onions, green peppers and mushrooms.

Old Fashioned Chicken in the Pot **18.95**
Haley's favorite! Home style serving of tender chicken simmered with garden vegetables
and egg noodles, served in a rich chicken broth.

Barbecue Baby Back Ribs **18.95**

Jr. Filet Mignon and Shrimp De Jonghe **28.95**
A combination of two Chicago classics.

Eli's Dinner Select .... per person **40.00**
A complete menu of the foods made famous at Eli's. Sauteéd Calves Liver Eli; Chicago's Famous
Garbage Salad; Eli's Special Sirloin Steak (seasoned with crushed black peppercorns); Cottage
Fries or Potato Pancakes; and Eli's Chicago's Finest Cheesecake ... of course.

Steaks & Chops

Broiled New York Cut Sirloin Strip Steak **25.95**

Broiled Jr. New York Cut Sirloin Strip Steak **22.95**

T-Bone Steak (20 oz.) **29.95**

Filet Mignon of Beef Tenderloin **24.95**

Jr. Filet Mignon of Beef Tenderloin **21.95**

Chateaubriand of Beef Tenderloin ....(serves two) **48.00**
Served with bouquetiere of vegetables.

Broiled Duet of Prime Lamb Chops **26.95**
With minted stone ground mustard.

Broiled Chopped Steak Esther **17.95**

Roast Prime Rib-Eye of Beef **22.95**

Pepper Steak **20.95**
Sirloin medallions, onions, tomato, peppers and mushrooms sauteéd with Eli's pepper steak sauce.

Gibsons Steakhouse

A top-notch steakhouse that believes in BIG. The booths are big, the drinks are big, the steaks and lobster are big—even some of the waiters are big. This equals great dining in a real steakhouse atmosphere. And if you can tear your eyes away from the food, look around; you're sure to spot a celebrity.

Menu Changes Seasonally

SIDE DISHES

French Fries 3.00
Baked Potato 3.00
Onion Rings 3.00
Sauteed Spinach with Garlic 4.25
Broccoli...........................3.50

APPETIZERS

Shrimp Cocktail.....................8.75
Snow Crab Claws 12.50
Chopped Chicken Livers...............3.75
Soup...............................3.50
Crabmeat Avocado 8.00

SALADS

Spinach, Hot Bacon Dressing 6.25
Tomato & Scallion 3.75
Caesar 4.25
Garbage...........................8.75

1028 North Rush St • Near North/Gold Coast • (312) 266-8999

STEAKS AND CHOPS

Filet Mignon 22.00
Small Filet 16.25
New York Sirloin .26.50
Small New York Sirloin 21.50
Sliced Sirloin, Red Wine Sauce 27.00
Porterhouse Steak 27.50
Bone In Sirloin 31.00
Veal Chop 20.25
Double Lamb Chops 22.50
Chopped Steak 11.00

RIBS AND CHICKEN

Gibsons Baby Back Ribs 14.50
Whole Spit-Roasted Chicken 14.75

FISH AND SEAFOOD

Planked Whitefish 15.25
Broiled Salmon 19.50
Chargrilled Swordfish 22.00
Giant Lobster Tail 60.00
Lobster Tail 30.00
Surf & Turf 42.00
Colossal Surf & Turf 75.00

DESSERTS

Carrot Cake 3.75
Ice Cream 3.50
Sherbet 3.50
Chocolate Hazelnut Tart 3.75

Dinner: 7 Days a Week 5:15 - 12

Palm, The

Sawdust on the floor, walls alive with colorful caricatures of Chicago celebrities, deep and comfortable wood booths, waiters who steer you with a smile...this is the Palm, and it serves up its own brand of delicious steaks, lobsters and humongous side dishes that take more than two to tangle with.

APPETIZERS

Clams Oreganato 7.50
Melon & Prosciutto 7.50
Shrimp Bruno 7.50
Calamari 7.00
Soup of the Day 3.50

PASTA

Linguine with White Clam Sauce . . . 12.50
Linguine with Red Clam Sauce 12.50
Linguine Marinara 12.50
Linguine Aglio E Olio 12.50
Pasta of the Day 12.50

VEAL

Veal Milanese 18.00
Veal Piccata 18.00
Veal Marsala 18.00
Veal Franchese 18.00
Veal Parmigiana 18.00
Veal Porterhouse (20 oz.) 24.50

181 East Lake Shore Dr • Near North/Gold Coast • (312) 944-0135

SEAFOOD

> **HOUSE SPECIALTY**
> Jumbo Lobsters . . . . Market
> Sizes (3 lbs) and Higher

Swordfish Steak 19.50
Salmon 19.50
Fish of the Day . . . . market
Jumbo Shrimp Saute 18.00
Clam & Shrimp Posillipo 20.00
Scallops 18.00

POULTRY

Broiled Chicken 14.00
Chicken Saute 16.50
Blackened Chicken 16.00
Chicken Vesuvio 16.50

STEAKS and CHOPS
(U.S. Prime Aged)

Prime Aged New York Sirloin (19 oz.) 25.00
Steak A La Stone (19 oz.) 25.00
Filet Mignon (16 oz.) 23.00
Lamb Chops (three double cut) (25 oz.) 24.00
Pork Chops (three) (18 oz.) 16.00
Prime Rib of Beef (25 oz.) 23.00
Porterhouse Steak (24 oz.) . . . . · 29.00
Rib Eye Steak (16 oz.) . . . . · · · · 21.00

Bearnaise Sauce 1.50

> **HOUSE SPECIALTY**
> Double Steak 44.00
> 32 ounce New York Sirloin served for two

Dinner: Mon - Fri until 10:30, Sat 5 - 10:30, Sun 5 - 10

Ruth's Chris Steakhouse

Part of a nationwide chain, this is the steakhouse for the traveling man who doesn't like surprises. Aged steaks of high quality are quite good, but the great choice of potatoes is not to be missed.

Home of _Serious_ Steaks

APPETIZERS

Smoked Salmon	7.95	Escargot Borré	6.95
Barbecued Shrimp Orleans	6.95	Mushrooms Stuffed with Crabmeat	6.95
Shrimp Remoulade	6.95	French Fried Onion Rings	2.95
Shrimp Cocktail	6.95	Toasted Garlic Bread	1.95
APPETIZER OF THE DAY			

SALADS

Italian	3.95	Caesar	3.95
Combination	3.50	Artichoke Hearts and Hearts of Palm	5.50
Sliced Tomato	3.50	Fresh Asparagus (in season)	4.75
Sliced Tomato and Onion	3.50	Head Lettuce	3.00

Bleu Cheese, Remoulade, Thousand Island, French, Italian, Ranch, Honey Mustard and Olive Oil and Vinegar Dressing (all made fresh daily from our exclusive recipes)

SOUP

Gumbo Louisiane	4.95	Turtle Soup Lafitte	4.95	Du Jour	

POTATOES

Au Gratin, (in cream sauce, topped with thick sharp melted cheddar)	3.50	Loaded Baked Potato (loaded with your choice of butter, sour cream,	
Lyonnaise (sauteed with onions)	2.75	chives and bacon)	3.00

VEGETABLES

Broccoli or Cauliflower	2.75	Sauteed Mushrooms	3.50
Au Gratin	3.50	Petite Peas	2.25
Broiled Tomatoes	3.50	French Fried Onion Rings	2.95

DESSERTS

Blueberry Cheesecake	3.50	Ice Cream Freezes - Amaretto,	
Chocolate Mousse Cheesecake	3.50	Praline, Raspberry Ruth	5.00
Bread Pudding with Jack Daniel's Whiskey Sauce	2.95	Pecan Pie	3.25
		Apple Pie	3.00
Hot Fudge Sundae with Pecans	2.95	A la mode	3.75
Ice Cream Pie	3.50	Ice Cream -	
		Vanilla, Chocolate & Sherbet	2.50

431 North Dearborn St • River North • (312) 321-2725

PETITE FILET OF BEEF TENDERLOIN 8 oz.   15.95
With Sauteed Jumbo Gulf Shrimp   21.95

LARGE FILET OF BEEF TENDERLOIN 14 oz.   19.95

RIBEYE OF BEEF 16 oz.   19.95
An outstanding example of U.S. Prime at its best.
This steak has the most marbling of all prime cuts,
which makes the ribeye flavorful and tender.

NEW YORK STRIP 16 oz.   22.95
This specially aged U.S. Prime sirloin strip if the favorite
of many steak connoisseurs. It is a little firmer than a ribeye,
and has a full-bodied flavor.

TOP SIRLOIN 14 oz.   15.95
Old Chicago stockyard's cut, outstanding flavor.

T-BONE 20 oz.   23.95
The favorite of steak lovers!

PORTERHOUSE   For Two **44.00**
A massive cut of finest quality beef, suitable for sharing, combining   For Three **56.00**
the rich flavor of the strip steak with the tenderness of the filet.

CENTER CUT PORK CHOP 12 oz.   8.95
The meatiest prime cut of pork chops. Extra-fine grained   Two Chops **17.95**
and flavorful. Served with sweet and spicy apple slices.

PRIME LAMB CHOPS   21.95
Two double cut U.S. Prime rib chops, hand cut extra thick. Extremely
tender, thanks to the natural marbling. Served with mint jelly.

PROVIMI VEAL CHOP 12 oz.   18.95
A succulent veal rib chop. Served sizzling!

SWEETBREADS JOSEF   15.95
Lightly dusted and sauteed -- unique!

OUR MEAT IS THE FINEST SELECTED CORN-FED AGED U.S. PRIME AVAILABLE.

CLASSIC SAUCES
To complement your entree or side item.

Hollandaise, Bearnaise, and Spicy Garlic   1.95

Dinner: Mon - Fri until 11, Sat 5 - 12

411

One of the newer entries in this great steak town, The Saloon has already built up a loyal and steady clientele. They come back time and again for great steaks, chops and saloon specialties such as baby back ribs, Caesar salad, and a scintillating selection of spuds. The atmosphere is comfortable and cozy, and the service is excellent.

The SALOON

Beverages

Soda/Coffee/Tea	1.25
Cappuccino	2.50
Espresso	2.00
Mineral Water	2.25

Appetizers

Crispy Calamari	4.95
House Smoked BBQ Chicken Skewers	4.95
Oysters on the Half Shell	5.95
Artichoke Vinaigrette	5.95
Blackened Scallops	5.95
Tuna Tartare	5.95
Jumbo Asparagus with Vinaigrette	5.95
Pan Fried Maryland Lump Crab Cake	6.95
Carpaccio	6.95
Appetizer Sampler	7.95
Smoked Scottish Salmon with Garnish	7.95
Shrimp Cocktail	7.95
Lobster Cocktail	7.95
Saloon T-shirt	13.95

Soup

Spicy Gumbo	1.95/3.95
The Other Soup	1.95/3.95

Chili

Black Angus Chili	3.95/7.95
White Chicken Chili	3.95/7.95

Salads

Beefsteak Tomato & Onion	3.50
Caesar Salad	3.50
Wedge of Iceberg	1.95
Confetti Slaw	1.95
Cobb Salad	9.95
Garbage Salad Small	4.95/9.95

Steaks and Chops

Porterhouse Steak for 2, 3, or 4	24.50 per person
Filet Mignon 14 oz.	19.95
Small Filet Mignon 8 oz.	13.95
New York Sirloin Steak 20 oz.	26.95
Small New York Strip 10 oz.	14.95

200 East Chestnut St • Near North/Gold Coast • (312) 280-5454

Kansas City Bone-in Strip,
Chili Corn Relish 18.95
Lamb Chops 19.95
Slow Smoked One Pound
Pork Chop 14.95
Wood Grilled Spice Rubbed
Veal Chop 19.95

Saloon Specialties

Surf & Turf Market
BBQ Meatloaf with
Mashed Potatoes 8.95
Whole Roasted
Lemon Pepper Chicken 12.95
Blackened Prime Rib
Queen 14.95
Reg. 22.95
Stuffed Chopped Sirloin/Mashed
Potatoes 9.95
101 Spice Fried Chicken 12.95
Smoked Chicken Hash 9.95

Mixed Grill Seafood

Tuna, Salsa Cruda 14.95
Swordfish, Avocado Relish 14.95
Blackened Salmon 14.95
Lobster Market
Wood Grilled Lobster Tail Market
Seafood Hash 10.95

Slow Smoked Barbeque

BBQ Baby Back Ribs 1/2 9.95
Whole 13.95
BBQ Chicken 1/2 9.95
Whole 13.95
Ribs and Chicken Combo 13.95
Daily Barbeque Platter 9.95

Sides

Cayenne Spiced Onion
Rings 2.95
Sauteed Spinach and
Mushrooms 2.95
Sauteed Mushrooms and
Onions 2.95
Broccoli 2.95
Jumbo Asparagus or
Artichoke 5.95
Cold with Vinaigrette
Hot with Jalapeno Hollandaise

Potatoes

Crispy Potato Cake 1.95
Hash Browns with Onion 1.95
Giant Baked 1.95
Skins 1.95
Bacon Scallion Mashed
Potatoes 1.95

Dinner: 7 Days a Week until 12

Arun's

Elegant and beautiful are the right words to use for the atmosphere, classy appointments, and the food and service as well. This is one classy Thai restaurant.

Menu Changes Seasonally

APPETIZERS:

A2.   KHAO KRIAB   (Steamed Rice Dumplings)
Steamed rice dumplings filled with dungeness crabmeat, shrimp, chicken and peanuts, dusted with fragrant fried garlic and served with a tangy sweet & sour chili vinaigrette. $7.95

A3.   KHANOM BUANG   (Thai-Style Crepe)
An authentic Thai crepe, flavored with kaffir lime leaf and turmeric, filled with shrimp, sweet daikon turnips and peanuts. Served with julienned cucumber and a chili-shallot vinaigrette. $7.95

A18.   POR-PIA POO   (Crab Spring Rolls)
Spring rolls with dungeness crabmeat, tofu, jicama, cilantro, scallion and beansprouts, drizzled with a caramelized tamarind sauce and hot mustard. $7.95

A5.   KRATONG THONG   (Golden Baskets)
Flower-shaped, bite-sized pastry baskets filled with a delicate mixture of shrimp, chicken, sweet corn and shiitake mushrooms. Garnished with an exquisitely carved basket. $7.95

A6.   KAI (MOO) SATAY   (Chicken or Pork Satay)
Spiced chicken (or pork) strips grilled on bamboo skewers, served with Thai cucumber salad and curried peanut sauce. $7.95

A7.   LARB MOO YANG   (Spicy Grilled Pork Salad)
Grilled pork cubes spiced with lemon grass, hot chili peppers, shallot, mint, cilantro and lime. Accompanied by garden fresh vegetables. $8.95

A8.   HO MOK TALAY   (Curried Seafood Casserole)
Red snapper, shrimp and rock crabmeat in a spicy red curry sauce, steamed on a bed of napa cabbage and sweet basil leaves, securely wrapped in a banana leaf. $ 8.95

4156 North Kedzie Ave • Uptown/Lincolnwood • (312) 539-1909

PORK

P1. MOO PA   (Spiced Pork Curry)
Pork medallions sauteed with baby eggplants and string beans, in an aromatic yellow curry sauce, flavors ranging from peppercorns and Krachai (aromatic Thai ginger) to sweet basil leaves. $17.95

P2. CHIANGMAI LARB   (Minced Pork Salad Chiangmai-Style)
Minced pork salad with special spices from Chiangmai, accentuated with roasted dried chili peppers, chopped scallion and aromatic saw leaves. $17.95

CHICKEN

C1. KAI PHAD KHING   (Ginger Chicken)
Sauteed slices of chicken breast dressed with shredded ginger, cloud ears, golden needles (lily blossoms) and scallion. $15.95

C2. KAI HIMAPARN   (Cashew Chicken)
Sauteed chicken breast with Indian cashew nuts, crushed garlic, diced onion and sweet peppers. $15.95

BEEF/VEAL

B6. NUA BUA BARN   (Gingery Veal)
Exquisite veal medallions fanned on a subtle gingery sauce of lemon grass and miso. Accompanied by fried vegetable rolls and lightly glazed with a sweet & sour tamarind sauce. $19.95

B7. NUA ORN PHAD PHASOM   (Veal with Mixed Vegetables)
Thin-sliced veal in a savory sauce with crushed garlic and chili peppers. Accompanied by fresh shiitake mushrooms and assorted vegetables in season. $19.95

SEAFOOD

SE7. PLA SARM ROSE   (Three-Flavored Red Snapper)
Crispily fried whole red snapper with traditional Bangkok three-flavored tamarind sauce: spicy, sweet and sour. $23.95

SE8. MAKHUA SONG KRUANG   (Spicy Roasted Eggplant)
Fragrantly roasted Thai eggplant, tender and succulent, topped with a flavorful sauce of chopped shallot, cilantro, chili pepper, sweet basil leaves and shrimp. A House specialty. $18.95

SE9. KANG SARM SAHAI   (Three Combination Curry)
Authentic country-style yellow curry with shrimp quenelle, chicken, kabocha squash and fuzzy melon in a curry sauce, hot, spicy and peppery, featuring kaffir lime and sweet basil leaves. $18.95

Dinner: Tues - Sat 5 - 10, Sun 5 - 9

Small and intimate, this suburban Thai is wildly popular with the locals, as it is one of the few fine Thai restaurants in the burbs.

Menu Changes Seasonally

◊Appetizers◊

Egg Roll 4.95

Baby Egg Roll 4.95
Tiny Egg Rolls filled with minced shrimps and pork.

Stuffed Chicken Wing 4.95
Marinated chicken wings stuffed with a blend of selected spices, ground pork and cabbages, dipped in batter, then deep fried.

Satay
•Pork, chicken, beef or combination 5.95
•Shrimps 6.95
Marinated in a light curry sauce, served with creamy peanut sauce and cucumber salad.

Thai Escargot 5.95
Baked snails in spicy Thai sauce.

Tod Mun PLA: Fish Cakes 5.95
Ground fillet of fish beat with chili paste, deep fried to a golden brown, served with ground peanuts in a sweet & sour cucumber salad.

Tod Mun Goong: Shrimp Cakes 5.95

Pour Pear 5.95
•Topped with crabmeat 6.95
Avocado, cucumber, bean sprouts, fried eggs and cream cheese wrapped in spring roll skin and basted with: house special, sweet tart tamarind or peanut sauce.

Pot Sticker 4.95
Grilled to perfection.thin pastry filled with shrimp accompanied with vegetables.

Mee Krob 5.95
Crispy vermicelli noodles tossed in sweet tart tomato sauce and topped with crispy fried eggs and shrimps, served in a crispy noodle basket.

Crab Rangoon 5.95
Crispy pastry shell stuffed with crabmeat, celery and cream cheese

◊Thai Salads◊

Cucumber Salad 5.95
Fresh cucumber, onions on a bed of lettuce and tomatoes with sweet & sour dressing.

Som Tum 5.95
Choice of carrot or cabbage, tomatoes and string beans with spicy hot & sour dressing, topped with shrimps.

Nam Sod 5.95
Cooked ground chicken tossed with onions, fresh ginger, roasted peanuts, chili and lime juice.

Egg Roll or Baby Egg Roll Salad 6.95
Deep fried Egg Rolls or Baby Egg Rolls placed on a bed of lettuce and tomatoes, with creamy peanut dressing.

House Salad 6.95
Fresh mixed vegetables topped with your choice of creamy peanut or house special dressing.

Bangkok Tofu 6.95
Fried tofu with creamy peanut sauce, on a bed of spinach.

Yam Neau 7.95
Broiled Beef, onions, roasted rice and spices blended to perfection, served on a bed of lettuce and tomatoes.

Yam Goong 8.95
Shrimps, quickly broiled with tangy lime juice dressing, served on a bed of lettuce and tomatoes.

◊Soups◊

Tom Yam
• Vegetables or chicken 5.95
• Shrimps or seafood 6.95
Famous Thai Hot and Sour Soup with tomatoes and straw mushrooms in a tart lime broth, seasoned with lemon grass citrus leaves and hot peppers .

Tom Kar
• Vegetables or chicken 5.95
• Shrimps or seafood 6.95
Spicy coconut soup simmered in a coconut milk, spiced with Thai ginger,hot peppers and lime juice.

3542 North Halsted St • Lincoln Park/DePaul • (312) 327-2870

◊Classic Curries◊

Green Curry
A typical Bangkok green curry fresh hot pepper curry paste, bamboo shoots, string beans, green peas and straw mushrooms simmered in coconut milk with distinctive flavors of lemon grass and sweet basil leaves.

Red Curry
Roasted hot pepper curry paste...prepared in a similar manner as above.
Choice of : Tofu, vegetables, beef, chicken or pork . **7.95**
Shrimps, squids, scallops, seafood or fish balls **8.95**

◊Beef ◊

Beef Broccoli **7.95**
Beef stir-fried with a broccoli in delicate oyster sauce.

Rama Beef **8.95**
Stir-fried beef and broccoli topped with curry peanut sauce.

Beef Basil Leaves **8.95**

Beef Pad Ped **7.95**
Beef pan fried with hot peppers, onions, and mushrooms in oriental sauce.

Beef Snow Pea **7.95**

Ginger Beef **8.95**
Sliced tender beef sauteed with fresh ginger root, hot peppers, onions, and oriental dried mushrooms.

Pepper Beef **7.95**

Beef Cashew **8.95**

◊Chicken ◊

Char Broiled Chicken **7.95**

Sesame Chicken **8.95**
Chicken breast stuffed with sesame seeds, fried eggs, spinach and crab meat dipped in batter and deep-fried, then topped with creamy coconut sauce or peanut sauce.

Sweet & Sour Chicken **7.95**

Chicken Broccoli **7.95**

Garlic Chicken **7.95**

Oriental Vegetable Chicken **7.95**
Sliced chicken stir-fried with fresh ginger root, onions, hot peppers, and Oriental dried mushrooms.

Spicy Oriental Chicken - Hot! **7.95**
Sliced chicken stir-fried with Oriental vegetables and hot peppers in oyster flavored sauce.

Ginger Chicken **8.95**

Cashew Chicken **8.95**

Chicken Pad Ped **7.95**
Sliced chicken stir-fried with hot peppers, onions and mushrooms in an Oriental sauce.

Chicken Basil Leaves **8.95**

◊Noodles◊

Pad Thai **6.95**
The most famous Thai Noodle Dish. Your choice of : Thin rice noodles, egg noodles, wide rice noodles, spinach noodles or glass noodles, stir-fried with eggs, chilli, ground peanut, vegetables and a sweet tart tamarind sauce. *With choice of :*
Tofu, oriental vegetables, beef, chicken or shrimp. **7.95**

Spicy Crazy Noodles **6.95**
Noodles stir- fried with ground chicken, onions, Thai egg plants, sweet basil leaves and hot peppers...Hot!

Pad Woon Sen **7.95**
Delicately seasoned glass noodles stir-fried with chicken, shrimps, eggs and vegetables.

Pad See-ewe
•Beef or chicken **6.95**
•Shrimps or seafood **7.95**
Your choice of crispy of soft wide rice noodles pan fried with broccoli, eggs and oriental sauce.

◊Frog Legs ◊

Dipped in batter and deep fried, with

Garlic Sauce **8.95**
Stir-fried with minced garlic, black peppers and our own special sauce, served with sauteed vegetables.

Pad Ped Sauce **8.95**
Stir-fried with hot peppers, onions and mushrooms.

◊Seafood ◊

Three Delights **8.95**
Shrimps stir-fried with baby corn, snow peas and Oriental mushroom in a flavorful oyster sauce.

Oriental Vegetables Shrimp **8.95**
A mixture of oriental vegetables and stir-fried with shrimps in a oyster flavored sauce.

Spicy Vegetable Shrimp **8.95**
A mixture of oriental vegetables and hot peppers stir-fried with shrimps in a oyster flavored sauce.

Seafood in Hot Sauce **9.95**
Seafood Combination sauteed with snow peas, onions, baby corn and hot peppers in a hot chili sauce.

◊ Specialties ◊

Spicy Pad Ped **9.95**
Shrimps, beef and chicken stir-fried with a mixture of Oriental vegetables in a tangy sauce of sweet basil leaves and hot peppers.

Panang Combination **9.95**
Beef, chicken and shrimp sauteed with panang curry paste and coconut milk.

Dinner: 7 Days a Week until 10:30

Pattaya Thai Restuarant

This pleasant and carefully-appointed restaurant doesn't get the recognition it rightly deserves. The kitchen has a deft touch when it comes to blending the complex flavors of Thai cooking. Service is friendly and attentive.

Appetizers

Satay .... (lnch) 5.00 (dn) 5.50
Char-Broiled chicken on skewers with peanut sauce

Spring Rolls (fresh) .... (s) 2.25
Fried wonton stuffed with crab meat, cheese, spinach   (l) 3.95

Pot Stickers (8) 3.95
Thin patty with ground shrimp chicken spinach

Shu Mai 2.95
Crab dumpling

Salad

	Lunch	Dinner
*Yum Nua	5.75	5.95
Grilled tenderloin beef, cucumber, lime juice		
*Nam Sod	5.50	5.95
Ground chicken, fresh ginger roasted peanuts, lime juice		
*Larb Gai	5.50	5.95
Ground chicken, roasted rice, lime juice		
Pad Thai Gai	5.25	5.50
Thin rice noodle, egg, peanut, bean sprout		
Lad Na Gai	5.50	5.95
Chicken, wide rice noodle, broccoli, gravy, garlic		
*Pad Kee Mau Gai (drunken noodle)	5.75	6.25
Chicken, wide rice noodle, egg, hot pepper, bean sprouts, tomato, garlic, basil		
Pai See-ew gai	5.75	6.25
Chicken, wide rice noodles, egg, broccoli, bean sprout, garlic		

114 West Chicago Ave • River North • (312) 944-3753

Entree
Your choice of Pork or Beef

	Lunch	Dinner

*Bangkok Chicken 6.75
Battered chicken, cashew nut, mixed vegetable, chili paste, garlic

*Chicken Cashew Nut 6.75
Chicken, cashew nut, mixed vegetable, chili sauce, garlic

Garlic Chicken 6.50
Chicken, fresh garlic, black pepper, peapod

*Rama Pattaya Chicken 6.50
Chicken, fresh ginger, garlic, broccoli, topped with
creamy peanut sauce

*Mongolian Beef 6.50
Beef with mushroom, chili sauce, mixed vegetable

Pad Voon Sen Gai .... 5.75...6.50
Bean thread, egg, mushroom, garlic, mixed vegetable

*Chicken Basil .... 5.75...6.50
Ground chicken, bell pepper, mushrooms, garlic, onion, basil

*Chicken Eggplant Basil .... 5.75...6.50
Chicken, eggplant, bell pepper, basil, garlic
Beef, oyster sauce, broccoli

Sea Food Entree

*Pattaya Sea Food Combination 9.95
Shrimp, squid, mussel, crab meat in red curry sauce
mixed vegetable, wrapped with rich cabbage leaf

*Catfish Tod Grob 6.25
Sliced Catfish in red curry, mixed vegetable

Goong Pad Hed 7.50
Shrimp with chili paste, pea pod, mushroom, garlic

Pad Ped Talay 8.50
Shrimp, mussel, squid, eggplant, bamboo, red curry sauce

*Slightly spicy   **Mildly spicy

Dinner: Mon - Sat until 10

A gem on the second floor, which means peace and tranquility while dining on exellent Thai food served in conventional or Asian mode (no shoes in the raised parlor area).

APPETIZERS

GOONG SABAI
(Fried Shrimp Roll)
Shrimp wrapped in a thin tofu sheet, served with sweet and sour plum sauce.   5.95

KAI SATAY (Chicken Satay)
Spiced chicken strips grilled on bamboo skewers, served with cucumber salad and curried peanut sauce.   5.50

POT STICKER
A Thai Borrahn appetizer favorite. Delicious fried dumplings stuffed with spinach and chicken.   5.95

GOLDEN BASKET
Flower-Shaped, bite sized pastry baskets filled with a delicate mixture of shrimp, chicken and corn. Served around a ound of shredded cabbage leaves.   4.50

SALAD

LARB
(Spicy Chicken Salad, Northeastern Thai-style) Cooked ground chicken freshly seasoned with lemon-grass, mint leaves, chili peppers, cilantro and lime. Accompanied by garden fresh vegetables.   6.95

YUM MOO YANG THAI BORRAHN
(Spicy Grilled Pork Salad) Grilled pork cubes spiced with fresh lemon-grass, hot chili peppers, mint leaves, cilantro, shallot and lime. Served with garden fresh vegetables.   7.95

NOODLES

MEEFUN DELIGHT
(Soft-Fried Noodles)
Fine vermicelli noodles stir-fried in light chicken bouillon with fresh shrimp, chicken and scallion.   6.95

PHAD THAI
(Thai-Style Noodles)
Thin rice noodles with shredded pork, shrimp, sweet turnip and tofu stir-fried in a light sweet & sour tamarind sauce.   6.95

247 East Ontario • Near North/Gold Coast • (312) 642-1385

ENTREES

Chicken

KAI HIMAPARN
(Cashew Chicken)
Sauteed sliced chicken breast with
roasted Indian cashews, sweet
peppers and onion.   7.95

KANG KAI (Chicken Curry)
Chicken curry in coconut milk with
choice of either a delicate red or an
aromatic green curry including Thai
vegetables in season.   7.50

KAI KRAPRAO
(Basil Chicken)
Minced chicken with crushed garlic,
chili peppers and sweet
basil leaves.   6.95

KAI YANG
(Marinated Grilled Chicken)
Chicken breast marinated in garlic
and special spices, grilled and served
with a sweet chili-garlic sauce.   7.95

KAI KRAPRAO
(Basil Chicken)
Minced chicken with crushed garlic,
chili peppers and sweet
basil leaves.   6.95

KAI PHAD KHING
(Ginger Chicken)
Sauteed sliced chicken breast with
shredded ginger, cloud ears,
golden needles and scallions.   6.95

KAI KRATIAM
(Garlic Chicken)
Sauteed sliced chicken breast with
crushed garlic, ground pepper,
shredded chili peppers and
scallions.   7.95

Pork

PANANG MOO
(Pork Panang Curry)
A fragrantly roasted pork curry
flavored with an aromatic mixture of
spices and ground peanuts.   7.95

MOO KRATIAM (Garlic Pork)
Sauteed pork in a peppery garlic sauce,
or in a garlic-lime sauce   7.95

Beef

BEEF BROCCOLI
A sumtuous platter of fresh broccoli
spears topped with beef sauteed
in our special oyster sauce.7.95

THAI BORRAHN JAN RONT
(Sesame Beef In Hot Plate)
Sauteed beef slices in oyster sauce
and wine with green onion
and sesame seed.   8.95

PANANG NUA
(Panang Beef Curry)
Fragrantly roasted beef curry with
pronouning flavors of roasted comino,
coriander and ground peanuts.   7.95

Seafood

PHAD TALAY
(Seafood Combination)
Seafood combination of red snapper,
prawn, sea scallops and squid
sauteed in a sauce, with zucchini,
young corn, mushrooms, basil
leaves, and red and green pepper.   9.95

PHAD KRAPRAO
(Prawn & Chicken Basil)
Prawns and minced chicken sauteed
with crushed garlic, chopped chili
peppers and sweet basil leaves.   8.50

Dinner: Mon - Sat 4-10

421

Konak

Don't let the decor put you off; this is the place in Chicago for Turkish food. The prices are right, the portions are impressive, and it's a nice change if you're bored with the ordinary.

MEZELER (APPETIZERS)

SOGUK MEZELER (COLD APPETIZERS)

ISPANAK	SPINACH, ONIONS AND RICE COOKED IN OLIVE OIL AND TOPPED WITH YOGURT	2.75
PATLICAN SALATASI	BAKED EGGPLANT, TOMATOES, PEPPERS MIXED WITH OIL AND GARLIC	3.50
KISIR	BULGHUR RICE MIXED WITH PARSLEY, TOMATOES, FRESH ONIONS AND OLIVE OIL	2.50
PILAKI	PINTO BEANS COOKED WITH ONIONS AND CARROTS, PARSLEY IN OLIVE OIL WITH TOMATO SAUCE	2.75
PIYAZ	BOILED NAVY BEANS WITH ONIONS, PARSLEY, TOMATOES, EGGS AND BLACK OLIVES	2.75
HUMMUS	BOILED CHICK PEAS GROUNDED AND MIXED WITH TAHINI, CUMIN, LEMON JUICE AND OLIVE OIL	2.75
CACIK	HOMEMADE YOGURT MIXED WITH DICED CUCUMBERS, DILL AND GARLIC TOPPED WITH OIL, PAPRIKA	2.50

SICAK MEZELER (HOT APPETIZERS)

KIYMALI BÖREK	LEAN GROUND BEEF SAUTEED WITH ONIONS AND WRAPPED WITH STRUDEL LEAVES	2.75
ISPANAKLI BÖREK	SPINACH SAUTEED WITH ONIONS AND WRAPPED WITH STRUDEL LEAVES	2.75
PEYNIRLI BÖREK	WHITE TURKISH CHEESE, PARSLEY AND EGGS MIXED TOGETHER AND WRAPPED WITH STRUDEL LEAVES	2.75
CIGER TAVA	LIGHTLY SEASONED LAMB'S LIVER, PAN FRIED AND TOPPED WITH RAW ONIONS AND PARSELY	3.25
BÖBREK TAVA	LIGHTLY SEASONED LAMB'S KIDNEY, PAN FRIED AND TOPPED WITH RAW ONIONS AND PARSLEY	3.25
MÜCVER	FRIED ZUCCINI PANCAKE (ZUCCINI MIXED WITH DILL, EGGS AND FLOUR)	2.75

5150 North Clark St • Uptown/Lincolnwood • (312) 271-6688

SALATALAR (SALADS)

COBAN SALATASI   DICED TOMATOES, CUCUMBERS, ONIONS AND .... PARSLEY MIXED TOGETHER AND TOPPED .... WITH HOUSE DRESSING 2.50

DOMATES SALATASI SLICES OF BEEFSTEAK TOMATOES AND RAW ONIONS .... TOPPED WITH OUR HOUSE DRESSING 2.00

MARUL SALATAS   LETTUCE, TOMATOES AND CUCUMBER, BLACK
(HOUSE SALAD)   OLIVES AND WHITE TURKISH CHEESE TOPPED WITH OUR HOUSE DRESSING 2.50

YEMEKLER (ENTREES)

ALL ENTREES ARE SERVED WITH CHOICE OF SOUP OR HOUSE SALAD

KÖFTE KEBAP   MINI PATTIES OF LEAN GROUND BEEF SPICED MODERATELY, CHAR BROILED AND SERVED ON A BED OF RICE WITH VEGETABLES 7.95

KONAK KEBAP   (YOUR CHOICE OF HOT OR REGULAR) STRIPS OF LEAN GROUND BEEF MODERATELY SPICED, CHAR-BROILED, SERVED ON TOASTED PITA BREAD WITH TOMATO SAUCE, SERVED WITH VEGETABLES AND RICE (HOMEMADE YOGURT SAUCE IS AVAILABLE UPON REQUEST) 8.95

TAVUK SIS   MARINATED CHUNKS OF CHICKEN BREAST CHAR-BROILED, SERVED ON A BED OF RICE WITH VEGETABLES, TOPPED WITH TOMATO SAUCE 8.95

SIS KEBAP   CHOICE CUT CHUNKS OF BEEF, MODERATELY MARINATED, CHAR-BROILED AND SERVED ON A BED OF RICE WITH VEGETABLES 9.95

KARISIK IZGARA   COMBINATION PLATE OF KIFTA, SHISH, CHICKEN SHISH, AND KONAK KEBAP, HOT, ALL CHAR-BROILED AND SERVED ON A BED OF RICE WITH VEGETABLES 9.95

YAPRAK DOLMASI   LEAN GROUND BEEF, MIXED WITH ONIONS AND MODERATELY SPICED, ROLLED IN GRAPE LEAVES, TOPPED WITH TOMATO SAUCE AND YOGURT, SERVED WITH RICE 8.95

TAVUK GÖGSÜ   BONELESS BREAST OF CHICKEN CHAR-BROILED, TOPPED WITH SAUCE ALA KONAK (LEMON, BUTTER, GARLIC) SERVED WITH RICE AND VEGETABLES 9.95

Dinner: Tues - Sun 4 - 10

A cozy oasis in Ukranian Village on Chicago's Near West Side, this is the place for a hearty, inexpensive, robust Ukranian feast. And the music and dancing adds a nice touch of authenticity.

GALAN'S
HOUSE SPECIALTY
THE KOZAK FEAST

BORSCH

GALANS HOUSE SALAD

HOLUBTSI
Cabbage Rolls

VARENYKY
Filled dough dumplings

KOVBASSA AND KAPUSTA
Ukrainian sausage
and mild sauerkraut

KOZAK SPYS
Chunks of beef tenderloin
and pork on a skewer

KARTOPLYANYK
Country-style potato pancake

COFFEE A LA GALANS

DESSERT

$15.95

APPETIZERS

Galan's Herring   Specially marinated by our Chef 3.95

Ikra   Creamy Roe dip served chilled, garnished
with black olives and lemon slices 3.95

Tulka   Lightly sauteed fish fillets abundantly topped with
a savory concoction of peppers, mushrooms,
carrots, celery, tomatoes and onions 5.95

ENTREES

Holubtsi   Cabbage rolls, filled with a meat and rice mixture and baked
with a mild tomato sauce, served with potatoes 6.25

*Bigos   A traditional "Hunter's Meal" of choice meats
and sausages, mixed with a hearty portion of
sauerkraut and potatoes... 5.95

*Kovbassa and Kapusta   Galans' specially blended homemade sausages,
cured in our smokehouse and served with
mild sauerkraut and potatoes 5.95

2210 West Chicago Ave • Lincoln Park/DePaul • (312) 292-1000

All following entrees are served with cup of soup and salad.
Side dishes may be substituted with: dumplings, potatoes, rice.

Chicken Lviv *House Specialty.* 2 Boneless chicken breasts gently sauteed in wine-sauce, served over rice pilaf **8.95**

Chicken Kiev 2 Boneless chicken breasts stuffed with seasoned butter, mushrooms, then deep-fried in a crisp breadcrumb-coating, served over rice pilaf **9.95**

Chicken Marsala Sauteed with shallots, mushrooms and wine sauce **9.95**

Roast Duck 1/2 Roast boneless duckling, served with a baked apple and rice **10.95**

Pork Cutlet *Chef's Favorite.* Simmered pork served with mild sauerkraut and potatoes **8.95**

Barbecued Baby Back Ribs Pre-cooked pork ribs, prepared in our smokehouse and basted with our special piquant sauce
Full slab **11.95**
1/2 slab **6.95**

Bytky A Ukrainian delicacy of braised beef enlivened by a spicy sauce and served with earthy buckwheat-kasha **9.95**

Volovyna a la Kiev Juicy strips of beef tenderloin, sauteed with onions and mushrooms in a Kiev white sauce **10.95**

Beef Stroganoff Strips of beef tenderloin sauteed with mushrooms in a spicy paprika sauce, served with dumplings **10.95**

Stuffed Kartoplyanyk *Our Own Creation.* A large-size potato pancake generously stuffed with a highly seasoned beef mixture, served with a spicy sauce **8.95**

SEA FOODS

Rumyantsi Tender-fried large shrimps, in a garlic-flavored butter sauce served with a creamy, homemade dip **10.95**

Walleye in a Kartoplyanyk Our award winning creation! Sauteed in butter, generously covered with mushroom sauce and wrapped in a potato pancake **13.95**

Walleye a la Galans Broiled, covered with spicy cabbage, served on a bed of rice **12.95**

Dinner: Tues - Thurs 4 - 10, Fri - Sat 4 - 11

Heartland Cafe

It's got the right atmosphere, the right food, and the right attitude. Every time I eat here (the breakfast grains are great) I feel like I've done my body a much-needed favor.

Menu Changes Seasonally

STARTERS

Nachos Grandes. A large platter of corn chips covered with beans and melted cheese and topped with lettuce, tomatoes, and sour cream. Served with salsa 5.25

Baked Avocado con Salsa y Queso. Slices of avocado baked in a casserole with salsa and cheese and served with corn chips 4.50

Stuffed Quesadilla. A flour tortilla filled with refried beans, cheese, avocado and onions, topped with sour cream and served with lettuce, tomato and salsa 4.95

SANDWICHES

Big Heart Lentil Burger. A lentil patty, seasoned and grilled and
served in pita bread with lettuce, tomato and yogurt dressing 4.50
    with cheese 5.50
    with soy cheese 5.75

Grilled Cheese-Avocado & Tomato Sandwich. Your choice of
Colby or Cheddar grilled on whole grain bread 4.75
    with avocado and tomato 4.75
    with soy cheese 3.25

Grilled Turkey Burger. Pure, ground turkey seasoned with sage,
pepper and onion and served on a wheat bun with lettuce,
tomato and red onion 4.75
    with cheese 5.75
    with soy cheese 6.00

Grilled Chicken Sandwich. A boneless breast of chicken seasoned and
grilled and served on a wheat bun with lettuce, tomato, red onion,
and mayonnaise 6.25

Tuna or Turkey Club Sandwich. Your choice of sliced turkey or tuna salad
with avocado, cheese, tomato, lettuce and sprouts with herbal
mayonnaise on wheat bread 6.50

Tania's Grilled Turkey Special. Sliced turkey, sauteed spinach and
onions, mayonnaise, grilled with cheese on wheat bread 5.95

ENTREES

Chicken Quesadilla. A grilled four tortilla filled with chicken,
refried beans, cheese, avocado, and onions. Served with brown
rice, lettuce and tomato, sour cream, and salsa 6.50

Mexican Style Chicken and Rice. Boned chicken stir-fried with brown rice
and served with beans, lettuce, tomatoes, corn tortillas and salsa 6.50

Heartland Chili & Cornbread. Our vegetarian chili made from light
red kidney beans, tomatoes, mushrooms, green peppers, and onions.
Served with warm cornbread 3.95
topped with a scoop of brown rice 4.50
topped with brown rice and avocado slices 5.50

Fried Bean Plate. Roll-your-own lunch. Refried beans, a scoop
of brown rice, lettuce & tomato mix, avocado slices, warm
corn tortillas and salsa 4.95

Vegetable Fried Rice. A variety of seasonal vegetables, seasoned
with tamari and stir-fried with brown rice. Served with your
choice of cornbread or wheat bread 4.95
with Tofu 6.25
with Chicken 6.25
with Shrimp 6.95

Stir Fried or Steamed Vegetables. Seasonal vegetables over brown rice,
served with ginger sauce 6.25
with Tofu and Curry 7.25

Heartland Tofu Plate. Seasoned with tamari and sesame seeds and
sauteed with green onions. Served with brown rice and vegetable 4.25

Beans and Rice. A bowl of lightly seasoned beans of the
day topped with brown rice and scallions 4.50

The storefront setting belies what is probably the best Vietnamese food in Chicago, which means that the dishes ring true with the right mix of French and Thai flavors.

Le Bistro

Restaurant

KHAI VA APPETIZERS

SPRING ROLLS - GOI CUON 2.95
Fresh vegetables, shrimp, and rice noodles
rolled in rice paper served with a special
side dish of plumsauce topped
with roasted peanuts, and carrots.

GRILLED SAUTEED BEEF -
BO NUONG CAY 2.95
Grilled sauteed beef sticks (3 sticks)

PAPAYA SALAD - GOI DU
DU TOM THIT 6.25
Shredded young papayas, topped with
tenderloin pork, and shrimp, served with
our special house sauce

EGG ROLLS - CHA GIO
RAU SONG 2.95
Three Egg Rolls deep fried ricepaper roll,
contains ground pork carrots, vermicelli,
served w/ vegetables & fish sauce

SPECIALTY OF THE HOUSE

SAUTEED CRAB -
CUA RANG MUOI .... Seasonal Price
Whole Dungeness Crab, sauteed in a
buttery spicy sauce.

GRILLED BEEF - BO NUONG VI . 10.50
(Serves 4 as an appetizer or 2 as an entree)
Marinated beef w/ sesame oil, garlic, &
lemon grass served with fresh vegetables
and rice paper, cooked at your table.

SHRIMP LE BISTRO 7.95
Jumbo shrimp, lightly breaded & deep
fried, then they are added to our own
special seafood sauce, served on a base
of lettuce w/ sliced tomato & cucumber.

SOUR THIN SOUP - LAU
CANH CHUA TOM
Sm: (Serves 2-4) 10.95
Lg: (Serves 4-6) 15.25
Shrimp soup with assorted vegetables, okra,
and pineapples in a tamarind soup base
served in a hot pot.

ORANGE BEEF - BO XAO
CAM (hot or mild) 7.95
Crunchy sliced beef sauteed with orange
peel cooked with a special hot pepper sauce
or regular sauce.

HU TIEU XAO
Chewy Pan Fried Rice Noodles

FRIED RICE NOODLES - HU
TIEU XAO GIA 7.50
Fried rice noodles with
chicken and vegetables.

BEEF FRIED RICE NOODLES -
HU TIEU XAO BO 7.50
Fried rice noodles with beef and vegetables.

SHRIMP FRIED RICE NOODLE -
HU TIEU XAO TOM 8.50
Fried rice noodles w/ shrimp

SEAFOOD NOODLES - HU TIEU XAO
DO BIEN 8.95
Fried rice noodles w/ seafood (shrimp, crab
meat, squid, fish cake & vegetables).

BUN - THIN RICE NOODLES

SHRIMP NOODLES -
BUN TOM NUONG 5.25
Rice noodles mixed w/ fresh vegetables,
topped with charbroiled jumbo shrimp and
ground peanuts.

GRILLED BEEF NOODLES -
BUN BO NUONG.............................. 4.25
Rice noodles mixed w/ fresh vegetables,
topped w/ grilled beef and ground peanuts.

(Every dish is made to order w/ the finest ingredients from authentic Vietnamese recipes)

GA - POULTRY

CHICKEN LEMON GRASS -
GA XAO XA OT................................. 7.95
Hot & spicy chicken stir-fried w/ lemon
grass and jalapeño

CHICKEN COMBINATION - ·
GA XAO THAP CAM 6.75
Chicken stir-fried w/ vegetable combination

CHICKEN CASHEWS -
GA XAO HOT DIEU 6.95
Chicken stir-fried w/ cashews.

SWEET & SOUR CHICKEN -
GA XAO CHUA NGOT 6.95

BO - BEEF

STEAK CUBE - BO LUC LAC 7.50
Vietnamese steak - chunk of tender
beef marinated in a rich wine sauce,
served on fresh salad.

COMBINATION BEEF -
BO XAO THAP CAM 7.95
Stir-fried sliced beef with mixed vegetables.

Dinner: 7 Days a Week until 11

Index

- *Cuisine*

- *Geographical*

- *Alphabetical*

Gift Order Form

THE MENU is the perfect gift for every food lover, and is available at bookstores and gift shops everywhere. If you would prefer to order copies by mail, please fill out the form below, and return it to us with your payment. For gift purchases, a personalized card announcing your gift will be enclosed.

The Menu, New York City & Vicinity, 448 pgs. $12.95 x Qty = _____

The Menu, Chicago & Vicinity, 448 pgs. $12.95 x Qty = _____

The Menu, Los Angeles & Vicinity, 448 pgs. $12.95 x Qty = _____

The Menu, San Francisco Bay Area, 448 pgs. $12.95 x Qty = _____

Subtotal = $ _____

Postage & Handling (each book) $2.00 x Qty = _____

Total Order = $ _____

❑ I enclose payment of $ _____ payable to **Menubooks, Inc.**

❑ Please charge this order to my credit card. Total order = $ _____

MasterCard # _____ Exp. Date _____

VISA # _____ Exp. Date _____

American Exp. # _____ Exp. Date _____

Approval Signature _____

Name _____ Phone _____

Address _____

City _____ State_____ Zip _____

Payment must accompany order. Please allow up to four weeks for delivery. Rush/overnight delivery available. Call for details.

Menubooks, Inc.
David Thomas Publishing
733 NW Everett St., Box 12
Portland, Oregon 97209
(503) 226-6233

(Please fill out shipping instructions on reverse side.)

Gift Order Form

Please Send:
    ❏ New York City   ❏ San Francisco   ❏ Chicago   ❏ Los Angeles

To:

Name _____ Phone _____

Address _____

City _____ State _____ Zip _____

Please Send:
    ❏ New York City   ❏ San Francisco   ❏ Chicago   ❏ Los Angeles

To:

Name _____ Phone _____

Address _____

City _____ State _____ Zip _____

Please Send:
    ❏ New York City   ❏ San Francisco   ❏ Chicago   ❏ Los Angeles

To:

Name _____ Phone _____

Address _____

City _____ State _____ Zip _____

Please Send:
    ❏ New York City   ❏ San Francisco   ❏ Chicago   ❏ Los Angeles

To:

Name _____ Phone _____

Address _____

City _____ State _____ Zip _____

Please Send:
    ❏ New York City   ❏ San Francisco   ❏ Chicago   ❏ Los Angeles

To:

Name _____ Phone _____

Address _____

City _____ State _____ Zip _____

Gift Order Form

THE MENU is the perfect gift for every food lover, and is available at bookstores and gift shops everywhere. If you would prefer to order copies by mail, please fill out the form below, and return it to us with your payment. For gift purchases, a personalized card announcing your gift will be enclosed.

The Menu, New York City & Vicinity, 448 pgs. $12.95 x Qty = _____

The Menu, Chicago & Vicinity, 448 pgs. $12.95 x Qty = _____

The Menu, Los Angeles & Vicinity, 448 pgs. $12.95 x Qty = _____

The Menu, San Francisco Bay Area, 448 pgs. $12.95 x Qty = _____

Subtotal = $ _____

Postage & Handling (each book) $2.00 x Qty = _____

Total Order = $ _____

❑ I enclose payment of $ _____ payable to **Menubooks, Inc.**

❑ Please charge this order to my credit card. Total order = $ _____

MasterCard # _____ Exp. Date _____

VISA # _____ Exp. Date _____

American Exp. # _____ Exp. Date _____

Approval Signature _____

Name _____ Phone _____

Address _____

City _____ State _____ Zip _____

Payment must accompany order. Please allow up to four weeks for delivery.
Rush/overnight delivery available. Call for details.

Menubooks, Inc.
David Thomas Publishing
733 NW Everett St., Box 12
Portland, Oregon 97209
(503) 226-6233

(Please fill out shipping instructions on reverse side.)

447

Gift Order Form

Please Send:
☐ New York City ☐ San Francisco ☐ Chicago ☐ Los Angeles
To:
Name _____ Phone _____

Address _____

City _____ State _____ Zip _____

Please Send:
☐ New York City ☐ San Francisco ☐ Chicago ☐ Los Angeles
To:
Name _____ Phone _____

Address _____

City _____ State _____ Zip _____

Please Send:
☐ New York City ☐ San Francisco ☐ Chicago ☐ Los Angeles
To:
Name _____ Phone _____

Address _____

City _____ State _____ Zip _____

Please Send:
☐ New York City ☐ San Francisco ☐ Chicago ☐ Los Angeles
To:
Name _____ Phone _____

Address _____

City _____ State _____ Zip _____

Please Send:
☐ New York City ☐ San Francisco ☐ Chicago ☐ Los Angeles
To:
Name _____ Phone _____

Address _____

City _____ State _____ Zip _____